𝔗𝔥𝔢 𝔇𝔞𝔦𝔩𝔶 𝔗𝔢𝔩𝔢𝔤𝔯𝔞𝔭𝔥
RECORD OF THE SECOND WORLD WAR

The Daily Telegraph
RECORD OF THE SECOND WORLD WAR
Month by Month from 1939 to 1945

Introduction by Max Hastings · Afterword by John Keegan

Commentaries by Edward Bishop, W.F. Deedes
Simon Heffer & Clare Hollingworth

Edited by Hugh Montgomery-Massingberd
Consultant Editor: Edward Bishop
Assistant Editor: Diana Heffer

SIDGWICK & JACKSON
LONDON
in association with
THE DAILY TELEGRAPH

First published in Great Britain in 1989
by Sidgwick & Jackson Limited

Designed by Paul Watkins and James Campus
Picture research by Diana Heffer

Page 1 illustration: Collecting saucepans for
aircraft manufacture, 1940
Frontispiece: BEF troops arriving at
Southampton

ISBN 0-283-99917-9

Typeset by Spectrum Typesetting Limited
227-229 Liverpool Road, London N1

Printed and bound in Great Britain by
Butler and Tanner Limited
Frome and London
for Sidgwick & Jackson Limited
1 Tavistock Chambers, Bloomsbury Way
London WC1A 2SG

Contents

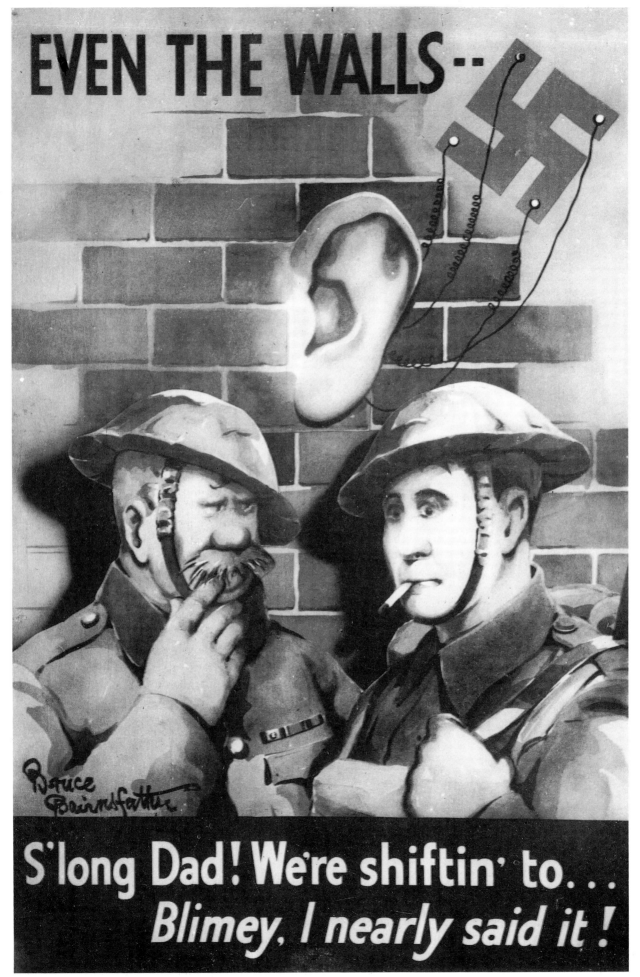

"Old Bill" reappears in 1939 poster warning troops on leave not to be too talkative

Introduction by Max Hastings

THE Second World War posed Britain with the greatest threat in her history. The reporting of it presented British newspapers with a challenge of matching importance. In time of peace, readers sometimes feel that they can miss a day or two of news without acute loss. But in war, information becomes literally a matter of life and death.

Beyond the grand campaigns that punctuated the six-year struggle for the nation's survival and ultimate victory between 1939 and 1945, everybody in the country possessed friends and loved ones fighting in theatres that extended from the defences of Broadstairs in 1940 to the last bitter battles for Burma in 1944–45. Fathers craved news of ordinary seamen manning cruisers off the Plate in December 1939; wives followed the daily detail of their pilot husbands' part in air battles over southern England in 1940; the whole nation hung in suspense in the weeks before and after the Normandy landings in 1944, for scarcely a home in the land did not have a personal stake in their outcome. The responsibility journalists and broadcasters bore in the 1939-45 period was arguably greater than at any other period in history, because the influence that they wielded over the morale and temper of the public was without parallel.

The British press laboured through the war under even greater difficulties than the rest of the nation's industries. Newsprint rationing reduced each day's papers to a few sheets. Most of the brightest and best of young journalists had gone to the forces, throwing the burden of daily editorial production principally upon middle-aged and elderly men and women. Fleet Street itself lay in the heart of London – the principal target of the Luftwaffe during the blitz, and also of the later V-weapon campaign.

Above all, of course, there were the immense difficulties first, of discovering the truth in time of war; and second, of determining what portion of it the nation could be told. Much is often made by the public of the chronic inaccuracy of newspapers in peacetime. In reality, it often seems remarkable that serious newspapers get as much right as they do, against the background of daily deadlines, and the normal ration of deceit and half-truth which is provided to them by politicians, business tycoons, and others with vested interests in ensuring that the public is only told what is good for it.

But in wartime, the problems of gaining accurate information increase many fold. With the best will in the world, the press of a combatant nation only has access to information from its own side. It cannot know much, if anything, about the view from "the other side of the hill" A submarine commander or a fighter pilot reports in perfect good faith to his superiors that he has hit an enemy ship or shot down an enemy aircraft. But, in the heat of action, he is often wrong.

The pages of this book are full of misinformation as well as information provided to *Daily Telegraph* readers by the paper, because nobody in Britain knew any better. That is a great part of the fascination of a work like this: to see the war unfold as people saw it at the time, uninfluenced for good or ill by hindsight. Historians can provide a sense of context, can show what really mattered about the war, and what did not. For instance, it is universally acknowledged by modern writers that the critical European struggle in the Second World War was waged between the German and Russian armies. It was on the Eastern Front that Hitler's legions suffered the devastating losses that so weakened them before the campaign in North-West Europe even began.

At the time, from 1941 to 1945, the British people were indeed encouraged to form an admiration and enthusiasm for "Uncle Joe" Stalin and the Russian people wholly at odds with prewar rhetoric about the evils of Soviet communism. But during these years, it is doubtful whether any event in the East made anything like the impact upon British public opinion of say, the Battle of Britain or the Battle of El Alamein, in which incomparably smaller forces were engaged. Military events that engaged one's own kith and kin inevitably exercised an influence upon popular imagination far greater than those which did not. Thus also the dismay many people here felt, when Americans began to arrive in this country in large numbers, and showed themselves woefully ignorant of the British war effort and achievements.

Any man or woman is likely to be more interested in the threat he or she directly faces, than that facing another nation, even an ally. This applies from the men in the line, to the very summits of the war's direction. Churchill himself possessed exceptional breadth of vision, even in the darkest days of the war, far in excess of that of any of his military advisers, with the possible exception of Alanbrooke. But even Churchill was liable to be carried away by the fascination of operations such as Dieppe; the fighter sweeps over France; the Middle East campaign. These, to an historian's eye, seem of moderate virtue and limited importance in the great sweep of world war. But they loomed very large indeed in the eyes of Britain's leaders, when they were the principal active operations in which their own nation was engaged. And thus, of course, they featured strongly in the columns of *The Daily Telegraph*. War is a great distorter of perspective; and total war is liable to distort perspective totally.

But the greatest dilemma for all nations in such circumstances is to decide how much they can afford to tell their own people about what is being done in their name; and how much will be directly helpful to the enemy. In the early months of the Second World War, as in the First World War, there was a bad-tempered debate

Fleet Street, 1939

between the press and government about censorship, and access to information. Thereafter, as both sides began to learn more about the realities they faced, a system evolved which worked tolerably well. Censorship remained notionally voluntary. But all press copy about military affairs was submitted for clearance. My father, a wartime war correspondent, wryly entitled a book of his own military reminiscences published in 1941 *Passed As Censored.* The debate about what should, and should not, be cleared for publication persisted with varying degrees of bad temper until VJ-Day.

The press required little urging, in a national conflict, to put the best possible face upon war news. Thus, *Daily Telegraph* readers were told that Singapore fell only "after a heroic defence", when in reality the British defeat was wholly ignominious. Throughout the Battle of Britain, the Air Ministry engaged in wilful self-delusion about the scale of German aircraft losses. During the British bomber offensive, the RAF published figures for the number of its aircraft which had "failed to return" from a given operation. But the many bombers which crashed on landing, becoming a total loss on British soil, were omitted – chiefly, of course, because such losses would be unknown to the Germans.

Many operations such as Dieppe, the Dambusters' Raid and St Nazaire, which achieved little or no strategic success but involved the utmost courage and sacrifice by those involved, were projected as triumphs. "The Commando raid on Dieppe... was completed according to plan when our troops had been nine hours in Dieppe", *The Daily Telegraph* told its readers on August 20 1942. Casualty figures were seldom published for ground operations, for obvious reasons of security. Constant emphasis was placed on the underlying weaknesses of German morale and the German economy – especially in the early years of the war – which reflected self-delusion on the part of the British government, as well as a desire to encourage the British people.

The need for the press to bolster the morale of the public, especially when the news was very black in 1940-41, will be self-evident to most people today. Some modern journalists have written books pouring scorn upon the performance of the British press in the Second World War, because it fostered so many false beliefs and misapprehensions. But to me, this seems absurd. If the British public had been told the objective truth about its military prospects in the autumn of 1940, it would have been justified in supposing that the government should sue for peace. When as a brash teenager I charged my father with writing wartime propaganda in his news reports, he remarked that like almost all his colleagues, he saw what he was doing as part of the war effort. This was surely quite right.

Yet if it was justifiable for the press to tell the public less than truth in dark days, there were also genuinely difficult dilemmas, in which it was hard to determine where the public interest lay. Newspapers were frequently angered by the government's decision to delay bad news, such as details of capital ship losses. When correspondents reported from the battlefield about the inferior quality of much British military equipment to that of the Wehrmacht, did their dispatches deserve to be published?

This was a problem during the desert campaign, and recurred even more seriously in Normandy, when the Sherman, Churchill and Cromwell tanks were perceived by their crews to be seriously outclassed by their German opponents. Churchill himself was angered by attempts to publicise the issue, arguing that it demoralised the men of the armoured regiments. Yet most journalists, and a handful of bold MPs, urged that only when a public outcry was raised about the poor quality of British tanks – matching the notorious Northcliffe "shell shortage" campaign of the First World War would something be done. Correspondents such as Alan Moorehead wrote with remarkable frankness from Normandy about the superiority of German equipment, and some at least of their despatches were published.

But whenever questions were raised in the House of Commons about the effectiveness of the RAF's strategic bomber offensive – and the immense sacrifice of crews it cost – political as well as journalistic debate was ruthlessly stifled, on the grounds that it would demoralise the men of Bomber Command. Here, indeed, was a case in which the censors were probably right, in the short term, that it would cause air crews unnecessary bewilderment and pain to have the value of their gallantry questioned. Yet in the broader context of the war, it may be argued that far better use could have been made of the strategic air forces, especially in the last months of the war, if there had been a more frank debate about the limits of what was being accomplished by the area bombing of German cities. It is a nice issue.

There were three principal sources of information open to British newspapers about the progress of the war. First, official communiqués were issued by government and service departments on a daily basis. Second, agency tapes brought news from Allied capitals, and from enemy sources via neutral countries. Third, each paper received despatches from its own reporters in the field.

The role of war correspondent was the most glamorous and sought-after in the journalism of the period. The youngest and ablest reporters were excused military service in order to report from the front, although they wore British uniform and bore the courtesy rank of captains. The best and bravest of them took greater risks than the average fighting soldier. One, a passenger in a British bomber attacked above the Mediterranean, took over the post of a dead gunner and shot down a German fighter – a feat that would have won him a decoration had he not been a journalist. Alan Moorehead of the *Daily Express* was twice mentioned in despatches in the desert campaign.

The Daily Telegraph featured the work of a galaxy of fine war correspondents, Christopher Buckley prominent among them. Buckley was one of a celebrated and inseparable trio of British journalists, the others being Alan Moorehead and Alexander Clifford. They commanded the confidence and respect of high commanders and fighting soldiers alike. Those postwar critics who suggest that war correspondents through the ages have played an ignoble role have never read the reports of Buckley, Moorehead and Clifford. They were as frank as circumstances ever allowed; they told as much as censorship or British knowledge made possible; they searched out their stories in the line as often as in headquarters messes; their understanding of tactical and strategic affairs became profound; they wrote superbly well. Their contribution to telling the British public the story of the Second World War as it unfolded is hard to overstate.

The picture of the war that emerges from the pages that follow is fragmented, because even at its best, journalists can provide no more than a rough draft for history; and the handicaps and exigencies of the 1939-45 period often made it difficult to achieve even this. But, read in parallel with a good modern history, this is a fascinating scrapbook of the greatest struggle in history, told through the columns of one of Britain's great newspapers.

An ornamented ARP shelter in Camberwell, London

SOME dates stick: The Battle of Hastings, 1066; Trafalgar, 1805; and in our century, the world wars which began in 1914 and 1939.

In the context of this chronicle, as Rob Wilton the contemporary BBC radio comedian reminded listeners remorselessly, September 3 1939, was "The Day War Broke Out".

It was not unexpected. After Germany invaded Poland on September 1, Britain honoured its pledge under an Anglo-Polish treaty to a courageous people.

When Neville Chamberlain, the Conservative Prime Minister, broadcast at 11.15 a.m. that autumn Sunday ". . .this country is now at war with Germany," a house parlourmaid summoned to the drawing room for the occasion asked her mistress, "Are they *black* there, madam?"

Announcements forbidding whistle-blowing and horn-hooting followed Chamberlain's sad little address and then, as the national anthem was played, air raid sirens began to wail. As if on cue, the rise and fall of their haunting warble sounded the death knell of his appeasement policy.

In the New Year of 1939 in the wake of the Munich Agreement of the previous September, Chamberlain's "peace for our time" had still seemed possible. Perhaps, it was hoped, after clawing the Czech Sudetenland into the Reich, Adolf Hitler, the German Chancellor – whom Chamberlain and the Press still courteously prefixed "Herr" – had truthfully realised his "last territorial ambition in Europe."

More immediately the activities of Europe's senior dictator, also styled politely, Signor Mussolini, and of a junior dictator-in-the-making, General Franco, were of concern. In Rome, Benito Mussolini, the Italian Duce, made boisterous claims to French territories in the Mediterranean. In the Spanish civil war Franco was set to defeat the Republican government.

The Far East was also unsettled. In China the armies of Chiang Kai-shek's Kuomintang and Mao Tse-tung's Communists were beset by Japan. In Russia, Stalin sustained power through purge. In the Middle East, Britain, continuing to administer mandated Palestine, bore the obloquy of policing Arab efforts to frustrate Jewish immigration.

If, apart from IRA explosions, the island begetter of the British Empire remained at peace, there were daily indications that time was running out. Golf club secretaries fumed at fairways being pegged out as possible anti-aircraft sites; a Savile Row firm marketed a tailor-made air raid shelter.

Rearmament had yet to reduce the jobless, but those not suffering the desperation of unemployment found escape in the picture palaces where Walt Disney's sugary *Snow White and the Seven Dwarfs* was pulling them in.

Meanwhile, indiscriminate bombing by German and Italian aircraft in support of Franco did not deter Chamberlain's appeasement journeys. The Prime Minister's wing collar and ubiquitous umbrella, if verging on the farcical, were quaintly reassuring in company with the uniformed and belligerently-jawed Duce who greeted him in Rome that January.

The measure of Chamberlain's ingratiation of the dictator emerged at a banquet when, raising his glass, he toasted the Emperor of Ethiopia; no longer the exiled Haile Selassie, but Mussolini's puppet, the King of Italy.

As Franco approached victory – under the United States's Neutrality Act arms for Republican Spain were embargoed – Hollywood, celluloid stockade of an introspective, isolationist America, resurrected an earlier civil war. Vivien Leigh, it announced, would play Scarlett O'Hara in *Gone With The Wind.*

In March Germany, marching into Prague, completed its occupation of Czechoslovakia, hardening resolve in Britain. Gas masks were distributed. If Poland was next on Hitler's list war seemed inevitable.

Even a slumbering America began to stir. Addressing a restrained warning to Hitler and Mussolini, President Roosevelt told them the "possibility of conflict" was "of definite concern to the people of the United States." Shortly afterwards he welcomed King George VI and Queen Elizabeth in Washington, a fortuitous spin-off of their visit that summer to Canada.

At home the nation was shocked out of its August idyll by the compulsory call-up of 200,000 men, aged 20 to 21, conscripted into khaki. Hitler brought home his conquering, battle-hardened Condor Legion from Spain and even Lord Halifax, Foreign Secretary, and Chamberlain's high priest of appeasement, hardened his heart.

And then, as Chamberlain acknowledged, came the "bombshell" of Germany's non-aggression pact with Russia, followed shortly by Stalin's intervention in Poland and invasion of Finland.

For Britain, the dominions and colonies of the Empire, the reality of going to war was quickly apparent. If the air raid warning of September 3 was a false alarm, that afternoon the unarmed America-bound Donaldson liner, *Athenia*, was torpedoed and sunk off the Hebrides. Within days a British Expeditionary Force was in France.

As what was to become known as the 'phoney war' set in, the combatants confronted one another from behind their Maginot and Siegfried concrete fortress lines and at home a phrase, reminiscent of 1914, was whispered in the blackout: "It will all be over by Christmas."

Mostly, the action was at sea. Germany sank the aircraft-carrier *Courageous*, the battleship *Royal Oak*, and took an ever-rising toll of British merchantmen. Maritime disaster provided a grim return to the Admiralty for Winston Churchill.

Then, before the year ended, came the fillip the First Lord and the people needed. In the South Atlantic the Royal Navy fought a brilliant action which enforced the scuttling of the German pocket battleship, *Graf Spee.*

But celebration was momentary. Poland had been crushed. The war would not be over by Christmas.

September 4 1939

GREAT BRITAIN AT WAR

THE Prime Minister announced yesterday in a message broadcast to the Empire, that as from 11 o'clock in the morning, Great Britain was at war with Germany.

The Commonwealth of Australia proclaimed a state of war three hours later, New Zealand followed and France was at war from 5 o'clock in the afternoon. Canada has given an assurance of effective co-operation.

The House of Commons met at noon to hear from Mr Chamberlain the declaration that Britain was at war.

In the Lords a similar announcement was made by Lord Halifax. MPs will meet again to-day at 3 o'clock.

At 6 o'clock in the evening the King broadcast a rallying call to the Empire. An hour later Mr Chamberlain had an audience of his Majesty.

It was later announced that the Prime Minister has established a War Cabinet, consisting of eight members in addition to himself.

It includes Mr Winston Churchill, who has joined the Government as First Lord of the Admiralty, the post he held at the outbreak of war in 1914.

Mr Eden returns to the Government as Dominions Secretary, without a seat in the War Cabinet, to which he will have special access.

Half an hour after Britain entered the war there was an air raid warning. It proved to be a false alarm, but it provided a test for the machinery.

An Order in Council makes to-day a banking holiday and no savings bank business will be transacted.

New regulations for motorists provide that the running boards and bumpers of cars must be painted white. Petrol to be rationed from Sept. 16.

The Admiralty announced that all British merchant ships are liable to be examined for contraband. The Navy is at its war

War is declared: September 3 1939

stations in full strength, supplemented by armed merchant ships as auxiliary cruisers. The naval convoy system has already been reintroduced.

Hitler is to take over supreme command of the German forces on the Eastern front. In a proclamation to the German people he found it necessary to state that whoever offended against national unity "need expect nothing other than annihilation as an enemy of the nation."

September 4 1939

War Orders to Civilians

GOVERNMENT announcements affecting the life of the civil population in war were issued yesterday.

The instructions include the procedure to be followed during air raids, closing of places of entertainment, prohibition of sports gatherings, and arrangements for schools and unemployed persons.

Air Raid Warnings
In the event of threatened air raids, warnings will be given in urban areas by means of sirens or hooters, which will be sounded in some places by short intermittent blasts and in other places by a warbling note changing every few seconds.

The warning may also be given by short blasts on police whistles. No hooter or siren may be sounded except on the instructions of the police. When you hear any of these sounds — take shelter.

Do not leave your shelter until you hear the "raiders passed"

signal, which will be given by continuously sounding the sirens or hooters for two minutes on the same note.

Poison Gas
If poison gas has been used, you will be warned by means of hand rattles. If you hear hand rattles do not leave your shelter until the poison gas has been cleared away. Hand bells will tell you when there is no longer any danger from poison gas.

General Instructions
Keep off the streets as much as possible. To expose yourself unnecessarily adds to your danger.

Carry a gas mask with you always.

Make sure that you and every member of your household, especially children able to run about, have on them their names and addresses clearly written. Do this on either an envelope or something like a luggage label, not an odd piece of paper which might get lost. Sew the label to your children's clothes where they cannot pull it off.

Tube Stations Not Shelters
London Tube railways are required for traffic purposes, and the stations are not available as air-raid shelters.

Cinemas and Theatres
All cinemas, theatres and other places of entertainment are to be closed immediately until further notice.

In the light of experience it may be possible to allow the reopening of such places in some areas. They are being closed because if they were hit by a bomb large numbers would be killed or injured.

No Sports Meetings
Sports gatherings and all gatherings for entertainment and amusement, whether outdoor or indoor, which involve large numbers congregating together are prohibited until further notice.

This refers especially to gatherings for entertainment. But people are earnestly requested not to crowd together unnecessarily in any circumstances.

Churches and other places of public worship will not be closed.

Schools
All day schools in evacuation and neutral areas in England, Wales and Scotland are to be closed for lessons for at least a week.

In reception areas schools should be reopened as soon as arrangements for the education of the children evacuated to the locality can be completed. The date of reopening schools in reception areas will be decided by the school authorities.

To Unemployed Persons
If you are already claiming benefit or allowances do not attend at the Ministry of Labour local offices until your next pay day. If you become unemployed and want to claim benefit or allowances you should attend at the Ministry of Labour local office.

To avoid congestion, claims will be taken from nine o'clock in alphabetical order, surnames beginning with A-H in the morning, the rest in the afternoon.

The British Expeditionary Force sets off for France

September 6 1939

America Proclaims Neutrality

PRESIDENT Roosevelt, at 1 p.m. Washington time to-day, signed a proclamation of United States neutrality. It became effective a few minutes later when it was signed by Mr Cordell Hull, Secretary of State, and carried from the White House to the State Department, where the seal of the United States was affixed to the document.

The proclamation names Germany, France, Poland, the United Kingdom, India, Australia, and New Zealand as the seven belligerents involved in war.

It declares that whereas war exists between these nations the United States is "on terms of friendship and amity with the contending Powers and with persons inhabiting their several Dominions."

It asserts that nationals of the United States should observe strict neutrality toward all nations involved in the European War.

The proclamation provides, among other things, that no person shall enlist as a soldier or seaman in the service of any Power at war; forbids any national from participating in the fitting out and arming of ships which may be in the service of a warring Power and lays down that no belligerent warship shall repair, refuel, take water or other supplies within the jurisdiction of the United States.

September 6 1939

SINKING OF THE ATHENIA

From Our Special
Correspondent, Glasgow

I learn from Galway that Capt. James Cook, of the Athenia, when he landed there to-day, stated definitely that the liner was shelled by the submarine after she had been torpedoed.

The captain says that the torpedo went right through the ship to the engine room. After this the submarine broke surface and fired a shell which was aimed at the wireless equipment. It missed its mark.

As far as can be ascertained to-night the number of those who perished was about 380,

out of a total of 1,102 passengers and 320 crew. One member of the crew estimates that 23 per cent of the American travellers were killed by the explosion of the torpedo and the liner's boilers.

Undaunted by their nightmare experience of the past 48 hours, most of the 500 odd survivors who arrived here to-day in two British destroyers surrounded the company's officials and clamoured for accommodation on the first available ship to North America.

The majority of these survivors were Americans, but also included among them were many of British nationality.

September 5 1939

GERMAN FLEET BOMBED

IT was officially announced last night that a successful attack was carried out yesterday afternoon by units of the RAF on vessels of the German fleet at Wilhelmshaven and Brunsbuttel, at the entrance of Kiel Canal.

Several direct hits with heavy bombs were registered on a

German battleship in Schilling Roads, off Wilhelmshaven, which resulted in severe damage.

At Brunsbuttel an attack was carried out on a battleship lying alongside the mole, causing heavy damage. During the operation, which was carried out in very unfavourable weather conditions, our aircraft encountered air attack and anti-aircraft fire, resulting in some casualties.

Another successful British air operation was carried out in the night of Sept. 3-4, the first night of the war, when aircraft of the Royal Air Force carried out extensive reconnaissance over Northern and Western Germany.

They were not engaged by enemy aircraft. More than 6,000,000 copies of a note to the German people were dropped over a wide area.

The Admiralty announced that naval activity continues on all seas, but as yet there are no major operations to report. The port of Dover is closed to commercial shipping.

The first communiqué of the war issued from Paris read: "Communiqué No. 1. On the morning of Sept. 4 the land, sea, and air force operations began."

Heavy fighting was reported yesterday on the Polish fronts, and the Poles claimed the recovery of several towns in the north-west. Polish bombers reached Frankfort-on-Oder, only 50 miles east of Berlin.

Evacuees departing for the country assisted by members of the WVS

September 15 1939

Children Best Off in Country

EARL De La Warr, President of the Board of Education, in a broadcast last night, reassured mothers anxious about their children who have been evacuated from danger zones. He said:

"I do wish that some of you parents of evacuated children could see the effects on your children of only a few days in the country. If you are feeling anxious about them, I think it would reassure you.

"Our task must be to save your children as far as possible from the sufferings and beastliness of modern war. So, however much you may miss them, don't take your children back just because nothing has happened during the first few days of war.

"The time may come when air raids are a grim reality. The Government felt it to be sufficiently important, to save the nation's childhood, to put the whole transport system at its disposal for nearly four days. But it would hardly be possible to do the same again."

September 29 1939

Tidying Up Germany

AMONG the more admirable qualities of the German character has always been its intense love of order. True, this national virtue is merely the reverse side of a most unpleasant national fault — the passion for regimentation which gets the average German into uniform on the slightest pretext, and sets him marching in any prescribed direction without pretext at all. Still, it remains that in Germany an Anti-Litter League would be a ridiculously redundant institution.

Conceive then what agonies the tidy-minded Teuton must have had to bear recently while 18,000,000 British leaflets have been floating down on him from the skies. How he must have writhed under the last merciless rain of eyesores, set adrift in a high wind across 50 miles of country. How deeply injured, in particular, must the German policeman be feeling.

If paper was thrown about in the good old days, it was his gratifying duty to compel the offender to pick it up again. Now, by a Nazi decree, he has got to pick it all up himself, with the inadequate assistance of the children under the age of reason.

September 28 1939

Income Tax 7s 6d in the £

THE Chancellor of the Exchequer, Sir John Simon, introduced his War Budget in the House of Commons yesterday and announced that Income Tax is to be raised to 7s 6d in the pound — the highest figure ever reached in this country.

It is 2s higher than the rate fixed when the Budget was introduced in April and is 1s 6d more than at the end of the last war. Other increases in taxation are:

Surtax — Graduated scales will run from 1s 3d on £2,000 to 9s 6d for incomes over £30,000.

Excess Profits Tax — An impost of 60 per cent. on any excess of profits over those of a pre-war standard period; this is to replace the Armaments Profits Duty. The National Defence Contribution remains as an alternative to the EPT, and the taxpayer will pay whichever is higher.

Estate Duty — To be raised by 10 per cent. on estates from £10,000 to £50,000; surcharge of 10 per cent. on estates over £50,000 to become 20 per cent.

Beer — Duty increase equal to a penny a pint.

September 11 1939

Public Welcome Cinema Opening

By Campbell Dixon

QUEUEING up with smiling faces, and gas masks in their hands, people in neutral and reception areas welcomed the reopening of cinemas on Saturday.

Audiences in the morning were not large. They rarely are, even in normal times; and on Saturday many people were not aware of the reopening.

Last night attendances were large enough to prove the wisdom of the decision to lift the ban. When programmes ended at 10 p.m. people trooped out cheerfully, agreeing that entertainment in these dull, anxious evenings was cheap at the cost of a little stumbling in the dark.

Twenty cinemas were open at Brighton and Hove. Capt. W. J. Hutchinson, Chief Constable of Brighton, has established a working relationship with the Sussex branch of the Cinematograph Exhibitors' Association, to achieve a reasonable balance of entertainment and safety.

On an air raid signal being given programmes will stop for five minutes, and audiences will be told where the nearest shelter is. Those who wish to leave will do so, and the rest will be able to see the continuation of the films.

Surprise has been expressed in the trade that the ban should have been lifted in some neutral and reception areas, but not all. Exhibitors at Liverpool complain that there has been discrimination, and they have petitioned the Home Office for a general reopening up till 10 p.m.

Spirits — Duty raised by 10s per gallon; price of whisky will rise from 12s 6d to 13s 9d a bottle.

Wines — Increases in duty of 2s per gallon on imported light wines and 4s on imported heavy wines.

Tobacco — Duty to be put up by 1½d per ounce on tobacco, with corresponding increase for cigars; it is equivalent to 1d on 20 cigarettes.

Sugar — Duties rise by 1d on the lb.

While the increases in the rates of duty take effect forthwith, the rise in Income Tax is being applied in two instalments.

The effect is that the rate of tax payable on Jan. 1 will be 7s in the pound; the full rate of 7s 6d will apply to the 1940-41 Budget.

Concessions for small incomes will be reduced so that instead of the first £135 of taxable income being charged, as to-day, at 1s 8d in the pound, on Jan. 1 the charge will be 2s 4d.

Relief will be given to persons who have experienced a substantial drop in earned income as a result of the war; where income is reduced by as much as 20 per cent. the taxpayer will be entitled to substitute this year's actual income for last year's as the basis of tax assessment.

The direction of the German and Russian advances in Poland

September 18 1939

RUSSIAN INVADERS IN POLAND

SOVIET troops began the invasion of Eastern Poland, along the whole length of the frontier, yesterday, and may make contact with the German advanced forces to-day.

Late last night the Moscow wireless announced that they were more than 30 miles from the frontier and had occupied six towns.

The invasion began at 4 a.m. without warning, almost concurrently with the delivery in Moscow by M. Potemkin, Vice-Commissar of Foreign Affairs, of a Note to the Polish Ambassador, M. Grzybowski. This declared that Russia was sending troops over the border to protect the population of Western Ukraine and Western White Russia.

Copies of the Note were handed to representatives of all States with which Russia maintains diplomatic relations, including Britain, France, the United States, and Germany, together with a declaration that the Soviet Government would continue to preserve a policy of neutrality towards those countries.

Our Diplomatic Correspondent states that this development in Poland, which was discussed by the Prime Minister and Viscount Halifax, the Foreign Secretary, yesterday, will be considered at its next meeting by the War Cabinet. Information last night was that Poland does not intend to declare the existence of a state of war with Russia.

THE DAILY TELEGRAPH

October 2 1939

Virtues in Rationing

NOW that the National Register has been taken, the imposition of national rationing, which is to be founded on the Register, is approaching. Not that any shortage of food has declared itself, but as no one can predict how long the war will last or what vicissitudes will mark the course of it, common prudence suggests that the habit of ordered living should be early acquired. As Cassius counselled Brutus —

> Since the affairs of men rest still incertain,
> Let's reason with the worst that may befall.

To be prepared for the worst is to be beforehand with the world; it transforms anything short of the worst from an affliction into a relief; and, as the experience of the last war showed, there is nothing to be afraid of in rationing, if only the system of distribution is well devised.

A Blessing in Disguise

Indeed, rationing, by imposing a restricted dietary, may prove a positive blessing in disguise to very many of those who yet regard themselves as moderate eaters. It is only an equivalent of the limitations and inhibitions which the wise men of Harley-street dictate to patients afflicted with dyspepsia or an excess of adipose.

The renunciation of some of those apparently innocent self-indulgences to which human nature is so prone, instead of resulting in a sense of privation and lowered vitality, may claim with the quack-remedy of a former day that it "strengthens the nerves, enriches the blood, and imparts tone and energy to the system."

A Gain in Health

Those who went through the last war know how the loss in weight — often measured not merely in pounds avoirdupois, but in stones — was a gain in health. This time we should begin rationing not only with ampler supplies, but with a system of distribution not hastily improvised — a system based on past experience, and free alike from the defects and the abuses of the food-queues of the last war.

In fact, in entering on the experience of rationing, we can tell ourselves that we shall be doing no more than undergoing a fashionable cure, and that, too, without a fee.

German troops parade triumphantly through desolate Warsaw

September 26 1939

ALL CENTRAL WARSAW IN FLAMES

THE entire business centre of Warsaw was reported to be in flames last night after shelling and dive-bombing that had continued without a pause since Saturday.

Inhabitants were unable to fight the fires owing to the scarcity of water and the danger of splinters and flying debris.

Not a building in Warsaw is now intact and not a building without its loss in killed and wounded following a bombardment that has continued day and night since Saturday.

Still there is no thought of yielding. Every broadcast message speaks of the determination of the people of the city and of the defending troops to fight to the end.

On Sunday alone over 1,000 civilians were killed and four churches and three hospitals filled with wounded destroyed, according to a communiqué issued by the defending garrison.

The Church of the Saviour and the Ujazden Red Cross Hospital, with the red cross clearly marked on the roof, were among the buildings hit in the central districts.

The German communiqué describes the operations as attacks on important military objectives.

All attempts by the Germans to penetrate the real military defences of the city continue to fail.

Bayonet charges have brought the German forces to a halt in territory where the tank has been rendered largely ineffective by the trenches and barricades which the citizens prepared more than a fortnight ago.

The people of Warsaw are starving, according to a Soviet broadcast from Minsk.

For the last 24 hours, the report added, there had been no bread in the city.

British troops march through a French village

October 12 1939

BEF of 158,000 Men Now in France

MR Hore-Belisha, Secretary for War, made a statement in the House of Commons yesterday on the situation of the Army. He announced that:

By the end of last week 158,000 men of the Expeditionary Force had been transported to France;

This involved the transport of 25,000 vehicles; volunteers for the Army will again be accepted; Home Defence Battalions and Auxiliary Military Pioneer Corps are to be formed, giving opportunities for elder men.

Mr Hore-Belisha also stated that under the Commander-in-Chief of the BEF, Gen. Viscount Gort, VC, there are two Corps Commanders — Lt-Gen. Sir John Dill and Lt-Gen. Alan F. Brooke.

October 19 1939

Twice As Many Road Deaths

ROAD deaths in Great Britain have more than doubled since the introduction of the black-out, it was revealed by the Ministry of Transport accident figures for September, issued yesterday.

Last month 1,130 people were killed, compared with 617 in August and 554 in September last year. Of these, 633 were pedestrians.

In the House of Commons last night the Transport Minister, Capt. Euan Wallace, made an earnest appeal to all motor-drivers to recognise the need for a general and substantial reduction of speed in black-out conditions.

The public, he said, could help by exercising increased care on the roads and by refraining from using motor-vehicles after dark except for absolutely essential purposes.

The Government viewed this increase in road deaths, said Capt. Wallace, with deep concern. Since the first days of the emergency efforts had been made to achieve the maximum possible safety in road conditions consistent with the overriding demands of defence against attack from the air.

The measures taken included the relaxation of headlamps lighting restrictions, compulsory rear lights for cyclists, the use of hand torches by pedestrians, and the provision on a large scale of aids-to-movement, such as the marking of roads, kerbstones and pedestrian crossings.

"The black-out," he added, "must remain an essential part of our defence measures, and any beneficial effect which a relaxation would have on road accidents has to be set against an increased exposure to the risk of heavy casualties from air raids."

October 18 1939

ROYAL OAK SUNK AT ANCHOR

SURVIVORS of the Royal Oak last night told the story of the sinking of the 29,150 tons British battleship by a submarine in Scapa Flow.

Earlier Mr Winston Churchill, First Lord of the Admiralty, in a statement in the House of Commons, said that the battleship was sunk at anchor at Scapa Flow. Three or four torpedoes, striking in quick succession, caused the ship to capsize and sink.

Vincent Marchant, 18, of Doncaster, described how he was asleep in his hammock when the first explosion occurred.

"I ran to the upper deck to see what happened," he said. "There was a second explosion 20 minutes later, followed by a third and then a fourth. By that time the ship was tilting. She was sinking rapidly.

"Remembering what happened on the Courageous and the lesson that taught us, I stripped myself of all my clothing and, tying my safety belt around my waist, dived into the water. Searchlights were playing over the surface and I could see hundreds of heads bobbing around.

"Great volumes of oil started to belch up to the surface. My eyes started to smart and the faces of all the men swimming in the water turned a greasy black. I was caught in a searchlight for several minutes and saw that two of my pals were swimming alongside me. Later, however, they had cramp and disappeared.

"A small boat passed near at hand with someone on board shouting for survivors. I 'ahoyed' but they evidently did not hear me and the boat disappeared into the darkness.

"I swam and swam for I don't know how long, but I must have gone about a mile and half when I felt the rock under me. I scarcely remember what happened after that. It was like a nightmare.

"I have just a vague recollection of climbing up the sheer face of a cliff about 20 to 30 feet high.

"Another figure was climbing behind me but he slipped and crashed among the rocks below. He must have been killed or drowned. I lay down on the top of the cliff and lost consciousness."

A Land Army girl haystacking

October 5 1939

Looking After the Land Girls

THE moral welfare of Land Army girls was discussed at a meeting of the Glamorgan Agricultural Committee yesterday. "Gossip and goings-on" concerning soldiers billeted around farms was mentioned, and it was urged that it was unwise for land girls to be out after nine o'clock in a black-out.

It was explained by the Agricultural Director, Mr J. A. Davidson, that a number of the Land Army girls, aged from 17 to 40, had been sent to the farms. Regulations existed governing the authorities responsible for their own peace-time girl trainees on the farms, and he suggested that reasonable regulations should be imposed on the Land Army girls, also, after they had finished work.

Some members protested that they should not accept responsibility for the moral welfare of the girls — a matter for the authorities controlling them. The county's responsibility should end when they ceased work.

The Agricultural Director suggested that the girls should be at home by nine o'clock and steps be taken to call at all their billets to see if they were in.

Alderman David Davis said: "They are good-looking English girls, imbued with the right spirit. Good girls do not need looking after."

Alderman Hubert Jenkins said: "Nine o'clock is late for anyone to be out in a black-out. I know there are things going on quite apart from the Land Army. Some of the young men who are not in the Army are not behaving themselves as they should."

The committee decided that the chairman and director should interview the Land Army authorities on the question.

October 31 1939

HORRORS OF THE NAZI CAMPS

CONDITIONS in the dreaded Nazi concentration camps are described in a series of documents which were issued as a White Paper last night. A foreword states:

"The German Government has complained of the maltreatment of German minorities in foreign countries and of the 'Macedonian conditions' reigning there.

"It will be seen from the published papers that under the present régime the conditions in Germany itself and the treatment accorded to Germans are reminiscent not of Macedonia but of the darkest ages in the history of man."

It is explained that the documents were not written for publication and they are published now only because of the "shameless propaganda" being issued by Berlin "accusing Britain of atrocities in South Africa forty years ago."

So long as there was the slightest prospect of reaching any settlement with the German Government it would have been wrong to do anything to embitter relations between the two countries.

In fact, one British Consul-General who sent a report of atrocities to his chief asked that his information should be treated as confidential on the ground that "if broadcast it would probably rouse world opinion to a higher pitch of indignation."

Even after the outbreak of war the British Government felt reluctant to take action which might have the effect of inspiring hatred.

"But the attitude of the German Government and the unscrupulous propaganda which they are spreading compels his Majesty's Government to publish these documents so that public opinion both here and abroad may be able to judge for itself."

The documents are of unimpeachable authenticity. They consist of reports from Sir Nevile Henderson, when he was in Berlin as British Ambassador, and from former British Consuls General in Vienna, Cologne and Munich, and of statements made by ex-prisoners to charity organisations.

Commenting on the ex-prisoners' reports it is stated: "Accounts of brutal treatment are too consistent to have been mere fabrications.

"It is evident from the documents," it is added, "that neither the consolidation of the régime nor the passage of time have in any way mitigated the Nazi party's savagery."

Much of the White Paper, which consists of about 15,000 words, is devoted to the two concentration camps at Dachau and Buchenwald. The tortures inflicted at the latter camp are summed up by one ex-prisoner as "indescribable." They were not exceptional but of daily occurrence.

Some details of the concentration camp at Dachau (31 miles north-west of Munich) where Jews arrested in South and West Germany are interned, are contained in a message from the Consul-General at Munich, Mr J. E. M. Carvell, to Viscount Halifax, dated Jan. 5 of the present year:

"Apparently the first day of captivity was one of indescribable horror, since no released prisoner has been able or willing to speak about it. On entering the camp every prisoner had his head shaved, and was given a coarse linen prison suit with a 'Star of David' stamped in yellow upon it.

"It seems that no other clothing was provided, even after the onset of extreme winter weather. Underclothing could, however, be bought at the canteen at a price. Two hundred to 300 persons were crowded together in huts originally built for 60 to 80 persons. Some prisoners appear to have slept on the bare boards, but most had straw.

"Prisoners have been buffeted, kicked, and even beaten and bastinadoed with steel birches. Some guards never speak to prisoners without hitting them across the mouth with the back of the hand. The medical attendants are particularly callous in their disregard for prisoners requiring medical attention. Sixty sufferers from frost-bite were dismissed without treatment on being told that their affliction would eventually cure itself."

Sachsenhausen concentration camp, 1941

November 1 1939

Russia to Stay Neutral

M. MOLOTOFF, Soviet Premier and Foreign Minister, last night addressed the Supreme Soviet Council in the former Throne Room of the Kremlin. He declared that:

Germany was striving for peace, and Britain was now the aggressor. The continuation of the war for the restoration of Poland was senseless. To fight under the pretence of defending democracy was a crime.

The main points of Russian foreign policy were: a free hand in international affairs; the continuation of the policy of neutrality; not to help in spreading the war, but to try to halt it.

Finland, he disclosed, had rejected Soviet proposals for the exchange of territory and the handing over of islands for military purposes.

November 16 1939

Launching A Daughter

LAUNCHING a daughter is viewed from a new angle, now that wartime conditions have called a halt to ordinary social life on the one hand, while prospects of junior posts that will lead to a career have almost vanished.

More and more parents realise that training for interesting future employment is the best programme for girls shortly leaving school. The great advantage of training at this period is in keeping girls out of the overcrowded labour market and preparing them for a remunerative career when conditions become normal again.

"How can I launch my daughter for £50?" is typical of readers' inquiries.

This sum, or even less, spread over one or two years without maintenance, can open a number of careers. It would provide training in radiography, pharmacy, secretarial work, institutional management, cookery.

Parents with a little more to spend on fees, without maintenance, can equip a girl for a social service career such as hospital almonry, or enable her to take a university degree followed by a short secretarial training to qualify for higher secretarial work.

HERE are Do's and Don'ts of the war-time careers problem.

DO'S: Go ahead with domestic science training. Prospects good. Dental surgery prospects good, if training facilities obtainable.

DON'T choose beauty culture, hairdressing, journalism, art, political organising, sanitary inspection, advertising. Prospects slight, poor or nil.

You can still get a Ministry of Health grant for training in midwifery.

November 14 1939

AIR RAIDS ON THE SHETLANDS

TWO air raids on the Shetlands, in which eight bombs were dropped, and an attempted raid on the East Coast, which was foiled by RAF 'planes, were made by German aircraft yesterday.

Four planes took part in the Shetlands attack. All were driven off by heavy anti-aircraft fire.

Of the eight bombs dropped, four fell on land, for the first time since war began, and the remaining four in the sea.

One uninhabited house was damaged and windows of crofters' cottages were broken either by the blast of the explosions or by fragments of AA shells.

Holes six feet deep were made in the ground and a road was temporarily blocked, but no further damage was done on land, and at sea no ships were hit.

This was the second time that bombs had been dropped in an air raid on Britain. On the first occasion bombs fell in the waters of the Firth of Forth.

December 2 1939

FINNS CLAIM 1,200 PRISONERS

AN official Finnish communiqué issued late last night claimed that 1,200 prisoners had been captured in yesterday's fighting with the Russians. It was also claimed that:

A Soviet destroyer was sunk in a duel with a fort; 16 planes shot down and eight tanks captured, making 19 in all; and two companies of Russians annihilated by a new weapon.

The Russians captured Petsamo, Finland's Arctic port, where they mercilessly bombed and shelled fugitives, including women and children.

While a new Finnish Government has been formed at Helsinki under M. Ryti, Governor of the Bank of Finland, the Russians have set up a puppet Government at Terijoki, on the Karelian Isthmus, near the Soviet border.

The policy of M. Ryti's Government is understood to be to seek to negotiate but not to surrender. M. Molotoff, the Soviet Premier, refused last night to negotiate with the new Finnish Government.

December 15 1939

THE GRAF SPEE: BRITISH CRUISERS' BRILLIANT TACTICS

From Our Special Correspondent, Monte Video

ONE of the 10,000-ton, £3,750,000 pocket battleships, on which Germany had staked such high hopes, to-day swung at anchor in Monte Video harbour, crippled by at least 13 hits from the smaller guns of three British cruisers.

She had suffered disastrous defeat in the first serious naval engagement of the war and one of the most thrilling fights in the annals of the sea.

Her opponents were the Ajax, 6,985 tons; Achilles, 7,030 tons, and Exeter, 8,390 tons.

Bigger and stronger than the British vessels that pursued her like terriers in an all-day running fight along the Uruguayan coast, the German ship had been forced to turn tail and seek refuge in this neutral port with 36 dead and 60 seriously wounded and with 30 or 40 minor casualties.

Her captain is reported to have said that he would have stood and fought two ships, but three against him made continued action impossible.

An inspection of the battleship's exterior to-day made it evident that British gunners had done a fine job.

The German Legation this afternoon submitted a formal request to the Uruguayan Government for permission to keep the Admiral Graf Spee in port long enough to carry out repairs necessary to make the vessel seaworthy.

Her stay is governed by the Uruguayan Neutrality Law of Aug. 14, 1914. It provides that no foreign warship may remain more than 48 hours. Article 7, however, states that a damaged warship may request permission to extend its stay for the minimum period required to put the vessel into navigable condition.

All day to-day the battleship's personnel have been working desperately to repair damage and plug the holes in the plating. The large hole in the side was being stopped by planks.

If this pocket battleship should ever try to leave Monte Video, it is perfectly certain that a superior force of British ships would catch her before she escaped from the River Plate and send her to the bottom.

Naval experts here are amazed at the success of the three small British cruisers in forcing the pocket battleship, in her first real test, to run away from her far less formidable pursuers at the utmost speed.

The fight began soon after dawn yesterday when the German ship encountered the French steamer Formose, 9,975 tons, en route from Rio de Janeiro to Monte Video. She promptly attacked the British cruiser, Ajax, convoying the Formose.

Commodore Harwood commanded the British squadron from the bridge of the Ajax. She returned the fire while calling for help.

Before Cmdre Harwood went into action, newspapers here state that he hoisted Nelson's famous signal: "England expects every man this day will do his duty."

Very soon two other cruisers of the British South Atlantic Squadron, the Exeter and the Achilles, appeared on the horizon and an intense gunnery duel began.

The Achilles was the first to arrive, and passengers in the Formose saw the opening round of the fight.

While the Formose departed safely from the scene, the cruisers threw a heavy smoke screen around the battleship. They took up positions on each side and in the rear and poured shells into her.

The Exeter's eight-inch shells wrecked the battleship's forward turret and control tower almost immediately. The German commander, realising the danger from this cruiser, which is larger and more heavily gunned than the other two, concentrated his fire on her.

As a result the Exeter was severely damaged and forced out of the fight.

All the time the four ships were running in a southerly direction. When the Exeter had to drop out, the pocket battleship herself was so badly damaged that it was obvious she would have to seek refuge in the River Plate.

December 21 1939

The Graf Spee Captain Shoots Himself

From Our Special Correspondent, Buenos Aires

DISILLUSIONED about the Nazi régime and deeply hurt at the charges of being a coward and a traitor to the traditions of the sea, Capt. Hans Langsdorf, the commander of the scuttled pocket battleship, Admiral Graf Spee, shot himself with a revolver in his room at the Argentine naval arsenal here during the night.

Capt. Langsdorf, it is reported here, violently disagreed with Hitler when the Fuehrer ordered him by telephone from Berlin to scuttle his ship, which was driven to shelter in Monte Video last week.

As he had no choice but to obey, he decided to share the fate of his ship once he had seen to the safety of his men.

The *Admiral Graf Spee* is scuttled in the River Plate

December 18 1939

Graf Spee Goes Down in Flames

From Our Special Correspondent, Monte Video

ONE OF THE MOST AMAZING CHAPTERS IN NAVAL HISTORY WAS ENDED TO-NIGHT AT 7.25 (10.55 GMT) BY A TERRIFIC EXPLOSION, WHICH SENT GERMANY'S NEWEST POCKET BATTLESHIP, THE £3,750,000, 10,000-TON ADMIRAL GRAF SPEE TO THE BOTTOM OF THE PLATE RIVER.

This deliberate act of self-destruction was ordered by Hitler personally. Capt. Hans Langsdorf, the commander, was rescued and is being taken to Buenos Aires. All the crew aboard, numbering 180, are reported to be saved.

The battleship, which the Nazis did not want interned and which they did not want the British to sink in battle, was about five miles off Monte Video harbour when the first blast occurred. It shook the harbour.

A great column of smoke rose and flames quickly began to spread the entire length of the ship. Five minutes later there was another explosion. This must have been the magazine.

The ship was sunk, it is stated, by the exploding of a number of large bombs placed in the hull, fore and aft.

Standing at the waterside, jostled by crowds of people who in awed silence watched this fearful scene, I could now see the Admiral Graf Spee sinking fast.

Much of her superstructure was blown away, but the funnel and control tower could still be seen outlined against the sky.

After a time she seemed to come to rest on the bottom of the river. There, it was said, she would be a danger to navigation as the wreck obstructed the anchorage off the harbour.

Merchantmen and colliers steaming in convoy in the North Sea

December 19 1939

CANADIAN ARMY ARRIVES

THE first contingent of the Canadian active service force has arrived in Britain.

Without a mishap, or the loss of a man, an army has been convoyed across the Atlantic by the Navy, and is now installed in camp for the completion of its training before going to France.

Conditions of secrecy, essential for the success of so great an operation, had prevented any announcement of their coming.

At their first parade on British soil, the Canadians heard, from the GOC of the port area, a message from the King. It said:

"On behalf of the people of this country I extend the warmest welcome to the first contingent of the Canadian forces to reach these shores.

"The British Army will be proud to have as comrades-in-arms the successors of those who came from Canada in the Great War, and fought with a heroism that has never been forgotten."

From a vantage point outside the harbour I watched the great grey troopships glide by, with their naval escort. It was a bleak morning, but the spirits of the men on board were proof against it.

Cheer after cheer from the khaki-manned decks was heard. From one troopship came the skirl of the pipes. From another we heard "Pack up your troubles." Reconnaissance 'planes circled and swooped over the vessels.

The whole span of Canada was represented in the first men who came ashore. In the entire contingent there are lumbermen from New Brunswick, wheat farmers from Alberta, trappers from the North-West, and fruit-growers from British Columbia.

There are Americans who have crossed the border and enlisted as Canadians, Canadians who speak only French, coloured Canadians, and Red Indians.

The King visits Canadian troops newly arrived in Britain

December 19 1939

Nicknames of the War

SO far the war has produced no new nicknames, even for the enemy, whom the troops still refer to as Jerry. A section of the Press insists on referring to Lord Gort as "Tiger", but he has never been called this by anybody else. In the Grenadiers he was always "Fat Boy".

As far as I know there is only one RAF officer who is universally known by his nickname. He is Sir Hugh Dowding, who is almost universally referred to as "Stuffy".

This is in recognition of a certain asperity in dealing with those who have let him down. It need not be thought, however, that the name is other than an affectionate one. There is not a man in his Command who has not the greatest confidence in Sir Hugh's tenacity and strength of character.

December 30 1939

A Momentous Year

WE stand at the end of the year looking back upon four months of war. Their events have been very different from what we expected on that brilliant Sunday in September when the country heard "with composure and resolution" that it was at war with Germany, still more different from the anticipations of the Fuehrer and his deluded people.

Before long we may be fighting a strenuous air campaign, but four months' testing time has given us no reason to fear the quality of the German machines or pilots, and each day that passes brings us nearer the attainment of power to command the air. HITLER boasted that Britain was no longer an island, yet his navy has been as impotent as his air force to close our seaways. In a campaign of reckless brutality against British and neutral shipping the German submarine service has again earned the detestation of the world, but its power of destruction has been so checked by the Allied navies that the tide of the U-boat war "flows steadily and strongly in our favour."

A battleship and a large aircraft carrier have been actually sunk by Nazi torpedoes and many more capital ships by the mouth of Dr GOEBBELS. The Deutschland's big guns sank an armed merchant cruiser. But the one naval action, the running fight of the other "pocket battleship" Graf Spee with Adml. HARWOOD's three light cruisers, brought no renown to the Nazi navy, and its issue saw the Fuehrer wrapping himself in ignominy. The disappointments and humiliations of the naval war appear to have made Hitlerism hopeless of any future on the seas. No other explanation accounts for the policy of destruction by scuttling of German ships safe in neutral harbours. On land the war has been static as regards movement, but active in the strengthening of defences.

Mr CHURCHILL predicted that if we came through the winter without any serious blow we should have "gained the first campaign of the war." At the outset Poland was overrun and shamelessly partitioned between the Nazi and the Soviet. Then the Fuehrer thought fit to talk peace. The reply from the Allies was concentration of all their resources "for the effective prosecution of the war." From the neutral States HITLER received no encouragement. Italy and

Japan made it plain that the alliance of Nazi with Bolshevik lacked any charm for them.

Soon enough the enormous price which the Fuehrer had promised for the pleasure of wreaking his spite on Poland was exacted and startled the world. STALIN advanced from establishing his control of the Eastern Baltic to devour Finland. Not a tongue might wag in comment so that it could be heard in Germany, though all the Teutonic traditions and the Nazi racial creed, the old German policy and HITLER's

most precious purposes, were alike abandoned.

But the rest of the world knew that the Fuehrer had lost the initiative, that what happened on his eastern frontier and round the Baltic would be determined in his despite, while he could find no means to break through the grip of the blockade in the West. It must be dawning on him that Britain has never in her history taken up arms with unity so complete. The Empire has rallied to a common effort with more than loyalty, with a conviction

that liberty in every Dominion and Colony is threatened by Hitlerism. We have worked out such close concord with France as to multiply the strength of each country.

Yet the power of the enemy must not be underrated. Efforts of some hundred million people driven on under a desperate régime will only be overcome by tenacity. But we are assured of the final issue.

> For all men's native land and worth the price
> Of all men's service and their sacrifice.

The BEF in cheerful spirits in a French village

December 27 1939

CHRISTMAS IN THE FRONT LINE

From Richard Capell with the French Army

MY hosts this Christmas are well in front of the Maginot Line. Part of the unit is manning the outposts; and the scene of our festivities is but a little way from the frontier and the Germans.

It is a unit that knows as well as any the ins and outs of the peculiar frontier warfare of recent months. But Christmas Eve was profoundly calm, and in scattered billets there was the liveliest merrymaking.

The long winter evening was not long enough for my round of visits paid to various squadrons and companies in straggling villages. In the uncanny moonlight suffusing the mist the villages looked dead, but every now and then a door opened to the colonel and his guests, admitting us here to the stripping of a Christmas tree or there to an improvised concert.

Roads were icy, trees whitened with hoar frost, the

air utterly soundless. But within doors all was joyously uproarious with song and the clinking of glasses.

I began to forget how often the sons of Burgundy had sung the cheerful chant of their province, "Joyeux enfants de la Bourgogne." It is such a good song for that matter that it can bear any amount of repetition.

The big guard room was full of soldiers, winning presents at a sort of game of blind man's buff. A soldier priest was master of ceremonies, and a sergeant-major gave us a rousing song. The old walls must have seen the fighting men of five or six centuries. But never a more useful lot than these machine-gunners of my Christmas Eve party.

Elsewhere, how could the English guest not be touched, when he put in an appearance at a sing-song of a squadron of cavalry, at seeing "Wishes for a Merry Christmas" inscribed in English on the wall in his honour, or rather in honour of his country and fellow countrymen? Or by the three "Hurrahs!" heartily shouted as a farewell?

Christmas Day is at hand and we make our way to church for Midnight Mass. It is a church where for months no civilian has set foot. Only a day or two before permission had not been granted for the service to be held so near the front, but now it has come through and the church is full.

My unit has no official chaplain, but there are two priests who are serving in the ranks. One who celebrates Mass wears vestments over his machine-gunner's uniform. The other, who preaches the sermon is simply in the uniform of a stretcher-bearer.

It is a fully musical service. The organist is a young lieutenant who has been on outpost duty for three days. He is just back and has had not much more than time for a quick wash and shave before he goes up into the organ loft.

The Christmas hymn is Adeste Fidelis. And one who was present will never again hear the grand old tune without thinking of that freezing Christmas in the village of XYZ, of the soldier priests and a khaki-clad congregation.

1940

Mr and Mrs Churchill inspect bomb damage in the City

IN retrospect, the dire events of the generally calamitous year, 1940, are dwarfed by the deliverance of the Battle of Britain. The invasions of Denmark and Norway, Belgium, Holland and France in spring and early summer were catastrophic in their consequences. But neither they, nor the subsequent Italian invasion of Egypt, the start of the siege of Malta and the counter-blow to the Italian Fleet at Taranto, diminish the place in history of the air battle which swayed across the south of England that decisive summer.

If, 50 years on, Chamberlain's bromide opinion of April 4 that Hitler had "missed the bus" seems ludicrous, set in the context of the "phoney war" of the winter and early spring it was almost credible. After months of little more than routine patrols on the western front – the "phoney war" – feared slaughter on the scale of 1914-18 had not happened, nor had London been devastated. The call-up, the acceptance of volunteers in the armed services and on the home front, the gradual if slow expansion of munitions industries created jobs in and out of uniform. Moreover, as housewives were introduced to rationing in easy stages, supplies of food and consumer goods had yet to suffer the full rigour of a wartime economy. There seemed scant hardship in the counsel, "one spoonful of tea for each person and none for the pot".

Blitzkrieg ("Lightning War") changed all that. Germany's sudden, swift and simultaneous assault on France and the Low Countries on the morning of May 10 by-passed, then pierced France's concrete Maginot Line. Tanks and infantry, bombers and dive-bombers in support – an airborne artillery – thrust for the Channel and for Paris. On May 15 the Dutch stopped fighting. On May 28 Belgium capitulated. On June 10 Italy, anticipating cheap spoils, joined its Axis partner. On June 14 the German Army entered Paris and on June 22 France signed an armistice. The extension of German rule from Poland to Paris had been rapid indeed.

Yet in this sorry business two events, bearing the seeds of his future frustration, soured the overt joy which was symbolically expressed in Hitler's little jig (according to the newsreels) as he descended the steps of the historic Armistice railway coach in the Forest of Compiègne after reversing the humiliation of the post-1914-18 War Treaty of Versailles. On May 10 Winston Churchill had replaced Neville Chamberlain as prime minister and from May 27 to June 4 more than 338,000 British and French troops had been evacuated in the Dunkirk miracle.

Discovering the "Dunkirk spirit" (a phrase since hackneyed as the source of some mystical national inner strength), Britain imagined victory in defeat and counted its blessings. The millstone of a demoralised ally had been removed and with it the suicidal drain on military, particularly fighter resources. King George VI, writing to his mother, Queen Mary, put it plainly: "Personally, I feel happier now that we have no allies to be polite to…" This sentiment was given some force by the Navy's action on July 3 against the French fleet at Mers-el-Kebir and subsequent measures to recruit or neutralise its ships.

Would "he" come? In pub, café and parlour "he" invaded conversation. "He" was Hitler. In mid-May, in case "he" did come, Anthony Eden, War Minister in Churchill's national coalition government, appealed for Local Defence Volunteers. Within 24 hours the LDV (self-deprecatingly called "the Local Duck and Vanish Brigade") had enlisted 250,000 civilian men to wear its armlet and soon its scruffy khaki denims. In August when Churchill re-named it Home Guard, "Dad's Army" had more than one million men coming under arms. To confuse and combat the awaited sea and airborne professionals they uprooted road signposts, patrolled concrete tank obstacles and lay in ambush with pike, pitchfork, shotgun, Molotov cocktail (crude petrol bomb) and such more effective weapons as could be issued.

At the opposite end of the scale the newspaper proprietor, Lord Beaverbrook, brought into the government as Minister of Aircraft Production – or Aircraft Minister as suited better his Canadian accent and brisk style – hurled himself into making good RAF losses in France and conjuring more fighters from the factories. In the event, the RAF's victory in the Battle of Britain (it is described separately) obliged Hitler to call off Sealion, the planned invasion operation. When on the evening of September 7 scattered churches pealed out the pre-arranged invasion alert it was a false alarm.

As it turned out, invasion came elsewhere as Mussolini's Sicily-based air force laid aerial siege to Malta and, out-numbering British Empire forces seven-to-one, his North African army advanced into Egypt. It was the beginning of a series of tidal desert advances and retreats in which, until in 1943 Montgomery defeated Rommel, the "Desert Fox", many military reputations would be made and lost.

Amid much mayhem in the Mediterranean, aggravated in late October by Italy's invasion of Greece, one daring stroke brightened a dismal November. Fleet Air Arm Swordfish biplane torpedo-bombers of the aircraft carrier, *Illustrious,* attacked the Italian fleet at Taranto and accounted for three battleships. It was a much needed tonic in a month which saw the night bombing of Coventry and destruction of its cathedral.

There was cheer to be derived, too, from political events in the United States. Franklin Roosevelt became the first American president to be elected for a third term and beneficial consequences to Britain were quickly evident. Hard on the heels of the exchange of 50 elderly American four-stacker destroyers for the right to fortify and defend eight bases from Newfoundland to British Guiana, came Roosevelt's trailing of Lend-Lease, the Bill which would breathe new life into Britain's over-stretched war effort. It made the prospect of 1941 at war slightly less bleak.

THE DAILY TELEGRAPH

January 4 1940

War on Haw-Haw

LORD Haw-Haw's nightly sermons from Hamburg are the subject of an inquiry by the BBC. A fair proportion of the listening public, it is understood, lend ears however ribald to him every night. Partly, of course, the concentration on the noble lord in that "other place" is due to the fact that this is a slow-moving war, with only an occasional duel to curl imagination's toes. Haw-Haw – would not Hee-Haw be more appropriate? – therefore more gently titillates. His approach, besides, is speciously correct. He is the most liberal-minded of men, and his intentions are strictly honourable. He exploits the British dislike of war, the inexpressive isolationism of an island race, our customary wartime grievances against intangible things like "profiteering" and "shirking"; and last of all he exploits the differences of class and wealth which exist in Britain (and the rest of the world, including Germany, if the pistol poked into Haw-Haw's ermine allowed him to say so).

It is a liability of a democratic people that his glib voice should be one of the weapons wielded against them. But he can, to "broaden the strategy" of British democracy in Hyde Park, be heckled simultaneously on his own wavelength. His fallacies can be exposed in a series of talks. Or a broadcaster, preferably with a ready-made reputation, can answer him regularly at a given time after he has gone to bed. In this way, our answer would be given the institutional regularity, so dear to listeners, of the train home from town in the evening and the daily paper at breakfast. Since attack is the best posture for propaganda, we could carry the war into the enemy's rather unctuous camp with British weapons of humour and scepticism. It is for the BBC to decide which is the better way; but the public should soon be advised of the perversion of the truth which gives the Hamburg announcer a superficial power to attract.

January 22 1940

Minister Takes to Porridge

Daily Telegraph
Woman Reporter

MR Walter Elliot, Minister of Health, has given up bacon and eggs for breakfast since rationing began. He is Scottish, and every morning has porridge with milk and salt instead.

January 26 1940

Hitler Prepares to Rule Britain: Not Quite Sure of Date

From Our Own Correspondent, Amsterdam

THE Nazis, with typical German thoroughness, are now training officials who are intended to take over the civil administration in Britain after her annexation by Hitler's Reich.

The "leadership school" where this instruction is given is in the beautiful university town of Marburg, on the Lahn. All the pupils are picked men with a talent for languages.

Britain's future Gauleiter and Kreisleiter are not only taught the English language and English customs. They must learn everything about the particular area which they have been appointed to govern.

I have been told, for instance, about one man who has been assigned to a mining district in South Wales. He must pore over large-scale maps of the area and learn all about its industrial output and the character of the workers.

This report may at first sight seem fantastic, but it must be remembered that a similar system was followed in the case of all Nazi Germany's previous adventures.

In the past, however, Germany's rulers usually had some idea about the date when they would take over the latest addition to the Greater Reich. No exact date seems to have been fixed for the annexation of Britain.

Women tapping shells in an ordnance factory

At her offices in Tothill-street, Mrs Elliot, who is chairman of the London Committee of the Women's Land Army, discussed rationing problems with me.

Rationing need not affect people very much, she considered. Her household of six in Eaton Square found the allowances sufficient.

"Lunching out helps," said Mrs Elliot. "After breakfast I leave at 9.30 for my office. My husband and I do not meet again till dinner at 8 p.m."

There is no butter ration problem in the Minister of Health's home. Mrs Elliot has always used margarine for cooking, because it is cheaper and in her opinion just as good. Now it also appears on the breakfast and dinner table.

"The meat ration will require a little more thinking out," Mrs Elliot said. "I like meat, and dinner is my main meal."

"My husband would just as soon have eggs or fish. He likes omelettes and scrambled eggs, and we sometimes have egg and haddock as a savoury."

The chief meat ration substitute dish at Mrs Elliot's home will be haggis. The Scottish cook will make it once a week. Its ingredients are oatmeal and offal, which is unrationed.

Rabbit pie is another of Mrs Elliot's dishes, which will be served more frequently when meat rationing begins. It is made with a short crust and hard boiled egg and, in pre-war days, thin slices of bacon were an ingredient.

January 4 1940

Miss Mitford Returns from Germany

MISS Unity Mitford's return would better have been marked by silence. But she has only herself to blame if she finds herself starred in the sensational Press.

In normal times the vagaries of a young woman who uses her social position to try and make a role in international politics may be dismissed with a smile. This is a free country as cranks of every political colour know well enough.

Unfortunately for Miss Mitford, however, the times are not normal, and her vagaries became rather a nuisance. Her wearing of a Swastika badge at election time in Prague in the summer of 1938 infringed the law and caused diplomatic complications.

January 16 1940

VC KILLED IN FRANCE

LT Edward Benn Smith, VC, DCM, who was the youngest holder of the Cross in the last war, having won the distinction at the age of 19, has died from wounds in France.

His parents, Mr and Mrs C. Smith, North Quay, Maryport, Cumberland, have just received news of his death from the War Office.

Joining the Army in 1917, when he was 18, Lieut. Smith served as a corporal in the infantry in France. Soon after his 19th birthday in the same year he won the DCM when, single handed, he scattered a party of 40 Germans in no-man's land.

Not long afterwards he won the VC "for most conspicuous bravery, leadership and personal example during an attack and in subsequent operations."

On the outbreak of this war he re-joined as regimental sergeant-major, but had been in France only a few weeks with the first contingent of the BEF when he was promoted lieutenant and gazetted to the Lancashire Fusiliers.

January 30 1940

Sgt Muggeridge

UNTIL six weeks ago Mr Malcolm Muggeridge was in the Ministry of Information. Then he joined up. He has now been promoted sergeant, and is not a little proud of himself.

During the last few days he has been busy correcting the proofs of his new book, "The Thirties," which is a survey of the last decade. To find the time and the quiet in the barracks, he tells me, was no easy matter.

He says that only one thing recalled his days with "Minnie." This was the pay parade. Literary as always, he found this "tedious but remunerative."

Canadian Palace Guards march over Westminster Bridge

February 24 1940

Mr Churchill: "Island Race Has Not Lost Its Daring"

WITH peace-time magnificence of civic state, London yesterday paid honour to the officers and men of the cruisers Ajax and Exeter for their victory over the German "pocket battleship" Admiral Graf Spee.

Their march through the streets packed 20 deep in some places by wildly cheering crowds, and the Royal Investiture at the Horse Guards Parade, culminated in a proud and happy luncheon party in the City's ancient Guildhall.

Here, amid flowers and a blaze of light, was celebrated, in the words of the Lord Mayor, the Navy's "victory over the King's enemies."

MR CHURCHILL, First Lord of the Admiralty, was received with loud and prolonged cheers.

He said that his colleagues of the Board of Admiralty and of the War Cabinet were very grateful to the Lord Mayor for inviting them to the ancient Guildhall to share the hospitality which the City of London had extended to the brave sea captains and hardy tars who won the battle of the River Plate. (Cheers.)

"It is an action," added Mr Churchill, "at once joyous, memorable and unique. It is the highest compliment which your Corporation can give to the officers and men of the Ajax and Exeter, and through them to the whole of the Navy, upon whom our lives and the State depend.

"I do not suppose that the bonds which unite the British Navy to the British nation – and they have taken a long time to form – or those which join the Navy to the Mercantile Marine were ever so strong as they are today. (Cheers.)

"The brunt of the war has fallen upon the sailormen and upon their comrades of the Coastal Command of the RAF, and we have lost nearly 3,000 lives in a hard, unrelenting struggle which goes on night and day and is going on now without a moment's respite.

"The brilliant sea-fight which Adml Harwood conceived and which those who are here executed takes its place in our Naval annals, and I might add that, in a dark, cold winter, it warmed the cockles of the British heart. (Cheers.)

"Warriors of the past may look down, as Nelson's memorial looks down upon us now, without any feeling that the island race has lost its daring or that the examples they set in bygone centuries have faded as the generations have succeeded one another.

"To the glorious action of the Plate there has recently been added an epilogue – the rescue last week by the Cossack and her flotilla – (prolonged cheers) – under the noses of the enemy, and amid the tangles of one-sided neutrality – the rescue of British captives taken from the sunken German raider – your friend, the one you sunk.

"Their rescue, at the very moment when those unhappy men were about to be delivered over to indefinite German bondage, proves that the long arm of British power can be stretched out, not only for foes, but also for faithful friends. And to Nelson's immortal signal of 135 years ago: 'England expects that every man will do his duty' – there may now be added last week's not less proud reply: 'The Navy is here.'" (Loud cheers.)

February 2 1940

Pheasant Season Extended

AN Order in Council was signed last night extending the pheasant shooting season until March 1. The season normally closes on Feb.1.

The suggestion was made in THE DAILY TELEGRAPH that the season should be extended in view of the large carryover of pheasants, which might result in damage to farm crops. The Government at first considered the possibility of extension under the Defence Regulations, but legal difficulties prevented this.

Since the outbreak of war many shoots have found difficulty in securing sufficient guns. Furthermore, conditions early this year were unsuitable for pheasant shooting.

The result has been that the normal close season arrived with an unusually large number of pheasants in the country.

Landowners and farmers, faced with a big expansion of their arable acreage, will welcome the extension of the season. While pheasants are not wholly harmful to agriculture – they devour enormous quantities of wire worms—they can do much damage to wheat and other cereals, and to some market garden crops.

The severe winter has deprived them of their natural food, and this has accentuated the danger to crops. There is also the possibility of disease being spread by the birds.

February 8 1940

Rationing the Tongue

No one will say that the Ministry of Information is ill-occupied in launching a campaign to warn the public of the dangers of careless talk. The universal preoccupation with one subject, the war, makes perfect strangers kin. Whatever their occupation or social environment, they are confident of having a major interest in common, one sure and obvious conversational lead. Nor can most of this exchange of comment, conjecture and hearsay which makes up casual conversation serve other than as a relief to "the stuffed bosom." It may be that, amid the flood of insignificant chit-chat a grain of real enlightenment may be found in unsuspected suspense, as minute traces of gold are recoverable from the salt, estranging sea. But the rewards of the listener with intent would be scanty indeed.

It must be admitted that the humorous drawings which the Ministry of Information are issuing by the million, to illustrate the perils of careless talk, are admirably contrived to arrest attention. But it is no small ambition to attempt to impose on free and friendly people, long accustomed, as TENNYSON observed, "to fling whate'er they felt, not fearing, into words," the habit of taciturnity. They will still be talking, even when nobody marks them. The parish-pump is no longer a feature of the English scene; but the genial social habits which it has bred persist. It may be hoped, therefore, that the Ministry of Information exaggerate a little the prevalence of enemy agents in our midst; for it would be easier to accept uncomplainingly the severest rationing, rather than a Trappist discipline.

"Of course there's no harm in your knowing!"

CARELESS TALK COSTS LIVES

Laying mines off the east coast of England

February 19 1940

"GERMANS DID NOT FIGHT: MORE LIKE RAT-HUNT"

THE Foreign Office announced last night that the British Government had sent a Note to the Norwegian Government pressing for the internment of the German prison ship Altmark, from which over 300 British merchant seamen were rescued by the destroyer Cossack in the action in Joessing Fjord on Friday night.

The note complained that the Norwegian Government failed in its duty as a neutral by not noting the presence of British prisoners aboard the Altmark when she was searched at Bergen.

From the lips of some of the 303 British prisoners rescued from the Altmark, our Special Correspondent learned of their suffering in the German prison ship and how they were released from their ordeal by the destroyer Cossack.

After being landed here yesterday evening from the Cossack, about 250 of the men were taken to hospitals in the district. Today, 150 of them were able to leave hospital, and they were sent to their homes in various parts of the country.

Frank Hill, of Melbourne, Australia, a fireman, who had been taken on to the Altmark after the torpedoing of the Tairoa in December, told me how a German sailor who befriended the English prisoners was shot by one of his own officers from the bridge.

"We were kept in separate companies about the ship," he said, "and to prevent us from coming out on deck the Germans not only locked the door of the hatch but bound it round with wire hawsers.

"The first thing that we knew about the approaching rescue was the sound of shots. Then a German pumpman, who could speak English, and who had been good to us, came to the bulkhead, took off the wire ropes, and opened the door.

"'Englanders,' he shouted, 'a warship is here. Come up.' Before any of us could get through the door, a German officer on the bridge drew his revolver and shot the man through the thigh.

"He fell to the deck bleeding, and I just stopped long enough to ask him if I could do anything for him, and gave him a cigarette. Then we rushed on to the deck.

"The Navy men were having a brisk scrap with the Altmark fellows round the bridge and on the forward well deck. There were one or two bodies lying about.

"We heard a shot, and others coming from the engine-room, but the Germans did not attempt to stand up and fight. It was a hit-and-run affair along the deck and round corners, and it was more like a rat-hunt than anything."

April 5 1940

"Hitler Missed the Bus"

IN a speech in London yesterday Mr Chamberlain declared that after seven months of war he felt ten times as confident of victory as he did when war began.

The Prime Minister was addressing the Central Council of the National Union of Conservative and Unionist Associations at Westminster. He said that the Germans might have been expected to take advantage of their initial superiority to try to overwhelm the Allies. No such attempt was made, and whatever the reason one thing was certain. Hitler missed the 'bus.

Other points in the speech were:

We have beaten off successfully all attempts to starve us out by attacks on our shipping from raiders, or aircraft, or from secret weapons, or any old thing that the Nazis can think of.

Our relative position towards the enemy has become a great deal stronger than it was.

Seven months have enabled us to make good and remove our weaknesses, to consolidate and to tune up every arm, offensive and defensive, and so enormously add to our fighting strength that we can face the future with a calm and steady mind.

One by one the leaks and loopholes in the blockade are being stopped, and as the war goes on the strangling effect of the blockade will more and more drain the lifeblood out of our enemy. This is a war of wills.

April 12 1940

FIRST MAIN CRUNCH OF THE WAR

IN a graphic speech in the House of Commons yesterday, Mr Churchill, First Lord of the Admiralty, declared that the German fleet had "sustained the most grievous losses" and been "crippled in important respects" during the sea and air fighting which had been going on continuously, especially in Norwegian waters, since Sunday. Actions were still going on.

Mr Churchill's eagerly awaited statement on naval operations may have disappointed some members of the House of Commons. There were clear indications that it impressed far more by its frankness and sober veracity.

The House gave the fullest accord to his declared policy of telling the news, good or bad, as soon as he was satisfied of its authenticity, and of restricting his observations to past events. His request that the public should temper its hunger for news with faith and confidence and not mind "three or four days' darkness" on such occasions as this was well received.

Control of Germany's supply channels, suggested in his confident reference to our activities in the Skagerrak and Kattegat, gave great satisfaction. So, also, did his cool analysis of the difficulties which the Nazis had created for themselves by the Scandinavian invasion.

Misgivings were, however, expressed at the disquieting tone of the first Admiralty bulletin of the Narvik engagement, and also at the fact that erroneous reports of the reoccupation of Norwegian centres had been allowed to circulate for so long without an official warning as to their truth.

MR CHURCHILL spoke for just over an hour. As he warned the House at the beginning, the urgency of events had left him no opportunity for polishing and preparing his material, but Churchillian vigour and humour were by no means lacking.

Particularly vivid was his warning that we were probably arriving at "the first main crunch" of the war. His contempt for the recklessness of the Nazis which had resulted in the "deep mutilation" of their navy was that of the naval expert.

It could not be said that artistry was lacking in Mr Churchill's vivid word-pictures of the loss of the Glow-worm and of the Renown's destructive encounter with the Scharnhorst and a Hipper-class cruiser in heavy seas and a snowstorm.

The general impression left by his speech was one of restraint born of a complete confidence in the outcome of the operations in progress.

"Lured by the old master's dream"

April 22 1940
GEN. DE WIART IN NORWAY

ONE of the British landing forces in central Norway is commanded by Major-Gen. A. Carton de Wiart, VC, DSO.

A veteran of three wars and numerous wounds, he was in Poland as a member of the British military mission last September, and escaped into Rumania a few hours ahead of German and Russian troops. He was later decorated by Gen. Sikorski, the Polish Prime Minister, at the Polish Embassy in Paris.

April 10 1940
BRITISH SHIPS IN ACTION OFF NORWAY

LATE last night it was reported from various sources that hotly-contested naval engagements between British and German warships were taking place in stormy weather off the West Coast of Norway, following Germany's invasion of both Norway and Denmark. A big battle was said to be taking place in the Skagerrak.

A communiqué issued by the German High Command admitted the presence of Allied warships west of Bergen.

Early this morning, the British Admiralty denied a German claim that two battleships had been damaged by bombs. Two cruisers, it was added, had received very slight damage from splinters. Otherwise no official details of these actions were available.

The statement that at least one naval engagement had taken place was broadcast by the American short-wave station Schenectady. Other reports were that:

The 26,000-ton Gneisenau, one of Germany's largest battleships, had been sunk by Norwegian coastal batteries;

Germany's biggest liner, the 51,000-ton Bremen, had gone down with 1,300 men on board;

Two German ships were sunk off Narvik; and a British submarine had sunk the 7,129-ton German steamer Amasis.

Arctic attire for the BEF in Norway

April 17 1940
SEVERE FIGHTING AT NARVIK

IT is learned in London that the Allied Expeditionary Force to Norway has now in part disembarked and is being reinforced.

According to a message from the Norwegian-Swedish frontier early this morning bitter fighting is taking place in the Narvik area.

Part of the German landing party has moved along the iron ore railway to the frontier, coming in contact with a Norwegian force. It is thought that the whole German force may be forced across the frontier by the advancing British troops.

British, French and Polish ships were used to transport the Allied Force to Norway. Famous liners of the three countries had been quickly assembled at various ports. Among the first contingent are Canadian units originally intended for Finland who have been intensively trained for warfare in mountainous and snow-bound country. The British troops represent regiments from all parts of Britain.

Eye-witnesses of the embarkation were impressed by the magnificent equipment of the men. Tribute was paid to the

The Norwegian War Zone

launching of such an expedition as one of the greatest feats of rapid organisation accomplished by the British Army.

Equipment included white fur jackets, white jerseys and pullovers, fur caps and leather jerkins.

May 8 1940

Premier Defends the Allies' Withdrawal

THE Prime Minister, Mr Neville Chamberlain, in the House of Commons yesterday, defended the Government's policy concerning Norway and the Allies' withdrawal. Among his points were:

The argument that, by dispersing the Anglo-Finnish force, we missed an opportunity of successfully attacking the Germans in Norway was founded on a complete misconception.

The main body of this force, which had been sent to France, would have been transported to Norway with no delay if the advanced troops already landed could have been established there; but this was not the case.

The withdrawal from Central Norway was not comparable with the Gallipoli withdrawal. Not much more than a single division was involved.

The expedition against Trondheim was made, despite its hazardous nature, in response to most urgent and repeated appeals from the Norwegian Commander-in-Chief. Plans for a direct attack, combined with the land forces, were carefully considered.

Sir Roger Keyes, wearing the uniform of Admiral of the Fleet, made a strong impression on the House by a critical speech, in which he declared he had been told at the Admiralty that there was no difficulty in going into Trondheim, but it was not considered necessary.

Sir Roger ended with a personal tribute to Mr Churchill. He was longing to see proper use made of his great abilities, and that could not be done under the existing system. War could not be won by committees. Those responsible for its progress must have full power to act.

Mr Churchill would be loyal to his colleagues, but Sir Roger hoped he would take steps to see that vigorous action in Norway was no longer delayed.

There was prolonged cheering when Sir Roger sat down after his speech, to which Mr Churchill had listened intently.

The Conservative attack on the Government was resumed by Mr AMERY, who declared that once again they had locked the stable after the horse had gone.

There was a roar of delight from the Socialist benches when he quoted Cromwell's famous description of Fairfax's troops as "old, decayed serving men," in pointed reference to the Front Bench. The cheers were renewed at another quotation from Cromwell's dismissal of the Long Parliament, ending with the words: "Depart, I say, and let us have done with you. In the name of God, go."

Less well received was his insistence that the Socialist front bench should take its share of responsibility in the Government: that there should be "a real National Government."

May 15 1940

A Little Imagination

By J. B. Priestley

A little imagination goes a long way to help us in these difficult days. The thing to do is to try and stand away from yourself for a moment, just before you are beginning to boil over. And then you calm down. You may even laugh.

For example, the other day I was on the main line train, and as usual it was crowded and looked like being late, and as usual I was feeling annoyed. Through the dining-car there passed a thick bumpy stream of young soldiers, who all seemed rather lost, not knowing which end of the train they really wanted. Also, like all young soldiers, who seem to be all elbows and knees and equipment, each one seemed to take up twice the space of an ordinary passenger.

Well, just as my irritation began to boil up, I suddenly remembered the beginning of the last war, when I was an awkward young soldier, all elbows and knees and equipment. And I remembered how I felt then that when I had been given a few days' precious leave, and had struggled on to a train, every train had been filled with fat, complacent, middle-aged civilians, gobbling and guzzling away in the dining-cars.

Instantly then, the real ME, which pretended once to be an awkward young soldier, and pretends now to be a plump, middle-aged civilian, began to laugh in its own silent and invisible fashion, and all was well. I grinned at the lads pushing past, and they grinned back at me, and we all knew the train was doing its best for us.

A little imagination, a touch of

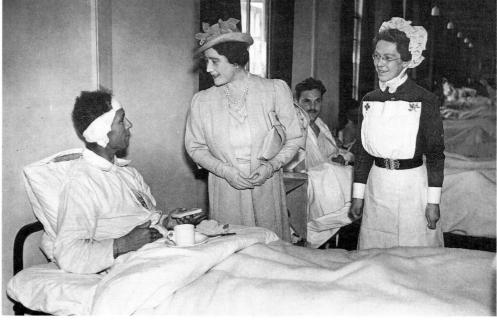

The Queen chats to wounded members of the BEF in a military hospital

humour, a slight change in the point of view, they help wonderfully. And you won't find them in *Mein Kampf*.

May 18 1940

Prof. F. A. Lindemann

THE Prime Minister has appointed Prof. F. A. Lindemann, whose researches led to the use by Britain of the balloon barrage, as one of his two personal assistants. The professor, an Oxford don, has been performing experimental work in an Admiralty laboratory during the war. As an experimental pilot in the last war he proved by his own flights the value of the spiral dive in saving the lives of airmen.

May 25 1940

King's Call to His Peoples

IN a vigorous and inspiring broadcast to the Empire last night on the occasion of Empire Day the King said:

"The decisive struggle is now upon us. Let no one be mistaken: It is no mere territorial conquest that our enemies are seeking. It is the overthrow, complete and final, of this Empire and of everything for which it stands: and after that the conquest of the world.

"It is the issue of life or death for us all. And if their will prevails, they will bring to its accomplishment all the hatred and cruelty which they have already displayed.

"But confidence alone is not enough. It must be armed with courage and resolution, with endurance and self-sacrifice.

"Keep your hearts proud and your resolve unshaken. Let us go forward to that task as one man, a smile on our lips, and our heads held high, and with God's help we shall not fail."

The broadcast, the longest his Majesty has made, lasted 12½ minutes. Reports last night indicated that every word was heard with perfect clarity throughout the United States and in distant parts of the Empire.

May 11 1940

MR CHURCHILL BECOMES PRIME MINISTER

Mr Chamberlain saw the King at Buckingham Palace yesterday evening and tendered his resignation. He advised the King to send for Mr Winston Churchill.

Mr Churchill was immediately summoned to the Palace and entrusted with the formation of a new Government.

This is to be on an all-party basis. While every Minister has placed his office at the disposal of the new Prime Minister, all are at his request carrying on at present in their posts pending the formation of a new Administration.

Mr Churchill, in addition to being Prime Minister, will act as Minister of Defence, supervising the work of the three Service Ministers. I understand that he will appoint Mr Chamberlain Leader of the House of Commons, following the example of Mr Lloyd George, who in the Coalition Government in the last war delegated to Mr Bonar Law the task of leading the House.

Mr Chamberlain will, at Mr Churchill's express desire, be a member of the War Cabinet. He will also, I understand, retain the leadership of the Conservative party.

Mr Attlee and Mr Greenwood, the Leader and Deputy Leader of the Socialist party, spent some time late last night at Admiralty House discussing with Mr Churchill the composition of the new Government.

A slight reduction in the size of the War Cabinet is a change Mr Churchill is expected to make. It will be largely, though not entirely, composed of Ministers without departmental duties. Viscount Halifax will remain a member, and representatives of both Opposition parties will be included.

In some quarters it is believed that Mr Greenwood will be the Socialist member of the War Cabinet.

Trade Union leaders as well as members of the Opposition Front Bench will, it was predicted last night, be given posts in the new Administration. The names of Sir Walter Citrine and Mr Ernest Bevin are being mentioned for important offices.

May 11 1940

A Government of Victory

Mr WINSTON CHURCHILL takes up the duty of national leadership at a great hour in the life of our country. By the inspiration of a bold and fertile genius, by long study and aptitude for the direction of war, by experience in administration hardly to be rivalled, and above all by force of will and hearty understanding of that stubbornness and fire which have made the British Nation great in arms, he has the qualities to make his arduous task glorious. He will be able to command from the leaders of the several parties support making easy the establishment of a Government completely representative of the nation and uniting the ability and the energy which will bring forth the utmost power of the country and direct it to the swiftest and greatest advantage.

Socialist leaders were quick to realise their duty. Their position was not without its difficulty, for their party has been sensitively jealous of association with any other in a Coalition Government. They might have waited for permission from the Conference about to meet. The National Executive unanimously supported Mr ATTLEE and Mr GREENWOOD in the right course of taking their share of responsibility as full partners in a Government under a new Prime Minister. They will now do their part – as the part which both the political and the industrial wings of Labour can play is of high importance – to ensure that the new Government holds and keeps the complete confidence of the nation.

In France, M. REYNAUD, who was able to set the example of including the Socialist organisation in a Cabinet of union, has given it further strength by the representatives of all parties. The Allies are each established in a unity which tyranny can never compass. We have a Government of victory.

The new Prime Minister: Winston Churchill

May 15 1940

"CEASE FIRE" ORDER TO DUTCH TROOPS

THE end of resistance in Holland to the German invasion was announced in the following statement issued at one o'clock this morning by the Netherlands Legation in London:

"The Commander-in-Chief of the Netherlands Army has issued a proclamation to the troops concerned that fighting is to cease."

Throughout yesterday the German armies continued their concerted push on a front of over 120 miles from Liège, in Belgium, down to Longwy, in France.

The attacks were pressed with the greatest severity in the Sedan sector where, according to last night's French communiqué, "a momentous effort was made with furious obstinacy and at the expense of heavy casualties."

It is clear that a supreme effort is being made to break through. Gen. Gamelin, the Commander-in-Chief, has, it was stated in Paris, chosen the line on which the Allied Armies, with all the forces at their command, will join battle.

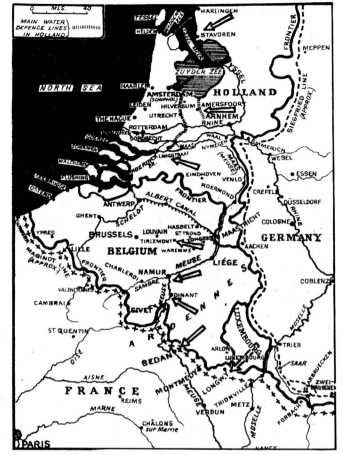

The German Army pushes through Holland and Belgium

Sir Oswald Mosley, Bt, founder of the British Union of Fascists

May 14 1940

"Blood, Toil, Tears and Sweat"

MR Churchill delivered his first speech as Prime Minister in the House of Commons yesterday, when a resolution of confidence in the new Government was agreed to. "I have nothing to offer but blood, toil, tears and sweat," he declared in a statement which was loudly cheered from all sides of the House.

Other points were:

To form an Administration of this scale and complexity is a serious undertaking, but it must be remembered that we are in the preliminary phase of one of the greatest battles in history.

If you ask what is our aim I can answer in one word – it is victory.

May 24 1940

Sir O. Mosley and 33 Fascists Arrested

THE Home Office last night issued the following statement:

"Leading members of the British Union of Fascists were arrested today by the direction of the Home Secretary.

"As announced in the House of Commons this afternoon, Regulation 18B of the Defence Regulations was amended last night by the addition of a provision enabling the Home Secretary to order the detention of members of organisations which have had associations with the enemy or

subject to foreign influence or control and which may be used for purposes prejudicial to the national security.

"Under new powers conferred by the amended regulations the Home Secretary made orders last night for the detention of a number of the leading members of the British Union of Fascists. Among those arrested during the course of the day in pursuance of these orders were:

"Sir Oswald Mosley, A. Raven Thomson, N. Francis-Hawkins, F. E. Burdett, Capt. U. A. Hick, C. F. Watts, H. McKechnie, G. Bruning and Mrs Dacre-Fox.

"In a statement in the House of Commons to-day Sir John

Anderson made it clear that this action had been taken not on account of any opinion held or expressed by the British Union of Fascists nor on account of their propagandist activities, but because of the danger that the organisation might be used in the execution of acts prejudicial to the security of the State.

"Other persons arrested to-day under Regulation 18B, but not connected with the arrest of members of the British Union of Fascists, included:

"Capt. A. M. Ramsay, MP, president of the Right Club, and Mr John Beckett, secretary of the British People's party."

June 3 1940

CLIMAX OF BEF EVACUATION

By Douglas Williams
A South-East Port

THE evacuation of the BEF from Dunkirk and the adjacent beaches was approaching its climax this evening. All through the week-end thousands of troops continued to pour into this port, to vanish onto waiting trains for unknown destinations at camps and barracks all over England.

I am not permitted to estimate the number of those who have got away and those who are still left. By dusk this evening it was safe to state that the numbers still remaining, apart from the rearguard and the casualties, are surprisingly small.

At Dunkirk dive-bombing and machine-gunning by enemy 'planes, as well as direct fire from German howitzers, continues to render entry into and exit from the port a hazardous business. For troops on the beaches there is little protection.

Scarcely a ship returns to this port without some visible evidence of German violence – splinter scars on her superstructure or bullet holes in her funnel.

If the crews of the naval vessels have been magnificent in their superb indifference to risk in the task they are now completing, equal praise must be given to the masters of the innumerable auxiliary vessels, many of them lacking any defence save a Bren gun or two, which have fearlessly run in and out of Dunkirk.

One such vessel, formerly a well-known pleasure steamer, nosed into Dunkirk harbour about four this morning, just as dawn was breaking. It was her fourth or fifth trip, and she had already had some miraculous escapes. She eased alongside the Mole in the half-light and looked around for passengers.

Two hundred weary, grimy, hungry men scrambled aboard. An hour before they said there had been two or three thousand waiting, but as no steamers were there at that time, they had gone back to dig in on the sands as protection against air bombardment.

The steamer waited two hours despite heavy shelling when a German battery started to register on the Mole. Another party of 12 men arrived together with a couple of wounded.

The captain then decided he could risk his ship no longer. The shelling was getting hotter and visibility perfect. He backed out and as he steamed away had the chagrin of seeing another party of 12 men running down the Mole.

But it was too late: he could not return for them.

A view from the air of the Dunkirk evacuation

June 1 1940

DEFEAT TURNED TO VICTORY

AT an early hour this morning it was estimated that some 75 per cent. of the BEF had been evacuated from Dunkirk.

Some of the men who arrived home last night had been engaged in a rearguard action as late as yesterday morning. For days they had been fighting their way back to the coast without rest from near the Luxembourg border.

While these troops were being taken off in one of the most hazardous, and brilliantly executed, evacuations of all time, other forces continued throughout yesterday to bar the way to the Germans attempting to encircle them and reach the port.

Gallant French soldiers, side by side with the British, fought like cats in defence of what has appropriately been termed the Corunna Line, recalling the historic exploit of Sir John Moore in Spain, in 1809.

Little remained of Dunkirk itself, which was subjected to terrific bombing. But the defences protecting the area remained intact, and it was authoritatively stated that there is no intention that they or Dunkirk shall be abandoned.

Apart from a narrow corridor through which the Allied troops were withdrawing, the whole region to the north-east and south-west had been flooded to a depth of nearly two feet, making it impracticable for enemy infantry and mechanised units alike.

This inundation, let loose by Allied engineers, released much-needed troops to defend the Line of the Flanders Hill, 25 miles to the south.

Here a particularly fierce battle was raging as the Germans, foiled in their attack on Dunkirk by the rising flood waters, redoubled their efforts to cut off the French forces under Gen. Prioux, who were hacking a way through to Dunkirk from the Lille region – a distance of 70 miles.

At Dunkirk, the evacuation went on day and night. Troops, who were constantly shelled as hour after hour they waited uncomplainingly on the beaches, were embarked, packed like sardines, as rapidly as accommodation could be provided

There was continual coming and going of an armada of vessels of every conceivable type. Ships which had crossed the Channel loaded with men returned at once with supplies of food, medical stores and ammunition for those still to be taken off and defending the withdrawal.

Troops leaving Dunkirk

June 4 1940

Place Names to be Painted Out

By Our Motoring Correspondent

FOLLOWING on the removal of road signposts throughout the country, which is now practically completed, the Postmaster-General has given instructions that the names on all post offices and telephone exchanges are to be painted out.

But there still remain many place names attached to shops and garages and other private premises which must be removed if the scheme is to be complete. So far, no orders on this point have been issued.

Some counties are painting out street names where they betray a direction. Others are even removing the signs to and from local beauty spots. Elsewhere, the sign "Please drive slowly through So-and-so" is still seen.

June 5 1940

Britain Will Ride Out Storms of War: "Never Surrender"

THE last Allied troops in Dunkirk were evacuated yesterday and the ruined and useless fort left in the hands of the enemy.

The rearguard was embarked after fighting from house to house through the town. Adml Abriel, the French naval commander, who was the last man to leave, arrived in London with two other French admirals and three French generals.

Mr Churchill described the operations of the past week to the House of Commons yesterday. The evacuation, he said, was "a miracle of deliverance" following "a colossal military defeat."

The number of British and French troops taken off was 335,000. This was largely due to the RAF which "decisively defeated the main strength of the German Air Force and inflicted losses of four to one."

BEF losses in personnel exceeded 30,000 killed, wounded and missing. Losses in material embraced 1,000 guns and all transport and armoured vehicles. But they would be replaced speedily.

The Prime Minister announced that a secret session would be held next Tuesday to discuss the organisation of defensive measures against possible invasion.

Mr CHURCHILL said: "I have myself full confidence that if all do their duty and nothing is neglected and if the best arrangements are made, as they are being made, we shall prove ourselves once again able to defend our island home, ride out the storms of war, and outlive the menace of tyranny if necessary for years, if necessary alone. (Cheers.)

"At any rate, that is what we are trying to do. That is the resolve of the Government, every man of them. It is the will of Parliament and of the nation.

"The British Empire with the French Republic, linked together in their cause and in their need, will defend to the death their native soil, aiding each other like good comrades to the utmost of their strength, even though large tracts of Europe and many old and famous States have fallen or may fall into the grip of the Gestapo and all the odious apparatus of Nazi rule.

"We cannot flag or fail. We shall go on to the end. We shall fight in France, we shall fight on the seas and oceans, we shall fight with growing confidence and growing strength in the air.

"We shall defend our island whatever the cost may be. We shall fight on the beaches, we shall fight on the landing grounds, in the fields, in the streets and in the hills.

"We shall never surrender, and even if, which I do not for a moment believe, this island or a large part of it were subjugated and starving, then our Empire beyond the seas, armed and guarded by the British Fleet, will carry on the struggle until in God's good time the New World, with all its power and might, sets forth to the liberation and rescue of the old." (Loud cheers.)

June 5 1940

"On to the End"

RESOLVE to see things as they are and conceal nothing of their sombre menace from the country was the first element in the Prime Minister's survey of the war yesterday. Its absolute candour, as Lord CREWE remarked in the House of Lords, made a marked contrast to the German bulletins. Mr CHURCHILL's speech was instinct also with high courage and a determination to "go on to the end," however distant, whatever the sacrifices. He sounded the clarion of the spirit of attack. War to him is not a grand defensive. He declared full confidence in our power to defeat the march of tyranny.

In all this Mr CHURCHILL spoke the very temper with which the British people are facing the future. They are well aware that "no easy hopes or lies shall bring them to their goal." Their minds are made up to throw everything into the fight. What they ask from their leaders is wise foresight and planning and the boldest action. No British Government, it may be, has ever had a more difficult task.

The tidings which Mr CHURCHILL had to tell were much less "hard and heavy" than he himself expected last week. Then he thought that only

Refreshments for troops back from Dunkirk

some 30,000 men would be re-embarked from the Flanders coast. In fact over 335,000, French and British, have been brought "out of the jaws of death." British losses, killed, wounded and missing, he put at something over 30,000. While we mourn those who fell to save their comrades, fighting "with a joyful courage, a passionate pride," we may be glad to remember that the loss is only a

third of that sustained in the great German onslaught of March 1918.

Yet Mr CHURCHILL was right to pronounce with grim candour that the German success has been a "colossal military disaster". There is no consoling mist over the prospect. We have to multiply productive exertions in days when the danger of attack on our island has been brought nearer.

June 8 1940

FIRST VC OF THE WAR

THE first VC of the war has been awarded posthumously to Capt. B. A. W. Warburton-Lee, of the destroyer Hardy, who led the 2nd Destroyer Flotilla in the first Battle of Narvik on April 10 and successfully engaged a superior enemy force.

The Western Front: the Germans advance through France

June 19 1940

PREMIER ON EMPIRE'S "FINEST HOUR"

"LET us brace ourselves to our duty, and so to bear ourselves that, if the British Commonwealth and Empire lasts for a thousand years, men will still say: 'This was their finest hour.'"

With these inspiring words Mr Churchill ended his war survey in the House of Commons yesterday. In it he dealt with the effect of the French move for a separate peace and reviewed the possibilities of an invasion of this country.

"Our professional advisers of the three Services," he said, "unitedly advise that we should continue the war, and that there are good and reasonable hopes of final victory."

He stressed the point that it was not yet certain that military resistance would come to an end in France, and continued:

"The French Government will be throwing away great opportunities, and casting away their future if they do not continue the war in accordance with their Treaty obligations, from which we have not felt able to release them."

Britain would fight on, if necessary for years. While the battle of France was over, he expected that the battle of Britain was about to begin. "Hitler knows he will have to break us in these islands or lose the war."

June 11 1940

Mussolini Declares War on the Allies

THE Italian Foreign Minister, Count Ciano, yesterday informed the French and British Ambassadors in Rome at 4.30 and 4.45 p.m. respectively that Italy had decided to enter the war on the side of Germany.

Britain and France were formally notified that hostilities would begin at midnight. Switzerland, Jugoslavia, Turkey, Egypt and Greece were told by Mussolini that Italy did not intend to drag "other peoples" into the conflict, but it would "depend entirely on their own attitude."

President Roosevelt, who was informed by telephone of the Italian decision, declared in a broadcast at 12.15 a.m. today (British time) that Italy had "scorned the rights of security of other nations."

The United States, he said, would extend to the opponents of force the material resources of the nation.

M. Reynaud, the French Prime Minister, broadcasting at 7.45 p.m., said: "When, at 4.30 this afternoon, our Ambassador in Rome asked Count Ciano for what reason Mussolini had decided that blood must flow, the reply was, 'Mussolini is only carrying out the plans which he has made with Hitler.'"

In a broadcast to Germany last night Paris Radio said: "We know how vulnerable Italy is. The Alps are insurmountable. All gates to France are barred."

A statement issued in London by the Ministry of Information said that the Allies' preparations against the entry of Italy were complete and "they will know how to meet the sword with the sword."

June 17 1940

RESIGNATION OF REYNAUD CABINET

FOLLOWING all day meetings of the French Cabinet in Bordeaux yesterday it was announced by the French radio last night that the Reynaud Government had resigned.

A new Ministry, the announcement stated, had been formed under the leadership of Marshal Petain with Gen. Weygand as Vice-Premier and Defence Minister.

June 19 1940

Rules for Civilians in Invasion

RULES for the guidance of the civilian population "if the invader comes" are set out in a leaflet, prepared by the Ministry of Information, which is to be issued to all households in the next few days. It states:

The Germans threaten to invade Great Britain. If they do so they will be driven out by our Navy, our Army and our Air Force. Yet the ordinary men and women of the civilian population will also have their part to play.

Hitler's invasions of Poland, Holland and Belgium were greatly helped by the fact that the civilian population was taken by surprise. They did not know what to do when the moment came. You must not be taken by surprise.

When Holland and Belgium were invaded the civilian population fled from their homes, they crowded on the roads in cars, in carts, on bicycles and on foot, and so helped the enemy by preventing their own armies from advancing against the invaders. You must not allow that to happen here. Your first rule therefore, is:

If the Germans come by parachute, aeroplane or ship you must remain where you are: the order is "stay put."

There is another method which the Germans adopt in their invasion. They make use of the civilian population to create confusion and panic. They spread false rumours and issue false instructions. To prevent this you should obey the second rule, which is:

Do not believe rumours and do not spread them.

When you receive an order, make quite sure it is a true order and not a faked order. Most of you know your policemen and your ARP wardens by sight. You can trust them. If you keep your heads you can also tell whether a military officer is really British or only pretending to be so. If in doubt, ask the policeman or the ARP warden. Use your common sense.

Be calm, quick and exact. The third rule, therefore, is as follows:

Keep watch. If you see anything suspicious, note it carefully and go at once to the nearest police officer or station, or to the nearest military officer. Do not rush about spreading vague rumours. Go quickly to the nearest authority and give him the facts.

Remember that if parachutists come down near your home, they will not be feeling at all brave. They will not know where they are, they will have no food, they will not know where their companions are. The fourth rule, therefore, is as follows:

Do not give any German anything. Do not tell him anything.

Hide your food and your bicycles. Hide your maps. See that the enemy gets no petrol. If you have a car or motor-bicycle, put it out of action when not in use. It is not enough to remove the ignition key: you must make it useless to anyone except yourself.

If you are a garage proprietor, you must work out a plan to protect your stock of petrol and your customers' cars. Remember that transport and petrol will be the invader's main difficulties. Make sure that no invader will be able to get hold of your cars, petrol, maps or bicycles.

Signing the French Armistice in a railway carriage, Compiègne June 22

June 24 1940
DE GAULLE'S RALLYING CALL

GEN. de Gaulle, who was Under-Secretary for War in the Reynaud Cabinet, broadcasting last night in French from London, said that the Armistice accepted by the Bordeaux Government was a capitulation.

"This capitulation was signed before all means of resistance had been exhausted. This capitulation delivers into the hands of the enemy, who will use them against our Allies, our arms, our aeroplanes, our warships, our gold. This capitulation utterly reduces France and places the Government at Bordeaux in immediate and direct dependence on the Germans and Italians.

"There is no longer on the soil of France herself an independent Government capable of upholding the interests of France and the French overseas. Moreover our political institutions are no longer in a position to function freely, and the people of France have at the moment no opportunity of expressing their true will.

"Consequently, and owing to force majeure, a French National Committee will be formed in agreement with the British Government, representing the interests of the country and the people, and resolved to maintain the independence of France; to honour the alliances to which she is committed, and to contribute to the war efforts of the Allies until the final victory.

"The war is not lost, the country is not dead, hope is not extinct. Vive la France!"

Zone of the German occupation under Armistice terms

June 25 1940
Pig Clubs in Villages

PARISH councils, young farmers clubs, women's institutes and other rural organisations are co-operating in the Ministry of Agriculture's efforts to establish village pig clubs on a co-operative basis to utilise household and vegetable waste.

By forming clubs, allotment holders, owners of large and small gardens and smallholders can make a valuable contribution to the nation's food supplies.

Specialist pig breeders are being forced to reduce their herds through lack of imported feeding stuffs, and the clubs could provide an alternative source of pig meat besides giving the specialists an outlet for their young stock.

It is estimated that if one out of every five allotment holders and rural householders fattened only one pig a year, half a million pigs would be available for food annually in addition to those fed on farms.

Mr Alec Hobson, secretary to the Small Pig Keepers' Council set up by the Ministry, said that there had been a most encouraging response to the scheme.

July 1 1940
Lady Mosley Detained

A number of people were detained by police during the week-end under the Defence Regulations. They included Lady Mosley, wife of Sir Oswald Mosley, and Capt. George Henry Lane Fox Pitt-Rivers, a well-known anthropologist.

Lady Mosley, who is 30, is the third daughter of Lord Redesdale and a sister of Miss Unity Mitford. She was formerly Mrs Diana Guinness.

The arrest was carried out by senior officers of the Buckinghamshire police at Lady Mosley's home, Savehay Farm, Denham, on Saturday. She was driven direct to Holloway Prison. Afterwards, a search of the house was carried out.

Lady Mosley visited her husband several times at Brixton Prison, and it is believed she has kept in touch with members of the Fascist party.

It was revealed on Saturday that Lady Mosley gave birth in a nursing home 11 weeks ago to a second child of her marriage to Sir Oswald. It is learned that Lady Mosley was given an opportunity of taking her baby with her, but she left it behind. The child is being looked after at her house.

Capt. Pitt-Rivers is Lord of the Manor of Hinton St Mary, and is a prominent landowner in Dorset and Wiltshire. He contested the North Dorset seat at the 1935 general election as Independent agricultural candidate, and forfeited his deposit.

The Rev. H. E. B. Nye, Rector of Scampton, near Lincoln, and the Rev. John Vivian Thomas, Vicar of Langton by Wragby, near Lincoln, have also been detained by police.

July 10 1940
Duke of Windsor

THE Colonial Office announced last night that the Duke of Windsor has been appointed Governor and Commander-in-Chief of the Bahama Islands.

Until the French Armistice the Duke was at French GHQ, where he acted as liaison officer between the British and French forces.

The Duke and Duchess of Windsor are at present at Lisbon.

Emptying waste into the "pig bin"

Spitfires on patrol over England

The Battle of Britain

THE *Battle of Britain was fought between July 10 and October 31 1940. These are the official dates for the eligibility of Fighter Command aircrew to wear the prized rose gilt emblem on the ribbon of the 1939-45 Star and for inclusion on the roll of honour at Westminster Abbey. They relate to the critical summer weeks when invasion seemed likely until air superiority achieved by the RAF removed the threat.*

Churchill anticipated and named it when he told the Commons on June 18: "What General Weygand called the Battle of France is over. I expect the Battle of Britain is about to begin…The whole fury and might of the enemy must very soon be turned on us."

The odds were daunting. Three Air Fleets, including 800 Me 109 single-engined and 290 Me 110 twin-engined fighters, assembled – Air Fleets 2 and 3 in France, Holland and Belgium and Air Fleet 5 in Norway and Denmark – to escort 1,260 medium, and 320 dive-bombers. Facing them Air Chief Marshal Sir Hugh Dowding's battle order as C-in-C, Fighter Command, could call on 19 squadrons totalling some 200 operationally serviceable Hurricanes and Spitfires – only six squadrons of Spitfires – in Air Vice-Marshal Keith Park's No. 11 Group, standing between London and the coast of south-east England. Three other groups, Nos 10, 12 and 13, guarded the rest of the country with 16 Hurricane or Spitfire fighter squadrons, one squadron of biplane Gladiators, six squadrons of Blenheims (mostly experimental as night fighters) and two squadrons of Defiants, an ill-starred power-turreted fighter.

Dowding entered the battle with some 600 fighters, mostly Hurricanes, of varying performance and 1,253 pilots of whom more than 50 were on loan from the Fleet Air Arm. He knew that anti-aircraft and balloon barrage defences were inadequate and that the early warning radar system upon which so much depended was only now nearing completion. He also had access (a well kept secret at the time) to limited Ultra readings of the enemy's Enigma coded signals.

The battle began on July 10 with an attack on a Channel convoy and Park responded cautiously. An error could lose the war in a matter of hours. Soon his parsimony in confronting enemy waves with small formations, even pairs of Hurricanes, frustrated pilots who were on the fringe – not least Sqdn Ldr Douglas Bader, the legless commander of No. 242 Squadron, mostly Canadians, stationed behind London in Air Vice-Marshal Trafford Leigh-Mallory's 12 Group.

But as the pattern of the German onslaught emerged, Dowding and Park's husbandry paid off. On August 12 grouse shooting began and the significance of the date in the British sporting calendar was not lost on Berlin radio which broadcast that on the previous day "the Nazi cads unsportingly had bagged 90 RAF warplanes for the loss of 32 German." (The true tally was 38 Luftwaffe aircraft for the loss of 32 RAF.)

After the convoy attacks the Luftwaffe concentrated on the coastal radar chain, moving on to 11 Group's airfields that were essential to fighter squadrons defending the invasion corner of England. On August 13 Goering signalled "Eagle Day," expecting air superiority to be achieved within four days. It unleashed a frenzied attempt to rub out Biggin Hill and Park's other crucial airfields. Fortunately, just when the radar stations were at risk of becoming inoperable, Goering again switched the emphasis of the attack. With 11 Group's airfields becoming untenable he turned on London. The day raids on the capital between September 7 and 15, relieved the pressure on the radar sites, fighter airfields and aircraft factories.

This gave Dowding the miracle he had prayed for; and Churchill his immortal words: "Never in the field of human conflict was so much owed by so many to so few."

June 29 1940

NIGHT SORTIE BY RAF BOMBERS

By Douglas Williams
An RAF Station in East Anglia

THE light was failing fast as we stood in a little group on the tarmac watching the second pilots taxi the big Wellington bombers over to the edge of the field. The moon had already risen, but was half hidden behind a bank of clouds. The evening was clear and mild, with a hint of rain.

Members of the crew of the machines selected to make the raid over Germany stood in little groups, awaiting their machines, tugging on overalls, adjusting parachute harness, testing earphones. Laughing and chatting with each other, they seemed as little concerned about their dangerous mission as though they were about to take a night train to Scotland.

Each machine had a separate target, several hundred miles away, into the heart of Germany, involving a dangerous night flight over hostile country and the correct location of a tiny spot on the map where an important railway junction, a munitions factory or a petrol dump was to be attacked.

This particular raid had a special significance because it was the "christening" of a new aerodrome – the first time machines had made a raid from it. And to mark the event almost the entire station personnel had gathered in the darkness to say bon voyage to the "sortie" – the Group Captain, the padre, pilots and men off duty were all there gazing silently at the huge machines as with their double motors roaring they were manoeuvred into position for the take-off.

Each was loaded with more than a ton of bombs, explosive and incendiary – the type carefully selected in accordance with the target to be attacked. Then as each machine in turn pulled up in front of the headquarters building the crew of six climbed in: the two pilots, the observer and navigator, the wireless operator and, finally, the two airgunners who, each ensconced in splendid isolation in his transparent turret, one in the nose and the other in the tail of the aircraft, play their important rôle of defending the bomber from hostile machines.

All is order and method. There is no fuss or confusion. No sense of drama or that any of that gallant crew is involved in anything but his normal day's work. From the young 19-year-old airgunner to the 40-year-old pilot, who, married and with children, emerged from his retirement to rejoin the service for the war, all are calm and supremely confident.

One by one the machines take off and disappear into the eastern sky.

Off they go, flying high, at nearly 200 miles an hour, resolutely determined to find their target, regardless of fierce anti-aircraft defences, of the stabbing beams of searchlights, of attacks by enemy fighters.

Two-thirty a.m. and the eastern sky is already faintly streaked with the pearl grey of dawn. We walk back to the field and strain our ears for the engine beat of the returning machines.

In his signal cabin the wireless operator twirls his dials seeking to pick up a call. Suddenly we hear a machine and there, drifting in from the east, we see a homing plane. The ground officer dashes over to the signal hut – "OK to come in – OK in," he shouts through the microphone, and the pilot's voice, as clear as though he were in the same room instead of thousands of feet up in the air, answers, "OK – coming in – OK coming in." And down he comes, following the flare of the landing searchlight, to make a perfect landing. The crew climb out, stretch their legs, light cigarettes.

"How was it?" someone asks. "Very dull," is the laconic answer. "Very cloudy all the way. Jerry didn't bother us at all. But we found our target and saw a lot of flame and smoke after we had dropped our bombs."

The machine-gunner complained to me, "Hadn't a chance to fire a round. That's the trouble of this night flying.

"But the fireworks are fine. From my seat in the tail I get a wonderful view of the show – the AA bursts, the searchlights, the tracer bullets and, better than all else, the explosion of our bombs. It's better than the Crystal Palace!"

July 11 1940

FIGHTERS' GREAT FEATS AGAINST BIG ODDS

GERMAN air losses in a great air battle over the south-east coast of England and in other engagements with the RAF yesterday are believed to total 37 'planes.

The Air Ministry announced early to-day that, in addition to 14 machines definitely shot down, 23 were so badly damaged that they were unlikely to reach home.

The Royal Air Force, said the statement, inflicted the greatest damage in any day since air raids began, at a cost of only two fighters. One of the pilots, however, was safe.

About 150 'planes were engaged in the south-east coast air battle, circling, diving and zooming with machine-guns blazing. Spectators said that Spitfires shot down three German bombers in less than three minutes.

One machine had its tail shot off; a bomber and fighter collided and crashed; several badly damaged raiders turned back across the Channel with trails of black smoke pouring from their tails.

Describing this action the Air Ministry statement said that late in the afternoon Spitfires and Hurricanes engaged about 70 enemy bombers and protecting fighters. In the dog fights which followed the British pilots shot down six ME 110 twin-engined fighters and damaged four ME 110s, four ME 109s, and an HE 111 bomber without loss.

Sqn Ldr Douglas Bader on the wing of his Hurricane

July 15 1940

IDENTITY OF LEGLESS PILOT

By Major C. C. Turner

I learn that the Hurricane pilot who, although he lost both legs in a pre-war crash, shot down a Dornier 17 in a weekend raid was D. R. S. Bader.

He is the 30-year-old son of Mrs Hobbs, wife of the Rector of Sprotborough, near Doncaster. He performed some daring aerobatics in the RAF display at Hendon in 1931. He played Rugby for the RAF, the Combined Services and Harlequins, and was so good a scrum-half that he would in all probability have got his England cap. He also played cricket and squash.

In December, 1931, he lost control when flying over his aerodrome and crashed heavily. After the loss of both legs, he was invalided out of the service, but he became so skilful in the use of his metal legs that he could still play cricket, tennis and squash. He became the representative of an oil combine, and had the pedals of his car altered so that he could drive. He even learned to play golf.

Within nine months he was in the air again, a fully qualified civil pilot. When war broke out, in the words of a friend, "he almost went down on his hands and knees to the Air Ministry to take him back into the RAF." He passed a test with flying colours and was posted to a fighter squadron.

A few months ago he was taking off when his engine failed and he had a minor crash. Both his metal legs were badly bent, but an artificer straightened them and half an hour later he was up in the air again. Now he is leading a squadron of Canadians.

July 20 1940

Hitler on "One Last Appeal for Peace"

HITLER appealed for a Nazi peace when he addressed the Reichstag in Berlin last night. Ciano, the Italian Foreign Secretary, was present to demonstrate the solidarity of the Axis.

The speech, which occupied one hour and 36 minutes, consisted mainly of a long survey of history as he sees it, to which Hitler has accustomed his Nazi audiences. The purpose for which the speech was staged was apparently contained in the following phrases:

"I realise that if this struggle continues it can only end in the annihilation of one of us. Mr Churchill thinks it will be Germany. I know it will be Britain . . . I see no reason why this war must go on."

There were the customary protestations of Germany's innocence, much talk about the "war-mongering Jews" and threats of reprisals for the RAF raids.

In diplomatic quarters in London last night, Hitler's speech was not thought worthy of comment. America was similarly unimpressed, the view being taken that such "peace threats" were now a recognised part of Nazi propaganda.

One of the more interesting features was Hitler's adherence to the Napoleonic tradition in creating Goering, Marshal of the Reich; Keitel, his Chief of Staff, General Field-Marshal, and promoting several of the army and air force generals to the rank of marshal.

July 13 1940

'PLANES TURN TAIL AND DUMP BOMBS IN SEA

A further 11 German raiders, all bombers, were shot down round the coasts of Britain yesterday – nine by Spitfires and Hurricanes, one by an Anson of the Coastal Command, and one by anti-aircraft gunners. Others were damaged.

Seven out of 16 Germans which attempted to bomb shipping were destroyed. None of the ships were damaged.

Two bombers which presumably hoped to raid the South-East coast turned tail and dumped their bombs in the sea when a British fighter appeared. One was shot down before his inglorious attempt to escape could succeed.

Another bomber fell to the accurate firing of an AA battery in South-West England which had collected a bag of four 'planes on Thursday.

Germany has lost 108 bombers and fighters since she began mass raids on this country on June 18. Of these no fewer than 72 have been brought down this week. Many others, severely damaged, were unlikely to reach home.

Germany's losses for the week are: Sunday 7, Monday 8, Tuesday 9, Wednesday 14 and Thursday 23.

July 16 1940

AIR FIGHT SEEN FROM CLIFF

From a Special American
Correspondent
Straits of Dover

I sat on a cliff for a solid hour yesterday afternoon while 40 Stukas, German dive-bombing 'planes, attacked a convoy. It was the great air battle in which, according to the official account, seven German 'planes were shot down and the convoy escaped damage.

A flaring Junkers 87 glided down and knifed into the sea half a mile from where I sat. Minutes later a German pilot came floating down out of the clouds, frantically trying to make the beach. He landed half a mile out to sea and was drowned before anybody could reach him.

Back to the west a Hurricane dived on a Messerschmitt 109 and drove him down with smoke trailing behind. He roared over me at 500ft, the smoke suddenly stopped, and he seemed to right himself. Then his engine began to rattle like a kettledrum and he went staggering back toward France.

Over to the right the Stukas soared like hawks, then hurtled down to the roar of racing engines to bomb the convoy. There were incredible concussions, and the ships were shut off from view by smoke, flame and spray.

A warship seemed surrounded in fire as all its guns blazed away at the soaring, diving German machines.

I had come down in the morning for the avowed purpose of seeing a German bombardment. In glorious summer sunshine the cliffs north of Cape Gris Nez, 22 miles away, seemed within arm's reach.

When the fight was in full swing, the noise in the skies and down in the Channel never seemed to end. Hurricanes and Spitfires came dashing in early in the attack and were chasing German 'planes all over the skies. Just at the back of the cliffs, 5,000ft up, one Hurricane got on the tail of a Messerschmitt 109 and gave it a long burst. The Hurricane whipped round and went after another as the Messerschmitt came hurtling down toward my "one man Press gallery" with smoke pouring out behind him.

As the British fighters took care of the Messerschmitts and then dived on the Stukas themselves the battle finally began to peter out and the Germans went off.

Back in the neighbouring town I found streets were crowded with Sunday afternoon strollers. Nobody seemed to be talking about the air raid, although most of them had been sitting in shelters holding their ears a bare hour before.

A crater caused by enemy bombs in Ashdown Forest

July 10 1940

Appeal for Aluminium

LORD Beaverbrook, Minister of Air Production, issues the following appeal to the women of Britain: "We want aluminium and we want it now.

"New and old, of every type and description, and all of it. We will turn your pots and pans into Spitfires and Hurricanes, Blenheims and Wellingtons.

"Everyone who has pots and pans, kettles, vacuum cleaners, hat pegs, coat hangers, shoe trees, household ornaments, cigarette boxes or any other articles made wholly or in part of aluminium should hand them over at once to the local headquarters of the Women's Voluntary Services.

"There are branches of this organisation in every town and village in the country.

"If you are in any doubt, or if you have difficulty in finding the local office of the Women's Voluntary Services, please inquire at the nearest police station or town hall."

The Minister adds that the need for aluminium is urgent and imperative in the national interest.

A Luftwaffe pilot is taken prisoner during the Battle of Britain

July 22 1940
LDV Captures Nazi Airmen

THE story of the capture of three German airmen by an LDV officer was told last evening by Mrs Phillips, wife of the officer, Capt. A. H. Phillips. He and his wife and their son, a private in the RAMC, had travelled by car to visit the young man's grandmother.

On their way back through the country they noticed a big aeroplane flying low overhead. Capt. Phillips said: "That looks like a Jerry." Then two RAF fighters swept down out of the sky.

There were a few bursts of machine-gun fire and the other 'plane, which they could now see was a German, landed on its fuselage in a field.

Capt. Phillips covered the Germans with his revolver, and the uninjured man at once handed over his pistol. Meanwhile, Pte Phillips gave first aid to the others.

July 29 1940
Church Bell Problem

INQUIRY among the clergy shows that no precise instructions have been given on the Government order to discontinue the use of church bells except as an alarm against parachutists.

It was stated that the bells would in future be rung only by the military or the local defence volunteers. For the most part, however, the clergy have received no instructions and no requests for giving access at all times to the bells.

Moreover, it appears to have been overlooked that the ringing of bells requires much practice and skill. When the anticipated emergency arises there is likely to be bewilderment and exasperation in the belfry when an inexperienced soldier or volunteer tries to give the alarm. He will pull the rope, but no sound will be heard. The harder he pulls the less likely he is to make the bell ring.

On the other hand, the bell set for ringing can be made to speak with very little effort by the practised bellringer, but the novice who pulls the rope with the bell in its proper ringing position runs the growing risk of wringing his own neck.

A bell rope whipping round the belfry with a ton weight of metal agitating it is like a live thing and very dangerous. It is also possible for the inexpert ringer to be carried up and to crack his skull on the belfry roof.

It would seem a wise plan to have enlisted bell-ringers for the express purpose of sounding the tocsin. It is estimated that there are about 35,000 in England, almost all of whom would be only too glad to give their services.

July 25 1940
Village Home Guard

By Richard Capell

BETWEEN the great elms the village church shows its sandstone tower and the cottages their high-pitched roofs of thatch. Dear and homely scene, to-day doubly dear!

Not, I suppose since the days of Cromwell and his Ironsides has this valley echoed to any but the sounds of peace. When will it hear again those familiar sounds – the foxhounds at the meet on a winter morning, the cheering at our Saturday afternoon cricket matches in the park, the church bells?

To-day the village is thinking of other things. The captain of the cricket club has not worn flannels this summer. Instead, he has unearthed the khaki uniform he had put away in 1919. He commands the village LDV, (now designated Home Guard), which parades night by night as the sunset fades on park and summer elms and sleeping meadows. He scores a good mark, I think, by being able, after 21 years, to get into that old uniform so comfortably.

There is not a possible man in the village who does not belong to the Guard. A few are young fellows who still await their call to the Colours.

What would come as a surprise to the stranger to our pastoral scene, a scene that speaks so intimately of an age-old peace, is the number of men with experience of soldiering.

The stranger who should see these men in hayfield or rickyard might fancy that this Midland horizon was the only one they had ever known. But here, at the evening parade, is a man who sports a North-West Frontier medal, and next to him is a veteran of the South African war, while everyone who is in their 40's or 50's has memories of 1914-18.

The Home Guard's orderly room is in the rectory stables. To see the roses in his garden you would say that the rector had given them half a lifetime's attention to the exclusion of the outer world. You would be wrong. The rector is an old Army chaplain with a long record of overseas service, from which he retains the liveliest and most affectionate memories of the Andaman Islanders. He is a keen member of the Guard, and at field exercises the other night impersonated (with an umbrella) an alien parachutist. A patrol spotted him; a rifle clicked – for while not yet completely equipped, the village Guard is already partially armed – and the rector's dramatic leap and cry were the admiration of the parish.

War talk in the village is less speculative than the talk one hears in towns. The day's task is accepted as it comes. To-day's task or to-night's – the patrolling of these familiar fields, of these woods that have not for a whole age known any more considerable enemy of society than a poacher – still strikes the imagination as fantastic; but that is the fault of imagination. The village Home Guard is facing the facts squarely.

Men of the Home Guard practice with a Vickers machine gun

August 5 1940
Hollywood Points the Moral

By Campbell Dixon

"THE Sea Hawk" (Warner) is another notable proof of Hollywood's sympathy with the British cause. Sabatini's original corsair, the scourge of the Mediterranean, becomes Francis Thorpe the privateer, harrying the aggressive Spaniards.

If he plunders galleons it is to give his Queen the gold she needs to build ships without exorbitant taxation; and her last speech, pledging a stronger fleet and the destruction of the invading Armada, might have been spoken by Mr Churchill.

The producer's eye to contemporary events is revealed again in the debates of Elizabeth's cousellors, some urging defiance to the dictator who wants to overrun the world, others advising appeasement and delay. England's hero is played by Errol Flynn, who recently took out American naturalisation papers – partly to save income-tax, it seems.

August 13 1940

DRAMATIC US ACCOUNTS OF AIR BATTLES

From Our Own Correspondent, New York

THE air battle over Southern England yesterday dominated today's American newspapers.

Although handicapped by the difficulty of weaving stories out of scores of dog fights into a narrative, American correspondents now appear to have access to much more vivid material than before, and every newspaper has given a detailed and thrilling account of the Nazi onslaught.

So far, however, the British authorities have apparently declined to release photographs for radio transmission to the United States, and the papers here are anxious to show their readers what air-fighting of this kind means.

One story which appealed to the imagination of all American editors was the description of a new and terrifying British weapon – the spider-web net of steel cables fired from guns to snare the Nazi 'planes.

Pride of place is given to the dramatic eye-witness messages written by Americans who watched some of the raids from towns on the south-east coast.

"From a balcony spattered with machine-gun bullets and jarred by deafening bombardment," says Robert Bunnelle, of the Associated Press, "I saw a new chapter in the Battle for Britain written today in a sky thick with aeroplanes and spotted with mushroom puffs from anti-aircraft shells.

"During one attack, I saw four German 'planes apparently bagged by British fighters and anti-aircraft shells. The battle raged so furiously that it was impossible to keep accurate count of the 'planes which fell. Throughout the firing balloon barrage crews worked calmly preparing new balloons to replace those shot down."

A writer in Weymouth was impressed by a British pilot who, shot down over the sea and rescued, immediately telephoned his base from a police station, saying "I will be back this afternoon and do not forget to have a 'plane ready."

A United Press correspondent says: "All day long the sky has been filled with Nazi 'planes. It seemed as if they never would stop coming over."

Comparatively little space is given to the Berlin side of the story, for the reason that the American public does not attach much faith to the German communiqués. Distrust was further emphasised by printing the German figures in small type.

Typical of the intense interest with which Americans are following this phase of the Battle for Britain is the amount of space devoted to yesterday's raids by the Herald-Tribune, which prints six columns and has five-column headlines on the front page. All the evening papers have banner headlines across their front pages.

Scramble!

Bombs exploding on the south coast of England

August 23 1940

DOVER AREA SHELLED FROM FRANCE

GERMAN heavy guns on the French coast bombarded the Dover area last night, following an attempt by the gunners earlier in the day to destroy a convoy steaming through the Straits of Dover.

The attack on the convoy was the first occasion on which the enemy brought into action the high-velocity guns which he has massed along the French coast from Boulogne to Calais as part of his plans for the invasion of Britain.

A War Office, Air Ministry and Ministry of Home Security communiqué, issued at 2.50 a.m. today, said:

"Yesterday evening enemy artillery on the French coast opened fire on the Dover area. Enemy shells caused some damage to buildings. There were a number of casualties."

The bombardment began soon after 9 p.m. and lasted for nearly three-quarters of an hour.

August 22 1940

Trotsky Dies of Injuries

From Our Own Correspondent
Mexico City

M. Leon Trotsky, the exiled Bolshevik leader, died tonight from the injuries he received when he was attacked yesterday at his home here. He received a fractured skull.

A trepanning operation was performed last night, but he gradually sank.

The attack on Trotsky was made by an American citizen known as Frank Jackson, said to be one of his closest friends. For this reason he was admitted freely to the closely-guarded house. He attacked Trotsky at his writing desk with an instrument resembling an alpenstock, striking his head repeatedly.

August 17 1940

DELIBERATE ATTACK ON EASTBOURNE

MORE than 71 Nazi raiders yesterday paid the penalty of the invader, when the German air force engaged in a series of intensive raids. These included the indiscriminate bombing of south-western suburbs of London and what was officially described as "a deliberate attack on Eastbourne."

The following communiqué was issued by the Air Ministry and Ministry of Home Security shortly before 3 a.m. today:

"On several occasions during yesterday evening waves of enemy aircraft crossed our coasts but most of them scattered over a wide area and dropped bombs at many points in country districts of Herts, Essex, Surrey, Hants and Oxfordshire. Little damage was done. Some people were injured but reports so far received indicated that the number of killed was small.

"A deliberate attack was made on the residential town of Eastbourne where damage was caused and several persons were fatally injured.

"Casualties, including some deaths to service personnel, were caused at Royal Air Force aerodromes, at one of which considerable damage was done to buildings.

"Although full reports are not yet available, the total of enemy aircraft now known to have been destroyed yesterday is 71. Eighteen of our fighters were lost but the pilots of 10 of them are safe."

Swift retribution, it was announced, overtook the raiders who bombed Croydon airport on Thursday – every enemy machine which took part in the attack was destroyed.

Civilians sheltering at Aldwych tube station

September 2 1940

'Planes Litter Countryside

From H. A. Flower
South-East Coast

THE beautiful countryside of Southern England is littered with broken Dorniers, Heinkels, Junkers and Messerschmitts.

Today I drove through the highways and byways of a south-eastern district with the idea of estimating bomb damage. I found little, although many fields, gardens and stretches of heath and beach were pitted with craters. But what I did discover in a two-hour run were the wrecks of no fewer than 13 raiders.

As I drove back towards the coast I saw, flying low along the coast, the huge black mass of a Dornier 17 bomber which was shortly to be added to the litter of Marshal Goering's fleet of crashed 'planes. The 'plane appeared to be attempting a photographic survey of a number of gun and searchlight positions.

Suddenly from a camouflaged strong point which the Nazi had obviously not observed there came a sharp blast of machine-gun fire. Almost at the same moment a skilfully concealed gun came into action when the Dornier's nose was pointed directly at it.

All of the Dornier's guns opened up at once and I watched from my car barely 100 yards from the scene a short, sharp and thrilling battle. With its gun spurting explosive bullets, the pilot tried vainly to "lift" his machine over and away from the

Wreckage of a German Dornier bomber

hidden posts. The duel lasted for perhaps 20 secs. Then, after half a dozen rattling exchanges of fire, the Dornier pancaked on the beach a yard from the water's edge with tell-tale wisps of smoke pouring from the engine.

A moment later men from the posts were racing to the rescue of the Dornier's crew. They lifted the four occupants from their seats a few seconds before the machine became a mass of flames. Two of them were wounded.

The German sergeant-pilot told me before an ambulance took him to the hospital that this was his first flight over England. His gunner, a young officer, had been before and wore an Iron Cross.

August 30 1940

GREAT FIRES IN BERLIN AFTER RAF RAID

BERLIN experienced the full weight of the Royal Air Force offensive early yesterday, when, in a three-hour raid, great explosions and fires that could be seen 50 miles away followed intensive bombing of a number of selected military objectives.

The raid was carried out in clear moonlight. One of the British 'planes, after launching its bombs, cruised over Berlin for 50 minutes, another made a rectangular run all round the city.

'Planes selected from two squadrons, the Air Ministry stated last night, made a special attack on one objective only four miles from the centre of Berlin.

The nature of this objective was not disclosed.

The Berlin raid was only one feature in a night of sustained and systematic devastation of military objectives in many parts of Germany and enemy-occupied territory.

More than 15 tons of high-explosive and incendiary bombs were rained down on the great Junkers factory at Dessau, 65 miles south-west of Berlin.

"Panic in England" as portrayed by the *Detroit News*

THE BLUE GOOSE

I BETCHA TWO BOB THE BLIGHTER MISSES THE IRON MONGERS

RIGHTO — YOU'RE ON

AIR RAID SHELTER 50 FT. ▶

September 5 1940

Threat to Wipe Out Towns

CHAGRIN at the failure of his blitzkrieg attempts across Britain, and rage at the success of RAF raids on Germany, were the dominant notes in a speech which Hitler addressed to the German nation yesterday.

Mouthing his well-worn threats against Britain, shrieking his oft-repeated gibes at her statesmen, he left no doubt in the minds of neutral listeners that his plans have gone awry, and that the present situation is not to his liking.

In his threat of devastating reprisals for British night raids was an obvious attempt to apologise to the German people for Goering's failure to sustain his boast that not an enemy bomb would drop on their territory.

"For three months," he shouted, "I have waited for the British to cease the nuisance of nightly and planless bomb throwing." Then, after this demonstration of his magnanimity came the threats.

"The British will know now that we are now giving our answer night after night. If they attack our cities we will simply erase theirs. We will call a halt to these night pirates. The hour will come when one of us two will break up, and it won't be Nazi Germany.

"If the British throw two or three thousand pounds of bombs we will unload 150, 180, yes, 200 thousand . . ."

Apparently he intended to continue the progression of figures, but the shouts of the crowd halted him.

Salvaging possessions in the aftermath of a bombing attack

September 9 1940

AIR ATTACK ON LONDON RENEWED LAST NIGHT

T HE big air attack on London, which began with a mass daylight raid on Saturday evening and continued during the night, was resumed last night, when the warning was given at 7.59 as dusk fell.

Goering, creator of the German Air Force, is directing the attack. He said in a broadcast yesterday from his headquarters in Northern France that he could see waves of 'planes headed for England.

He did not mention the price which the raiders paid, though the German radio had admitted "great sacrifices."

Immediately after last night's warning there was one of the heaviest AA bombardments in the London area since the raids began. Windows and doors were shaken by gunfire. In the half light eight Nazi machines could be observed approaching from the south-east at a great height.

Shells burst around the 'planes, which were forced to change their course. Some bombs were dropped on a suburb, including incendiaries, which started a blaze.

Raiders also approached London from the north-west, where anti-aircraft guns immediately went into action. A few minutes after the warning several enemy 'planes passed over a London suburb. Anti-aircraft guns opened fire in the gathering twilight.

Within a few seconds of the alarm sirens ceasing, violent AA fire broke out in Central London. This was followed by the sound of a screaming bomb and an explosion.

Three-quarters of an hour later a second wave of raiders approached the East London area. Bombs fell at scattered points, some in the district affected in Saturday's raids.

After a sleepless night, while their Anderson shelters rocked with the explosion of bombs and the crash of guns, the people of East London carried on yesterday with their usual amazing spirit.

Several hundred began their search for new homes as soon as the all clear sounded. Whole streets had been destroyed and many other houses demolished. But people gathered their possessions together and piled them into perambulators. With children in their arms they started their walk to friends or relatives.

Their morale was astonishing. As they were walking to their new homes, many were laughing and joking among themselves.

Some families took care of children whose parents were dead or injured, and made long journeys across London to escort them to the homes of relatives.

Women went on preparing the Sunday dinner, even though they had no water or gas. They borrowed water from more fortunate neighbours and lit fires to roast the joints. One of them, Mrs W. Johnson, who had spent the night in a shelter, was preparing her meal in a house where the dividing wall between dining-room and drawing-room lay in chunks across the floors.

In a dockland tavern, where every window had been blown out by a bomb which fell across the road, they were collecting for a Spitfire fund.

The licensee of a hotel gave up his saloon bar for housing people whose houses were no longer tenable.

In several streets neighbours were making a whip round for those who had lost their belongings.

"It was an experience far worse than the Silvertown explosion in the last war," Mrs Cook, who with her husband and five children escaped injury, said to me. "The heat from the fires was terrific. We do not intend moving from the district despite this ghastly raid."

The morale of the people was summed up in the words of one Mayor, who said, "They have taken it on the chin."

Mrs D. Adams, MP for South Poplar and an alderman of the borough, said: "Wherever you meet our people today, they are not worrying. If all the country is as good as we are in Poplar, then the Government or the people has no cause for fear. The morale of the people is very high."

A similar tribute was paid by the Rev. R. A. Kingdon, vicar of St John's, Isle of Dogs, who said: "There was no panic. If it is any barometer whether we are going to win or not, the people here are going to stick it. There is no lack of confidence."

The Queen emerges from an air raid shelter

September 12 1940
King and Queen take tea after "All Clear"

THE King and Queen, caught by the sirens in a street in South-East London, yesterday went into a shelter beneath a police station. Only a few yards away was a heap of rubble which was a court-house before a German airman dropped a bomb there on Saturday night.

In the bleak, starkly lit room was gathered a strange cross-section of London life.

In the centre sat their Majesties on bare wooden chairs, the King in the Service dress of a field-marshal and the Queen in a two-piece suit. On the forms around the walls sat policemen in uniform and in plain clothes, Court officials now without a Court, overalled ARP workers, fresh from the ruins next door, and white-smocked women from the police canteen.

Their Majesties, who, accompanied by Sir John Anderson, Minister of Home Security, spent the morning inspecting bomb damage in the outer suburbs of South-East London, were driven to the police station led by the police car which had been guiding them.

When the King and Queen walked into the shelter about 30 people were already there. They stared in astonishment and then clapped their hands. The King leaned back in his chair, crossed his legs comfortably and lit a cigarette. The Queen sat composedly and smiling.

One of the canteen women bustled about to make some tea, but it was not quite ready when the sirens again sounded. The King, who was the first to hear them, remarked, "That is the 'all clear,' but I am going to wait for some of this tea." In a few moments the King and Queen were drinking tea from thick china cups which have the mark of the police canteen upon them. Their Majesties were in the shelter for about 20 minutes.

During the morning the King and Queen saw a dozen scenes of devastation and were touched by the cheerful spirit of the people around them. As they came from a bomb crater marking the spot where a bomb had fallen in the middle of a block of workers' flats, men and women pressed about them cheering and began to sing, "There'll always be an England."

September 14 1940
Palace Chapel Hit

LONDON'S seventh night of intensive air raids saw relays of German bombers attempt, for the most part singly, to elude the formidable box barrage which has proved an effective check on their activities.

Gun flashes in the east heralded the arrival of the first raiders at 9.2 p.m. and from then on until the all clear was sounded shortly before dawn the anti-aircraft batteries were constantly in action.

A communiqué issued by the Air Ministry and Ministry of Home Security at 3.15 p.m. stated:

Following last night's ineffective attacks, in which bombs were dropped in London, at random through heavy clouds, a small number of enemy aircraft have today deliberately bombed a number of conspicuous buildings in various parts of London irrespective of their nature.

It is feared that the enemy has succeeded in killing and injuring a number of civilians.

Buckingham Palace was attacked, several bombs falling within the precincts, one of which damaged the Palace Chapel. Their Majesties were in residence, but fortunately escaped injuries. Three members of the Palace staff were injured.

September 16 1940
St Paul's Saved

ST Paul's Cathedral has been saved by the magnificent courage of a handful of men. The high explosive bomb which had menaced it since Wednesday was safely removed last evening by a bomb disposal section under Lt R. Davies, after three days' unremitting struggle.

The missile proved to be a ton in weight and looked like a vast hog, about 8 ft long. It was fitted with fuses which made it extremely dangerous to touch or move.

The bomb fell in Dean's-yard, close to the west end of the cathedral. It entered the roadway at the end of the pavement.

When the Bomb Disposal Section began to dig they found that a 6in gas main had been fractured. Three men were overcome by fumes at an early stage.

The gas company were called in to deal with the main which had caught fire. No one then knew how close to the flaming main the bomb might have been.

When the gas had at last been cut off the bomb disposal section had to dig for 27ft 6in into the subsoil before they found the bomb.

To save devastating damage to St Paul's the risk of removal had to be undertaken, and with great difficulty the bomb was drawn up with special tackle. High polish had been imparted to it in its passage through the soil, making it difficult to handle.

Two lorries in tandem were required to haul it out of the hole. The streets were cleared by the police from St Paul's to Hackney Marshes. The bomb was placed on a fast lorry and driven away by Lt Davies at high speed, the risk of explosion being imminent all the time.

At Hackney Marshes the bomb was blown up by the Bomb Disposal Section. It caused a 100ft crater and rattled windows, and in one case loosened plaster, in houses far away on the Marshes.

Only the courage and tenacity of the officer, his NCOs and men prevented St Paul's from being levelled to the ground, states the Ministry of Home Security.

September 18 1940

NAZI INVASION FLEET SCATTERED

HITLER'S invasion armada, which, as Mr Churchill emphasised in a statement on the war situation in the House of Commons yesterday, the Germans have been steadily massing for the attack on Britain, has been scattered.

From dawn yesterday reconnaissance aircraft of the RAF Coastal Command combed the enemy coastline over the entire Channel area to ascertain sudden changes in the dispositions of the German sea forces.

These changes were imposed on the enemy after a day of harassing bombing action on Monday and in consequence of the strong westerly wind which swept the Channel throughout the night.

The wind blew with gale force in the exposed places where the German surface craft had been last sighted by RAF patrols.

Most of the Channel was very rough and, as was expected, the enemy's ships and small craft scattered and scurried to seek shelter.

September 23 1940

Evacuee Ship Sunk

EIGHTY-THREE child evacuees bound for Canada, nearly all from State-aided schools, have lost their lives through the torpedoing of their liner in the Atlantic, 600 miles from land, by a German submarine. When survivors arrived here it was disclosed that the attack was made without warning after dark on Tuesday, and in a very heavy sea.

There were 421 passengers and crew in the ship, and the total death-roll is 306. The passengers included eight children not travelling under the evacuation scheme and nine escorts for the evacuees. Two of these eight children and seven of the escorts lost their lives. The casualties were the first in the transport overseas of nearly 3,000 children.

Anti-saboteur poster in the London Docks

FRUSTRATE HIS KNAVISH TRICKS !!!

PREVENT

SABOTAGE

(Fire and Wrecking)

Report suspicious persons & things AT ONCE

September 24 1940

FREE FRENCH FIGHT FOR DAKAR

IT was announced in London last night that Gen. de Gaulle and a force of Free French troops, yesterday, arrived at Dakar to forestall German occupation of this port and naval base in French West Africa.

He sent an envoy ashore appealing to his followers at Dakar to rally to him and urging the French authorities to accept his leadership. The French Governor-General, M. de Boisson, however, ordered resistance to be offered.

A British force is at Dakar with Gen. de Gaulle, lending him full assistance.

According to an announcement on behalf of the Pétain Government at Vichy last night, the naval forces escorting the troops to Dakar opened fire on the town after the Governor-General had declined to surrender.

The Pétain Government, it was added, would not regard this as an occasion for declaring war on Britain. The Cabinet would, however, "reply to force with force."

September 24 1940

King Institutes George Cross

THE King broadcast to the nation last night: "It is just over a year now since the war began. The British peoples entered it with open eyes, recognising how formidable were the forces against them, but confident in the justice of their cause.

"Many and glorious are the deeds of gallantry done during these perilous but famous days. In order that they should be worthily and promptly recognised I have decided to create at once a new mark of honour for men and women in all walks of civilian life.

"I propose to give my name to this new distinction, which will consist of the George Cross, ranking next to the Victoria Cross, and the George Medal for wider distribution.

"As we look around us we see on every side that in the hour of her trial the Mother City of the British Commonwealth is proving herself to be built as a city that is at unity in itself. It is not the walls that make the city but the people who live within them.

"The walls of London may be battered, but the spirit of the Londoner stands resolute and undismayed.

"As in London, so throughout Great Britain, buildings rich in beauty and historic interest may be wantonly attacked, humbler houses, no less dear and familiar, may be destroyed. But 'there'll always be an England' to stand before the world as the symbol and citadel of freedom, and to be our own dear home."

The London Fire Brigade tackling the blitzed Eastcheap in the City

September 26 1940

With London's Fire Fighters

By Helen Kirkpatrick
(Chicago Daily News London Staff)

OUR first alarm of the evening had been caused by a handsome combination of a few high explosives and a "Molotoff breadbasket," and it was a pretty good blaze even in the eyes of the AFS, who do not consider anything less than a five-alarm fire worthy of mention.

Strictly speaking, it was not the first alarm that had been sounded, but it was the first our fire-fighting friends in the gigantic control room, feet underground, thought we should bother with. So we piled into a fire car and dashed off to a well-known Central London street. About 30 pumps were working on it when we got there after making our way along the glass-covered street.

A building opposite to the one afire had been razed by explosive and we had to climb over heaps of bricks to get up to the front line where hoses were playing on the top of an office building.

"Watch it. Hose coming up," and we jumped aside as another powerful stream leapt into the air. The accumulation of hoses, firemen and police in the small area suggested that we had better make way, so we stood on the steps of an adjacent building. Just then came the now familiar whizz of an approaching bomb and someone yelled, "Down flat, everybody."

Our fireman guide stuck out his foot to trip me up, but I was already flat by then inside a door. A thud and boom sounded down the street and everyone picked himself up.

It was well under control and only smoke with an occasional flicker poured from the top floors. It occurred to someone that an old-fashioned gas street light was going as merrily as in peacetime. "Anyone got a piece of soap?"

A policeman disappeared into the building and returned with a cake. As it smothered the gas out he called: "Hey, mate, don't forget to return it. I might want to wash me hands."

Roosevelt Pledges Further Aid

From Our Special Correspondent, Boston

MR Roosevelt announced, in a major campaign speech here today, that he had approved a further extension of the policy of aid for Britain by giving his approval to British orders for artillery, machine-guns, rifles, tanks and ammunition.

He said he asked the Priorities Board, which deals with defence orders, to give sympathetic consideration to a British request for 12,000 additional 'planes. This would bring Britain's present orders to more than 26,000 'planes.

America's objective, he declared, was to keep the potential attacker from the shores of the Continent. Mr Joseph Kennedy, the United States Ambassador to Britain, had told him how the small nations in Europe "live in terror of destruction of their independence by Nazi military might." "We are free to live and love and laugh," the President said.

October 26 1940

Women to Fly Hurricanes

I understand that women are to be allowed to pilot Hurricane fighters. Their task will be to take the Hurricanes from the factories to units at which equipment is added, and then to fly them to the squadrons.

Hitherto they have only been permitted to take training types from the factories.

They do so under a special scheme which came into operation at the beginning of this year, when eight women pilots began work under the leadership of Miss Pauline Gower, daughter of Sir Robert Gower, MP. The number has since been increased to 20.

The reply of the women to the doubters of their ability is to be found in the splendid work they have done. They hope that before long this permission will be extended to all types.

October 7 1940

Planning the Winter Siren Suit

By Our Fashion Expert

WOMEN are planning winter outfits for the shelter. There are many converts to the practical choice of trousers with jumper of rather severe design and short tailored coat. It is the kind of attire in which one remains trim and presentable whatever happens, and it keeps out cold and damp better than most garments.

The shelter trousers (DAILY TELEGRAPH Vogue Fashion Service Pattern No.8774) are cut with dart fitted built-up waistline and slightly rounded hips and are narrow at the ankles.

Princess Elizabeth makes her broadcasting début with Princess Margaret

October 14 1940

Princess's Radio Debut

WITH the King and Queen and her sister standing nearby and with "Uncle Mac," of the Children's Hour, in an adjoining room, Princess Elizabeth made her first broadcast yesterday afternoon, when she addressed evacuee children at home and in the Empire.

The Princess said: "In wishing you all 'Good evening,' I feel that I am speaking to friends and companions who have shared with my sister and myself many a happy Children's Hour.

"Thousands of you in this country have had to leave your homes and be separated from your fathers and mothers. My sister, Margaret Rose, and I feel so much for you, as we know from experience what it means to be away from those we love most of all. To you, living in new surroundings, we send a message of true sympathy, and at the same time we would like to thank the kind people who have welcomed you to their homes in the country.

"Before I finish I can truthfully say to you all that we children at home are full of cheerfulness and courage. We are trying to do all we can to help our gallant sailors, soldiers and airmen, and we are trying, too, to bear our own share of the danger and sadness of war. We know, every one of us, that in the end all will be well: for God will care for us and give us victory and peace. And when peace comes, remember it will be for us, the children of today, to make the world of tomorrow a better and happier place.

"My sister is by my side, and we are both going to say goodnight to you.

"Come on, Margaret."

Princess Margaret: "Goodnight."

Princess Elizabeth: "Goodnight and good luck to you all."

Many a public personage, hardened to broadcasting, might have envied the clearness and precision of the Princess's voice (writes a DAILY TELEGRAPH reporter).

The likeness of her delivery to her mother's, both in tone and enunciation, was very striking.

November 7 1940

ITALIAN PILOTS FIND OUR SKIES TOO COLD

IN contrast to the trumpetings of Rome Radio is the admission in the Giornale d'Italia that Italian pilots are finding increasing difficulties in their much vaunted attacks on Britain.

The paper admits the disadvantages of a personnel untrained for night flying in unknown climatic conditions, in fog, and in skies "where bad weather and tempests are a normal thing. The British pilots are quite at home in these conditions, which is a great advantage."

November 12 1940

Tribute by Premier to Mr Chamberlain

LEADERS of the political parties in the House of Commons have today expressed the nation's sense of loss in the passing of Mr Neville Chamberlain.

Mr Churchill spoke of the dead statesman as the man of peace, whose strivings had established for Great Britain and the Empire a verdict from future generations that we were guiltless of the blood and terror and misery of our time.

Bitter controversy had been stilled by his death. "At the lychgate we may all pass our own conduct, our own judgment, under searching review." History would always provide new proportions and another scale of values. Man's only guide was his conscience, his only shield the rectitude and sincerity of his actions.

"It fell to Neville Chamberlain," said the Prime Minister, "in one of the supreme crises of the world, to be contradicted by events, to be disappointed in his hopes, and to be deceived and cheated by a wicked man."

November 13 1940

HEROIC LAST FIGHT OF THE JERVIS BAY

AN epic story of gallantry at sea was made known last night with the return to ports in Britain of 24 of the ships of the convoy which were attacked by the Nazi raider in mid-Atlantic on Nov. 5.

The Admiralty announced in a communiqué at 11.15 p.m. that:

Of the 38 ships in the convoy, which the Germans claimed to have sunk in its entirety 29 are known to be safe;

They owe their escape to the armed merchant cruiser Jervis Bay, which was escorting the convoy and which fought the raider for two hours, though heavily outclassed in guns, and sacrificed herself so that ships in the convoy might have time to elude the German warship.

The armed raider is believed to have been a pocket battleship; the Jervis Bay was a merchantman of 14,164 tons armed with guns of lesser calibre. Nevertheless, the British ship steered for the enemy and engaged her.

Like the former P. & O. liner Rawalpindi, in similar circumstances, the Jervis Bay went on fighting while blazing furiously with her decks awash and her guns roaring to the last as she fell a victim to the enemy.

An eighteen-year-old ship of the Aberdeen Commonwealth line, the Jervis Bay was acting as escort to the convoy. Of her crew 65 are known to have been saved.

The 16,698-ton New Zealand liner Rangitiki was in the convoy and she was heavily shelled. Nevertheless, she made her escape, thanks to the action of the Jervis Bay, and has now made port in Britain.

Of the nine convoy ships not accounted for, some may yet prove to have escaped.

November 26 1940

Road Deaths Higher

By Our Motoring Correspondent

ROAD deaths last month numbered 1,012. This is roughly 10 per cent. more than in October 1939.

Of the 1,012 persons killed 535 were pedestrians, compared with 572 a year ago; 170 were motorcyclists, 68 more than a year ago; and 146 were pedal cyclists – 14 more.

Fifty per cent. of the fatalities occurred in the black-out hours: in October last year it was 60 per cent. Of the pedestrian victims 313, or not quite 60 per cent., were killed at night and 222 in daylight, last year 74 per cent. of the fatal accidents to pedestrians occurred at night.

Commenting on the return, the Minister of Transport, Col. Moore-Brabazon, says: "Road accidents are up. The number of cars on the roads is down. There is something very wrong here. The black-out, I know, makes driving difficult. Pedestrians are invisible and yet think they are not."

November 26 1940

More Digging for Victory

MR Tom Williams, Parliamentary Secretary to the Ministry of Agriculture, will this week complete a tour of England and Wales undertaken to forward the campaign for 500,000 allotments.

He has addressed regional conferences of local authorities covering the whole country and has stressed the urgent need for immediate action to increase food production.

Almost as important as expansion of the allotments movement is the greater use of gardens for vegetable production. The necessity of war demands that the space devoted to flowers shall be reduced and that every garden shall grow its share of food.

November 16 1940

Nazi Vandalism on Coventry

TO-DAY the people of Coventry have given a proud display of stubborn courage and indomitable spirit as they carried on amid the ruins left by the Nazi terror raid of last night.

All the powers of destruction which go to make an air raid on Greater London, with its 7,000,000 inhabitants, were for the space of a night concentrated on the Midland city of 225,000.

The damage, concentrated in the confines of Coventry, seems today to be on a catastrophic scale. The heart of the town is a shambles of broken glass, piles of brickwork and masonry, and smouldering woodwork. The ancient cathedral is a shell.

The German vandals sought to reproduce the Spanish tragedy of Guernica on a larger scale. They did havoc to buildings, but the spirit of the people is undaunted.

As Mr Morrison, the Home Secretary, found during his tour today, the people have gone about their tasks with "courage and cheerfulness" despite the damage on every hand, reminder of the ten-hours ordeal of the night.

These Germans assert that Coventry was devastated as a reprisal for what the RAF did to Munich. In fact, the methods of the RAF are not to be compared with the indiscriminate Nazi devastation at Coventry.

There was not even a pretence at an attempt to select military targets. For 10 hours raider after raider flew over at an immense height and dumped bombs haphazard at the rate of nearly one a minute on the town.

The result is that factories which are legitimate military targets have escaped comparatively lightly. The brunt of the destruction has fallen on shopping centres and residential areas – hotels, offices, banks, churches and – no Nazi raid is complete without this – on hospitals.

Hundreds of people were killed and many more were seriously injured. It is officially estimated that the casualties numbered about 1,000.

Allotment workers "digging for victory"

Coventry Cathedral devastated in an enemy raid

November 14 1940

TORPEDOES CRIPPLED ITALIAN FLEET

L AST night the Admiralty announced further successes against Italian naval forces, following on the crippling blow inflicted by the Fleet Air Arm which cost the Italians the loss of three latest battleships and two cruisers.

Almost at the hour on Monday night that the 'planes of the Fleet were making the attack on the main Italian forces at Taranto, a British light naval squadron inflicted heavy damage on a convoy of enemy supply ships bound for Albania, presumably with arms and men for the campaign against Greece.

Italian naval losses in operations announced yesterday are:

At Taranto –
Battleships: Two half sunk, third severely damaged.
Cruisers: Two put out of action, listing badly.
Fleet Auxiliaries: Two badly damaged, sterns under water.

Straits of Otranto –
Supply Ships: One sunk, two set on fire, fourth damaged.
Destroyer: Hit and damaged.

The Italian Fleet is attacked by the British Royal Navy and Air Force

THE DAILY TELEGRAPH learns that the devastation at Taranto was caused not by bombs but by aerial torpedoes, a new technique of torpedo attack which had been perfected by the Fleet Air Arm not long before the war began.

These losses were inflicted at the cost of two British 'planes. Italy's battleship strength has been reduced by half and the Italian Fleet no longer has, even on paper, numerical superiority compared with our own forces in the Mediterranean. Mr Churchill, in announcing the successes to a cheering House of Commons yesterday, stated: "The result, while it affected decisively the balance of naval power in the Mediterranean, also carried reactions in the entire naval situation in every quarter of the globe."

December 10 1940

BRITISH OPEN ATTACK AGAINST ITALIANS

T HE first major British offensive by land against the Italians was launched in Northern Africa at dawn yesterday.

British forces in the Western Desert, that separates Egypt from Libya, attacked at several points to the south of the port of Sidi Barrani and surprised the enemy. By night they had taken more than 1,000 prisoners; killed an Italian General and captured his second-in-command; and captured an Italian camp.

The operations are on a bigger scale than any yet carried out on this front. They have been launched with the object of forcing Graziani to fight at a moment when the Italians are embarrassed by the debacle in Albania.

The Navy and the Air Force assisted the troops in their dawn attack.

Gen. Sir Archibald Wavell, British C-in-C in the Middle East, himself gave the first news of the British offensive to British, American and Turkish war correspondents less than four hours after the attack was begun at dawn.

Leaning cross-legged against his desk, with his hands in his pockets, he said: "Gentlemen, I have asked you here to tell you that our forces began to carry out an engagement against the Italian armies in the Western Desert at dawn this morning."

After describing how British troops had steadily approached within striking distance of the enemy, he added: "Two hours ago I received word that we had captured an Italian camp."

Wreckage of an Italian fighter in the Western Desert

December 12 1940

BRITISH CAPTURE SIDI BARRANI

SIDI Barrani, hub of the Italian positions in the Western Desert of Egypt, was captured yesterday afternoon by detachments of Britain's Army of the Nile, not much more than 50 hours after the offensive was launched at dawn on Monday.

A special communiqué issued from British Headquarters in Cairo last night stated: "This afternoon Sidi Barrani was captured, with a large number of prisoners, including three generals.

"Advance elements of our mechanised forces are now operating westwards, and considerable additional captures have been made."

The Prime Minister inspects bomb damage in London

December 3 1940

Queen Mary Sees Bristol

QUEEN Mary and the Princess Royal, accompanied by the Duke of Beaufort, on Sunday inspected some of the damage caused by the recent German raid on Bristol.

In a statement to the Press yesterday Sir Hugh Elles, Regional Commissioner for the South-West, said the city had suffered a violent attack lasting several hours, designed by the enemy as an act of terrorism against the civil population and the city.

As the result there has been extensive loss of private property, and a loss of life which was widely and deeply deplored. A magnificent effort was being made to restore the damaged part of the city, and this was being done with remarkable efficiency.

December 27 1940

Writing Novel in Nazi Padded Cell

MR P. G. Wodehouse, who disappeared on June 26, following the German advance on Le Touquet, is writing a new naval in the padded cell of what was once an insane asylum in Upper Silesia. His 1,100 fellow internees include lorry-drivers, coalmen, seamen and artists.

In an interview, says the Associated Press, Mr Wodehouse said: "This must be the first book written in the padded cell of an insane asylum. I have been thinking of calling it 'Money for Jam.'"

He related that after being kept under police supervision at Le Touquet he and other British subjects were arrested on July 21 and sent to prison at Loos and from there to Huis, in Belgium, where they spent five weeks before going to the present camp.

Mr Wodehouse is president of the camp library, which consists of 14 of his own books. The early to bed schedule, he declared, was giving him health such as he never had achieved in private life.

"The food is of the same amount and quality as given to the German population. I am becoming a great admirer of the German potato," he remarked.

December 31 1940

Historic Buildings in Ruins

WORKING ceaselessly throughout Sunday night and yesterday thousands of firemen, aided by soldiers and civilians, fought the many fires which had been started by the Nazis in what was officially described as a "deliberate attempt to set fire" to the City of London.

When dusk fell only a few buildings were still smouldering, though many a charred and blackened shell bore witness to the wanton nature of the most concentrated fire-raising raid of the war.

Some 150 'planes are estimated to have taken part in the attack which appeared to have been cut abruptly short at a time when numerous fires, blazing brightly, offered excellent targets for explosive bombs. At least 10,000 fire bombs were dropped.

Mr and Mrs Churchill motored to the City during the afternoon to inspect the damage.

The Premier noted the still smoking ruins of St Bride's Church in Fleet-street, its beautiful Wren spire still standing. He stopped in St Paul's Churchyard to see the havoc there and to comment on the remarkable escape from further harm of the cathedral itself.

Then through Cheapside to King-street and Guildhall, where, stepping over hosepipes littering the ground and through pools of water, he made a careful inspection of the fire damage to the historic building.

Mr Churchill called attention to the Union Jack still flying at the top of the flagstaff over the main doorway and remarked on its symbolic expression of British defiance to vandalism. He went to the doorway of the famous dining hall where he had made speeches at many Lord Mayor's banquets.

As he walked away, the Prime Minister was recognised by many people. Firemen perched on roofs, demolition squads, police all joined in the cheering that greeted Mr and Mrs Churchill in their two hours' tour.

As they left a deep underground shelter a woman ran forward and asked "When will the war be over?" Mr Churchill paused in his walk, turned to the woman and said, "When we have beaten 'em." Those standing by cheered.

Others shouted, "Good old Winston. Give it to them back and remember we can take what we had and much more."

1941

A German submarine captured by aircraft of the Coastal Command and British warships

IN the New Year of 1941 any suggestion that by Christmas Germany would be locked in conflict with Russia, America would be at war with Germany and Japan, Hongkong and Malaya invaded and Hongkong seized, would have been scoffed at as fanciful. Lacking such foreknowledge the outlook was complex and chilling. The possibility of invasion, while no longer imminent, could not be written off entirely, but shipping losses along the Atlantic lifeline presented the principal threat to island survival. Elsewhere, German intervention in the Mediterranean, North Africa and Greece imposed increasing strains on Britain's dispersed resources.

Strangulation by U-boat blockade compelled tighter belts along the Food Minister Lord Woolton's "Kitchen Front" where Woolton Pie (a concoction leaning principally on vegetables and potatoes) was commended as a staple meal and basic civilian groceries were four ounces of bacon, two ounces of butter and two ounces of tea a week. A meat ration to the value of 1s 2d a week bought three-quarters of a pound of stewing steak or two tiny chops. An egg a fortnight was a treat. Cabbages flourished in the moat of the Tower of London and many other unlikely places. Civilian morale ebbed, absenteeism rose in war factories, 'bus drivers cried off during raids and dockers went slow. Deprived of hope, the Dunkirk spirit had dissolved into listless apathy.

Overseas, as German troops, sent in to retrieve a discredited Italian campaign, invaded Yugoslavia and Greece, the obstinate determination of Eden, now Foreign Secretary, and chivalrous desire of Churchill to rally to the aid of Greece, resulted in the disastrous depletion of army and air force units in the desert. If it went down well in Washington as representing fight yet in the old lion, it sold the pass on Wavell's triumph in Libya where the Italians had suffered humiliating defeat.

British intervention in Greece, coupled with the arrival in Libya of Rommel and his Afrika Korps and of the Luftwaffe in Sicily, resulted in a reversal in the desert and all hell let loose for Malta. There were, though, some saving graces. Troops, enduring siege in the coastal enclave of Tobruk, gave birth to the legend of the Desert Rats (the name later adopted by Monty's 7th Armoured Division) and a shared sentiment among opposing forces assured *Lili Marlene* a place in history as a desert anthem in common. At sea, the Navy, routing the Italian fleet off Cape Matapan, compensated some of the shambles and humiliation of the enforced evacuations of Greece and Crete. In Ethiopia, British arms restored Emperor Haile Selassie to the throne.

Meanwhile, a Pro-Axis revolt further tested British resolution. As Rommel schemed to march on the Nile, a complementary scare developed east of the Suez Canal where Iraqi rebels momentarily threatened the British base at Habbaniya.

Much had happened since the invasion of France, but nothing to match the bizarre parachute arrival in Scotland on its first anniversary (May 10) of Hitler's deputy, Rudolf Hess. Speculation on his motive, never satisfactorily explained, provided a diversion from such distressing losses as the battle-cruiser *Hood,* though morale lifted when shortly afterwards she was avenged by the sinking of her adversary, the battleship *Bismarck.*

Yet all such incidents were minnowed on June 22 when Germany invaded Russia – Operation Barbarossa, the opportunity, Hitler briefed his senior commanders, "to smash Russia while our own back is free." For Britain Barbarossa was a godsend, its implications lending added purpose to Churchill's first meeting of the war with Roosevelt. Taking place in August at Newfoundland's Placentia Bay this produced the Atlantic Charter, a side gain of which was to prepare Americans, short of the declaration so desired by Churchill and the Russian leader, Joseph Stalin, for the acceptance of war.

Short of the Second Front, for which Stalin would ceaselessly campaign, Britain's military assistance to Russia could amount to little more than the RAF's Luftwaffe-containing fighter sweeps over occupied Channel areas and such inaccurate attacks on German industry as an as yet inadequately equipped Bomber Command could attempt. By November the fall of Kiev, investment of Leningrad and Sevastopol and thrust on Moscow had, despite increasing American assistance short of war ("I shall never declare war," Roosevelt had told Churchill at Placentia, "I shall make it") rendered her entry imperative.

On December 7, a surprise Japanese air attack on the American base at Pearl Harbor relieved Roosevelt of the onus. If to Churchill's and Stalin's relief Pearl Harbor brought America in, it also introduced a new and desperate dimension to the British Empire's responsibilities. The sinking on May 10 off Malaya of the battleship, *Prince of Wales,* which had steamed the Prime Minister to the President, and battle-cruiser, *Repulse,* helped to pre-ordain the fall early in the New Year of the naval base at Singapore – and much more besides.

Australian troops entering Bardia, Libya

January 1 1941

BRITAIN READY IN AIR, ON LAND AND SEA

Britain entered the New Year today with her three fighting Services full of determination and confidence. It was pointed out in authoritative circles in London yesterday that:

The Royal Navy is in complete command of the vital Mediterranean Sea and is steadily countering the submarine menace.

A new Army is being equipped on the most modern lines, and will be ready for any purpose this year.

The Royal Air Force, which has proved itself superior to the Luftwaffe, has done more damage to Germany's war effort than she has to ours. The Fighter Command destroyed 3,090 enemy 'planes in the year and AA gunners claimed 444. The balloon barrage also obtained some victims.

Italy, dependent on many supplies from overseas and with her Empire in Africa cut off, may lose Libya, Eritrea, Somaliland and Abyssinia in the year now opening. Her East African possessions locked up at the "end of a British drainpipe" will be "ours for the asking," and will be delivered to their rightful occupants.

Her fleet has been largely paralysed and has done nothing to back up Mussolini's boast of the Mediterranean being "Mare Nostrum."

The vigorous offensive of Admiral Sir Andrew Cunningham's Mediterranean Fleet has completely changed the situation, has probably altered the balance of naval power, and directly affected the eventual outcome of the war. Its pressure on the weaker partner in the Axis is continually increasing.

It is doubtful whether the Germans can make up Italy's deficiency in coal. Her oil, for ships, aircraft, mechanised troops and industries, normally comes from Rumania and Russia through the Black Sea and the Dardanelles, from the Persian Gulf through the Suez Canal, and from America through the Straits of Gibraltar.

With these last two channels in British hands and a long line of communication from the Black Sea liable to interruption, Italy's oil situation is serious indeed. She may have built up a large war reserve, but her ally has none to spare.

January 6 1941

BARDIA GARRISON SURRENDERS

Bardia, Italy's Libyan stronghold, has fallen. This was announced in the following special communiqué issued last night from British GHQ, Cairo:

All resistance at Bardia ceased at 1.30 p.m. today. The town, with total forces defending it and all stores and equipment, is now in our hands. Gen. Bergonzoli, commanding the Italian forces at Bardia, another corps commander, and four senior Generals are prisoners of war.

It is not yet possible to make a full count, but prisoners so far captured exceed 25,000. Among other booty captured or destroyed are 45 light and five medium tanks.

The Italian flag was hauled down from Government House on Saturday evening by the officer commanding the Australian Infantry. Thereafter, pockets of resistance were mopped up. Thus in two days the Australians, fighting in co-operation with British mechanised units, the RAF, and the big ships of the Navy, smashed the defences of the port.

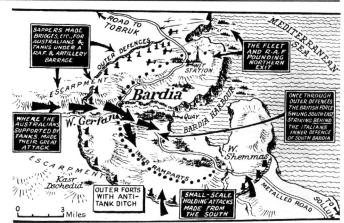

How the Australians broke through Bardia

Italian prisoners captured at Bardia

January 7 1941

Amy Johnson Drowned in Air Crash

MISS Amy Johnson, the air-woman, who made flying history by her 10,000-mile solo trip to Australia ten years ago, was last night reported to have lost her life in an air accident off the Thames Estuary

An official announcement stated that she was "missing and believed drowned," but an eye-witness of the accident, which occurred on Sunday, said that there was no ground for the faintest hope for her survival.

Amy Johnson, who was 32, was engaged in her duties as ferry pilot for Air Transport Auxiliary, piloting aircraft from factories to RAF aerodromes.

January 11 1941

FIRST MASS DAYLIGHT RAID BY RAF

The RAF has made a new departure in its offensive strategy.

Last night the Air Ministry announced that aerodromes in Northern France were successfully attacked in daylight yesterday by a strong combined force of fighters and bombers.

Over 100 fighters escorted the bombers.

Aircraft on the ground and German troops were machine-gunned.

While the waves of raiders were over France no attempt was made to intercept them

On the return flight three enemy fighters which attempted to interfere were shot down.

All our 'planes got back safely.

January 14 1941

James Joyce Dead

By George W. Bishop

Mr James Joyce, the Irish-born author, who died in a Zurich hospital yesterday, first came into the literary limelight with his sensational book "Ulysses," which was originally banned in Great Britain.

At an early age Joyce went to live abroad, and in Paris he made a startling figure dressed in a white frock-coat, white trousers and a white hat. He stated that he found this costume soothing to his eyes.

"Ulysses" was published in Paris in 1922, and, despite the ban, some copies managed to get into this country and were sold at £2.2s. Some of them changed hands in a few weeks at £10.

The book dealt frankly and freely, and very obscurely, with a squalid side of Dublin life and introduced words that are not usually seen in print. A few critics hailed "Ulysses" as a masterpiece; others derided it; but the book has undoubtedly had a tremendous influence on young English and American writers.

Italian prisoners marching through captured Tobruk

January 22 1941

BRITISH STORM WAY INTO TOBRUK

LATE last night it was announced that British Imperial forces were inside Tobruk, Italy's chief naval base in Libya. This success, coming quickly after the opening of the final assault at dawn, was revealed in the following special communiqué from GHQ, Cairo:

Shortly after noon to-day Imperial troops, actively supported by the Royal Navy and the RAF, successfully penetrated both the outer and inner defences of Tobruk to a depth of over five miles on a broad front.

The advance is continuing. Many prisoners have already been taken, including one Italian General. The Italian cruiser San Giorgio, in Tobruk Harbour, is in flames, together with a number of dumps of stores, petrol and the like.

A famous British regiment led the attack, charging the defenders with the Australians, and supported by tanks and artillery.

January 24 1941

ANZAC HAT FLOWN AS FLAG

From Arthur Merton
Tobruk

AN Anzac's hat hoisted on the flagstaff in the central square of Tobruk was one of the first signs of the occupation of the town by the Imperial Forces.

When they entered, their first thought was to haul down the Italian flag and replace it by the Union Jack, but not one could be found. They solved the problem in their own way.

The garrison at Tobruk actually surrendered at 10.15 yesterday morning. An advance guard of an Australian cavalry regiment in Bren gun carriers drove up the main road to the city and broke down the steel and concrete barrier.

As they proceeded into the town, they were met by a couple of bursts of machine-gun fire to which they promptly replied, but this was the last sign of resistance.

Area of Libya now in British hands

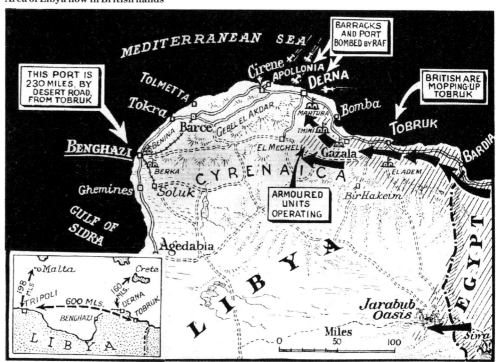

January 22 1941

Mr Boothby Resigns from Government

MR Robert Boothby wrote to the Prime Minister last night resigning his post as Parliamentary Secretary to the Ministry of Food after a Select Committee of the House of Commons had published its report on his conduct and activities in the realisation of Czech assets.

The Committee found that:

"Mr Boothby's conduct was contrary to the usage and derogatory to the dignity of the House and inconsistent with the standards which Parliament is entitled to expect from its members."

Mr Boothby had a claim to participation to the extent of £24,200 on the understanding that he would render services in the realisation of Czech assets by political speeches and pressure on Ministers.

He took no steps to disclose his personal financial interest either to the House of Commons or to the Treasury. He denied to the Chancellor of the Exchequer on his honour that he had any such interest.

January 24 1941

Col. Bingham Relieved of Command

LT-Col. R. C. Bingham, who, in a letter which appeared in the Times on Jan.15, criticised officers of the new Army drawn from the middle, lower middle, and working classes, has been relieved of his command of the 168th Officer Cadet Training Unit.

This was announced in the House of Commons yesterday by Capt. Margesson, Secretary for War.

Col. Bingham, at his home in Evelyn Gardens, South Kensington, declined to be interviewed, but sent the following brief and pointed statement to a DAILY TELEGRAPH reporter:

"An officer is not allowed to open his mouth. Unfortunately, I did so, and am paying for it. It is the privilege of an officer to be shot at without answering back."

January 28 1941

Earl May Have Been Shot

THE Earl of Erroll, it was revealed at the inquest at Nairobi yesterday, may have been murdered.

Lord Erroll was found dead in a car early on Friday morning. It was reported at the time that death was the result of a car accident.

A doctor stated at the inquest, however, that death was due to a revolver wound behind the left ear. It was most unlikely, in his opinion, that the wound could have been self-inflicted.

Civilians practise fire-fighting with a stirrup pump

January 20 1941

Mr Kennedy Urges All Aid for Britain: But US Must Stay Out of War

New York

MR Joseph Kennedy, the retiring United States Ambassador in London, in a broadcast to the nation to-night, declared himself in favour of the utmost aid for Britain.

"But such aid," he said, "should not and must not go to the point where war becomes inevitable."

Mr Kennedy denied that he wanted appeasement in the sense of a "deal with the Dictators contrary to British desires," or that he had predicted the defeat of Britain.

Mr Kennedy began by recalling that when he returned from London he declared that the United States ought to stay out of the war and could stay out of the war, and that he urged his country to give England all possible aid.

"I feel the same way about it to-day," he observed.

"I never thought that it was my function to report pleasant stories that were not true. When I reported to our Government the seriousness of the problems that faced the British people, I did it in considerable detail and purposely, because I wanted our Government to have all the information possible affecting the plight of Great Britain, so that this country, in the days to come, could guide itself more intelligently in its foreign policy, regardless of what the outcome of the war might be."

Mr Kennedy denied that he predicted the defeat of Britain. "I am aware of, and have reported on, serious obstacles to the British victory," he added. "I know many of Britain's weaknesses, but a prediction can be based only on complete knowledge of the strength and weaknesses of both sides."

January 28 1941

Heel Click As Clue

From Our Sheffield Correspondent

HOW an escaped Nazi prisoner gave himself away by clicking his heels and bowing his head in the German manner was described to me today by a Sheffield 'bus conductor, who effected his recapture.

The conductor is Mr Colin Spittle, Studfield-hill, Wisewood Estate, Sheffield. He was acting as conductor on a 'bus going from Gainsborough to Sheffield. On reaching Retford, police informed him that three German prisoners had escaped in the north of England, and he was given a description of the men.

When the 'bus was 16 miles from Sheffield a young man got on. He was dressed in a sports jacket and grey flannels, and carried a small travelling case which was later found to contain chocolate.

"He asked for a ticket to Sheffield in fluent if unnatural English," said Mr Spittle. "As I gave him a ticket I heard a sharp click of his heels and saw a forward movement of his head. My suspicions were aroused, and I told the driver to stop if we saw a policeman.

"We came on a sergeant and a constable and stopped. I told them of my suspicions. When asked for his identification card the passenger replied, 'I have not got one.' He was quite self-possessed till he was asked if he was one of the three escaped men. Then he appeared startled and was taken into custody."

January 31 1941

"Lipstick, the Use of"

LIPSTICK, women, in the Services, for the use of.

This has become a Parliamentary matter. It is to be referred to shortly by the Ministers, Service, Three, from the Bench, Front, Government.

Capt L. F. Plugge, Conservative MP for Rochester and Chatham, is to ask the Secretaries for War and Air and the First Lord of the Admiralty to state their policy about the use of lipstick by women attached to the Services under their control.

Their reply, I understand, will be: "Moderation in all things, including lipstick and nail varnish. We do not object to either, but their application must be unobtrusive. Hair styles must be neat and dressed above the collar."

Definitions of "unobtrusiveness" and "inconspicuousness" will be left to the good sense of company commanders. Members of the ATS, WRNS, WAAFs and Army nurses will be guided by their own officers.

In other words, the sergeant-major will lay it on thick if they lay it on thick.

February 6 1941

New Loaf and "Blitz Broth"

Daily Telegraph Woman Reporter

THE new Government wholemeal loaf of 85 per cent extraction flour has, I learn, a flavour all its own. It differs from many brown breads as it contains no malt and no flakes of bran. It is easy to digest and should be popular.

The loaf will be tried out in thousands of homes this weekend. I could not get it in London yesterday, but the bakeries have their machinery ready and are now waiting for deliveries of the wholemeal flour.

Here are the ingredients of the "Blitz Broth" which experts of the Ministry of Food evolved as the most sustaining and nourishing soup that could be stored in bulk at emergency dumps. To make 100 gallons of carrot soup use:

Carrots 240 lb; Potatoes 480 lb; Turnips 32 lb; Oatmeal, fine 24 lb; Stock – yeast extract watered down 22 galls; Salt 16 lb; Pepper 8 oz.

As flavouring, thyme, celery seed, parsley, mint, marjoram and basil are used in equal quantities of 1½oz. plus 11¼oz. of dark-brown caramel.

February 18 1941

Fire Watch on the Temple

WELL-known barristers, including King's Counsel, are among the many lawyers who are taking duty nightly to guard the buildings of the Temple against fire bombs. Already some damage has been caused in this historic area.

Sir Patrick Hastings, Treasurer of Middle Temple, presided yesterday at a meeting of the Middle and Inner Temples held to discuss an extension of the fire guard system, to bring it into line with the fire-fighting order.

Meanwhile, several readers of THE DAILY TELEGRAPH, attracted by statements about "fancy" rates of pay obtained by full-time fire-fighters at some City and West End premises, have written seeking employment of this nature.

One states that he and his wife are prepared to take on fire-fighting, either singly or as a team, at wages of £6 and £4 a week respectively.

An ex-sergeant-major now working as a Government clerk at £4 a week would like to be put in touch with any firm prepared to pay £6 or £8 a week.

February 26 1941

Gas Mask Test for Horses

THE use of gas masks for horses is to be tested at a demonstration arranged by the National ARP Animals Committee. In general the use of masks for animals is not advocated by those who have been going into the matter.

For cats and dogs it is suggested that the best method is to provide them with special boxes. Caged birds are particularly susceptible to poison gas. For them a cloth soaked in a weak solution of hypochlorite or permanganate, and then wrung out and hung over the cage, is advised.

March 8 1941

Lowest Total of Workless

UNEMPLOYMENT has reached a record low level, and the situation now is that reserves of male labour are practically exhausted.

On Feb. 10 the total unemployed was 580,849. This was 114,757 less than the previous month and 923,251 less than in February last year.

A shelter buried after a bomb attack; the occupants survived

March 12 1941

ROOSEVELT SIGNS THE AID BILL

From Our Washington Correspondent

A T 9.51 p.m. today, British time, President Roosevelt signed the Lease and Lend Bill, which thereby became law.

Immediately afterwards the President approved the transfer of the first allotment of Army and Navy material to Britain and Greece.

The Bill, which throws practically the whole of the United States war production on the side of Britain and her Allies, received its final Congressional approval earlier in the day when, by 317 votes to 71, the House of Representatives passed it as amended by the Senate.

It was taken straight to the White House, where the President appended his signature only 15 minutes after it had left the Capitol.

When newspapermen crowded into his study for a Press conference, the President triumphantly announced that he had already taken action under the new powers granted him.

He refused to reveal what Army and Navy materials had been made available. "Details of a military nature will only be given," the President said, "when knowledge of them is unlikely to be of benefit to anyone else."

Most of the materials released today will go to Britain, but some will go to Greece.

The President also declared that sometime next week he would give a fireside radio talk to the nation explaining the significance of the Act and what the United States' task would be now that its objectives had been accepted by all save a small minority.

He added that no deal or trade had been made over with today's transfer.

Although the list of weapons is being kept secret, the President indicated that the swift movement of these weapons was contemplated.

Smouldering ruins of St Andrew's, Plymouth

March 21 1941

2,659 Churches Bombed

By Our Ecclesiastical Correspondent

HITHERTO unpublished figures, giving what is thought to be a reasonably accurate account of damage done in air raids to churches and other church properties up to the beginning of February, is given by the Ministry of Information.

Churches destroyed and seriously damaged were:

Anglican – England 282, Wales 5.

Free Churches – Baptist 89, Congregational 123, Methodist 118, Presbyterian Church of England 17, other Free Churches 22, making a Free Church total of 369.

Roman Catholic – 58.

Making a total of 714.

Churches damaged less seriously were:

Anglican – England 1,070, Wales 30.

Free Churches – Baptist 106, Congregational 98, Methodist 448, Presbyterian Church of England 18, Other Free Churches 40, making a total of 710.

Roman Catholic – 135.

Making a total of 1,945.

Among cathedrals destroyed or seriously damaged are Coventry and St Paul's (although the main fabric stands unhurt). Cathedrals damaged but in most cases not too seriously include those of Liverpool, Manchester, Sheffield, Rochester, Canterbury, and Westminster Cathedral.

Many other church properties have been destroyed or damaged, including Westminster Abbey.

March 18 1941

De Valera's Pledge

Mr de Valera, Prime Minister of Eire, in a St Patrick's Day broadcast to America yesterday, said: "We have pledged ourselves that our country will not be used as a base of attack against Britain.

"We are determined that no one of the belligerents shall use the territory of our State as a base of attack on another. For us to permit such a thing to be done would be to involve ourselves in war."

He added: "It has taken an effort of centuries to win back the independence we have got. We are determined that it shall not be lost again."

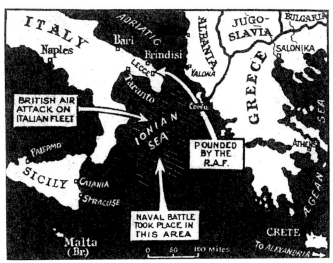

Where the British attacked the Italian Navy

March 14 1941

Privileged Pilots of Aircraft Delivery Service

By J. Wentworth Day

LITTLE is heard of the war work of the Air Transport Auxiliary: it does not attract the spotlight. Twice within a few days it lost gallant members with the loss of a 'plane – Amy Johnson and Capt. Horsey – and the tragedy of their death drew brief attention to that body of pilots of no Service rank or status, who, on flying duties of a special kind, have the right to fly anywhere in Britain at any time.

What, then, is the work of the Air Transport Auxiliary?

They pilot Spitfires, Hurricanes, Wellingtons, Ansons and the most hush-hush aircraft that were ever wheeled on the tarmac. They wear a private uniform of their own – or just civilian clothes. They must be ready to fly anything, anywhere, in almost any weather.

They are paid, but some of them refuse to take the money. Yet they fly more types of aircraft than many a Service pilot has ever seen, and though they are sometimes found in areas thick with the enemy, they carry no arms and fly machines without guns or bombs. In fine – they have all the fun of war, some of the risks, none of the glory; and nothing to hit back with.

An ATA pilot's job would not be easy for the best all-round pilot in the world. He is almost invariably a man who has been refused for the RAF because of age or disability. His job is to collect new aircraft, either from the factory or from the "collecting point" and fly them to whatever units of the Service need them.

Every one is a volunteer in the ATA. Some are millionaires and some are farmers. Several are stockbrokers and one is a professional huntsman. Three of them have only one arm and one man has one arm and one eye.

They have their own sense of humour – a little boyish, sometimes macabre.

There was the case of my host, flying north at 1,200 feet. He had expected no German lower than 20,000 feet when, out of a cloud, a couple of hundred yards away, four Stuka dive bombers flew straight past him.

"Passed me on my starboard bow – so close I could see the chaps sitting in 'em."

"What did you do?"

"What could I do? Couldn't shoot them as I hadn't a gun. So I waved. They didn't wave back. No sense of humour, these Germans."

March 20 1941

Vegetable Sausages

Daily Telegraph Woman Reporter

VEGETABLE sausages are being produced on a considerable scale. They are called "rissoles" because as they contain little or no meat, they may not be sold as sausages.

A famous sausage manufacturer is making them. West End butchers are experimenting with their own recipes. One butcher told me that he is using carrot and potato and a small amount of meat, and expects the selling price to be 8d lb.

I saw rabbits arrive in the poultry department of a West End store. In a few minutes women were crowding round to buy them. "The retailer is willing to take rabbits now that the price has been adjusted to give him a little more profit," was the explanation given me of their sudden appearance. "He has been selling a rabbit at a profit of ½d or 1d or even at a loss. We hope that supplies from Ireland will continue."

Cod's roe is one of the useful foods of the moment that help with breakfast catering. It is 2s 4d lb.

Housewives should register at once for their monthly ½lb a head of preserves to enable them to get their allowance of jam, marmalade, syrup or treacle. No coupons are used, but the retailer marks the ration book to show what you have had, and you must enter his name and address and your own in the two bottom squares on page 16 (page 15 in a child's book). The retailer keeps the left-hand square.

March 31 1941

BIGGEST MEDITERRANEAN BATTLE: FIVE MORE ITALIAN WARSHIPS SUNK

THREE of Italy's most powerful cruisers and two of her destroyers sunk, one of her newest battleships damaged – such are the latest established facts in the great Mediterranean naval battle, in which the Italian fleet, ordered to sea by its new German masters, has been caught and smashed by a combined British-Greek fleet.

In command of the Allied fleet was Adml Sir Andrew Cunningham, Commander-in-Chief, Mediterranean, who thus had the supreme satisfaction of bringing to action the fleet which had escaped him off Sicily last November.

Further details of the Italian losses in this, the first real action of the war between rival fleets, which began on Friday, were given in the following Admiralty communiqué last night:

The Commander-in-Chief Mediterranean reports that no casualties or damage were sustained by HM ships throughout recent operations. Two of our aircraft are, however, not yet accounted for.

So far it is confirmed that the following Italian warships have been sunk: the 8in cruisers Fiume, Pola and Zara; the large destroyer Vincenzo Gioberti and the destroyer Maestrale.

To prevent enemy air interference with the action the RAF made a heavy attack on Lecce, the Italian air base south of Brindisi, during which grounded aircraft were machine-gunned and set on fire.

It was pointed out in naval circles last night that the figure of five ships actually sunk may by no means represent the final sum of the Italian losses.

Referring to the battle on Saturday Mr A.V. Alexander, First Lord of the Admiralty, said: "I don't think there is much left of their destroyers."

April 3 1941

Noted Writer Feared Dead

MRS Virginia Woolf, the essayist and novelist, has, her family fear, been drowned in the River Ouse, near Lewes, where she and her husband, Mr Leonard Woolf, lived.

Mr Woolf said last night: "Mrs Woolf is presumed to be dead. She went for a walk on Friday, leaving a letter behind, and it is thought she has been drowned. Her body has, however, not been recovered."

Virginia Woolf was one of the most remarkable writers of her time. Her first novel, "The Voyage Out," appeared in 1915.

She went on to develop a technique that attracted wide attention in, among other novels, "Night and Day," "Mrs Dalloway," "Orlando," "A Room of One's Own," "The Waves" and "The Years."

The German attacks in Yugoslavia and Greece

April 7 1941

BRITISH ARMY IN THE LINE IN GREECE

WITHIN a few hours of the attack Germany launched at dawn yesterday against Jugoslavia and Greece, it was officially announced in London that a British Army is in the field in the Balkans.

According to reports in Berlin last night, the British troops are taking part in the tenacious resistance which the Germans are meeting in the Struma Valley, which runs from Bulgaria into Greece, north of Salonika, and down which one of the main Nazi thrusts is directed.

Both in Germany and in the Press of the United States, reports have appeared for some days past of the presence of British troops in the Balkans, but it was not until early this morning that they were officially confirmed here in the following announcement:

After the entry of German troops into Bulgaria had brought to a head the long-threatened German invasion of the Balkans the British Government, in full consultation with the Dominion Governments concerned, have sent an army to Greece comprising troops of Great Britain, Australia, and New Zealand, to stand in the line with the soldiers of our brave Allies in defence of their native soil.

The British Air Force, which has for some time been operating in Greece against the Italians, has been strongly reinforced.

Gen. Sir Archibald Wavell, C-in-C in the Middle East, who directed the victorious campaigns in Africa, is in supreme command, our Political Correspondent states. It must not be assumed that the BEF in the Balkans consists only of troops drawn from the Libyan and East African fronts.

A British artillery column passes through a Greek village

Ludgate Circus at dawn after the Blitz

April 18 1941

London Recovers from War's Worst Raid

LONDON made a quick recovery yesterday from Wednesday night's raid, the worst night raid yet made on any place in Britain, and described by the Germans as a reprisal for the RAF raid on Berlin a week before.

Between 450 and 500 German 'planes took part in the night-long attack – at least twice as many as have been used in any recent raid.

The bombing was indiscriminate and incessant – Berlin radio stated that thousands of high-explosive and more than 100,000 fire bombs were dropped. Six of the raiders were shot down.

Within a few hours of the end of the raid, which caused heavy casualties, severe damage and the greatest strain ever put on civil defence workers, London's essential services were in make-shift working order.

The city's civil defence services rallied magnificently and battled heroically and successfully throughout the night.

Transport plans which were prepared after the great fire-raid in December came into immediate operation.

Fleets of 'buses, including 500 extra vehicles, were mobilised while the blitz was at its height and took the load from interrupted rail services, avoiding damaged streets where firemen, demolition squads and rescue parties still dealt with the havoc of the night.

Managements and staffs of businesses damaged or out of bounds were accommodated by neighbour firms and given every facility to carry on.

This latest Nazi terror raid on London, officially described as "very heavy and sustained," lasted without respite from dusk to dawn.

Parachute flares turned night into day, showers of fire bombs started fires in many parts of the capital, and high explosive bombs fell over a wide area, as wave after wave of German bombers flew through a heavy barrage of anti-aircraft fire.

Besides those raiders shot down, many others must have been badly damaged.

The main features of the attack were:

Eight hospitals were hit.

Churches suffered in many parts.

Several department stores and hotels were damaged.

Many office buildings, blocks of flats, shops, restaurants and public houses were destroyed.

Cinemas and theatres were struck.

Many people were trapped and rescuers worked all day to free them.

Numbers of civil defence workers were among the killed.

A great many streets were closed.

Yesterday afternoon Mr and Mrs Winston Churchill toured the areas of damage.

Mr Churchill, at one point of his tour, clambered to the rim of a fuming crater and there, catching sight of people on the roof of a building near, took off his hat and waved it with a jaunty air.

The people as jauntily waved back, and others who had gathered in the street clapped and cheered and shouted, "Are we downhearted? – No!"

April 21 1941

MIDNIGHT TOAST TO HITLER

HITLER spent his 52nd birthday yesterday at his headquarters near the zone of operations of the Balkan campaign, according to the official German news agency.

On Saturday night he gave a reception to his staff in the special train forming his headquarters. On the stroke of midnight Field-Marshal Keitel, Chief of Staff, offered his congratulation, and a toast to victory was drunk.

Hess, the deputy Fuehrer, in an obsequious speech on behalf of the civil population, said that the German nation sent Hitler its wishes and prayers, "coupled with gratitude that, through your powerful and far-sighted leadership, you have preserved Germany against the destructive designs of the enemies."

Goering, speaking on behalf of the armed forces, stated: "You gave your thoughts to the question of what weapons were best for the coming struggle, to perfecting the armoured weapon of the army and building new warships, and constructing the most modern 'planes."

Goebbels, the Propaganda Minister, in a broadcast speech of adulation, said: "We are experiencing the greatest miracle in history. A genius is creating a new world."

The whole German nation, and countless millions beyond the German frontiers, were, he said, about to express to the Fuehrer their "Gratitude, reverence, admiration and unshakable faith in his historic mission."

Rome radio, in its birthday greetings, stated that Hitler was "the greatest leader of all time," and Mussolini was the "greatest statesman of all time." Therefore it was impossible for these two men not to become friends.

April 28 1941

MR CHURCHILL: WE CONQUER OR DIE

MR Churchill, in a stirring broadcast to the nation last night, expressed the conviction that the British people meant to "conquer or die" and that it was in the West that victory would be won.

Nothing that was happening now, the Prime Minister said, was comparable in gravity with the dangers through which we had passed; nothing that could happen in the East was comparable with what was happening in the West.

Hitler, he declared, could not find safety from justice in the East, the Middle East or the Far East. To win, he must conquer this island or cut the Atlantic lifeline to the United States.

Against the 70,000,000 malignant Huns, were 200,000,000 people of the British Empire and the United States possessing unchallengeable command of the oceans and with more technical resources than the rest of the world put together.

The King and Queen on one of their morale-raising tours of the East End

May 12 1941

NAZI BOMBERS WRECK HOUSE OF COMMONS

IT was revealed last night that several of London's most famous buildings were damaged on Saturday night, when German 'planes unloaded their bombs indiscriminately in the heaviest attack since the "reprisal raid" of April 16, which was the worst the capital has experienced.

Among places hit were:

House of Commons – St Stephen's Hall, the Chamber where MPs meet, reduced to a heap of rubble and may never be used again. Big Ben and its famous clock scarred, but still going. Roof of Members' Lobby destroyed.

House of Lords – Chamber damaged. The Resident Superintendent, Capt. E. L. H. Elliott, was killed.

Westminster Hall – Historic roof, dating back to 12th century, damaged.

Westminster Abbey – Roof of the Lantern, the square tower on the centre of the building, has fallen in. The Deanery has been destroyed, but the main fabric of the Abbey is undamaged.

British Museum – Fire damage to back of building.

Blitz rescue workers bring out a man buried by rubble

May 5 1941

THREE RAF RAIDS ON IRAKI AIRFIELD

BRITAIN has taken strong action against the pro-Nazi usurper, Rashid Ali, in Irak. The latest developments are:

It was stated at midnight last night that RAF 'planes on three occasions bombed Moasar Rashid aerodrome, outside Baghdad, where 23 'planes – nearly half the estimated strength of the Iraki air force of 50 – were put out of action and hits scored on petrol dumps and magazines.

The airport, dock area and power station were occupied at Basra, the port on the Shatt-el-Arab, near the head of the Persian Gulf.

The RAF bombed and machine-gunned Iraki mechanised troops and transport after the Irakis had resumed the shelling of Habbaniyah aerodrome, 60 miles south-west of Baghdad, occupied by British troops.

Non-combatants were injured in the shelling at Habbaniyah, where, it was stated yesterday in Simla, British women and children from Baghdad were sheltering.

The deposed Regent of Irak, Emir Abdul Ilah, in a proclamation issued from Palestine to all Irakis, declared that he was returning to lead his native country back to prosperity under a lawfully constituted Government. He called on the people to "drive out this band of traitors."

May 12 1941

LINDBERGH'S CAMPAIGN

From Our Washington Correspondent

MR Charles Lindbergh carried his "Knuckle under to Germany" campaign to the Middle West last night when he addressed a cheering mass meeting at Minneapolis and once more expressed his conviction that Britain could not win even with American aid.

Obviously feeling that he is not making much headway, he made the fantastic charge that American people are no longer allowed to express their will through the ballot-box. He also made the curious claim that, "for years the true facts about Europe have been hidden from us."

Finally, Mr Lindbergh somewhat modified his earlier assertions that Germany could not be invaded by saying: "Even if invasion were possible, the resulting devastation would be so great that Europe could not recover for generations, if it could recover at all."

This rather weakens his major thesis that it is no use going on with the war because the Nazis are unassailable on the Continent.

May 13 1941

HITLER'S DEPUTY FLEES FROM GERMANY

RUDOLF Hess, Hitler's Deputy and third man in the German Reich, has escaped by 'plane from Germany, and last night was lying with an injured leg in hospital in Glasgow.

This dramatic announcement was made in a statement issued from 10, Downing-street, shortly before midnight. It followed within three hours of the disclosure by the German radio that he had set off on a flight and had not returned.

The Nazi announcement, which was broadcast from all their stations, alleged that he was suffering from hallucinations and had been forbidden to fly. He was represented as having in all probability taken his life by jumping overboard in mid-air.

The Downing-street statement was made in the following terms:

"Rudolf Hess, the Deputy Fuehrer of Germany and party leader of the National Socialist party, has landed in Scotland under the following circumstances:

On the night of Saturday the 10th an Me. 110 was reported by our patrols to have crossed the coast of Scotland and to be flying in the direction of Glasgow. Since an Me. 110 would not have the fuel to return to Germany this report was at first disbelieved.

"Later on an Me. 110 crashed near Glasgow with its guns unloaded. Shortly afterwards a German officer who had baled out was found with his parachute in the neighbourhood suffering from a broken ankle.

"He was taken to a hospital in Glasgow where he at first gave his name as Horn but later on he declared he was Rudolf Hess.

"He brought with him various photographs of himself at different ages apparently in order to establish his identity. These photographs were deemed to be photographs of Hess by several people who knew him personally.

"Accordingly an officer of the Foreign Office who was closely acquainted with Hess before the war has been sent up by aeroplane to see him in hospital."

Later it was announced that his identity as Hess had been established beyond all doubt.

May 13 1941

Hess Found in Field by Ploughman

DAVID McLean, a West of Scotland ploughman, found Hess lying injured in a field. He assisted Hess to his house, where the Deputy Fuehrer gossiped with McLean's mother and other relatives for nearly an hour before being taken away by officials.

"I was in the house and everyone else was in bed late at night when I heard the 'plane roaring overhead," McLean stated. "As I ran on to the back of the farm I heard a crash and saw the 'plane burst into flames in a field about 200 yards away.

"I was amazed and a bit frightened when I saw a parachute dropping slowly downwards through the gathering darkness. Peering upwards I could see a man swinging from the harness.

"I immediately concluded it was a German airman baling out and raced back to the house for help. They were all asleep, however.

Rudolf Hess: Hitler's deputy until his mysterious flight to Britain

"I looked round hastily for some weapon, but could find nothing except a hayfork.

"Fearing I might lose the airman, I hurried round by myself again to the back of the house, and in the field there I saw the man lying on the ground with his parachute nearby.

"He smiled, and as I assisted him to his feet he thanked me, but I could see that he had injured his foot in some way.

"He said there were no ammunition or bombs on his 'plane. Stealing an aircraft which had been refuelled near Munich, he took off solo and headed for Scotland. When his petrol supply was almost exhausted he decided to bale out."

"I helped him into the house. By this time my old mother and my sister had got out of bed and made tea. The stranger declined any tea and smiled when we told him we were very fond of it in this country.

"He said, 'I never drink tea as late as this. I will only have a glass of water.'

"Word was sent to the military authorities and in the meantime our visitor chatted freely to us.

"He told us he had left Germany about four hours previously.

"I could see from the way he spoke that he was a man of culture. His English, although it had a foreign accent, was very clear and he understood every word we said to him.

"He was a striking looking man, standing over six feet. He was wearing a very magnificent flying suit. His watch and identity bracelet were of gold.

"He did not discuss his journey, and he seemed to treat what seemed to us a most hazardous flight as a pleasure flip.

"He seemed quite confident that he would be well treated, and repeatedly expressed how lucky he had been in landing without mishap.

"He was most gentlemanly in his attitude to my old mother and my sisters, and stiffly bowed to them when he came in and before he left.

"He thanked us profusely for what we had done for him.

"He was anxious about only one thing, and that was his parachute. He said to me: 'I should like to keep that parachute, for I think I owe my life to it.

"He would not tell us who he was and we did not like to press the question as we assumed he was just another German airman who had been brought down."

May 15 1941

Hess Hoped to Meet Duke of Hamilton

RUDOLF Hess, Nazi No. 3, who flew from Germany to Scotland on Saturday, came, it was disclosed last night, to see the Duke of Hamilton.

He is reported to have told the farm people in the district where he landed of tyranny prevailing in the Reich and of great distress and suffering as a result of the RAF's heavy raids.

He further said that he had a message of great importance to deliver to the Duke of Hamilton, whom he had known well as the Marquess of Douglas and Clydesdale.

The information he had to give the Duke would be of great use to the British in overthrowing the tyranny that now prevailed in the Reich.

Hess added that he was "fed up with the war and with life in Germany," and had made the most pains-taking preparations for his flight.

According to the German radio, documents which Hess left behind reveal that he wanted to meet the Duke in an attempt to effect a peace between Germany and Britain. It was his belief that the Duke, whom he had met on one or two occasions some years ago at sporting events, would be likely to have influence with circles in England which might be interested in securing a negotiated peace.

Hess, in fact, landed 12 miles from the Duke of Hamilton's house. He met the Duke in Berlin in 1936 when he was Marquess of Clydesdale and was attending the Olympic Games.

The *Bismarck* fires at HMS *Hood* in the Denmark Strait

May 28 1941

1,750-MILE DEATH HUNT OF THE BISMARCK

HM Cruiser Dorsetshire (Capt. B. C. S. Martin, RN) was ordered to sink the Bismarck with torpedoes. Bismarck sank at 11.01 this morning.

"So far as is known at present the only damage sustained by HM ships other than HM Battle-cruiser Hood is the slight damage to HM Battleship Prince of Wales" (suffered on Saturday morning, when Bismarck was first engaged).

Such are the closing paragraphs of a graphic account issued by the Admiralty last night of the running battle with Germany's newest and biggest 35,000-ton battleship which enemy propagandists claimed to be unsinkable. The operations lasted from Friday evening till 11 a.m. yesterday and extended over 1,750 miles of sea, from Denmark Strait, between Iceland and Greenland, to a position less than 400 miles west of Brest.

The communiqué shows that the greatest concentration of warships ever assembled for a chase at sea took part in the pursuit. These included the main body of the Home Fleet, coming down from the north, vessels from the Mediterranean Fleet, coming up from the south, and at least two battleships detached from escorting convoys in the North Atlantic.

No official indication is given of the total number of warships involved, but our Naval Correspondent estimates that at least 100 took part.

The cruiser Norfolk was actually engaged throughout the whole operations. She shadowed the Bismarck from Friday evening and was the last ship mentioned as being in action with the Nazi warship. She is a sister-ship of the Dorsetshire, which administered the coup-de-grace.

Throughout the hunt invaluable service was rendered by shadowing aircraft of the Coastal Command and by Royal Canadian Air Force 'planes from Newfoundland. American-built Hudsons bombed the Bismarck when first she left Bergen, Norway, and an American-built Catalina scouting 'plane located her on Monday after she had been lost sight of for 31 hours.

Mr Churchill, who announced the sinking of the Bismarck, in the House of Commons yesterday, revealed that the Hood had been sunk by a shell which hit her from a range of 23,000 yards, over 13 miles – but not before she had hit her opponent and set her on fire.

WOMEN OF BRITAIN!

ARM HIM

ISSUED BY THE MINISTRY OF LABOUR AND NATIONAL SERVICE

A recruitment poster urges women into the war effort

May 22 1941
DUKE OF AOSTA IN BRITISH HANDS

THE Duke of Aosta, Italian Viceroy of Abyssinia, formally surrendered himself to representatives of Lt-Gen. A. C. Cunningham, British C-in-C in East Africa, on Tuesday, it was officially announced in Cairo yesterday.

He surrendered on the day that Rome radio announced that the King of Italy had conferred on him the Golden Medal for valour in the field.

With the Duke were five Italian generals and a number of senior staff officers.

Their surrender follows the capitulation of the Italian Army in the Amba Alagi area.

May 28 1941
SINKING OF KELLY OFF CRETE

IT was learned in Alexandria yesterday that Capt. Lord Louis Mountbatten, a second cousin of the King, who was in command of HMS Kelly, was among the survivors.

He is 41 and has been in the Navy since he was a boy of 13. He received the DSO in January after a gallant exploit by the Kelly.

The destroyer was crippled by a torpedo in the Channel last May. Throughout four days of air attack her crew fought the guns entirely by hand, the electrical system being out of action, and the Kelly was towed safely into port.

May 30 1941
US WILL TRAIN 8,000 RAF MEN A YEAR

From Our Washington Correspondent

MR Stimson, Secretary for War, today announced details of the important scheme for the training of RAF pilots and navigators in the United States.

The scheme, which will ultimately provide training for 8,000 men a year, comes into operation on Saturday week. One-third of the entire American Army Air Force training facilities and all civilian flying schools will be placed progressively at the disposal of the British Government.

The first contingent of 700 members of the RAF either have arrived or will arrive soon. A fresh class will be begun every five weeks.

Mr Roosevelt's Stirring Call to the Americas

From Our Washington Correspondent

PRESIDENT Roosevelt's address to the nation last night dispelled the atmosphere of "business as usual" and called on the people to face the fact that the defeat of Hitler was not merely a sentimental hope, but a vital necessity.

It has drawn support from all sections of the country, which has evidently been waiting for just such a type of leadership.

Here are some extracts from Mr Roosevelt's historic "Fireside Chat":

The Battle of the Atlantic now extends from the icy waters of the North Pole to the frozen continent of the Antarctic. Throughout this huge area there have been sinkings of merchant ships in alarming and increasing numbers by Nazi raiders and submarines. There have been sinkings even of ships carrying neutral flags.

There have been sinkings in the South Atlantic, off West Africa and the Cape Verde Islands, between the Azores and the islands off the American coast, and between Greenland and Iceland. Great numbers of these sinkings have been actually within the waters of the Western Hemisphere.

The blunt truth is this – and I reveal this with the full knowledge of the British Government – the present rate of Nazi sinkings of merchant ships is more than three times as high as the capacity of British shipyards to replace them; it is more than twice the combined British and American output of merchant ships today.

We answer this peril by two simultaneous measures: First, by the speeding up and increasing of our great shipbuilding programme. Second, by helping to cut down the losses on the high seas.

The deadly facts of war compel the nations for simple self-preservation to make stern choices. It does not make sense, for instance, to say, "I believe in the defence of all the Western Hemisphere," and in the next breath to say, "I will not fight for that defence until the enemy has landed on our shores."

And if we believe in the independence and integrity of the Americas we must be willing to fight to defend them just as much as we would fight for the safety of our own homes.

Our patrols are helping now to insure the delivery of needed supplies to Britain. All additional measures necessary for the delivery of the goods will be taken.

Any and all further methods or combination of methods which can be utilised are being devised by our military and naval technicians who, with me, will work out and put into effect such new additional safeguards as may be needed.

The delivery of needed supplies to Britain is imperative. This can be done. It must be done. It will be done.

To the other American nations, 20 Republics and the Dominion of Canada I say this: The United States does not merely propose these purposes, but is actively engaged today in carrying them out.

I say to them further: You may disregard those few citizens of the United States who contend we are disunited and cannot act. There are some timid ones among us who say we must preserve peace at any price lest we lose our liberties forever.

To them I say: Never in the history of the world has a nation lost its democracy by a successful struggle to defend its democracy.

We must not be defeated by fear of the very danger which we are preparing to resist. Our freedom has shown its ability to survive war, but it would never survive surrender. The only thing we have to fear is fear itself.

Suda Bay falls to German hands, with heavy losses to the Allies

June 2 1941

CRETE EVACUATED: ORDEAL WORSE THAN DUNKIRK

CRETE has been evacuated and some 15,000 British troops have been withdrawn to Egypt. This was announced in a War Office communiqué last night, which stated:

"After 12 days of what has undoubtedly been the fiercest fighting in this war it was decided to withdraw our forces from Crete.

"Although the losses we inflicted on the enemy's troops and aircraft have been enormous, it became clear that our naval and military forces could not be expected to operate indefinitely in and near Crete without more air support than could be provided from our bases in Africa.

"Some 15,000 of our troops have been withdrawn to Egypt, but it must be admitted that our losses have been severe."

Up to a late hour last night, THE DAILY TELEGRAPH was informed, there was no information to show how many German prisoners had been removed from Crete, although it was regarded as certain that a number of them had been brought away.

Gen. Freyberg, the Allied C-in-C, was definitely known to be alive, despite German claims that he had been killed in an air crash. It was assumed that he came out with his troops.

The figure of 15,000 mentioned in the communique, it was stressed, related only to our own troops. Greek and Italian soldiers and some civilians have, however, arrived in Egypt with the Imperial Forces.

"We were lucky to escape ... Even Dunkirk and the battlefields of Greece were nothing compared with this show," said one survivor.

The German communiqué claimed yesterday that roughly 10,000 British and Greeks had been taken prisoner. Berlin radio stated the remnants of British units are trying to leave the island by any available means – in small schooners, fishing boats and rowing boats.

Ten thousand soldiers worn by the strain of 13 days' fierce fighting to hold Crete against the most furious attack yet launched by Nazi air might, arrived in Egypt last night.

Britons, Australians and New Zealanders brought with them Greek and Cretan soldiers and some civilians, including women who preferred the perilous voyage to living under Nazi domination.

Others have poured in since then, bombed for hours during the trip from the island.

The decision to evacuate was taken on Thursday afternoon as it was apparent that German air supremacy would enable the enemy to land an endless stream of men by air and simultaneously prevent the British from landing adequate reinforcements and supplies.

The Imperial soldiers were wearied by the days of air attacks, so continual that they wore on the strongest nerves, but their morale was high and their determination to continue the fight to hold the Near East was unflagging.

They had only contempt for the German parachutists, thousands of whom they had killed. Those from the Heraklion area said that every German landed there perished. Not knowing the more serious situation in the Canea and Suda Bay regions, they were surprised when ordered to withdraw.

Almost all the British in the Heraklion area escaped. Those around Suda Bay did not fare so well, though many got away by retiring along the coast to Heraklion or by climbing the rugged mountains, to be picked up on the wild south coast.

One soldier said: "Dive-bombing all day long was terrible. We hardly ever saw any of our fighters. If we had a few squadrons of them it would have been different."

A New Zealand officer stated: "The Germans employed a number of new tricks. We saw one bunch of parachutists, opened fire and thought we had killed them all. When they landed we found them to be dummies. The real parachutists descended nearby."

June 3 1941

NIGHT DRAMA OF THE CRETE EVACUATION

From Christopher Buckley
At Sea in the Eastern
Mediterranean

THIS despatch, giving the first eye-witness description of the evacuation of Crete, in which some 15,000 British troops have been withdrawn, is being written aboard an Australian cruiser.

A few hours ago the warship took off 1,200 men from Sphakia, on the southern coast of Crete.

It was an eerie, yet intensely impressive, process. In the dead of night we had lain off the little Cretan village of Sphakia – it cannot be called a port – where a week earlier the King of the Hellenes had made his dramatic departure from Greek soil.

We formed part of a fairly big convoy of cruisers, destroyers and a troopship engaged on the same task.

For three hours we lay alongside while our boats – large, flat-bottomed, and shallow-draughted, so that they could be run right on to the beach – plied backwards and forwards, carrying fully 50 a-piece, across glass-smooth waters under a tranquil starry sky.

The stillness of the night was not broken by a sound, and one might have thought that the ship was sleeping instead of being intensely and throbbingly alive.

The black mass of the island was totally unrelieved save for an occasional flash from the beach, answered by a recognition signal from the ship.

Boatload after boatload drew alongside, discharging silent cargoes of weary, stumbling, khaki-clad figures carrying what equipment they had been able to retain during their arduous trek across the bare Cretan Mountains from sea to sea. For these men, British and New Zealanders, had arrived from the Maleme-Canea sector.

They had been bombed and machine-gunned ruthlessly from the air without intermission day after day under conditions which, in the opinion of those who had experienced both, made even Dunkirk seem a picnic by comparison.

As the men came aboard they were guided between decks and given hot cocoa and biscuits. For the most part they were content to sit almost silent while they stretched their legs and enjoyed the luxury of relaxing for the first time for days. Even of those who were not wounded the largest number were limping.

Despite this and despite the burden of their kit, a portion had retained their rifles and tommy-guns.

"The temptation to throw away mine almost overcame me a dozen times during the climb over the mountains," a soldier said to me, "but every time I reflected that there is nothing that bucks up Jerry's morale more than piles of discarded arms, and I hung on."

A similar reflection appears to have occurred to many, judging by the armament brought away.

It was remarkable to note the way in which the cruiser seemed almost to expand and take on its additional complement of 1,200. Officers and men vied with one another in providing sleeping accommodation.

The gratitude of these weary men was pathetic. The two officers to whom I gave up my cabin gazed enraptured at the bunks. "It seems a miracle to see sheets again," one of them said. "All that belongs to another world."

There can be no doubt that the heroism shown by these men was comparable with that of any during the war. Why, then, was it necessary to evacuate Crete? The answer can be found in two words – air power.

The Allied troops in Crete did all and more than could be expected of them, despite the intense disadvantage at which they were placed by the decision rendered necessary by the development of events and the withdrawal of our fighter defences from Crete.

The decision was forced by the destruction wrought at our three Cretan aerodromes and by the enemy's tenure of positions at or near them. In consequence our forces in Crete were subjected to what almost certainly represented the mass strength of the Luftwaffe concentrated to capture the island.

Yet success for the Allies was not impossible of achievement, and the original decision to endeavour to hold Crete seems justified. Perhaps Crete will go down in military history among the campaigns in which decisive success only just eluded us.

June 3 1941

US Troops Reported in Greenland

REPORTS were current in Washington today that American troops have been sent to Greenland, where they are believed to be preparing aerodromes.

President Roosevelt stated at his Press Conference on April 25 that it was possible that Greenland had been partly occupied by Axis forces. The United States, he added, was taking steps to counteract any occupation.

United States industry was virtually placed on a war basis by the President today when he signed the mandatory Priorities Bill, which gives the Government the power to subordinate civilian production completely.

June 7 1941

PLANNED WAR IN ABYSSINIA

IT can now be revealed that one of the British officers responsible for recent operations in Abyssinia is Orde Charles Wingate, who when last officially mentioned was a captain in the Royal Artillery, but is now believed to hold the rank of Brigadier.

At the outbreak of the war he was in charge of anti-aircraft units in Kent. Later, however, it was decided to make use of his special abilities, and he was sent out to engineer the Abyssinian campaigns.

He became and has remained a believer in the Jews' powers as fighters. Disagreeing with the Government's view on a matter of policy, however, he resigned his appointment and returned to this country.

In looks, Capt. Wingate, who belongs to a well-known military family, bears a marked resemblance to Lawrence of Arabia. His work is comparable with that of Glubb Pasha, leader of the Arab Legion, which has done such good work in Irak.

June 2 1941

Clothes Coupons Needed

FOLLOWING the surprise announcement yesterday morning of the Government's Clothes Rationing Order, informal conferences were held by the heads of many firms during the day to try to forecast the probable effects of the scheme.

It will introduce a new feature in shop window display – a ticket showing, in addition to the price of the article, the number of coupons required.

A munitions girl models "no coupon" clogs for wear in explosives shops

The Order is designed to secure fair distribution of the country's supplies, which have had to be reduced to make way for munitions, and to protect the interests of the small consumer and the small retailer. The public are asked not to buy more than they need, nor before they must.

"This plan helps the fighting man, and it is fair to everyone," said Mr Oliver Lyttelton, President of the Board of Trade, in a broadcast yesterday.

Men, women and children, will have 66 coupons each to last them until the end of May, 1942. The margarine coupons in the current ration books will serve as the first 26. Clothing cards containing 40 more coupons will be issued later.

WAAFs plot enemy aircraft, guided by radio location – Britain's "secret weapon"

June 5 1941

The Ex-Kaiser

NEWS of the death of the ex-KAISER WILHELM II can be read with small emotion now in any of all the countries which still have bitter cause to remember his reign. He had long outlived the fierce resentment which he earned among the nations allied against Germany in her first war for world power. If he was not forgiven, he was forgotten.

Among his own people, too, oblivion covered his life long ago. No memory of him could Germany desire to preserve.

June 12 1941

BRITISH CAVALRY'S SWORD CHARGE

THE Allied forces in Syria, fully supported by the RAF, and continuing to make satisfactory progress, were yesterday threatening the vital towns of Beirut and Damascus.

Having broken the main French fortified line defending Beirut, Australian and British troops advancing along the Syrian coastal road, aided by British warships, were nearing Sidon, 20 miles from Beirut.

It was admitted in Vichy last night that the town of Merj Iyun, which had been holding up the Allied advance along the Litani valley towards Rayak, had been taken.

The Vichy forces, it was stated, had withdrawn to positions about 10 miles north on a level with Hasbeya.

During the operations in this sector British cavalry made a charge with drawn swords over open country against a squadron of Lebanese horsemen. These fled before the British reached them.

June 18 1941

Radio Ray Beating Nazi Bomber

By L. Marsland Gander
Radio Correspondent

REVEALING the best kept secret of the war last night, Air Chief Marshal Sir Philip Joubert, who was appointed Chief of Coastal Command last week, declared that "radio-location" is Britain's secret weapon against the German bomber.

"It is a system," he said, "whereby rays which are unaffected by fog or darkness are sent out far beyond the limits of our shores. Any aircraft or ship in the path of this ray immediately sends back a signal to the detecting station, where people are on watch.

"These ether waves keep a 24-hour watch year in and year out. They are always on duty."

A scientist's vision of the possibilities of certain electrical phenomena led to the development of this remarkable weapon, which, as Sir Philip pointed out, helped to win the Battle of Britain last autumn.

The scientist is a 49-year-old Scot, Mr Robert Alexander Watson Watt, the Scientific Adviser on Telecommunications at the Ministry of Aircraft Production. He made his early experiments, in 1935, with an ancient lorry on a country road near Daventry as a laboratory.

Today that ancient lorry has grown into an organisation which covers the whole country and which needs at once the services of about 7,000 men with a knowledge of radio work and 3,000 women for training.

Sir Philip Joubert said that this was a marvellous opportunity for young men to "get in on the ground floor" of one of the most remarkable developments of modern times.

Radio location has already had a profound influence in air, military and naval strategy.

So secret has it been that even in the Services it has been referred to only by three letters. Even these could not be whispered outside the Services.

June 23 1941

Britain Offers Aid to Russia

THREE points stood out in a world-wide broadcast made last night by Mr Churchill on the German invasion of Russia. They were:

We shall give whatever help we can to Russia. We have offered any technical or economic assistance in our power.

We are resolved to destroy Hitler and every vestige of the Nazi régime. From this nothing will turn us. We will never parley, never.

I gave clear and precise warnings to Stalin of what was coming. I can only hope these warnings did not fall unheeded.

German panzers heading for Smolensk

The German Army's four lines of attack against Russia

June 23 1941

RUSSIA ATTACKED ON 1,800-MILE FRONT

FIGHTING by land and air on a front extending for 1,800 miles from Finland to the Black Sea was reported last night to be in progress following the Germans' dawn attack on Russia. The main centres of operations appeared to be:

Karelian Isthmus – In this area of north-western Russia, the scene of bitter fighting when the Russians broke through the Mannerheim line 18 months ago in their war with Finland, the Germans were attempting to push towards Leningrad. It was claimed in Berlin that Finnish troops were attacking with the Germans.

East Prussia – Air raiding by both sides. Russian airfields attacked. German troops' penetration after preventing Russians from blowing up bridges.

Poland – Many Russian 'planes destroyed in air raids near Warsaw. German troops crossed River Bug.

Rumania – Advance by German and Rumanian troops, who occupied several towns.

Ukraine – Towns and Black Sea ports bombed by the Germans.

The movement of troops by the Germans, who had about 100 divisions massed on the frontier, was described as "the greatest the world has ever seen" in a proclamation by Hitler, which was read over the radio by Goebbels. The strength of the opposing Russian forces, according to a declaration yesterday by Ribbentrop, the Nazi Foreign Minister, is 160 divisions. They are commanded by Marshal Timoshenko, who succeeded Voroshiloff as Defence Commissar in October.

June 27 1941

"Jeeves" in Durance

A report about Mr P. G. Wode-house, which would seem incred-ible even if it did not come from Berlin, states that he is about to broadcast weekly from Germany an account of his experiences to the United States. The German authorities are said to have given him complete freedom for this purpose.

The mere hint of such a possibility must distress those millions of readers on both sides of the Atlantic who have found such unfailing delight in the Wodehouse humour.

He is a writer so typically English in style and inspiration that it would be an affront to him to believe that he could contemplate bringing to our bitterest foe such aid and comfort as his testimony that he himself had made his peace with his Nazi captors.

The report states ingenuously that he is not interested in politics, but Mr Wodehouse, we may be sure, is too nimble-witted to believe that politics can be divorced from the Berlin wire-less.

July 3 1941

Noel Coward's Gay Ghosts

By W. A. Darlington

WE were thoroughly well back in the genuine first-night atmos-phere yesterday at the Piccadilly, when Noel Coward's "Blithe Spirit" opened its run.

All the familiar figures seemed to be there, though not in the familiar garb. There was the old chatter in the interval, the cheers and excitement at the end, the author's graceful speech. There were even, for good measure, one or two boos. They came, I suppose, from disgruntled spiri-tualists.

And why, you ask, should spritualists be disgruntled? Be-cause the play is about ghosts, and treats them frivolously.

Cecil Parker, that grand actor, is married to Fay Compton, at rather less than her sweetest. A séance, held for no reason that we need bother about, conjures up the spirit of his first wife from the vasty deep. This is Kay Hammond, looking enchanting in a wraith-grey make-up; and as she can be seen and heard only by Mrs Parker, trouble ensues.

July 3 1941

Sir D. Broughton Not Guilty

SIR Delves Broughton was found not guilty of the murder of the Earl of Erroll in the Kenya Supreme Court in Nairobi yes-terday.

The jury returned this verdict after an absence of $3\frac{1}{2}$ hours. The crowded court applauded when the verdict was announced, and Sir Delves was congratulated by his friends as he left the dock.

July 15 1941

Paris Taunts the Invader

I have just listened to a first-hand account of life in France today given by "Mrs A.," the French wife of an Englishman now serving in the RAF. I met her soon after she had arrived in Britain with her two children.

This is how she described France:

Occupied Territory – "So strong is the pro-British feeling that people walk about wearing in their coats the R.A.F. badge and the crossed flags of France,

WAAFs hauling up a large barrage balloon

as so many did in the early days of the war."

Unoccupied Territory – "People are not so pro-British as in the occupied zone, but emphatically they are not pro-German. The downfall of Lavall was cheered. Adml Darlan is regarded with suspicion. The people are pro-French, and the only hope they see for their country at the moment is Marshal Pétain, whose prestige is still high."

As for Vichy itself, there are, in "Mrs A.'s" own words, "as many Germans there as in the occupied zone."

"Paris," "Mrs A" said to me, "is a much-changed city, but the Parisian still laughs – usually at the expense of the invader.

"French wit and sarcasm may be the only weapons temporarily available to the people, but they are being mercilessly used, and the Germans feel the lash.

"Students and lads write tickets, saying, 'I am the advance guard of de Gaulle,' and stick them on the backs of German soldiers.

"If a German comes into a shop the women waiting there will make way for him and cry, 'Serve that gentleman first. He is in a hurry; he is going to England.'

"When a German officer goes into a restaurant or cabaret he clicks his heels, gives the Nazi salute, takes off his equipment and revolver and hangs them up.

"When a French lad goes in, he clicks his heels, gives the Nazi salute, and then, solemnly, unties a piece of string round his waist from which dangles a bicycle pump and hangs it up.

"The Germans do not like ridicule, but there is not much they can do about it. Last July they were confident that they would be leaving for England any day – and said so to the French. August and September came and the invasion was put off. The Germans became uneasy and showed it.

July 8 1941

Wodehouse in Berlin

To the Editor of
The Daily Telegraph

SIR – It is amusing to read the various wails about the villainy of Wodehouse. The harm done to England's cause and to England's dignity is not the poor man's babble in Berlin, but the acceptance of him by a childish part of the people and the academic government of Oxford, dead from the chin up, as a person of any importance whatsoever in English humorous literature, or any literature at all. It is an ironic twist of retribution on those who banished Joyce and honoured Wodehouse.

If England has any dignity left in the way of literature, she will forget for ever the pitiful antics of English Literature's performing flea. If Berlin thinks the poor fish great, so much the better for us.

Yours, &c.,
SEAN O'CASEY.
Totnes, Devon

July 25 1941

Another 3 Million for National Service

OVER 2,000,000 women and nearly 1,000,000 men are comprised in new age groups which will be called upon to register for national service between Aug. 2 and Dec. 6. The groups include women born in the years 1916 to 1910 and men born in 1897, 1896 and 1895.

By the end of the year registration will be complete of men up to 46 and women up to 31.

This new drive for increased man-power, announced by the Ministry of Labour yesterday, has been undertaken because it is now considered that the country can no longer afford:

To allow men to do jobs that can be done by women, or

To spare their services for work that is not essential to the war effort or to the civil life and well-being of the community.

July 14 1941

Stalin Toasts Soviet Pact with Britain

NEGOTIATIONS which had been taking place in Moscow between Sir Stafford Cripps, the British Ambassador, Stalin, and M. Molotoff, Foreign Commissar, supplemented by talks in London between Mr Eden, the Foreign Minister, and M. Maisky, the Soviet Ambassador, were brought to a successful conclusion yesterday.

The signature was simultaneously announced at 2 p.m. in Moscow and London of an Anglo-Russian agreement providing for mutual assistance and stipulating that neither country will conclude a separate armistice or peace treaty.

Throughout the negotiations the Dominions and the United States Governments were kept fully informed.

The final details of the agreement were settled by Stalin and Sir Stafford Cripps, and it was signed at 5.15 p.m. on Saturday in M. Molotoff's office in the Kremlin.

Stalin attended the ceremony and afterwards he and M. Molotoff toasted the British representatives in champagne.

Loading bombs on to a Flying Fortress

July 10 1941

FLYING FORTRESSES NOW IN ENGLAND

TWENTY Boeing Flying Fortress bombers have already been flown to this country from the United States. Some are now with operational units of the RAF, ready to take part in the ever-growing onslaught on Germany and Nazi-occupied territory.

These giant bombers – they have a wing span of 103ft 9in and are 67ft 10in in length – comprised the original order of the British Government, and delivery is now complete. Fresh arrivals, under the provisions of the Lease and Lend legislation, will take place regularly.

July 21 1941

All Europe Resounds to V Rhythm

ALL Europe resounded yesterday to the rhythm of the V as Britain's Victory Campaign surged across the Continent to the fateful opening theme of Beethoven's Vth Symphony.

Rat-ta-ta-taat – "Fate knocks at the door."

Dot-dot-dot-dash – "V for Victory."

V-ictoire, V-rijheid, V-ictory.

At midnight, zero hour of the campaign, Mr Churchill sent a message to the oppressed people of Europe: "The V sign is the symbol of the unconquerable will of the occupied territories and a portent of the fate awaiting the Nazi tyranny," he said.

August 15 1941

BRITAIN AND US UNITED FOR VICTORY AND PEACE

Mr Churchill and Mr Roosevelt have met at sea. After a series of conferences lasting three days they have drawn up a momentous eight-point declaration of the joint peace aims of Great Britain and the United States.

The secret of this dramatic meeting was broadcast yesterday by Mr Attlee, Lord Privy Seal and Deputy Prime Minister, to a world keyed up to a high state of expectancy.

The official statement disclosed that President and Premier were accompanied by high-ranking Service officers, but the complete list of names has yet to be made public.

From the United States came the news that among those who left England with Mr Churchill were Mr Harry Hopkins, administrator of the Lease-Lend Act, and Sir Alexander Cadogan, Permanent Under-Secretary of the Foreign Office.

Lord Beaverbrook, Minister of Supply, who left England after the Premier, joined Mr Churchill and subsequently proceeded in a B. 24 Consolidated bomber with British markings and flown by an American pilot, to Washington, where he arrived last night.

The declaration proclaims that:

First, their countries seek no aggrandisement, territorial or other.

Second, they desire to see no territorial changes that do not accord with the freely expressed wishes of the peoples concerned.

Third, they respect the right of all peoples to choose the form of government under which they will live; and they wish to see sovereign rights and self-government restored to those who have been forcibly deprived of them.

Fourth, they will endeavour, with due respect for their existing obligations, to further the enjoyment by all States, great or small, victor or vanquished, of access, on equal terms, to the trade and to the raw materials of the world which are needed for their economic prosperity.

Fifth, they desire to bring about the fullest collaboration between all nations in the economic field, with the object of securing for all improved labour standards, economic advancement and social security.

Sixth, after the final destruction of Nazi tyranny, they hope to see established a peace which will afford to all nations the means of dwelling in safety within their own boundaries, and which will afford assurance that all the men in all the lands may live out their lives in freedom from fear and want.

Seventh, such a peace should enable all men to traverse the high seas and oceans without hindrance.

Eighth, they believe all the nations of the world, for realistic as well as spiritual reasons, must come to the abandonment of the use of force. Since no future peace can be maintained if land, sea or air armaments continue to be employed by nations which threaten, or may threaten, aggression outside of their frontiers, they believe, pending the establishment of a wider and permanent system of general security, that the disarmament of such nations is essential. They will likewise aid and encourage all other practicable measures which will lighten for peace-loving peoples the crushing burden of armaments.

August 15 1941

A Momentous Meeting

History has no precedent or parallel for the declaration which was broadcast from London yesterday by Mr Attlee and later issued from the White House in Washington. It announced to the world that the non-belligerent United States is in agreement with the belligerent British Commonwealth upon the war aims which must be attained if the dangers threatening both democracies, and civilisation itself, from Nazism and the Axis are to be averted. President Roosevelt, though his country is still at peace, has conferred with Mr Churchill on the measures which the American and British peoples are taking for their security against the Nazi armaments. The achievement of this unison of policy and concord of action is momentous.

Every circumstance of the manner in which it was secured adds to its force. There is much more than picturesque drama behind the blunt statement that the President and the Prime Minister "met at sea." They met upon the battlefield of the Atlantic. It was a day presaging doom to Hitler when, traversing those ocean lanes kept by parallel patrols of American and British squadrons, the leaders of the two democracies came into counsel and the ensigns of their two countries saluted each other.

The world can have no better illustration of the course of the Atlantic battle. The meeting proclaims the change which by united effort has transformed 3,000 miles of ocean from an abyss dividing us into a means and a bond of union, an endless belt of communication and supply.

Two "naval persons": President Roosevelt and Mr Churchill meet at sea

August 19 1941

"BBC Poison in German Blood"

Goebbels, the Reich Propaganda Minister, has made a damaging admission of the effect BBC broadcasts are having on German listeners.

Writing in Das Reich, he says: "Their lies get into the blood, making listeners weak and tired of carrying on, thus showing that the BBC poison is beginning to work. This is the reason we fight with all our strength against the BBC.

"Some Germans say that they are strongminded enough to listen to the BBC lies and not be harmed by them. I reply that this is not true, as those who listen have not the means of checking and finding out whether or not the BBC is lying.

"To win the war Britain endeavours to make the German people distrust their Fuehrer, and were the British to succeed they would certainly win the war. Therefore we introduce the death penalty for listening to the BBC, and those who, despite all warnings, continue to do so deserve beheading."

August 4 1941

Nelson and His Emma

Film Notes by Campbell Dixon

ENTER a naval captain in a hurry, and one of the great love stories of history is under way. Mr Korda, in "Lady Hamilton" (Odeon), tells it very skilfully.

Vivien Leigh is perhaps too petite, too obviously a creature of fire and air, for Lady Hamilton, whose buxom charms have been etherealised by Romney; but it makes no matter. Emma's fascination and gay extravagances – these she recaptures brilliantly, while sparing us some of the gush that emerges in the letters. This is easily the finest performance Miss Leigh has given us, and it confirms her position among the first actresses of the screen.

As for Mr Olivier's Nelson, I can think of no other actor likely to suggest as well the genius, the nervous intensity and the fire that burned in this son of a commonplace Norfolk parson. Grenville and Keats, Marlowe and Nelson, Shelley and T. E. Lawrence – where, I wonder, does the world get the notion of the phlegmatic Englishman?

August 23 1941

The MacRoberts' Reply

LADY MacRobert, of Douneside, Tarland, Aberdeenshire, has bought a £25,000 Stirling bomber to strike back at the enemy, her reply to the news that one of her two sons in the RAF has been killed in action and the other is missing.

This memorial will be named "MacRobert's Reply." It will bear the family's crest and badge, which has the motto "Virtutis Gloria Merces" ("Glory is the Reward of Valour").

In a letter to Sir Archibald Sinclair, Secretary for Air, Lady MacRobert wrote:

"It is my wish to make a mother's immediate reply in the way that I know would be my boys' reply – attacking, striking sharply, straight to the mark – the gift of £25,000 to buy a bomber to carry on their work in the most effective way. This expresses my reaction on receiving the news about my sons.

"I never doubted that they would do their duty. I can only hope that my youngest son may yet return. In any case, they would be glad that their mother replied for them.

"Let it be used where it is most needed. May good fortune go with those who fly it.

"I have no more sons to wear the badge or carry it in the fight. If I had had 10 sons I know they would all have followed that line of duty.

"It is with a mother's pride that I enclose a cheque for £25,000 and with it goes my sympathy to those mothers who have also lost their sons and gratitude to all other mothers whose sons so gallantly carry on the fight."

Members of the Women's Institute at a jam-making centre

Poster encouraging voluntary care for war-workers' children

If *you* can't go to the factory help the neighbour who *can*

How you can help

Arrange now with a neighbour to look after her children when she goes to her war-work—or give your name to

CARING FOR WAR WORKERS' CHILDREN IS A NATIONAL SERVICE

Issued by the Ministry of Health

August 21 1941

BADER IN HOSPITAL

WING-Cmdr Douglas Bader, the legless airman, shot down over France last week, is among three British pilot-officers found wounded and taken to hospital, the German wireless stated yesterday.

Two artificial legs are reported to have been dropped for Wing-Cmdr Bader by parachute from an RAF 'plane during a daylight sweep over Northern France on Tuesday.

August 26 1941

BRITISH AND RUSSIAN TROOPS ENTER IRAN

RUSSIAN silence on the entry into Iran was broken at one o'clock this morning by Moscow radio, which announced: "Soviet troops crossed the Iranian frontier early yesterday morning and are moving in the direction of Ardebil and Tabriz. They have covered 28 miles and the advance continues."

Tabriz, 60 miles south of the Caucasus border, is the terminus of the railway linking it to Erzerum in Turkey and Tiflis on the Batum-Baku line. Ardebil is 100 miles inside the Iran frontier and 40 miles from the Caspian Sea.

Late last night it was reported from Baghdad that British and Indian mechanised troops, strongly supported by the RAF, had crossed the Iraki-Iranian frontier at several points.

September 20 1941

NAZIS CLAIM CAPTURE OF KIEV

From Ossian Goulding, Stockholm

THE German High Command, in a special communiqué tonight, claimed the capture of Kiev, capital of the Ukraine, and said that "the Reich flag had been flying from the citadel since this morning."

A Soviet communiqué issued at 10 p.m., several hours after the German communiqué, stated that the fighting near Kiev was "particularly serious."

Earlier, Moscow had described the situation as grave, and had stated that the Nazis had reached the outskirts of the city after a battle which had lasted 45 days.

German losses in the attack were estimated at four divisions, or about 70,000 men.

The fall of Kiev must be admitted to be a severe blow to the Russians, but it will also be costly to the Nazis, and they will gain little but a heap of ruins, stripped bare of everything useful to them.

Kiev has held out far longer than anyone believed it could, and now we must look east of Kiev where the Nazi horde menaces the far more important industrial city of Kharkov and the rich areas of the Donetz Basin.

Marshal Budenny's armies have suffered another hard blow and it would be useless to try to minimise the fact that the Nazis have won an important victory.

September 29 1941

BADER ESCAPES ON NEW LEG

REPORTS that Wing-Cmdr Bader, the RAF's legless pilot, escaped from a German hospital and was not recaptured for four days were received in Rome yesterday.

A few days after receiving the new artificial leg dropped by parachute by an RAF 'plane, said these reports, he climbed out of a window, reached the ground with the aid of a blanket and walked away.

When he was recaptured, it was added, he was 100 miles away and was making for the French coast. An American report said that after this incident the Germans remove one of Bader's legs at night and return it in the morning.

October 14 1941

Voice Butts in on BBC

THE radio war, begun so effectively by "Ivan the Terrible," the Russian voice on the German wireless, was taken a step further last night, when the Nazis invaded the BBC programmes, including the nine o'clock news.

Among the questions asked by the Nazi voice last night were: "Do you know how much money Churchill is being paid by the Jews?" and "Has Churchill played fair with you?"

Another comment was: "We are being swindled and led up the garden path and sold to America."

Later the Voice said, "Remember, Churchill lost you your Empire. It is your duty to throw out Churchill." Another remark was: "Churchill will never be a Duke of Marlborough."

Following is an extract from the dialogue during the news:

Announcer: The Germans are keeping up pressure in Ukraine.

Voice: Wait till tomorrow.

Announcer: The RAF made a big offensive over Northern France today.

Voice: And got shot down!

Announcer: Raid over Germany and fires started.

Voice: That is what you say.

Announcer: Great fires at Emderi.

Voice: Rot.

A reference by the announcer to bombs being dropped on a German coaling station brought the jeer: "Ha – five miles off it." Another passage in the news brought the remark: "That's a good one."

When the announcer said, "That is the end of the news," the Voice commented, "Thank God."

Later when bagpipe music was being announced, the Voice said: "Music does not give us food to eat."

But the Voice soon gave up the struggle against the pipes and the interruptions ceased.

October 9 1941

Rural Rides Up To Date

By J. Wentworth Day

IN three weeks I have travelled on horseback and by horsebox, with one long-distance excursion by train, through Hertfordshire, Essex, Suffolk, Cambridgeshire, the Isle of Ely, Huntingdonshire, Northamptonshire, Leicestershire and Warwickshire.

I have seen the heart and soul of farming England busy at the peak of its year – garnering this hard-won harvest which is the British farmer's answer to Hitler.

I have stayed with and talked with great landowners, great farmers who farm from 500 to 2,000 acres; small farmers, that sturdy backbone which lives and rears its families on less than 150 acres; with the small men who struggle wearily on five or 10 acres; and with the farm labourers, the men who drive the tractors, guide the plough horses, milk the cows, reap and bind, stack and thresh.

It has been a golden autumn pilgrimage, with unforgettable moments. Mist curling off the stubble fields in the innocent stillness of dawn; the heat of high noontide with the clack of threshing tackle, the swish and rattle of combine harvesters, the slow grumble of horse-drawn wains – these formed the setting of it all. Then the evenings, when we sat and talked in inns and farmhouse kitchens, in the squire's library and the labourer's back garden – quiet evenings, full of English philosophy, the sound wisdom of the soil.

From all this there emerge certain present-day facts and four major problems which stand out like lighthouses. They are the four factors which will govern the immediate future of farming. They will determine the long-term future of land ownership and land cultivation. Those four points are (a) wages, (b) prices, (c) soil fertility and (d) excess profits tax on farming profits.

It is no use continuing to feed the land on artificials. As well might one dose an invalid with repeated nips of whisky. We must get back to sound farmyard manure, to leys and, to a lesser degree, to green manuring, though that depends on rainfall.

I do not give this merely as a personal opinion, but as the considered view of practically every farmer without exception whom I have interviewed in the last three weeks. All admit that artificials have their uses. Nine out of ten of them good-humouredly accept the advice of professors and rural scientists who bombard them at NFU meetings and through the Press. But under it all is the conviction that grandfather's methods of manuring were the best and that the sooner we get back to them the better it will be for the land.

Land girls reaping wheat on the Sussex Downs

WAAF mechanics inspect an aircraft engine

October 20 1941

STATE OF SIEGE IN MOSCOW

DRASTIC steps to make Moscow's defences secure were announced by the Soviet radio early this morning.

A state of siege has been declared in the capital and in the adjoining districts from today and two new defence chiefs have been appointed, under an Order issued by the National Defence Committee.

General Zhukov, Vice-Commissar for Defence and Chief of the Soviet General Staff, has been appointed Supreme Commander of the Defence Forces operating 60-75 miles from Moscow. Defence of the city's approaches has been entrusted to Lt-Gen. Artemyev.

The Order forbids the movement of individuals or vehicles in the streets of the city between midnight and 5 a.m., without a special permit and makes it compulsory for all persons and vehicles to conform with ARP regulations during raid alarms.

"Spies and enemy agents who appeal to the population to break this Order will be shot on the spot," the decree declares.

The order, which is signed by Stalin, adds: "The State Committee of Defence appeals to all workers in the capital to keep calm and orderly and render the Red Army defending Moscow all possible help."

October 28 1941

Duke's Statue Disfigured

"V" signs and other inscriptions were found yesterday painted on the 25ft statue of Francis, 5th Duke of Bedford in Russell-square, London, WC. The fifth duke was an ancestor of the present Duke of Bedford, the 52-year-old pacifist peer, who was stated by Mr Herbert Morrison, the Home Secretary, last week to have been prohibited from visiting Ireland.

A Union Jack was draped around the waist of the statue. A beer-bottle was thrust into the right hand, and a can of treacle was perched on the head.

An inscription in yellow paint on the side of the pedestal read: "Grandfather of a Quisling." Others in yellow paint and white chalk were: "Traitor, 1941," "Melt It," "Down with the Duke" and "Down with the Railings."

The last inscription is a reference to a recent statement by the Duke that he was unwilling to have iron railings removed from Russell-square, Bedford-square and Bloomsbury-square.

October 29 1941

Girls Take to the New Careers

FOR thousands of girls adventure offers itself today in the form of war-time careers that did not exist for women two years ago. If you go into Britain's wooded countryside you may meet girls of the Forestry Corps whose special school label was "good at maths." and whose interesting open-air job is timber measuring.

At a West Country training school you will find young women – a good education is again the key to this job – completing their training as assistant examiners in aircraft factories, receiving 57s 6d a week while at the school, plus a Civil Service bonus. When they go into the factories to help win our air offensives by their scrupulous care in examining aeroplane parts before and during assembly, their inclusive rate, with overtime, is about £3 15s to £4. Those with excep-

tional ability will in time become full examiners.

You will soon see girls in the vans of the London Telephone Service, repairing wiring. If you live in London your electric meter may be read by a girl. No experience needed for this job, but accuracy and agility – meters are often in awkward places.

October 31 1941

Pikes for the Home Guard

SELECTED units of the Home Guard are to be armed with pikes instead of rifles. Close order combat, it is held, may be necessary in some localities defended by the Home Guard; hence the issue of this improvised mediaeval weapon. Permanently fixed on a steel tube is a sword bayonet.

It is a well-balanced instrument, about as long as a rifle with fixed bayonet. A special drill, similar to that laid down for the bayonet, has been arranged for men equipped with it.

The general equipment of the Home Guard now includes the anti-tank gun, light automatic, rifle and bayonet, hand grenade, flame thrower and the pike.

November 15 1941

ARK ROYAL'S END

From Ronald Legge
Gibraltar

FROM the bridge of a destroyer which had been escorting the Ark Royal I watched the last hours of this famous aircraft carrier which sank in the Western Mediterranean today after being torpedoed by the sneak shot of a U-boat yesterday.

She was taken in tow after being hit. This gallant ship met a gallant end, struggling to the last to reach the haven of dry dock where her wounds could be healed; but it was not to be.

Fourteen hours after the torpedo struck, the inky waters of the Mediterranean, which had been the scene of so many of her great exploits, closed over her. Few saw her passing, for the night was dark and cloudy.

For some hours she had been a mere smudge on the horizon, with puffs of black smoke occasionally discernible against a lighter patch of sky as witness to her game fight for survival. Then suddenly there was no smudge. "She's gone," said someone beside me, and no one spoke for a while.

No ship of his Majesty's Fleet was held in greater regard than the Ark Royal – "sunk" so many times by Axis propaganda. I sensed there was a lump in the throat of everyone in the little group of watchers.

The sense of disappointment was the more keen because it had seemed after the first shock of her crippling that the efforts to salve her would be successful.

November 17 1941

Miss Myra Hess

MYRA Hess and a Beethoven programme attracted a record audience at the Albert Hall yesterday. By special permission 500 spectators were admitted in excess of the numbers allowed during the "Prom." season, reckoned at 5,000.

Miss Hess's choice fell on the most gracious and lyrical of Beethoven's concertos – the fourth. Its rare poetry was fully realised.

December 2 1941

On the Brink

DURING the weekend the storm-laden atmosphere in the Far East has again perceptibly thickened.

Whether war impends is still the closely guarded secret of the war-lords of Tokyo, but their gesticulations have reached such a pitch of bellicosity that the threatened Powers are wisely taking every precaution as though the worst might happen at any moment.

November 20 1941

BRITAIN BEGINS BIG DRIVE INTO LIBYA

THE eagerly-awaited big drive into Libya by British Imperial Forces, under Gen. Sir Claude Auchinleck, C-in-C, Middle East, has begun. Advancing at dawn on Tuesday, our troops completely surprised the Germans and Italians, and penetrated to a depth of 50 miles on a front extending 130 miles southward from the coast.

The operations proceeded yesterday "according to plan." Reports received early today stated that some prisoners, all Germans, belonging to Gen. Rommel's Afrika Korps, had been taken.

The successful concealment of the preparations for the attack was largely due to skilful camouflage and the RAF's prevention of enemy reconnaissance. The Navy co-operated by bombarding German coastal positions at Halfaya (Hellfire) Pass and Sollum.

The greatest pressure was exerted by British armoured forces on a 25-mile sector near the coast. If the advance here attained a depth of 50 miles, the forward British troops were within easy reach of beleaguered Tobruk on Tuesday night.

All the land, air and naval forces taking part in the offensive had a message from Mr Churchill read to them on the eve of the offensive.

On land, it was officially stated in Cairo, the Imperial Forces are commanded by Lt-Gen. Sir Alan Cunningham, who was formerly in charge of the East African campaign. He has taken over command of the newly-formed Eighth Army, which, as announced earlier this week, is the new name for the British Army in the Western Desert.

In this first test of strength between the British and Germans since Crete, soldiers from the British Isles are playing a predominant part. The proportion of Dominion troops is smaller than in previous campaigns.

Our troops, it is stated, are engaging Germans in preference to Italians on the principle that one Nazi killed is worth a dozen Italians captured. The slogan is: "Smite the Hun and the Iti will run."

November 26 1941

SOUTH AFRICANS STOP ROMMEL'S TANKS

A desperate German attempt at Sidi Rezegh to force a way to the west between the Imperial Army and the Tobruk garrison has been smashed by the South Africans, as today's Cairo communiqué reveals.

When Rommel's tanks tried to smash their way out the South African anti-tank gunners went down on their knees and gave the Germans "all they had."

The South Africans were outnumbered, but their magnificent stand stopped the Germans till British tanks rumbled into action to turn them back.

Authoritative quarters in Cairo tonight stated that the great tank battle, which has been raging for three days, has now passed its climax of intensity. It is chiefly the Eighth Army's infantry, which has been reinforced, that is now engaging the German infantry.

November 26 1941

MAORIS ENJOY DESERT HUNT FOR GERMANS

SUPPORTED by British tanks, New Zealand shock troops are fighting their way along the coast from Gambut – the German supply centre the capture of which was announced yesterday – towards Tobruk.

They are fighting with anti-tank guns, grenades, Molotov cocktails – and bayonets. As they go north-westwards they send detachments to all sides to seek out and destroy the enemy petrol and ammunition dumps that are thickly dotted over this area.

They are marauders of the desert, raiding parties in trucks accompanied by armoured cars. They are mopping up many enemy posts as their wide sweep continues. Maori units particularly enjoy this grim non-stop fighting, but the whole New Zealand force is inspired with the same eagerness to avenge Greece and Crete.

A British Cruiser tank passes a German tank in the Western Desert

USS *Arizona*: one of the casualties of the Japanese attack on Pearl Harbor

December 8 1941

JAPAN DECLARES WAR ON BRITAIN AND US

IMPERIAL HEADQUARTERS IN TOKYO ANNOUNCED LAST NIGHT THAT JAPAN HAD ENTERED INTO A STATE OF WAR WITH BRITAIN AND THE UNITED STATES IN THE WESTERN PACIFIC AS FROM DAWN YESTERDAY.

Several hours before this announcement was made, news had been received that Japanese bombers had heavily attacked United States naval bases in the Pacific.

The first raid was made at 8.10 a.m. (7.40 a.m. BST) on Pearl Harbour, Oahu, the chief island of the Hawaii group. Much damage was done, and it was officially announced that casualties among army forces alone were 104 killed and 300 injured.

Honolulu city, also on Oahu island, was bombed.

According to a broadcast from the Honolulu representative of the Columbia Broadcasting Corporation, three United States warships in Pearl Harbour were hit by bombs and the battleship Oklahoma was set on fire.

United States forces were said to have sunk one Japanese aircraft carrier and four submarines and to have shot down six 'planes.

The broadcast report added that the United States fleet had steamed out of Pearl Harbour.

At the same time it was announced from the White House, Washington, that the island of Guam, another American naval base in the Pacific, had been attacked by a squadron of "unidentified" 'planes.

Yet another United States base, Wake Island, between Hawaii and Guam, was said to have been occupied by the Japanese.

December 8 1941

US Learns Technique of the "Blitz"

From Alex Faulkner
New York

"WHITE House says, Japanese attack Pearl Harbor."

That sentence, rapped out on the printers of the Associated Press at 2.22 New York Time – 8.22 BST – on this peaceful Sunday afternoon had the effect of an exploding bomb on the newspaper offices and news rooms of broadcasting stations.

In staccato bulletins from Washington the first available details followed in swift order.

Shortly after three p.m. the first messages describing the attack began to arrive from Honolulu. Very few afternoon newspapers are published in the United States on Sundays, but every radio station in the country has been interrupting its programmes at intervals of a few minutes to relay the amazing and totally unexpected news to the American public.

For the first time since the Nazis marched against Poland the war was not a theoretical matter concerning the other half of the world, but something happening in what the United States regards as its home waters.

Hans Kaltenborn, news analyst of the National Broadcasting Company, reduced the reaction of most of his fellow countrymen to the simplest terms when he commented: "The United States has been attacked and the United States will know how to answer that attack."

He recalled that the Japanese set a precedent for this kind of thing when they attacked the Russian Fleet without warning in the Russo-Japanese war.

For more than an hour after the White House announcement I watched thousands of people who were obviously unaware of what had happened, parading peacefully on Fifth-Avenue.

When the news began to spread, however, the scene changed. There was a stampede for bars and other places where radios were to be found, and crowds gathered round wireless-equipped taxis listening with an air of astonishment to the announcements.

December 9 1941

EMPEROR ON WAR

THE Emperor of Japan, declaring war on the United States and Britain, stated:

"It has been truly unavoidable and far from our wishes that our empire has now been brought to cross swords with America and Britain.

"We, by the grace of heaven, Emperor of Japan, seated on the throne of a line unbroken for ages eternal, enjoin upon you, our loyal and brave subjects: we hereby declare war on the United States of America and the British Empire.

"Men and officers of our army and navy will do their utmost in prosecuting the war, our public servants of various departments will perform faithfully and diligently their appointed tasks, and all other subjects of ours will pursue their respective duties.

"The entire nation, with united will, will mobilise its total strength so that nothing shall miscarry in the attainment of our war aims.

"To ensure the stability of East Asia and to contribute to world peace is the far-sighted policy which was formulated by our great, illustrious, imperial grandsire and by our great imperial sire, succeeding him, and which we take constantly to heart.

"To cultivate friendship among the nations and to enjoy prosperity in common with all nations has always been the guiding principle of our empire's foreign policy.

"The situation being such as it is, our empire, for its existence and self-defence, has no other recourse but to appeal to arms and to crush every obstacle in its path.

"Hallowed spirits of our imperial ancestors guarding us from above, we rely upon the loyalty and courage of our subjects in our confident expectation that the task bequeathed by our forefathers will be carried forward."

The Emperor concluded by expressing the hope that "the sources of evil will be speedily eradicated and enduring peace immutably established in East Asia, preserving thereby the glory of our empire."

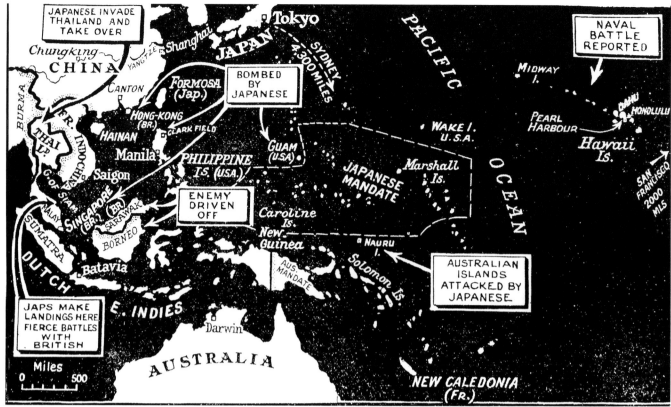

Developments in the Far East

December 10 1941

Hitler at War with US, Says Roosevelt

PRESIDENT Roosevelt broadcast to the American people at 10 o'clock last night (4 a.m. British Summer Time).

Five hours previously he had issued proclamations placing all Italians and Germans, as well as Japanese, in the United States in the category of "enemy aliens." He prescribed the conduct they must follow, giving as his reason that "an invasion or predatory incursion is threatened."

Washington opinion last night was that a severance of relations with all the Axis Powers might be expected soon, with a state of war soon after.

President Roosevelt in his broadcast stated:

America is in the war all the way.

We must begin the great task before us by abandoning once and for all the illusion that we can ever again isolate ourselves.

A serious setback has been suffered in Hawaii. Reports from Guam, Wake and Midway Islands are confused. We must be prepared for announcement that these three outposts have been seized.

Reports that the Japanese have gained naval supremacy in the Pacific are rumours. This is an old trick of propaganda used innumerable times by the Nazis to spread fear and confusion and goad us into revealing military information.

The United States Government has known for weeks that Germany has been telling Japan that if Japan did not attack the US, Japan would not share the spoils.

Japan was promised perpetual and complete control of the whole Pacific area, including a stranglehold on the west coast of North, Central and South America.

Germany and Japan are conducting military and naval operations in accordance with a joint plan.

Remember always that Germany and Italy, regardless of any formal declaration of war, consider themselves at war with the United States at this moment. Germany puts all other republics in the Americas in the category of enemies.

America expects to eliminate the danger to the world from Japan but it would serve us ill if we accomplished that and found the rest of the world dominated by Hitler and Mussolini. For the past decade Japan's course in Asia has been parallel to that of Hitler and Mussolini in Europe and Asia.

Today it has become far more than a parallel. It is collaboration so well calculated that all continents and all oceans are now considered by Axis strategists as one gigantic battlefield.

It will not only be a long war, it will be a hard war.

December 11 1941

SINKING OF PRINCE OF WALES AND REPULSE

LITTLE further news was received last night concerning the sinking of the British battleship Prince of Wales and the battle-cruiser Repulse early yesterday during operations against the Japanese attack on Malaya.

The warships, claimed by the Japanese to have been sunk by air attack, may well have been in action also against a Japanese fleet and have been hit by torpedoes fired from submarines.

December 13 1941

GERMANS SMASHED ON MOSCOW FRONT

SMASHING Russian successes on the Moscow front are officially announced tonight as a result of powerful counter-strokes launched by Gen. Zhukov against both the enemy flanks on Saturday last.

Both north and south of the Soviet capital the enemy has been hurled back with heavy losses.

Solnechnaya Gora, 40 miles north-west of Moscow, where the Nazi spearhead had reached nearest the capital, and the key towns of Stalinogorsk and Venev, to the south, have been recaptured.

December 20 1941

Princess as Star Turn

THE first Royal pantomime on record in this country was given somewhere in England yesterday, when Princess Elizabeth and Princess Margaret presented "Cinderella" in aid of the Royal Household wool fund.

Princess Margaret was Cinderella, and she was the big hit of the show. In addition to being word perfect, she acted cleverly, and when singing popular numbers invited the audience to join in the chorus. She also had several duets with her sister, who was a dashing Prince Charming in traditional tights.

HMS *Repulse* is bombed by the Japanese

December 23 1941

Mr Churchill Meets Mr Roosevelt

AT 1.4 O'CLOCK THIS MORNING THE FOLLOWING DRAMATIC ANNOUNCEMENT WAS MADE IN LONDON:

"THE BRITISH PRIME MINISTER HAS ARRIVED IN THE UNITED STATES TO DISCUSS WITH THE PRESIDENT ALL QUESTIONS RELEVANT TO A CONCERTED WAR EFFORT. MR CHURCHILL IS ACCOMPANIED BY LORD BEAVERBROOK, MINISTER OF SUPPLY, AND A TECHNICAL STAFF. MR CHURCHILL IS THE GUEST OF THE PRESIDENT."

A simultaneous announcement of the visit was made in Washington at 7.4 p.m., Eastern Standard Time.

The official announcement was quickly followed by the statement that the Prime Minister had arrived at the White House in Washington and had gone into immediate conference with the President.

December 22 1941

HITLER TAKES OVER AS C-IN-C

HITLER, who already holds the title of Supreme Commander of the German Armed Forces, has taken the drastic step of assuming the lesser post of Commander-in-Chief.

In an official announcement broadcast by Berlin radio last night, it was stated that the Fuehrer, "following his own intuitions," had superseded Field-Marshal von Brauchitsch, C-in-C of the German Army since February, 1938.

Von Brauchitsch, who has been in charge of the operations against Russia, is thus made the scapegoat for the serious reverses which the German Army has suffered all along the Eastern front.

In an appeal to the Army on assuming his new post the Fuehrer makes the significant admission that the armies in the East "must be brought from mobile progress into a stationary front." He calls on them to defend with fanaticism the territory they have conquered.

December 23 1941

"I RESIST TILL I AM CAPTURED" – HONG KONG GOVERNOR

SIR Mark Young, Governor of Hong Kong, will hold out until the end and until he is taken prisoner. The garrison of the colony is still resisting Japanese attacks.

This announcement was made by the British Embassy in Chung-king, seat of the Chinese Government, yesterday. The Embassy was in hourly contact by wireless with the garrison.

The Embassy had been informed that the Japanese had made "no substantial gain in the past 24 hours" at Hong Kong. They had suffered 15,000 casualties even before effecting a landing.

The Chinese Army HQ on the Canton front reported that part of the Japanese troops on Hong Kong had been driven off by the defenders. This news was received by long-distance telephone.

December 27 1941

Cheers in Congress Hold up Premier

Mr Winston Churchill today addressed both Houses of the United States Congress, delivering a fighting speech which evoked round after round of rousing cheers.

His reception when he entered the Chamber was electrifying.

Once, when he referred to the fate awaiting Japan, he was held up for a minute and a half by the clock while Senators and Representatives stood up and cheered to the echo. And as he concluded he was given an ovation such as Congress has seldom accorded any speaker.

As he left the rostrum at the conclusion of his speech Mr Churchill, walking slowly with shoulders hunched, turned and acknowledged the applause by lifting his right hand with two fingers making the V for victory sign. This act evoked a renewed storm of applause.

For half an hour his voice, of which most of his audience had heard only the radio reflection, played upon a whole series of emotions as he reminded them of the common ideals of Britain and America, analysed their common struggle, and proclaimed his hopes of Anglo-American collaboration in the peace to come.

They applauded enthusiastically as he echoed the Gettysburg ideal of Abraham Lincoln: "Government of the people, by the people, and for the people." They laughed with him as, in rasping tones of high disdain, he spoke of "the boastful Mussolini" as "a serf, the merest utensil of his master's will."

They cheered with him the determination of Russian and Chinese resistance to the Axis, and kept solemn silence as he spoke in quiet, earnest tones about the reverses of Britain and America in Malaya and the Pacific.

But a few moments later he roused them to a new pitch of enthusiasm as, with characteristic relish, he asked:

"What kind of a people do they think we are? Is it possible that they do not realise we shall never cease to persevere against them until they have been taught a lesson which they and the world will never forget?"

1942

Infantry attacking at El Alamein, October 1942

THE New Year is a time for a fresh start, for resolving to keep a diary until Christmas, but anyone embarking on a diary for 1942 would have been an optimist indeed. To note, Fall of Rangoon, capital of Burma, February 8; Fall of Singapore, February 15; and follow with Japanese bombing of Port Darwin, Australia; occupation of the Dutch East Indies; and, across the world, Rommel recaptures Benghazi, would have been sufficient to dishearten the most dedicated diarist.

Yet there was a credit side. If the war had become global, Britain was no longer alone, a partner bonded by the common cause of defeating Germany, Italy and Japan, with Russia, the United States, China, the Free French and Poles and such other remnants as had escaped from the occupied nations of Europe and Scandinavia.

On the home front the reality of such a string of disheartening disasters, however distant they might seem, reinforced a growing war weariness and pessimism that was fertilised by the fact that obtaining enough, and sufficiently nourishing, food was a daily preoccupation. White bread was banned and the disappearance of ice-cream removed one lingering luxury. Those engaged on unaccustomed manual work were particularly vulnerable to all-round austerity at a time when it was a measure of munitions industry desperation that women without dependants who did not take a job could be sent to prison. When in February the battle-cruisers *Scharnhorst* and *Gneisenau* and cruiser, *Prinz Eugen,* made their cheeky "Channel Dash" from Brest to the North Sea, only the courage of the intervention by the posthumous VC, Lt-Cdr Esmonde and his biplane Swordfish torpedo-bomber crews, brought some cheer to a dismal month.

If enemy capital ships could survive the confines of the Channel, in deep sea the situation was worse. Long since Churchill had warned, "We must now assume the Battle of the Atlantic has begun." U-boats, guided to target convoys by four-engined Focke-Wulf Condor reconnaissance aircraft, would remain on top until they could be frustrated and defeated by the introduction of long-range maritime aircraft (based east and west), merchantmen converted into escort carriers, naval hunter-killer convoy escort groups, and improving Ultra intelligence.

Meanwhile, losses in Arctic convoys supplying Russia – particularly the shattered PQ 17 – compounded mounting sinkings along the transatlantic Lend-Lease lifeline. As with the suicidal Swordfish operation in the Channel, it was temporarily left to a handful of brave RAF and Fleet Air Arm Hurricane pilots, catapulted from cargo decks, to fight off the prying Condors and, off Norway, land-based bomber attacks – survival depending on parachuting or crash-landing into the stormy Atlantic and living long enough to be picked up.

Ten days after the "Channel Dash" Air Marshal Arthur Harris was appointed to take over Bomber Command. On May 30 Bomber Command, scraping the barrel of the Operational Training Units, mounted its first 1,000 bomber raid against Cologne as retaliation for the Germans' "Baedeker" raids on Britain's cathedral cities.

Soon the RAF's new four-engined bombers – notably the Lancaster – supported by the versatile Mosquito (the "Wooden Wonder") and guided by the youthful Air Vice-Marshal Don Bennett's Pathfinder Force, would begin an ever-escalating assault on the industrial Ruhr, Hamburg, Berlin and other cities.

Short of Stalin's urgently pleaded Second Front in Europe – raised yet again at his Moscow meeting with Churchill in August – the Battle for Stalingrad began in September. Such disruption of munitions and communications as could be achieved by bombing was the most at this point that could be done to relieve Russia.

There were, however, two landing diversions: the disastrous and largely Canadian raid in August on the Channel port of Dieppe; and Operation Torch, the successful November landings in Morocco and Algeria. Designed to crush Axis forces in North Africa between the armies of Eisenhower and Montgomery advancing from west and east – once Montgomery's Eighth Army had won the morale-boosting Battle of Alamein on the edge of Egypt – "Torch" paid off and gave hope for the success of future invasions. It also served to ease the continuing plight of Malta, the George Cross island.

Further east, the Japanese, in occupation of much of Burma, imperilled India and Ceylon. The threat to India was brought home to the *Burra Sahib* members of the Bengal and Saturday clubs by Hurricane fighters taking off at Christmas from the nearby Red Road running parallel with Calcutta's Piccadilly, Chowringhee, to defend the Bengal capital. Japanese bombers were now in range.

Gas mask test in London street

January 2 1942

FASTEST RAF HEAVY BOMBER

By Our Air Correspondent

AMONG the new heavy bombers which are being delivered to the RAF is the Avro Lancaster. This is a 4-engined aircraft of monoplane design which should be capable of carrying a big load at a higher speed than any other of the new type bombers at present in service.

The Lancaster has some resemblance to the Avro Manchester which has two Rolls-Royce engines. According to reports from Canada, which is one of the places where the Lancaster is being made, the engines can be Bristol Hercules.

These are air-cooled radial engines with sleeve valves, and are of high power. But it is also believed that the Lancaster can be fitted with Rolls-Royce engines.

The need for speed in the new heavy bombers has been emphasised again and again in recent operations.

The success of the German defences in bringing down British aircraft when they are making raids on Germany is often attributed to the fact that our aircraft are of relatively slow speed. They can carry immense loads, but in relation to those loads the speed is low.

The Lancaster should to some extent improve this position. For a given load it is believed to be the fastest aircraft yet produced.

January 3 1942

GRAND ALLIANCE AGAINST AXIS

From Denys Smith, Washington

THE Grand Alliance against the aggressor States was formally concluded here to-day when the representatives of 26 nations, headed by the President of the United States and the Prime Minister of Great Britain, signed a solemn pact pledging themselves to fight the war to a finish.

The text of the Agreement is as follows:

Declaration by the United Nations:

Joint declaration by the United States, the United Kingdom of Great Britain and Northern Ireland, the Soviet Union, China, Australia, Belgium, Canada, Costa Rica, Cuba, Czechoslovakia, the Dominican Republic, Salvador, Greece, Guatemala, Haiti, Honduras, India, Luxembourg, the Netherlands, New Zealand, Nicaragua, Norway, Panama, Poland, South Africa and Jugoslavia.

The Governments signatory hereto,

Having subscribed to a common programme of purposes and principles embodied in the joint declaration of the President of the United States and the Prime Minister of Great Britain and Northern Ireland, dated Aug. 14, 1941, known as the Atlantic Charter,

Being convinced that complete victory over their enemies is essential to defend life, liberty, independence and religious freedom, and to preserve human rights and justice in their own lands as well as in other lands,

And that they are now engaged in a common struggle against savage, brutal forces seeking to subjugate the world, declare:

1 Each Government pledges itself to employ its full resources, military or economic, against those members of the Tripartite Pact and its adherents with which such a Government is at war.

2 Each Government pledges itself to co-operate with the Governments signatory hereto, and not to make a separate armistice or peace with the enemies.

The foregoing declaration may be adhered to by other nations which are or which may be rendering material assistance and contributions in the struggle for victory over Hitlerism.

Done at Washington, Jan 1, 1942.

On the wing: a Lancaster bomber *en route* for a raid on Germany

January 16 1942

AUSTRALIANS GO INTO ACTION IN MALAYA

From H. A. Standish
Singapore

AN official communiqué on the land fighting in Western Malaya, announcing a "local engagement," was issued in Singapore to-night; breaking a silence of 48 hours.

It disclosed that the Australian forces had been in action for the first time, advanced elements attacking and defeating a small Japanese column of infantry and tanks in the eastern part of Negri Sembilan.

The communiqué appears to belie the Japanese claim to be in Gemas, the important railway junction on the Negri Sembilan – Johore border, about 120 miles from Singapore.

Today I was given the first authoritative account of the Japanese landing which began the invasion of Malaya. It was given by the British brigadier commanding the force which defended Kota Bahru, the north-east coast port where the landing was made on Dec. 8.

He said that the Japanese troops were guided to the landing place by two lights hoisted over the house of Fifth Columnists.

At advanced British HQ the brigadier gave me his account of the grim fight for Kota Bahru. He said:

"From the morning of Dec. 7 the troops had been at their battle stations. That evening four ships were reported heading south toward Kota Bahru, and at 1.5 the next morning our 18-pounders on Badung Beach opened fire on ships lying off the beach.

"It was difficult to estimate how many landed at this spot. One Indian officer, who fought with the utmost gallantry commanding an 18-pounder battery on the beach, considered that about 60 boats, carrying 60 Japanese each, got through.

"The country around the river-mouth where the landing was effected was very bad mangrove jungle. We pinned them down there that day and endeavoured to reinforce our pill-boxes, which had suffered heavily.

"This proved difficult, partly because our own wire, anti-personnel mines and other defences hindered the approaches to the pillboxes except along the river, which the Japanese occupied.

"Air reinforcements were called to the three aerodromes in this area. The Japanese began to bomb the aerodromes heavily. On the aerodrome at Machang one bomb caused 26 casualties.

"That day 28 ships were reported off Badung Beach landing more troops. We lost a large proportion of our fighter 'planes.

"That evening (Dec. 8) our air strength ceased to function. The RAAF pilots were ordered to fly off all the serviceable 'planes.

"This meant that our long lines of communication were very vulnerable. We had limited troops. Our east coast sea front was 35 miles long and behind was a river front of about equal length.

"The Japanese continued landings on Badung Beach and later on Sabak Beach, despite the great gallantry of our beach defence posts, many of whom died at their posts fighting to the end.

"We managed to straighten the line north of Kota Bahru. The enemy were now using heavy mortar fire. More ships were reported off the coast, and it was also reported that troops were coming by railway from Thailand.

"The enemy concentrated on landing again on the Badung and Sabak Beaches. At this stage I decided to withdraw to Chanda Muchan."

The brigadier told how the Japanese troops used the same tactics as on the west coast, lying all day in flooded paddy fields, climbing trees to throw grenades into carriers, hiding under heaps of wood. One party crept under a bridge 100 yards from brigade headquarters.

The few enemy prisoners captured proved extremely talkative. One who subsequently died was so amazed at his treatment in hospital that he kissed the hands of the orderlies.

The rest of the brigadier's story was of a steady, orderly withdrawal about 200 miles down the railway, mostly a few miles at a time. All the major bridges were blown up.

"I doubt if they will ever be able to use that line again," the brigadier said.

"Our aircraft immediately 'bombed up' and took off. Before dawn they had hit a ship of 15,000 tons, which burned all day.

"All the shore lights had been extinguished, but as the ships arrived we saw two lights in a line appear over a house at the mouth of the small river Pa'pamat.

"Our men tore down the lights immediately, but the damage had been done. The Japanese troops came into that river mouth in small boats, thus avoiding our wire and land mines.

"They were subjected to a raking fire from our pill-boxes and suffered heavy casualties, because later they were seen picking up 60 or 70 dead around each pill-box. Some got through, however, and disappeared into the jungle.

January 24 1942
JAPANESE LANDINGS IN NEW GUINEA

IT was announced in a Melbourne communiqué tonight that Japanese landings had been reported during the day in New Guinea and the Solomon Islands.

Mr Forde, the Army Minister, stated that, in the Solomon Islands, one landing had been made, following a surprise air attack yesterday, at Kieta, which is about 850 miles from the Queensland mainland.

There are no details of where the landings have taken place in New Guinea, though it is stated that a number have taken place. At 9.20 this morning (12.20 a.m. BST) Bulolo, on the northern coast of the island, reported by radio: "Aircraft overhead." The station then closed down.

January 24 1942
Duke of Connaught

THE Duke of Connaught, whose funeral took place at St George's Chapel, Windsor, yesterday, in the presence of four kings, is to be laid to rest in the Royal Mausoleum at Frogmore, beside his wife and near the tomb of his mother and father, Queen Victoria and the Prince Consort.

Carole Lombard in her last film *To Be Or Not To Be*, with Jack Benny

January 19 1942
Carole Lombard Dies in Crash

From Campbell Dixon
Hollywood

MISS Carole Lombard, the film star, died as spectacularly as she had lived when the big Douglas 'plane carrying her, her mother and 20 other people crashed on Friday night on a precipitous green mountain in the region of Las Vegas, New Mexico.

Miss Lombard was returning to Los Angeles after taking part in a £500,000 Defence Bonds sale campaign in her native Indiana.

Seldom separated from her husband, Mr Clark Gable, she consented to make the journey only if her mother accompanied her.

Her Press agent, who urged her to return by train, tossed a coin to decide the issue. She won – and lost.

When I saw her at the film studio recently she was finishing a film comedy directed by Ernst Lubitsch which is to be entitled "To Be or Not To Be." A flip of the coin has supplied the answer.

January 8 1942
Attagirls!

By Peterborough

ANOTHER recruit for Attagirls, as the women ferry pilots are called in the Services, is Mrs. Allen – better known as that fearless parachutist, Miss Naomi Heron-Maxwell.

Mrs Allen tells me she had several narrow escapes from falling into enemy hands. When serving in the Passport Control Office she had to make a hurried exit from Jugoslavia at the time of the German invasion.

After a fortnight's comparative safety in Athens she again had to make her escape to Cairo. She reached England four months later in a troopship without any incident.

Air-minded even as a schoolgirl, Mrs Allen learnt parachuting as soon as she left school. Later she joined Sir Alan Cobham's air circus.

She tells me she is delighted at the thought of being in the air again after two years' absence. She is looking forward to the interesting work of ferrying different types of planes.

American troops arriving in Northern Ireland

January 27 1942

AMERICAN TROOPS IN NORTHERN IRELAND

TROOPS of the United States Army – the vanguard of the Second American Expeditionary Force to Europe – have crossed the Atlantic and are stationed in Northern Ireland, where they arrived yesterday morning.

The men, who number several thousands, belong to an infantry division. They are combat troops with the usual components of field artillery.

A small number of women nurses also made the history-making voyage, just 24 years and seven months after the first AEF landed in France.

Both the British and United States Navies took part in escorting the convoy.

While the troops were being disembarked anti-aircraft guns in the vicinity opened fire upon enemy raiders. The Ministry of Public Security later announced that no damage had been reported.

The first official news of the troops' arrival was given in Washington last night when the United States War Department issued the following communiqué:

"Northern Ireland: The Secretary of War announces the arrival in Northern Ireland of United States Army forces under the command of Maj.-Gen. Russell P. Hartle.

"The Secretary of War declined to make public designation of the units, their composition and strength, nor would he divulge the ports of embarkation, the dates of sailing, or other details of movement from the United States.

"There is nothing to report from other areas."

As Gen. Hartle stepped ashore he was greeted by the Duke of Abercorn, Governor of Northern Ireland, Sir Archibald Sinclair, Secretary for Air, and Mr Andrews, the Northern Ireland Prime Minister.

Welcoming the soldiers on behalf of the British Government, Sir Archibald, who had flown to Northern Ireland, said:

"Your safe arrival here marks a new stage in the world war. It is a gloomy portent for Mr Hitler; nor will its significance be lost on Gen. Tojo."

February 13 1942

NAZI WARSHIPS HIT IN RUNNING FIGHT

A RUNNING fight in the English Channel with three German warships, each of which was reported hit by bombs and torpedoes, was described in a dramatic communiqué issued by the Admiralty and the Air Ministry at 1.35 this morning.

The warships were the two 26,000-ton battleships Scharnhorst and Gneisenau and the heavy cruiser Prinz Eugen (10,000 tons). They were attempting to reach German ports from Brest, where they had been lying for months past.

They were engaged by RAF bombers, Swordfish torpedo-bombers and destroyers, but although hit were believed to have proceeded to ports in Heligoland Bight. At least six torpedo hits are thought to have been scored on them.

They began their run up-Channel under cover of the darkness, and in daylight yesterday limited visibility aided them. The official communiqué was in the following terms:

"At about 11 a.m. yesterday RAF aircraft reported that an enemy squadron, consisting of the Scharnhorst, Gneisenau and Prinz Eugen, accompanied by destroyers, torpedo-boats, E-boats and minesweepers, was approaching the Dover Straits from the westwards. The enemy squadron was also heavily escorted by fighter aircraft.

"Visibility at this time varied from three to five miles with low cloud and the enemy ships were never visible from the English Coast.

"On receipt of a report, coastal craft of the Dover naval command were immediately sent out to the attack together with Swordfish Aircraft of Fleet Air Arm, strongly escorted by RAF fighters.

"The attacks both by Swordfish and by the coastal craft were pressed close home in the face of intense fire from all enemy surface vessels and opposition by enemy fighters.

"The reports indicate that the Swordfish scored at least one hit on one of the enemy heavy ships and one of the motor torpedo-boats also claimed a possible hit, but owing to the intense barrage and the heavy smoke screen put up by the enemy it was impossible to see the results of the attacks.

"Six Swordfish aircraft are missing, but some of the crews have been saved. There were no casualties in the coastal craft.

"During this time the Dover defences opened fire at extreme range, which was replied to by the enemy shore batteries on the French coast.

"The enemy force was repeatedly attacked by aircraft of the Royal Air Force, strongly escorted by fighters. Results were difficult to see owing to low cloud, but according to

Vice-Admiral Ciliax, commander of the German battle cruisers, inspecting his men aboard the *Scharnhorst*

preliminary reports Coastal Command Beauforts claimed three hits with torpedoes, and Bomber Command crews are confident that each of the main enemy units was hit by bombs.

"The attacks were pressed home with the greatest determination in the face of heavy anti-aircraft fire and strong fighter opposition, which resulted in the loss of 20 of our bombers, including five aircraft of Coastal Command, and 16 fighters.

"Fifteen enemy fighters were destroyed by our fighter escort and at least three more by the bombers themselves.

"Destroyers under the command of Capt. C. T. M. Pizey, RN, in HMS Campbell, also proceeded to intercept and attack the enemy.

"At 15.45 our destroyers sighted the enemy and went into the attack in the face of a very heavy bombing by enemy aircraft and also heavy gunfire from all the enemy's surface ships.

"Our destroyers took advantage of a rain squall to press their attacks home. Owing to the low visibility and the heavy fire to which the destroyers were subjected, it was not possible to be certain of the result of the attack, but there is reason to believe that at least one torpedo hit was obtained.

"Casualties in our destroyers were not heavy.

"When last sighted the enemy, which had become separated, were making for the ports in the Heligoland Bight."

February 3 1942

THREAT TO THE BURMA ROAD

From Leland Stowe
Rangoon

WITH Gen. MacArthur's midget forces with their backs to the wall on the Batam Peninsula, with Singapore within range of Japanese guns, and with the enemy now holding Moulmein and the eastern shores of the Salween River, Allied troops in all these theatres must hereafter fight desperately to ward off the enemy at all costs.

The period of strategic withdrawals has now ended, and every yard held by our forces must be clung to grimly to avoid the possibility of disastrous consequences.

Since this is clearly realised by Gen. Sir Archibald Wavell and the Allied commanders, the bitterest fighting yet seen in the Far East seems unquestionably to lie directly ahead in each of these zones.

The Battle for Burma – it could also be called the battle for the Burma Road – is now beginning in earnest.

The Japanese are already bringing exploratory pressure along the lower Salween River line, particularly from Kadu Island, which might be used as a stepping-stone between Moulmein and Martaban, at the river-mouth, and along the river's banks for 50 miles north to the neighbourhood of Shwegun.

Since there is a ferry at Shwegun the Japanese may be expected to concentrate there.

Japanese strategy must inevitably be based on an attempt to force a passage across the Salween well below the Shan Mountains, whence the enemy could strike to cut the Burma Road and isolate Rangoon.

How soon this drive will be launched may depend on Singapore's resistance. Possibly, however, the enemy will not need troops from the Thai area before thrusting for Burma's central artery which Kipling immortalised as "the Road to Mandalay."

Anyhow the day is now near when the dawn will come up with Japanese thunder from Thailand across Martaban Bay – and this month is likely to provide the answer to the Battle of Burma.

February 10 1942

Last of the MacRoberts

"GLORY is the Reward of Valour." Thus runs the motto borne on the MacRobert coat of arms.

And no family motto in any war has been brought more vividly into focus by the deeds of its holders.

To-day there is but one MacRobert – Lady MacRobert, of Douneside, Aberdeenshire.

Yesterday an RAF casualty list announced that Pilot Offr Sir Iain MacRobert, previously reported missing last June, is now presumed killed.

He was 24, youngest of the three sons of Lady MacRobert, all of whom have been killed while flying – two during the present war.

He was lost while piloting a Blenheim over the North Sea.

Last August Lady MacRobert bought a £25,000 Stirling bomber and presented it to the Royal Air Force as a memorial to her sons.

The bomber was named "MacRobert's Reply," and carried the family's badge and coat of arms.

Lady MacRobert said last night: "My message to the crew of 'MacRobert's Reply' is 'I am with you in thought – all the time my heart is with you.'

"I wish I had been a man – I would have gone in her myself."

Japanese troops proceeding with their bicycles through the jungle

February 16 1942

PREMIER ANNOUNCES FALL OF SINGAPORE

THE fall of Singapore was announced by Mr Churchill in a broadcast last night.

He described the loss of the great naval base and fortress, which cost £30,000,000 to construct, as a "heavy and far-reaching military defeat."

Up to an early hour this morning no details of the capitulation were issued in London. A Tokyo communiqué declared that the Imperial Forces surrendered unconditionally at 7 p.m. Singapore time (12.30 p.m. BST) yesterday.

The Japanese claim that the surrender was negotiated by the British GOC, Lt-Gen. Percival, and the Japanese commander-in-chief in the Ford works at the foot of Bukit Timah Hill. Preliminary discussions were entered into under a flag of truce.

Berlin radio, quoting a Japanese newspaper, stated that the greater part of the British and Australian forces in Singapore left on Friday for Java in about 30 ships.

In his broadcast, which was relayed throughout the world, the Prime Minister warned the nation that many misfortunes and anxieties lay ahead.

"One crime only," he declared, "can rob the united nations of victory, a weakening in our purpose and therefore in unity – that is the mortal crime."

Calling for a renewal of the spirit of June, 1940, after Dunkirk and the French collapse, Mr Churchill said: 'Here is the moment to display that calm and poise combined with grim determination which not so long ago brought us out of the very jaws of death.

"Let us," he concluded, "move forward steadfastly together into the storm and through the storm."

Singapore fell after a nine-days' siege followed by seven days' assault. The Battle of Malaya, which opened on Dec. 8, ended on Jan. 31, and the Battle of Singapore began.

These are the vital dates in the 16 days of siege and assault:

Jan. 31: Siege began with the blowing up of the Johore Causeway after the successful all-night withdrawal of our troops from the mainland.

Feb. 2: Japanese massed for assault. Their attack grew in violence.

Feb. 5: Japanese moved into position while their batteries shelled the island. Artillery duels across Johore Strait.

Feb. 8: Singapore's heaviest day's shelling and bombing. Indications of strong attack impending.

Feb. 9: Singapore island invaded by Japanese, who landed at night in the moonless hours. British, Australian and Indian troops, with Chinese volunteers, harassed and attacked the enemy among the swamps and plantations of the low-lying coastal area.

Feb. 10: More Japanese troops landed. British forces made a withdrawal. The enemy claimed to be five miles from the city.

Feb. 11: Japanese claimed to be in the suburbs of the city. Their dive-bombers made non-stop attack. Naval base evacuated.

Feb. 12: Magnificent resistance of the outnumbered defenders of Singapore as the Japanese flung in more troops.

Lt-Gen Percival surrenders to the Japanese in Singapore

British command ignored a surrender demand and counter-attacked successfully.

Feb. 13: Singapore held the invaders on the fifth day of the attack. Singapore Command issued a communiqué saying that in 24 hours' land and air onslaught, the Japanese had not succeeded in piercing the British lines.

Feb. 14: British still resisting fiercely and holding the two reservoirs.

Feb. 15: Singapore surrendered after a heroic seven-day stand.

Japanese troops parade in Singapore

February 20 1942

New Chief of Bomber Command

THE appointment of a new Chief of the Bomber Command was announced last night by the Air Ministry.

The official announcement stated: "Air Marshal A. T. Harris has been appointed Commander-in-Chief, Bomber Command, in succession to Air Marshal Sir Richard E. C. Peirse, who has been given a special appointment."

Air Marshal Harris, 49, was Deputy Chief of the Air Staff until May, 1941, when he was appointed for special duty with the British Air Staff at Washington. He once flew in a bombing raid with a Polish squadron.

Important modifications in bombing policy are foreshadowed by the changes. Air Marshal Harris will have to choose between a long-term system or a policy designed to get the maximum effect from the existing fleet.

Air Marshal A.T. Harris, Commander-in-Chief, Bomber Command

March 3 1942

"Red Indian" Fighting on the Sittang

From Leland Stowe
Burma

THE fighting here is curiously like that in Finland two years ago. There the patrols glided on snowshoes; here they slide across heavy-crusted rice paddies. There the skirmishers crept at night through frozen forests; here through bamboo thickets and primitive jungles.

But here, along the Sittang, as once in the white wilderness of Karelia, the battle is one of stealth, surprise and boldness, as well as strength. In daylight the jungle is formidable enough, but at night, when it conceals thousands of the enemy, moving as silently as Redskins, it is pretty much like the Lapland front in January.

Only it was 35 below zero at night there, and here it is 90-something above at midday.

Despite climatic contrasts, it is still Red Indian warfare in essence, save that warriors here carry tommy guns or drag machine guns. The Japanese patrols are always out.

British and Indian patrols are reported to be harassing the enemy in the same fashion on the other side of the Sittang, under cover of darkness.

The nature of the terrain explains why most of the Southern Burma front remains fluid, as did Finland and many portions of the Greco-Italian front in Albania.

The only fairly consistent line seems to be that cut by the Sittang. On this side of the river the land extends flatly away from the jungles. Long rectangles of rice paddies are interrupted here and there by rough patches of bush and grove, all dried out by the pitiless sun and all heavy with dust.

That is in the sector where the main approaches to Pegu are heavily guarded. Above Pegu, along the Sittang, the contested territory stretches for many miles, giving the enemy innumerable opportunities to attempt infiltration.

During a single night the Japanese may send "feeler" patrols over in a dozen different places along the 150-mile front.

In all this area only a handful of east-to-west dirt cart roads exist. The rest is open country. That is why night operations persist on both sides and why every night is a challenge and gamble.

A raid by 15 Japanese bombers on Toungoo, about 100 miles north of Pegu, when many civilians were killed, showed incidentally what the susceptibility of Japan's own cities and towns to air raid destruction would be.

As we entered Toungoo three blocks of flimsy wooden houses were blazing furiously. Within three minutes nothing but the framework of the buildings remained. The ignition of a single house meant the destruction of the entire block.

But when you looked at the sagging skeletons of these wooden structures somehow you thought immediately of Japan.

Japanese buildings are made of the same kind of flimsy tinder-like material as these Burmese dwellings.

Halfway up the Pegu-Toungoo road we met a barefooted, dust-covered multitude. They were huddled by eights or tens in two-wheeled bullock-carts, already laden with bundles of belongings, while hundreds of men and women trudged alongside. They gazed at us with bewildered, pleading eyes.

Some of the children held both hands together in front of their faces, in the gesture of prayer for help so common in Oriental beggars. Several hundred of these bullock-carts completely clogged the highway.

We could only tell them they must keep moving north – they must not stay in the war zone. One man asked, "Is there a good road all the way to Mandalay?" We saw a thankful look in his eyes when we said "Yes."

Then he asked, "Is there any from Mandalay to India?" That was not so easy to answer. We knew that the last stretch of that road is no road at all.

But, after all, the refugees could not stay here. The must go on, day after day, perhaps for 600 miles – at the pace of oxen.

Oil storage tanks ablaze at Rangoon which has fallen to the Japanese

Supply route to China as the Burma Road and Rangoon port are closed

March 10 1942

RANGOON EVACUATED BY BRITISH FORCES

RANGOON, stated a communiqué issued in New Delhi last night, has been evacuated by the British forces, who are continuing to fight to the north of the capital.

They are falling back along the only line of communication left with the north – the Rangoon-Prome railway, leading to the River Irrawaddy and to Mandalay, Burma's second city, 350 miles away.

According to Japanese accounts the invaders are now pressing forward in two columns – northward in the direction of Prome and northwestward into the rich Irrawaddy Delta.

Rangoon fell to an encircling movement which started north of the important railway junction of Pegu, 40 miles north of the capital. The Japanese cut across the Rangoon-Mandalay railway and then infiltrated south, outflanking the British positions round Pegu.

March 11 1942

Horror at Japanese Atrocities

A profound feeling of horror was created in both Houses of Parliament yesterday when Mr Eden, Foreign Secretary, and Viscount Cranborne, Colonial Secretary, revealed the facts concerning the atrocities committed by the Japanese on the garrison at Hong Kong.

Mr Eden disclosed, among other infamies, that

Fifty officers and men of the British Army were bound hand and foot and then bayoneted to death.

Ten days after the capitulation wounded were still being collected from the hills and the Japanese were refusing permission to bury the dead.

Women, both Asiatic and European, were raped and murdered.

"Nauseating hypocrisy" was the description applied by Mr Eden to the Japanese claim that their forces were inspired by a lofty code of chivalry – bushido, the ethical code of the Samurai or military knighthood in feudal Japan.

It is enjoined upon the follower of bushido that he should "show a compassionate regard for the honour of the enemy," and cultivate the seven soldierly virtues of loyalty, valour, patriotism, obedience, humility, morality and honour.

It is known that 10 days after the capitulation wounded were still being collected from the hills and the Japanese were refusing permission to bury the dead. It is known that women, both Asiatic and European, were raped and murdered and that one entire Chinese district was declared a brothel regardless of the status of the inhabitants.

All survivors of the garrison, including Indians, Chinese and Portuguese, have been herded into a camp consisting of wrecked huts without doors, windows, light or sanitation. By the end of January 150 cases of dysentery had occurred in the camp, but no drugs or medical facilities were supplied. The dead have to be buried in a corner of the camp.

The Japanese guards are utterly callous, and repeated requests by Gen. Maltby, General Officer Commanding, for an interview with the Japanese Commander have been curtly refused. This presumably means that the Japanese High Command have connived at the conduct of their forces.

March 6 1942

Ban on White Bread

THE national wheatmeal loaf is to be made compulsory and baking of the white loaf will be prohibited. An announcement to this effect is expected soon from the Ministry of Food.

Despite the Ministry's campaign to popularise the wheatmeal loaf its consumption, more than a year after its introduction, is still negligible. Wheatmeal bread comprises about 7 per cent of all bread sold, according to the latest figures.

The compulsory wheatmeal loaf will save shipping space, estimated at about 700,000 tons a year, and will be more nutritive than the white loaf, but the amount of offals for feeding to live stock will be less.

Incorporation of potato flour in the loaf is a future possibility.

March 18 1942

MacArthur takes over in Australia

From Our Washington Correspondent

PRESIDENT Roosevelt told his Press conference to-day that Gen. MacArthur, who has arrived in Australia from the Philippines, would be in supreme command of all Allied forces, on land, at sea and in the air, east of Singapore.

The President made it plain that Gen. MacArthur had left the Philippines solely because he would be more useful in his new post, and the fight in the Batan Peninsula was still going on.

"I know," said Mr Roosevelt, "every man and woman in the United States is in agreement that all-important decisions must be made with a view to the termination of the war."

During the three months of Batan fighting, Gen. MacArthur has insisted that he would leave the Peninsula only if ordered by the President. He received this order on Feb. 22.

He asked for time to reorganise his command, to ensure that

resistance to the Japanese should be continued by his successor there, Major-Gen. Jonathan Wainwright

In announcing Gen. MacArthur's appointment the United States War Department stated that it had been made at the request of the Australian Government.

Gen. MacArthur's stand in the Philippines has made him America's greatest military hero since Robert E. Lee, Stonewall Jackson and Ulysses Grant, and his appointment has been greeted with great enthusiasm.

March 9 1942

"AUSTRALIA WILL BE HELD"

From Our Sydney Correspondent

A warning that Japan may be expected to attack Australia, and a pledge that, given air support, Australia will be held, were given by Major-Gen. Gordon Bennett, who commanded the Australian forces in Malaya, in a broadcast from Sydney to-day.

"If Australia's fighting men take the initiative, the Japanese will be defeated," he said. "Their infiltration tactics do not apply to Australia. Australian soldiers will adopt tactics suitable to local conditions, and given adequate air support, we will make Japan rue the day she attempted to capture our country."

March 19 1942

HOW THE 93RD HIGHLANDERS FOUGHT IN MALAYA

DESPATCHES from Malaya sometimes mentioned the gallant part the Argyll and Sutherland Highlanders were playing in the campaign. Here is their story told by Col. I. MacA. Stewart, their Commanding Officer.

As one of the units of the 12th Brigade this regiment, the old

The threat to Australia from the Japanese

93rd, met the Japanese at the very start of the invasion, fought endlessly against heavy odds and were the last battalion to cross the Causeway.

We prepared an ambush on the road with A Company, armoured cars, mortars and carriers well hidden; B Company, with armoured machine-gun carriers to be hidden away in the rubber trees and jungle, went forward on the flank, ready to pounce out on the enemy's rear.

The signal to do so was to be by bugle, since it is so much quicker and the decision must be taken at once – it would take time for runners to get there, even supposing that runners could get through. The bugle call was to be the regimental call followed by the advance if the order was "attack"; the stand fast if an order was to withdraw to a previously arranged rendezvous.

The ambush on the road had tremendous success. Two of the Jap companies were caught by our machine-guns in close order at 75 yards range and just about wiped out to a man. But their reinforcements quickly came up – they had any number of them – and the inevitable walking round each flank began.

Shortly after 11 o'clock it was evident that we couldn't do our job by just sitting still, and, well – to encourage our weary men I told the piper, whom I had with me, to get ready to play. He was Pipe-Major McKalmen and he comes from Islay.

McKalmen and I had a discussion on what we were to play. We discussed first "Highland Laddie," which is our regimental march-past, or "Blue Bonnets," or I'm afraid I suggested the march which in English is translated "The Highway," and happens to be that of my own Clan Appin.

Well, I told the bugler, who was Hardy, my batman, and also a very gallant man indeed, to sound the regimental call and the advance, the signal to attack. Attack we meant to do with all we'd got, and that was precious little. He sounded the regimental call. Then, wetting his lips, as a good bugler always does to get a good blow, he was about to sound the advance when a despatch rider came dashing up the road.

I stopped the bugler just in time – just as he was beginning to play – while I had a look at the message. It read, "You may withdraw at your discretion."

"Quick, sound the stand fast," I said to the bugler.

Well, it had been a matter of seconds.

The enemy tried his usual quick follow-up, but an ambush by our armoured cars under Tom Nuttall – we had seven armoured cars in the battalion – soon put an end to that. Their leading party of 15 was caught at about 50 yards range by two of our Vickers guns – those of you who have fired Vickers know what that means – and they got the lot.

That battle cost the Japs not less than 200 men – it cost us 10.

The Manchester Regiment in the Far East ready for action

HMS *Exeter* is bombed by Mitsubishi aeroplanes in the Battle of the Java Sea

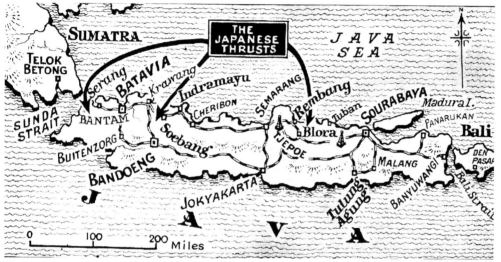

The Japanese attack in Java. Below: a blazing B-17 bomber after a Japanese air raid on Bandung airfield, Java

March 20 1942

EPIC OF JAVA SEA

From George Weller
Somewhere in Australia

AN American navy lifebelt, with a Holmes floating light attached to it, tossed overboard from the United States cruiser Houston in the battle of the Java Sea, saved the lives of 116 men, and enabled a Dutch destroyer commander to bring back the first comprehensive story of the action.

Struggling for their lives in oil-burdened waters after their destroyer, the Kortenaer, had been torpedoed, the 116 men managed to stay clinging to their rafts as the Allied squadron steamed past in the moonlight.

Their cries for help were answered by shouts from the Dutch cruisers De Ruyter and Java and the British cruiser Perth, but only some unknown friendly hand aboard the Houston had the quickness of mind to throw them the lifebelt.

It was the light attached to the lifebelt that guided a British destroyer to their rescue, although not before a radio operator had suffocated through fuel oil clogging his nose and throat.

Some 37 other members of the Kortenaer's crew perished when a Japanese torpedo, fired probably from a submarine, hit her near the engine room, destroying No. 2 boiler room and the magazines.

The Kortenaer split amidships, the two parts sinking perpendicularly within two minutes "like stakes driven into the sea."

April 1 1942

Life in a Nazi Prison Camp

THE first authentic account of life in a Nazi prison camp is given in "Prisoner of War," a sixpenny illustrated booklet published today on behalf of the War Organisation of the British Red Cross.

There are now more than 90,000 British prisoners of war in Europe. They are scattered over 39 camps. Here is a typical day described by an inmate of an Oflag:

Up at 6.45; parade 7.15; breakfast at 8; bath, make bed, read or work till 10, then canteen for beer.

Lunch at 11, sleep half-hour or more, read or lessons till 3; parade, then a swim if warm.

Tea; walk in field, not very interesting, nose to tail all the way, about one-tenth mile round.

Supper at 7; parade. If no concert, &c., bridge till 9.30.

The men are either kept in camp with a camp routine or sent out on working parties to do unskilled and strenuous manual labour.

This is a typical day's fare:

Breakfast: Half-litre of ersatz coffee.

Dinner: Soup and potatoes.

Tea: Soup and potatoes, or meat and potato mash, or cheese, or sausage, with tea or ersatz coffee.

Every day each prisoner is given 10oz of bread, and on Sundays a 2oz Camembert cheese and some jam.

The booklet comments: "This food will obviously keep a man from starving, but it is plain, dull and 'foreign,' of a sameness and a type that get you down, as the men say, consisting mainly of potatoes and acorn coffee. Men on heavy work especially need some supplement to the prison diet if their health is not to suffer."

Red Cross parcels – one a week per man – bring prison rations up to a proper nutritional standard. Four hundred tons of bulk supplies of food are being supplied monthly.

April 22 1942
Guards Cheer Their Princess

Princess Elizabeth was 16 yesterday. She celebrated the occasion by inspecting the Grenadier Guards, as their new Colonel, at a special birthday parade at Windsor Castle in the morning.

The occasion also marked her entry into the official life of the nation. The confidence and unhurried dignity with which she bore herself aroused wide appreciation among the spectators.

Clearing debris after a raid on Valletta

April 21 1942
Laval Proclaims His Nazi Policy

LAVAL publicly declared his whole-hearted submission to Germany in a broadcast speech last night to the people of France.

It was a speech confessing complete capitulation to Hitler – "a conqueror who did not abuse his victory." Yet while he attacked Britain bitterly he had no word of criticism for the United States.

His motive is to avoid a breach with Washington, and it is known in London that he has privately expressed his confidence that he can negotiate an understanding.

His belief that he can influence American opinion is one of his obsessions.

In general, as is characteristic of the man, Laval was careful to address his arguments to sections of the French people – especially the peasants and workers. He appealed to self-interest as against patriotic sentiment.

While Laval was paying tribute to the Germans for refraining from "humiliating France," the German authorities were executing 30 hostages in Rouen as a reprisal for an attack on a German troop train.

The Vichy report of the executions said that the hostages were chosen from a concentration camp where Communists and followers of Gen. de Gaulle are held.

The Germans announced that 80 more would be shot unless those guilty of the attack on the train, in which 44 Nazi soldiers were killed, surrendered by Thursday.

In future, it was added, French civilians are to be compelled to accompany Germans on troop trains.

In addition, 1,000 "Communists and Jews" are to be deported to Eastern Europe.

April 27 1942
MALTA'S 48 HOURS OF NON-STOP RAIDS

FOR 48 hours during the weekend Malta endured air-raids practically without cessation. The crump of bombs and the noise of machine-gun bullets were almost continuous.

The island found consolation, however, in the news of the RAF's intensive bombing of Germany and the fact that 14 Axis 'planes had been hit in what Rome calls "the hammering of the air bases of Malta."

In this week-end's three raids, four of the enemy's machines did not get home again. The RAF got three, the ground defences one.

The harbour area was heavily attacked, the aerodrome comparatively lightly.

Spitfires on stand-by, Malta

April 6 1942
FIRST ATTACK ON COLOMBO

ATTEMPTING to repeat in Ceylon their surprise attack on Pearl Harbour on the opening day of the Pacific war, the Japanese yesterday morning launched a heavy air raid on Colombo, the British naval and air base guarding the western approaches of the Bay of Bengal.

The enemy found the defences ready. Out of 75 raiders, 27 were shot down – 25 by fighters and two, engaged in a low-flying attack, by anti-aircraft fire.

The Colombo communiqué yesterday stated that five other raiders were probably shot down as well, while 25 others were damaged. Our losses were slight.

May 5 1942

"BAEDEKER" RAIDS

EXETER, city of churches, bears ghastly scars of German terrorism following the latest ferocious "Baedeker" raid during the early hours of this morning. On all sides there are scenes of devastation.

It was the third attack in 10 nights and it is feared that the casualties will prove higher than in the earlier raids on the nights of April 23 and 24, as the latest raid was on a much heavier scale.

The destruction of seven of the raiders is believed to be about a quarter of the total number – about 30 – engaged. Two others were probably destroyed.

The attack began at 2 a.m. and lasted for an hour. Flying low, the raiders dropped high explosive and incendiary bombs and machine-gunned streets.

Workmen going to their night-shifts were caught by the gunfire. A large number of fires were started, and many well-known streets suffered. Important buildings were hit, including a hospital college, a girls' school, almshouses, some churches and a terrace of Georgian houses. Many private houses were damaged.

Through it all there was fine team-work by civil defence services, soldiers, AFS workers and others. Many who had never before taken part in civil defence helped to fight the fires and rescue injured and trapped people, and some lost their lives in doing so.

At one church a bomb struck the tower, slicing half of it away and leaving some of the bells swinging in the open air.

The wife and young son of a doctor serving abroad were killed by a direct hit, and several fire-watchers and others on patrol duties are missing. Search parties are seeking women and children who were seen in a shopping centre in one locality shortly before bombs fell and damaged the buildings.

Street shelters saved hundreds of lives, including a number of mothers with young babies who were later cared for at a first-aid centre.

Supplies of static water were a great aid in fire-fighting. Fire-fighters and other defence services joined in the task of clearing streets and making way for essential services to-day, and rescue parties, reinforced by Pioneers and other Servicemen, set about the grim task of digging for those trapped beneath the ruins of old houses.

Exeter Cathedral is a victim of a "Baedeker" raid

May 5 1942

Women Outwit Austerity

Daily Telegraph
Woman Reporter

WOMEN have found a way to be smartly dressed despite clothes rationing and austerity styles. So many of them are having their old clothes remade that dress-makers are finding it difficult to cope with orders.

The trend of fashion just before the war enables the most to be made of the store of little-worn garments accumulated in women's wardrobes.

Then designers used up to 12 yards for a pleated day dress and up to 20 yards for a crinoline evening gown. These are now being converted into models of simple design.

Satin bridal dresses are being turned into lingerie. Fur coats are being made into capes and short coatees, or renovated with panels of suede or cloth.

One firm is converting men's lounge and evening suits into women's costumes. "Nothing is smarter than a black costume made from a dress suit," a representative of this firm said to me.

Fashion leaders of pre-war days now give a lead in economy ideas. Countess Beatty gave me these ideas for the home needlewoman:

"Old table napkins make very smart collars. I have them starched to wear with my working clothes.

"Silk stockings look more sheer if they are worn inside out.

"For women whose male relatives are overseas I suggest that shirts make very smart blouses."

Lady Beatty turns old evening frocks into blouses and day dresses and her husband's suits into boys' suits.

May 5 1942

Army's Carrier Pigeons

PIGEON fanciers are working in close collaboration with the Royal Corps of Signals.

At any time of the day you may see an elderly man – he must be nearly 70 – running up a certain street of this town. He is one of the keenest of a small army of private loft-owners whose pigeons are working for the Army.

The messages which arrive at his loft are always delivered "at the double" to Signals HQ.

These private pigeons earn 2d for their owners every time they fly for the Army. They are auxiliary to the Army's own organisation.

The birds are tended by experts – men who made a hobby of pigeon racing before they entered the Army.

The Japanese attempt to cut off the British and Chinese forces

May 4 1942

ENEMY ENTER RUINED MANDALAY

THE British and Chinese forces in Upper Burma are in a grim situation with the fall of Mandalay and Lashio and the loss of the railway running between those two towns. Mandalay, according to Tokyo, was a "blazing ruin" when the Japanese entered the city.

The British, having fallen back across the Irrawaddy, are now fighting a strong threat to their right flank at Monywa, on the River Chindwin 50 miles west of Mandalay – part of an attempt to trap the Allies.

The Chinese, for their part, are struggling to hold the Japanese advance beyond Lashio, which has now reached Kutkai (60 miles north and 30 miles from the China border).

The Japanese on this front are pouring in reinforcements and are aiming to reach Bhamo and then the railway north to Myitkyina, route of any Allied retreat from Mandalay

May 9 1942

"BRADSHAW" RAID

RAILWAY yards and a railway at Dieppe were attacked last night by Boston bombers which were escorted by fighters. All our aircraft returned safely.

With no German fighters to worry them, the Spitfire pilots had a grand-stand view of the raid. One said he saw what he believed to be a goods train on fire. Another pilot commented: "It was just like travelling to a Bradshaw time-table."

The King talks to a fighter pilot returned from a raid

May 9 1942
New Cochran Revue

THE predominant note in "Big Top," the revue last night at His Majesty's which brings Mr Cochran back to the London theatre, is mockery. The author is that witty writer, Herbert Farjeon, and he makes fun – sometimes gentle, occasionally almost savage, fun – of most things from Shakespeare to ballet fans.

He has several brilliant artists to point the satire. There is Beatrice Lillie, who must be the most economical comedienne in the world. With a shrug of her eloquent shoulders or the slightest lift of the eyebrows she speaks volumes of humour.

She is exquisitely funny as "The Lady in Grey" singing mournfully on the Embankment about "Wind Round the Heart," which is a perfect burlesque of the "Blues."

Fred Emney, with his air of nonchalant geniality, is always a joy. He is at his best in a scene which might have been regarded as out of his line of comedy – the sketch of the all too amiable gentleman who is no raconteur but insists on telling a long, rambling story without any point. He does it so well that what might have been very boring from almost anyone else is one of the most humorous things in the show.

The Canadian Beaver and the British Lion: war poster, April 1942

May 13 1942
GERMANS REPULSED IN CRIMEA

THE prelude to Hitler's much-publicised summer offensive on the Eastern front has come with a smashing onslaught by tanks and dive-bombers on the Soviet lines on the 15-mile front of the Kerch Peninsula in the Crimea.

To-night's Russian communiqué speaks of the "stubborn fighting" throughout to-day, the fifth day of the battle.

From Soviet official sources I learn that the Germans have been flung back with very heavy losses on all sectors except on the shores of the Bay of Arabat on the Russian right wing, where armoured units have made some progress towards the village of Arabat.

A Berlin military spokesman this afternoon informed the foreign Press that Gen. von Manstein's troops are using a new Nazi secret weapon, a newly-discovered gas which although non-poisonous, temporarily paralyses troops. This he claimed had enabled the Nazis to overwhelm the first line of the Soviet defences at Kerch.

Allied military circles, however, deny all knowledge of the existence of any such gas and state it is part of the Nazi nerve-war tactics.

May 13 1942
5s Meal Maximum

FROM June 1 no restaurant or hotel will be allowed to serve any meal costing more than 5s, subject to certain additional house charges, or consisting of more than three courses.

Simultaneously there will be a ban on meals between midnight and 5 a.m. in the London police area, and between 11 p.m. and 5 a.m. in the provinces, except in catering establishments licensed to serve night workers and travellers.

Lord Woolton, the Food Minister, announced in the House of Lords yesterday that he will shortly bring in an Order to impose the restrictions. The Order will also authorise him to prohibit the serving of fish, game and poultry in hotels on certain days when he considers it necessary to allow domestic consumers to purchase a reasonable share of supplies.

In addition to the 5s, restaurants will be allowed to charge up to 2s 6d for music, dancing or cabarets.

Special provision is to be made to meet the exceptional cases of establishments which, on account of high overhead charges, would have to close down if they were limited to the 5s maximum. They can apply for leave to levy a house charge. This will not be allowed to exceed 7s 6d.

May 15 1942
Big Queues for Ration Books

PEOPLE eager to get their new clothing cards and personal ration books formed long queues at collecting centres in London yesterday.

The rush was much greater than expected. At more than one centre police had to marshal the crowd. At Croydon Food Office clerks brought their tables out to the pavement and a queue was formed at each table.

Many people in the queues were under the impression that there was only one day to collect the documents. Actually there is about another fortnight.

Using the issue of the ration books as a means of checking identity cards has thrown a tremendous burden on food office staffs. In various parts of the country extra help has been practically unobtainable, women formerly available being now in munitions factories.

Lambeth food executive officer has adopted a novel method of facilitating the work. He has borrowed the town council's mobile information unit to carry the documents to people living in blocks of flats and big housing estates.

May 15 1942
"SHOT DOWN LIKE PARTRIDGES"

THE Ju.52 carriers which were shot down over the Mediterranean on Tuesday, were full of troops.

This was announced by the Air Ministry last night, in a statement giving details of the encounter.

RAF Kittihawk fighters were returning from a sweep when they encountered the large formation of troop carriers – about 20 'planes altogether. They shot down 13 Ju.52s and two Me.110s for the loss of only one of our 'planes.

It is known that the remaining 'planes in the formation were badly damaged.

Troops in the 'planes – each of which can carry 18 fully-equipped men in addition to the crew of five – were seen to be using tommy-guns against the RAF fighters in a desperate effort to avert their fate.

The German 'planes were flying in brilliant sunshine about 50ft over the sea when they were sighted. The RAF fighters immediately went into attack. In a few moments the first Ju.52 plunged into the waves.

"I have never seen anything like the next 15 minutes," said one fighter pilot. "One after another, at half-mile intervals, the Ju.'s crashed in flames."

The operation was led by an Australian-born wing commander, who holds the awards of DFC and Bar. He shot down one Ju.52. The rest of the

successes were shared by British, Australian and Canadian pilots.

A squadron leader, an Oxford graduate, who lives near Winchester, shot down two of the transports. He said, "My most vivid impression of the action was the sight of high columns of black smoke rising from the sea, like a long colonnade, visible at least 10 minutes after the engagement had been broken off."

Of the engagement, he said: "I hit two 'planes. I could see the face of the pilot twisted

with horror as his machine plunged into the sea, the starboard wing burning. It was like shooting partridges."

Two days before taking part in this battle an Australian flight lieutenant from Ross Bay, Sydney, had made a forced landing behind the enemy lines. On that occasion he was able to fly his aircraft back as he saw the enemy approaching.

Giving his account, in the vernacular, of the fight over the Mediterranean he said: "Well, I'm quits now for that flap they gave me."

May 29 1942

TANK BATTLE RAGES NEAR EL ADEM

From Our Cairo Correspondent

LATEST reports, received here early this morning, of the great tank battle raging in an area stretching from north-east of Bir Hacheim toward El Adem continue to be favourable.

They indicate that the Axis forces are taking severe punishment from the RAF, which has wrested the initiative from the German land units and is levying heavy toll of their supply columns.

The military situation appears to be that Gen.Rommel is thrusting for Tobruk, 20 miles north of El Adem, but that so far he has made little progress.

This thrust followed the repulse of heavy assaults on both our flanks (Bir Hacheim in the south, Gazala in the north).

In these abortive flank attacks terrible havoc was caused among the Axis transport and supply columns not only by the RAF but by our 25 and 30-pounder mobile artillery. At the end of the day the roads were strewn with the debris of burned-out Nazi vehicles.

One German tank column which came into contact at Bir Hacheim with our armoured forces sustained very heavy casualties, as did also an Italian force which attempted to advance south of Gazala.

It was officially stated here last night that "there is no cause for dissatisfaction" at the progress of the battle, which is developing on the lines anticipated by Gen. Auchinleck.

The ill-fated PQ17 convoy bound for Russia: it was savaged by U-boats following Admiralty orders to "scatter"

June 25 1942

Ice-Cream's Last Summer

THE manufacture of ice-cream is to be prohibited after Sept. 30.

Announcing this decision yesterday the Ministry of Food gave facts about the demands made by the ice-cream trade on materials, man-power, factory space and transport.

Among the materials required are fats and sugar. These, the Ministry says, should be used in foods which can be equitably distributed and equitable distribution of ice cream is impracticable.

The national manufacturers of ice cream employ more than 1,500 people and there are a number of smaller factories which all need skilled engineers.

Being perishable, the product is one which is very wasteful of specialised transport. The containers used for carrying it weigh more than the ice cream itself.

The refrigerated space set free in factories and depots will be available for storing more essential foods. There will be a saving of over 1,000 tons a year of paper and board used for tubs and wrappings.

Pursuing its policy of restricting canning to essential requirements, the Ministry of Food has also decided soon to stop the canning of spaghetti and macaroni and of vegetable salad with mayonnaise.

There was a big demand by housewives all over the country yesterday for dried eggs, which were on sale for the first time.

Nineteen million tins, each equal to 12 eggs, have already been distributed to shops. A further 15,000,000 will follow during the next three weeks. The retail price is 1s 9d a tin.

June 26 1942

EISENHOWER: C-in-C EUROPE

AT the same time as the United States War Department in Washington announced yesterday the "formal establishment of a European Theatre of Operations for the United States Forces," Major-Gen. Dwight D. Eisenhower, appointed Commanding General, took up his duties in London.

He had flown here from Washington, after conferences with President Roosevelt and Mr Churchill.

He is a 51-year-old Texan, clear-thinking, resolute and "tough." He is regarded as an expert in armoured force operations, and until recently was Assistant Chief of Staff, Operations Division, United States War Department General Staff.

Before then he was Gen. MacArthur's right-hand man in the Philippines, where, as Chief of Staff from 1935 to 1940, he took a leading part in organising the islands' defences.

Goebbels inspects the damage done to Cologne Cathedral by British bombers

A Halifax bomber comes home

June 1 1942

WORLD'S BIGGEST AIR RAID – ON COLOGNE

From Stewart Sale, Air Correspondent
At a Bomber Command Station

On the 1,001st day of the war more than 1,000 RAF bombers flew over Cologne, and in 95 minutes delivered the heaviest attack ever launched in the history of aerial warfare. It is officially described as "an outstanding success."

Involved in this great air bombardment were 13,000 men, roughly divided between the ground and the air.

The number of bombers employed was at least twice that of the heaviest single force sent over this country by the Luftwaffe. They carried some 3,000 tons of bombs – at least four times the weight that ever fell on a British town in any one raid.

Even then, it is considered that many of the German machines made two trips in one night. It is more probable that the latest RAF raid involved three or even four times the number of machines used by the Nazis in one night over Britain.

For the first time, all RAF commands were concerned in one night's operations, a notable feature being the participation of the Army Co-operation Command, which has not before been reported in action from this country. Its 'planes were engaged in diversionary attacks on enemy aerodromes.

All told it is probable that about 1,250 aircraft took part. In that case our loss of 44 'planes would be a fraction more than $3\frac{1}{2}$ per cent. of the whole.

The attack was delivered with such speed that the RAF bombers were going in over the target at the rate of 10 a minute – one every six seconds.

Halifax fliers, coming back at dawn to-day, told me of bombers milling over Cologne "like the traffic at Piccadilly Circus," and of vast fires that they could still see when they were over the coast of Holland 140 miles away on the journey home.

An air bomber, just back, put it in a sentence. "London at its worst," he said, "was only a patch on Cologne."

The 'planes, a mixed swarm with the heavier types in strong proportion, carried high explosive bombs of every calibre, including a large percentage of the new 4,000 pounders, and many thousands of incendiaries.

June 10 1942

"Cologne Just A Beginning"

Air Marshal A.T.Harris, who, as chief of Bomber Command, organised the 1,000-bomber raids on Cologne and Essen, in a talk recorded for a film, states:

"The Nazis, simple souls as they are, entered this war under the quaint illusion that they could bomb everybody who stood in their way – and that nobody could bomb them. That was Goering's boast.

"At Warsaw, Rotterdam, London, Coventry, Plymouth, and half a hundred other places, they put that naive theory into practice. They sowed the wind. They will reap the whirlwind. Luebeck, Rostock, Cologne – they are just the beginning.

"In the past Bomber Command was largely employed in bombing on a comparatively light scale those more immediately urgent targets dictated by the day-to-day war situation. A sort of strategic defensive. So much to do; so little to do it with. Now we pass increasingly to the strategic offensive.

"Do not imagine that we can yet put out 1,000 bombers a night whenever we please. That time will come. It may not be long delayed, but it is not yet.

"We have, however, proved that technically it can be done. Technically it can, and, if necessary, will be, far surpassed.

"We have not as yet in this country the force available to maintain that effort. But we shall obtain it, and we shall, if necessary, maintain it – from our own resources if need be.

"Let the Nazis take good note of the western horizon. There they will see a cloud as yet no bigger than a man's hand. Behind it lies the whole massive power of the United States of America.

"When the storm, gathering there and here, breaks in its full fury over Germany they will look back to the days of Lubeck, Rostock and Cologne as men lost in the raging typhoon think back to the gentle zephyr of a past summer.

"It may take a year; it may take two; but for the herrenvolk the writing is on the wall. Let them look out for themselves. The cure is in their own hands.

"A lot of people (generally those with no qualifications to speak, if to think) are in the habit of iterating the silly phrase 'bombing can never win a war.' Well, we shall see.

"It hasn't been tried yet, and Germany, more and more desperately clinging to her widespread conquests, and still foolishly enough striving for more, will make a most interesting subject for the initial experiment."

Leaflet to Germans warning that Cologne heralds intensive bombing

June 13 1942

BATTLES OF CORAL SEA AND MIDWAY

From Our Washington Correspondent

THE smashing nature of the United States victory over the Japanese in the battle of the Coral Sea at the beginning of May, which delayed for at least two months the enemy's plans to invade Australia, was officially disclosed here to-day.

A communiqué issued by the Navy Department gave the following figures:

Japan: 15 warships sunk, including the new aircraft-carrier Ryukaru and three heavy cruisers; two ships probably sunk and 20 damaged; more than 100 aircraft lost.

United States: Only three ships sunk, including the aircraft carrier Lexington.

To assess how large are the losses which the Japanese Navy has suffered this year, the damage done by United States Forces in the Midway Island battle on June 7 must be added.

The United States Navy spokesman at Honolulu revealed to-day that probably four Japanese aircraft carriers, including two of the heaviest type, were destroyed at Midway.

Earlier American estimates stated that two or three Japanese aircraft carriers and two destroyers were sunk in the Midway action, and 13 other vessels, including three battleships, were damaged.

The Coral Sea action was the first naval battle in history in which all the damage was done by aircraft. Surface craft were never in range of each other. They used their weapons only for anti-aircraft attacks. Fragments of an enemy battleship's shells were found in American aircraft.

Although outnumbered, the American forces smashed a Japanese invasion fleet and drove it back to its bases, giving valuable time for Australian and Pacific bases to be strengthened.

American sailors leap for their lives from the aircraft carrier *Lexington*, hit by the Japanese in the Coral Sea

June 30 1942

More than a Million Jews Killed

THE Germans have up to now slaughtered over 1,000,000 Jews in occupied Europe. This represents one-sixth of the Jewish population within that area.

It was recently revealed in a document published exclusively in THE DAILY TELEGRAPH that of this number 700,000 were killed in Poland alone.

It is the declared aim of the Nazis to wipe the race from the European continent. Goebbels, in a recent issue of Das Reich wrote:

"The Jews of Europe are playing a most detestable game in this war, and will pay with the extermination of their race in the whole of Europe and elsewhere, too."

I understand that the recent disclosures from Poland have moved London and Washington to open immediate discussions on counter-measures.

Reports of massacres, chiefly in the East European countries, have been reaching London recently. But there is also a volume of evidence to show that the declared Nazi policy of extermination of the Jews is intended to cover the West as well.

In France, Holland and Belgium executions are carried out on a large scale, and scores of thousands are imprisoned in concentration camps. A very large number have been deported for forced labour to Eastern Europe and to the ghettos and reserves there.

Vichy has already applied 70 of the specific Nazi anti-Jewish laws.

In Rumania 125,000 Jews have been murdered after signing a declaration which says, "I am responsible for the outbreak of the war and I have to accept my punishment for it."

Two trains leave Prague every week carrying Jews from Czechoslovakia to Poland. Over half the Jewish population had been deported up to the end of May.

One whole town within the country itself has been entirely evacuated of its Czech population to make a Jewish concentration camp.

In Hungary the expulsion of the entire Jewish population, numbering 800,000, is pending. All Jews have already been driven out of employment.

It is estimated that the casualties suffered by the Jewish people in Axis-controlled countries already far exceed those of any other race in any war.

Mr Arthur Greenwood, Leader of the Socialist Opposition, broadcasting greetings from the British Socialist Movement to Poland last night, said: "Do not think for a moment that we are forgetting you in your martyrdom, or that those guilty of the terrible crimes against you will escape their just retribution.

"We pledge ourselves that the independence and freedom, in defence of which we took up arms, shall be restored to you."

Tobruk under bombardment

June 22 1942

TOBRUK CAPTURED BY ROMMEL'S FORCES

IT was officially confirmed at midnight in London last night that the Libyan port and fortress of Tobruk had been captured by Gen. Rommel's forces.

Unofficial quarters in Cairo had earlier admitted the loss and that the enemy were also in Bardia, 20 miles from the Egyptian frontier.

According to the German and Italian communiqués issued early yesterday afternoon, Rommel took Tobruk with 25,000 prisoners and large quantities of war materials. This total of prisoners, it was stated in Cairo early to-day, was not unlikely.

The Axis communiqués said that Tobruk was captured by one overwhelming assault.

To the accompaniment of a terrific air bombardment all day on Saturday, heavy tanks crashed through the perimeter fences and were followed by masses of infantry and more heavy tanks.

Christopher Buckley, our Special Correspondent, describes how the Axis tanks, beginning their attack in the Ed Duda sector, smashed through regardless of losses.

The lack of official confirmation from Cairo up to early today of the fall of Tobruk, which was Rommel's main objective when he attacked on May 27, may have been due to interrupted communications.

It is also thought that isolated parties of the garrison troops may very probably have escaped across the desert to rejoin the main body. Boatloads may also have got away safely by sea; but

Libya-Egypt frontier area, three days after fall of Tobruk

the units forming the Tobruk garrison must be written off the 8th Army's strength.

In addition to Tobruk and Bardia, the Axis communiqués claimed the fall of Bir El Gobi, 28 miles south of Sidi Rezegh.

July 2 1942

MAIN BATTLE JOINED IN EGYPT BOTTLENECK

From Christopher Buckley with the Eighth Army

BATTLE was joined with Rommel's army at six o'clock this morning on the line of El Alamein, 60 miles from Alexandria. It is a battle which will probably decide the fate of Egypt.

The main armoured forces on both sides are engaged. Our losses have been heavy, but so have those of the enemy.

A bombardment of our positions at El Alamein by heavy artillery opened Rommel's attack. It has been met by determined counter-battery fire by British and New Zealand gunners.

The battle, probably the fiercest yet seen in Africa, is still in full swing to-night. There is little news of it, but no bad news.

Very heavy fighting is going on all along the 40-mile front from the sea to the escarpment above the Qattara depression. This is the "bottle-neck" which constitutes the Eighth Army's defensive line.

The enemy is attacking in considerable strength at the southern end of the front, near the lip of the depression, seeking to force our left flank backwards and exploit the strategy so familiar in this campaign of an outflanking movement to the south.

British help is being rushed to this vital front with all possible speed. The RAF and Allied air units are ceaselessly attacking Rommel's supply lines.

The enemy's aim is the speediest possible advance, irrespective of losses, towards Alexandria and Cairo.

Our aim is to draw out his forces, hitting him continuously meanwhile with our mobile columns, and thus preventing him from concentrating the weight of his armour when and where he desires.

A driver takes cover from a bombing attack

Troops digging trenches at the new positions

It is a grim, desperate race against time with tired men on either side struggling to get the last ounce of effort and endurance out of themselves and their machines.

The great majority of the troops on both sides have been fighting almost continuously for more than a month. During the next few days must come the final strain. Victory will go to the side which can bring up an extra gun or an extra round of ammunition.

The enemy is making the most of the dangerous period for us, when our armoured strength has been greatly reduced by losses and before the new guns, tanks and troops which are piling in can be brought into play.

To some extent it is a race between the impetus of his thrust and the speed with which our reinforcements can arrive. It is a race with tremendous stakes. Every hour saved matters now.

As far as the eye can see along the coast road there is a stream of supplies hastening towards the battle zone.

Tanks armed with two-pounders are going up, as well as the welcome spectacle of 25-pounder field guns, which have so often in the past stood us in good stead.

Besides using every scrap of armour he can lay his hands on, the enemy is pressing captured Gen. Grant tanks into his service – though these are likely to be of value only as long as captured ammunition holds out, since German 75mm. shells do not fit our guns – and also a number of 25-pounders.

Reinforcements, chiefly Italian, are being rushed up to Rommel, chiefly through Benghazi, to exploit his successes to the full. One Italian officer captured yesterday had been landed at Benghazi only a week before with fresh medium tank reinforcements.

Whatever the criticisms, and they will be numerous, of the handling of the Army and of military equipment, the RAF deserves nothing but praise. The part they have played and are playing has been superb.

From where I type these lines, in my temporary halting-place between sand dunes and roadside camel scrub, I have heard, hour after hour this afternoon with unbelievable frequency the reassuring hum of our bombers going in again and again to the attack.

July 3 1942

AXIS TANK ONSLAUGHT AT EL ALAMEIN

From Christopher Buckley with the Eighth Army

ROMMEL launched a powerful armoured attack this afternoon against the British defences at El Alamein, 60 miles west of Alexandria.

Immediately the Allied forces struck at the right flank and rear of his attacking forces – a manoeuvre which had been carefully planned.

Rommel delayed his assault until the full glare of the sun was in the eyes of the British troops. By attacking him from the west we turned this advantage against him.

The full ground strength of both sides has been thrown into this battle, which in the evening of its second day is still inconclusive.

Rommel's attack, however, is still being held, and late tonight it was learned that the El Alamein positions were still intact. This is his second blow at the positions, from which his tanks were thrown back yesterday.

Then, in the words of the official communiqué, "enemy armoured units effected a temporary break in a defended locality," but were later driven back.

Italian infantry of the Savoia and Brescia Divisions are heavily engaged, as well as the German 90th Light Division.

There can be no doubt that the battle now raging is of crucial importance for the defence of Egypt – with all that implies for our security in the Middle East.

While there are other defence zones in which the British could fight to defend Cairo and the Delta, the El Alamein front provides the best defensive position.

That the enemy will bring to bear the maximum force of which he is capable in this attack seems certain.

The Scots Guards attacking at El Alamein

July 3 1942

Premier's Censure Vote Triumph

The motion of censure of the Government's direction of the war was defeated in the House of Commons yesterday by the crushing majority of 475 to 25 after Mr Churchill had wound up a debate which had lasted 19 hours and 50 minutes, and in which 50 MPs had spoken.

After the division Mr Churchill left the Chamber making the V for Victory sign while the House stood cheering.

Perhaps as many as 30 MPs abstained from voting. Only about 75 were away, mostly either serving abroad or ill.

Points from Mr Churchill's speech were:

Battle in Egypt – At any moment we may receive news of grave importance.

At the opening of the battle we had 100,000 men to the enemy's 90,000, a tank superiority of 7 to 5, and an artillery superiority of 8 to 5.

On June 13 we had about 300 tanks in action. By nightfall no more than 70 remained. And this happened without any corresponding loss having been inflicted on the enemy.

Tanks for Overseas – We have sent 4,500 tanks to the Nile Valley, and over 2,000 to Russia.

Visit to Roosevelt – My conversations in the United States were concerned almost entirely with movements of ships, guns, troops, aircraft, and measures to be taken to combat losses at sea.

Shipbuilding – The United States is building now about four times as much gross tonnage as Britain, and I am assured she will range between eight and 10 times as much in 1943.

July 8 1942

VC FOR MEDITERRANEAN SUBMARINE EXPLOIT

THE award of the VC to Cdr Anthony Cecil Capel Miers, DSO, RN, for an exploit in the Mediterranean was announced in last night's London Gazette.

The official citation stated:

"For valour in command of HM submarine Torbay in a daring and successful raid on shipping in a defended enemy harbour, planned with full knowledge of the great hazards to be expected during 17 hours in waters closely patrolled by the enemy.

"On arriving in the harbour he had to charge his batteries lying on the surface in full moonlight, under the guns of the enemy. As he could not see his target he waited several hours and attacked in full daylight in a glassy calm.

"When he had fired his torpedoes he was heavily counter-attacked and had to withdraw through a long channel with anti-submarine craft all round and continuous air patrols overhead."

Cdr Miers's VC is the 43rd of the war and the 13th to go to the Navy.

During the past year in the Mediterranean the Torbay has sunk or damaged 70,000 tons of shipping, including 22 ships sunk by shell-fire.

Within three months of taking command of the Torbay Cdr Miers was mentioned in despatches in January 1941. He won the DSO in October "for courage, enterprise and devotion to duty in successful submarine patrols."

In April this year he was awarded a bar to the DSO as one of the two submarine commanders who played leading parts in sinking 11 Axis convoyed ships in the Mediterranean.

Cdr Miers is 36. He was a well-known Rugby football player in peace-time. In 1933, when he was a lieutenant, he was dismissed his ship, the fishery protection gunboat Dart, on being found guilty of attempting to strike a stoker.

At the court-martial it was pointed out on behalf of Lt Miers that if he had not reported it the matter need never have come to light. He was really self-convicted.

July 30 1942

Shadow Cast Before

ONE of the Nazi loudspeakers said that Sunday night's attack on Hamburg was among "the heaviest so far experienced by Germany." The vast damage done has now been multiplied by a second attack in strong force. Quick repetition of bombing, it has been proved abundantly, much expands its material and moral effects, and Hamburg, like Duisburg and the Ruhr last week, will provide more evidence of the power of a continuous air offensive.

This year's air offensive has already proved that British air attack disintegrates cities and regions. The Prime Minister said a month or two ago we could carry into Germany many times the tonnage of high explosive which HITLER could send and the proportion would continually increase to the end of the war. Cologne and Essen, Bremen and Duisburg and Hamburg bear out his words. Still Germans comfort themselves with assurances that heavy attacks cannot be frequent and cannot extend far across the Reich.

There is no doubt the intermission of attack for considerable periods of bad weather has steadied German nerves. Sir ARTHUR HARRIS promised them that soon American and English bombers will be "coming every night and every day, rain, blow or snow," and no part of the Reich will be safe. It is certain that we shall have the aircraft and the crews for a continuous offensive. The United States programme of 60,000 'planes this year is being fulfilled, and America and the British Commonwealth have trained personnel for large expansion of air fleets.

For some time past our bombers have been extending day flights over Germany. These are the shadows of things to come. When the offensive is maintained day by day and night by night through good weather and bad the breakdown of the Nazi war machine will be near.

"Making way for Victory"

August 11 1942

AMERICAN FORCES LAND IN THE SOLOMONS

From Our Washington Correspondent

AMERICAN forces have landed on the Japanese-occupied Solomon Islands. This was announced here to-night by Adml E. J. King, Chief of United States Naval Operations.

He revealed that the Allied attack, which began on Friday and is the first purely offensive action in the Pacific since the start of the war, took the enemy by surprise, and that the landings were effected as planned. The Japanese, however, had counter-attacked "with rapidity and vigour" and heavy fighting was still in progress.

Giving the lie to the fantastic Japanese claims to have sunk 22 Allied warships and transports, Adml King said that, so far as he knew at present, one United States cruiser had been sunk and two cruisers, two destroyers and one transport damaged. Many enemy 'planes had been destroyed and surface units disabled.

He warned Americans, however, that considerable losses must be expected as the price of such a difficult operation, the success of which could have far-reaching results.

Wing Cdr "Paddy" Finucane in his Spitfire

July 18 1942

"THIS IS IT, CHAPS"

"THIS is it, chaps." These were the last words, spoken in a quiet, self-possessed voice, of Wing Cdr Brendan – "Paddy" – Finucane, Fighter Command's 21-year-old "ace," before he crashed in the sea off France.

The pilot of the following machine watched Finucane struggling with his harness as his 'plane came down, and saw the machine sink as it crashed on the water. Finucane was unable to extricate himself.

It was not the Luftwaffe who ended the career of the young Irishman who in two years' fighting had shot down at least 32 enemy 'planes. To the end he was unbeaten in aerial combat.

In the words of his comrades it was "a million-to-one-chance" shot from a German machine-gun on the beach near Pointe du Touquet.

At the time Finucane, whose promotion to wing commander was announced last month, was leading his wing during the largest mass attack yet carried out by fighter pilots on targets in France.

As he flew low over the machine-gun post the gunner got in a lucky shot which penetrated the radiator of Finucane's Spitfire. Almost immediately afterwards the engine temperature began to climb dangerously, and Finucane, having carried on to attack his ground target, turned for home.

He was too low to bale out, and his engine was turning too slowly for him to gain height. He opened his sliding hood, took off his helmet and attempted to make a crash landing on the sea.

Instead of the Spitfire staying afloat for a few seconds it sank like a stone, carrying Finucane with it. The crash must have knocked him unconscious. His comrades circled the sea for a long time afterwards, but all they saw was a slowly-widening streak of oil which floated on the waters of the Channel.

While Finucane was leading his wing to the attack, his station commander was "listening in" to the radio-telephone conversation between the Spitfire pilots.

"Paddy did not know he had been hit until his 'No. 2' called him up to tell him," said the station commander. "He went on to attack his target, and I heard him say to his wing: 'Take the right target, chaps. Here we go!'

"As he was coming home, he continued to talk calmly over the radio. He was self-possessed and his last message – probably as his engine stopped – was 'This is it, chaps.'"

August 5 1942

Gandhi Schemed to Appease Japan

GANDHI's willingness to negotiate with Japan was exposed today by the Government of India, with the publication of records of Indian Congress proceedings seized in a raid at Allahabad.

In this raid on Congress headquarters the police secured proof that at the meeting of the Working Committee of Congress in April Gandhi's draft resolution stated: "If India were free her first step would probably be to negotiate with Japan."

In this draft resolution he also urged that only "non-violent" resistance should be offered to any invasion. He also opposed a "scorched earth" policy.

General de Gaulle visiting the Free French in Beirut

General Sir Harold Alexander

August 19 1942

GEN. ALEXANDER TO BE C-in-C MIDDLE EAST

CHANGES in the Middle East command were announced by the War Office last night.

Gen. the Hon. Sir Harold Alexander is to be C-in-C Middle East in succession to Gen. Sir Claude Auchinleck, whose future post is not named.

Lt-Gen. B. L. Montgomery is made commander of the Eighth Army in place of Gen. N. M. Ritchie, who returned to London last month.

Maj-Gen. H. Lumsden is given command of the 30th Corps in succession to Lt-Gen W. H. E. Gott, whose death in Egypt was first reported in THE DAILY TELEGRAPH.

It can now be revealed that had Gen. Gott not been killed – the 'plane in which he was travelling was shot down in the battle area – he would have been the new Commander of the Eighth Army.

It would be a fair inference that while in Cairo Mr Churchill discussed the changes with those responsible for operations in the Middle East on the spot.

During his stay in Egypt, on the way to his conference in Moscow with M. Stalin, Mr Churchill paid a visit to the El Alamein front.

The Prime Minister met brigade and divisional commanders, saw gun sites, and inspected personnel of Australian and South African divisions.

Wearing a tropical helmet and a tropical suit, his eyes protected against the glare by a pair of dark glasses, and with the inevitable cigar in his mouth, he spent some time at the Eighth Army's headquarters.

He walked down a road to make an informal inspection of Australian soldiers, to whom he gave his familiar V-sign, and from whom he received a rousing welcome.

A naval vessel putting down a smokescreen for the landing craft at Dieppe

August 20 1942

COMMANDOS BACK AFTER 9-HOUR DIEPPE RAID

THE Commando raid on Dieppe, the largest operation so far carried out by our forces on the Continent, was completed according to plan when our troops had been nine hours in Dieppe.

Re-embarkation of our main forces was begun within six minutes of scheduled time, according to the official communiqué on the operation issued last evening at 8.30. By that hour, many of the men who had taken part had been landed in this country and were on their way back to their bases. During the operations our forces:

Destroyed a six-gun battery, ammunition dump, radio-location station, and anti-aircraft battery.

Brought down 82 enemy aircraft for certain and probably destroyed 100 more, for the loss to ourselves of 95 aircraft, 21 fighter pilots being safe.

The air battle which developed out of the landing as the Luftwaffe attempted to smash our aerial "umbrella" was on a large scale, which rivalled and indeed excelled the engagements in the Battle of Britain. A German loss of 180 'planes would mean that a third of the Luftwaffe fighter strength available on the Western Front had been destroyed.

Heavy fighting developed during the landing. No statement on losses was available in London. The Germans claim to have taken 1,500 prisoners, including 60 Canadian officers, to have sunk three destroyers, four transports and three motor-torpedo boats.

The Allied Force, including British, Canadian, American and Fighting French troops, was much larger than has been employed in any of the eight preceding raids. According to the Germans, it consisted of a division.

The Channel was crossed under cover of darkness and the attack was launched about dawn. The Germans say that there were three landings – one to the east, a second to the west of the town and a third in the harbour.

It may be assumed that the two landings on the flanks were made at Puyes, where there is a breach in the chalk cliffs and a bathing beach, three miles to the north-east; and Veules, a small watering-place six miles to the south-west. Elsewhere the chalk cliffs rise about 100ft sheer from the sea.

The operation was promptly announced in a 6.45 a.m. communiqué from Combined Operations GHQ. At 7.30 in the morning, the French population were warned by our radio not to take any action to compromise themselves as this was no invasion of the Continent.

For purposes of propaganda, the Germans sought to represent the landing as an invasion. It was not on any such scale and the withdrawal was as much a part of the plan as the landing. Information was, however, gained which will prove of value when a full-scale invasion comes to be launched, and our new tank landing craft were in action for the first time.

Throughout the day wave after wave of bombers and fighters passed over the Channel to attack the enemy's defences and communications with Dieppe.

One of the heaviest attacks was made by Flying Fortresses of the United States Air Force, which bombed the German fighter base at Abbeville, north-east of Dieppe.

It was officially reported that many bombs burst upon a dispersal area as well as on the runways at Abbeville, and that clouds of smoke rose from fuel storage sites where hits were registered.

This was the first operation on European soil in which United States troops have taken part in this war, and the first in which Fighting Frenchmen have fought in their own country since Pétain capitulated.

August 21 1942

LOVAT'S MEN CARRIED OUT TOUGHEST JOB YET

By A. B. Austin

WE landed west of Dieppe at dawn. The British Commando troops to whom I was attached, Lord Lovat's No. 4 Commando, were the first men of the Dieppe raid force to jump ashore.

They had been told a few hours earlier by Adml Lord Louis Mountbatten, Chief of Combined Operations:

"Your task is most vital. If you don't knock out the German howitzer battery, the whole operation will go wrong. You have got to do it even at the greatest possible risk."

They had heard their Colonel, Lord Lovat, say: "This is the toughest job we've had. Remember that you represent the flower of the British Army."

And as we nosed in under the Dieppe cliffs, I heard a Commando trooper whisper to his mate: "Don't fergit the Germans is twice as scared as you."

They knew that if they failed, and the six German six-inch howitzers inland west of Dieppe bombarded the narrow Dieppe approach, there would be a great disaster.

They did not fail. The German guns were shattered. Their ammunition dump was blown up. The German gunners were wiped out at bayonet-point in hand-to-hand fighting.

Because of that and with superb support from the RAF and the Navy, the men of the Royal Regiment of Canada, the Saskatchewan Regiment, the Canadian Essex Scots, the Cameron Highlanders of Canada, the Calgary Regiment of Tanks, the Royal Hamilton Light Infantry, the Fusiliers de Montreal, and the small detachment of American Rangers, were able to land on their appointed beaches.

No German has ever been able to do that in England.

One question worried all of us in those last silent 20 minutes after the long, cramped voyage in the starlight: Would the Germans be ready for us?

A sergeant crouching in front of me kept up a whispered running commentary:

"About 500 yards now . . . see the cliffs? . . . There's the crack we want . . . Look at the tracer bullets . . . Don't think they're firing at us though . . . 100 yards now . . . 50 . . . There's a bloke on the cliff."

So our question was answered. I could just make out a figure, silhouetted for an instant in the half light.

At the next moment we grounded on the shingle at full tide, a few yards from the foot of the cold-looking, unscaleable, overhanging chalk-white cliffs.

Commandos back from Dieppe after nine hours of occupation

That was the worst moment, as we all said afterwards. The assault craft grounded, hesitated, nosed a little to port, grounded again and stayed put.

As we blundered, bending, across the shingle to the cliff foot a German machine-gun began to stutter from up above.

The Oerlikan guns from our support craft answered. Red hot tracer bullets flashed past each other between cliff top and sea.

But for the moment we were under cover, brought in at the exact spot at the exactly appointed time [4.50 a.m.] by the sound seamanship of the Navy.

At the same moment the other half of No. 4 Commando, led by Lord Lovat himself, had landed a little further west.

In a pause in the firing I looked up to find Lord Lovat sitting against a rock beside me. You could see that he was bubbling with happiness.

"We did the job all right!" he said. "We went in straight with the bayonet. Cut them to shreds. Not a man left in the battery. How glad I am I wasn't in the battery. But they fought hard."

He was easy to pick out anywhere in that day's battle. "Cool as a trout," a trooper said.

He had the only clean face among us, being the only one who had not blacked his face for the half light landing. He wore corduroy slacks instead of our denims or battledress trousers.

The enemy mortar banged down a bit of cliff near us.

"Getting a bit hot," said Lord Lovat. "I'm going aboard," and he strolled into the sea up to his knees, following the long lines of men who were clambering into the craft.

"Hi!" he yelled to the nearest craft, some way out. "You come in here. Why should I get my knees wet?" But it was too shallow for the craft, now the tide had fallen. We had to wade out.

After many hours' watching one of the most significant air battles of the war palled. We huddled slackly down in the boat, dead tired, filthy looking, ragged, lolling, happy men – happy because we knew that the Commando forces had made the battle of Dieppe possible.

The aftermath of the Dieppe raid

August 26 1942

Duke of Kent Killed in Air Disaster

IT is with profound regret that THE DAILY TELEGRAPH announces that the Duke of Kent, youngest brother of the King, was killed in an air crash yesterday.

The announcement was made in an official statement issued at 11.45 last night.

It added that His Royal Highness was on a flight to Iceland. The announcement stated:

"The Air Ministry deeply regrets to announce that Air Commodore HRH the Duke of Kent was killed on active service this afternoon when a Sunderland flying-boat crashed in the North of Scotland.

"His Royal Highness, who was attached to the staff of the Inspector-General of the RAF, was proceeding to Iceland on duty.

"All the crew of the flying-boat also lost their lives."

It was authoritatively stated in London that the crash was in no way due to enemy action.

Icy conditions on board HMS *Scylla* on patrol in the Atlantic

September 26 1942

ARCTIC CONVOY DEFIED 4-DAYS ASSAULT

FULL official details of the great battle fought in the Arctic a fortnight ago between a Russia-bound convoy and a force of German 'planes and U-boats were given in an Admiralty communiqué issued last night.

For four days, Sept. 12-15, the ships ran the gauntlet of ceaseless attacks by U-boats and relays of dive-bombers and torpedo-bombers, weaving their way through a minefield laid ahead of their course by enemy 'planes.

The Germans, in the words of Rear-Adml Burnett, who commanded the escort, delivered "the worst torpedo-bombing attack of the war" on the convoy, the largest ever sent to Russia. But they paid dearly.

At least 40 Nazi 'planes were shot down and many more seriously damaged, while two U-boats were almost certainly sunk and four others seriously damaged.

We lost four fighters, the destroyer Somali, the minesweeper Leda and certain merchant ships. The Germans claimed 38 out of 45 merchant ships and six naval vessels.

Some of the ships were lost when U-boats attacked a return convoy escorted by the same warships which took the first convoy to Russia. In this second series of attacks the Luftwaffe did not put in a single appearance, so severely had it been handled.

It was the first time the Germans had used torpedo-bombers on this convoy route. Their losses were probably heavier than officially reported, as it was impossible to see what happened to many of the damaged 'planes.

A prominent part in the rout of the Luftwaffe was played by Sea Hurricane fighters, which operated from an aircraft-carrier which was in the convoy. These were adapted for use from a flight-deck, with folding wings and a modified undercarriage. It was the first time Hurricanes had flown from an aircraft-carrier.

August 26 1942

MOSCOW ADMITS BATTLE NEAR STALINGRAD

STALINGRAD was mentioned by name for the first time in a Soviet communiqué late last night. It reported fighting north-west of the city. This constitutes an official admission of the extent of the German advance from the east bank of the Don against the Stalingrad defences.

The communiqué, received in London shortly after 11 o'clock, said that in this sector the "situation has become complicated."

Enemy attacks are being repelled with heavy losses, it is added, and Soviet tanks are counter-attacking numerically superior forces. Attacks north-east of Kotelnikovsk – south-west of Stalingrad – were also beaten off.

September 24 1942

Noel Coward's War Film

By Campbell Dixon

NOEL Coward's first screen production, "In Which We Serve," shown privately yesterday, is one of the few outstanding war films made on either side of the Atlantic. It contrives to be heroic and human, entertaining and yet real.

The chief character is a destroyer captain – a composite of a number of officers whose skill and daring have made history.

The heroine is the ship. We watch her building and her launching; she sees action in many seas, does her share at Dunkirk, suffers damage and casualties, sometimes limps home, and once is towed, and at last goes down, with guns blazing, off Crete.

This sequence is terrific. The shots of enemy 'planes dropping their bombs through a hail of fire, with one gun firing defiantly, till it is swallowed by the water, are thrilling in their intensity and realism.

But there is more to come. As a dozen men cling to a raft, machine-gunned at intervals from the air, we keep flashing back to episodes in their lives.

We meet their families and sweethearts: we come to know them, from the captain (Noel Coward) to the chief petty officer (Bernard Miles) and the young seaman (John Mills); and we understand why their captain, when at last they say good-bye, feels he has lost his friends.

October 6 1942

ACTION IF DIEPPE MEN ARE NOT FREED FROM BONDS

GERMANY'S action in carrying out her threat to chain the 2,500 British prisoners captured at Dieppe has been followed promptly by a British warning that German prisoners will be treated in the same way.

A statement issued by the War Office last night said: "The German Government having put into operation the illegal action threatened in their communiqué, the War Office announces that, unless the German Government releases the prisoners captured at Dieppe from their chains, an equal number of German prisoners of war will be manacled and chained as from 12 noon, Saturday, Oct.10."

This statement was made three hours after a German radio commentator had announced that the threat had been put into force. Describing the British reply to the German High Command announcement as "unsatisfactory," he said:

"Since noon to-day all British officers and men captured at Dieppe have been put into fetters as a reprisal for the same measure applied by the British Commando authorities against German prisoners."

Rock revue: the ENSA young ladies entertain troops in Gibraltar

Allied tanks moving forward to engage enemy armour

Alamein

On September 14 1942, General Montgomery delivered "Lightfoot," his masterplan for the defeat of Rommel, to corps and divisional commanders of the Eighth Army. This effectively put it under starter's orders – "Monty" had a predisposition for sporting metaphors – for the Battle of Alamein, the North African desert breakthrough which Churchill so impatiently awaited.

The battle began under a full moon on October 23. Nearly 1,000 guns subjected enemy batteries to intensive fire before ranging on to infantry positions. At Monty's disposal – reading from the Mediterranean coast in the north to the Qattara Depression in the south – were the 9th Australian Division, the 51st (Highland) Division, the 2nd New Zealand Division, the 1st South African Division, the 1st and 10th British Armoured Divisions, the 4th Indian Division, a Greek Brigade, the 7th Armoured Division and a Free French brigade.

But, above all he enjoyed air support on – for the desert war – an unsurpassed scale, including Wellington, Boston, Baltimore, Mitchell bombers and even land-based Fleet Air Arm Albacore torpedo-bombers. Spitfire, Kittihawk and Hurricane fighters provided cover and low-level ground attack support. Since smashing Axis armour was a prerequisite of a breakthrough, tank-buster fighters – particularly the Hurricane 11Ds of Nos 6 and 7 South African Air Force squadrons – played a critical part.

As the battle began, however, Rommel's presence was more evident in the portrait confronting Monty from his caravan wall than in the desert. He was in hospital in Germany and his place had been taken by General von Stumme. Within 24 hours of the first shots of the barrage, von Stumme had died of a heart attack. Ordered out of hospital by Hitler, the "Desert Fox" resumed command on October 25. His return produced what General Alexander, Monty's Commander-in-Chief, called "a big armoured counter-attack in the old style," employing German and Italian tanks. But the RAF, dropping 80 tons of bombs on the concentration area, devastated them.

In the early hours of November 2, after an Australian advance – achieved, as Churchill noted, "by ceaseless bitter fighting" – "Supercharge," the codename for the breakthrough, began. Covered by 300 guns, British brigades attached to the New Zealand Division penetrated Rommel's defended zone, enabling the 1st British Armoured Division to drive forward. Hitler signalled Rommel there must be no retreat, but on November 4 the 5th Indian Brigade broke through in its sector and deprived Rommel of any alternative. Monty's armour could now pursue the "Fox" across the open desert.

In the rout, German armour, reduced from 240 serviceable tanks to 38, took the lion's share of fuel, water and food, leaving six Italian divisions to the mercy of their captors. In the tally of Monty's victory, 30,000 prisoners were counted and four German and eight Italian divisions written off as fighting formations.

Infantry taking cover from enemy shells

October 27 1942

EIGHTH ARMY BATTERS AXIS INNER LINES

From Christopher Buckley and Ronald Legge with the Eighth Army

BITTER fighting continues without remission as the Allied ground and air forces batter mercilessly at the inner lines of the Axis defences.

Up to six o'clock last night 1,450 German and Italian prisoners had been taken.

We have consolidated all the positions gained by our first smashing blow against Rommel's positions on the 25-mile front from the Mediterranean to the Qattara Depression.

But obstacles to a complete breakthrough still lie ahead. The bottle-neck nature of the fighting zone makes it easy for the enemy to concentrate his minefields and anti-tank batteries in depth.

To sum up: We have pierced the enemy's defences. It now remains for our armour to round off the job with a decisive breach in Rommel's lines.

The fact that among the enemy's air losses are four Ju.52s – big troop carriers – shows that he is exerting every effort to reinforce his ground forces.

The battle is more like one of the vast conflicts of 1914-18 than anything yet seen in the Western Desert. Two armies are at grips in a confined area, where outflanking movements are impossible.

The guns are keeping up a ceaseless roar, which rumbles like a giant wave all along the line. The Eighth Army is giving Rommel no respite as it puts up barrage after barrage.

Though minor armoured clashes have occurred, there has as yet been no major battle between panzer and British tank divisions.

November 7 1942

GENERAL MONTGOMERY: "WE INTEND TO HIT THIS CHAP FOR SIX . . ."

From Christopher Buckley with the Eighth Army

"THIS is complete and absolute victory. The Boche is completely finished." With these words Gen. Montgomery, GOC Eighth Army, the British general who out-foxed Gen. Rommel, announced the outcome of the El Alamein battle in an address to war correspondents.

Gen Montgomery, who was wearing a tank beret and a grey pullover, received correspondents at his desert headquarters. He said:

"It has been a fine battle. There is no doubt of the result. Two nights ago I drove two armoured wedges into the enemy and I passed three armoured divisions through those places. They are now operating in enemy's rear.

"Those portions of the enemy's army which can get away are in full retreat. Those portions which are still facing our troops down in the south will be put 'in the bag.' It is complete finish.

"I did not hope for such a complete victory; or rather I hoped for it but I did not expect it.

"After 12 days of very hard fighting, the Eighth Army and the Allied air forces have gained a complete victory over the German and Italian forces. The enemy is completely smashed.

"For the last two nights the road behind the enemy lines has been blocked with stuff four deep trying to get away. They have been bombed day and night.

"But we must not think that the party is over. We have no intention of letting the enemy recover. We must keep up the pressure. We intend to hit this chap for six out of North Africa.

"Having done him in here, we are going to proceed with the job."

Gen. Montgomery further stressed, as he had done before the battle started, that the Eighth Army and the RAF were one entity and one fighting machine, and that was what had made victory possible. It could not have been done otherwise.

Gen. Montgomery told correspondents how Gen. Ritter von Thoma, commander of the Afrika Korps, had been captured and brought to his headquarters. He said:

"Thoma was reconnoitring in a forward position very near the front line. His tank was hit. He had to jump for it quick and he was promptly pounced upon and captured. He was brought to my headquarters, where he dined with me last night and had breakfast at my mess this morning. Now he has gone on to Cairo.

"Over the dinner table last night we fought over together, as two soldiers the two battles: that of Aug. 31 and now.

"We fought it out on the oilcloth on the table of my mess. I was able to tell him a lot he did not know about both battles. I told him particularly a lot he did not know about what was happening last night. He was surprised. He admitted the situation was critical.

"I told Thoma that I came to the desert in August. In September I met Rommel. In October I beat him."

Gen. Montgomery inquired about Rommel, but found Thoma was reluctant to talk. "I suggested that he must be a good general as he had made the Italians fight."

Gen. Montgomery then paid tribute to the soldiers. "They've been magnificent," he said, "quite magnificent."

Soldiers manning trenches in the Alamein positions

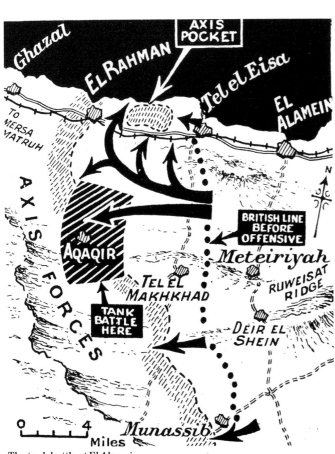

The tank battle at El Alamein

November 5 1942

Mrs Roosevelt has a Blitz Lunch

MRS Roosevelt lunched yesterday in a wayside hall in East Anglia, as if she had been bombed out of her home during the night and was being fed by the emergency blitz services.

Women of the WVS, of whom there are now nearly 1,000,000 in the country, showed her five types of emergency cooking stoves used after air raids.

Mrs Roosevelt saw pastry being made in an emergency oven, a main meal being prepared in an emergency stove which could be used in the blackout and cater for 200 people, an open fire which can be built in five minutes, a sawdust waterboiler and waste oil cooking.

Afterwards she went into the hall to have the lunch which she had just seen cooked. The menu was: Vitamin fortified vegetable soup, meat stew with potatoes, carrots and brussels sprouts, two kinds of puddings and coffee.

Mrs Roosevelt served herself at a long counter and sat at a small table squashed between two other "blitzed" women. Obviously she was thoroughly enjoying herself.

Unpacking the fuselage of an aircraft bound for Egypt

November 5 1942

Victory in the Desert

MORE swiftly than the highest expectation hoped a great victory has been won in Africa. The attack which Gen. ALEXANDER planned and which the Eighth Army under Gen. MONTGOMERY and the Allied air forces and the Navy have maintained through 12 days and nights of fighting as fierce as the world has ever known has already struck a blow which shakes the foundations of the Axis. It is not enough, it is not the end but the beginning of harder and longer tasks. Yet the Allies may now say with assured confidence that they are marching on to decision.

Nowhere in North Africa had the Germans and Italians of the Afrika Korps so strong a position as that between Qattara and the sea. They have been battered and hurled out of it, although on the last reports from the front the British tank divisions had not gone into action. The whole Afrika Korps is in full retreat from its narrow strongly-fortified front back into open country, where relentless pursuit by land and air can strike front, flanks and rear and the co-operation of the two arms will be still more deadly. It has already suffered disastrous loss. Such mutilation cannot soon be repaired with the means of repairing it so severely diminished.

Nevertheless, the Allies must regard what they have accomplished as no more than preparation. Chances and changes of desert warfare may still be many. Whatever power the Axis can bring together to halt the advance will certainly be hurled at it. There is good hope that the declared objective of Gen. MONTGOMERY, the destruction of ROMMEL's army, may be attained. That of itself is only the stepping stone to decision in the Mediterranean. The clearance of North Africa would set free great Allied forces, sea, air and land, for other campaigns; but the watchword now must be fiercer effort in the field and harder work by all.

November 2 1942

8TH ARMY STRIKES TO TRAP AXIS FORCE

From Ronald Legge and Christopher Buckley with the Eighth Army

THROUGHOUT the week-end violent fighting has continued in the coastal sector of the Alamein front, where a considerable body of enemy troops, mostly Germans, are threatened with encirclement following our renewed attack on Friday night.

This thrust was made in a northerly direction from a bulge previously driven into Rommel's lines somewhat to the south against a long narrow pocket in which the enemy held a series of heavily-manned strong points.

That pocket may now prove a trap for this Axis force, which numbers some thousands.

The British attack began shortly before moonrise – at 10 p.m., which had been zero hour for the start of the offensive exactly a week before.

Our artillery bombardment, which followed a day-long onslaught by the RAF, was the heaviest since the great "Somme barrage" which preceded the first assault.

It lasted for fully five hours. This time our troops went forward simultaneously with its opening. They consisted entirely of infantry, as the tactical conditions did not favour the employment of tanks.

All night long they fought their way across the white sand dunes and salt marshes where the enemy positions lay. By dawn one of our columns had achieved its object.

Although daylight brought many advantages to the defenders, our men battled on, and two hours later came news of further vantage points gained.

As was to be expected, Rommel has since put in several strong counter-attacks, but these so far have all been beaten back, with substantial losses to the enemy.

British tank crews say they are getting a higher proportion of "brew-ups" than ever before. "Brew-up" – tankmen's slang for a cup of tea – is the term they are now applying to burned out panzers.

November 7 1942

STALIN SAYS: "A SECOND FRONT WILL COME"

M. Stalin had a tremendous ovation both at the beginning and at the end of a speech yesterday in which he reviewed the events of the past year at a meeting of the Moscow Soviet marking the 25th anniversary of the Soviet Revolution.

He declared his confidence that a second front in Europe would come, and said that in his talks with Mr Churchill there was complete agreement on all important matters.

These events, he said, meant a progressive development of friendship between Soviet Russia, Britain and the United States.

A British Tommy gives the Victory sign to a German prisoner

November 4 1942

EIGHTH ARMY BREACH ROMMEL'S LINE

From Christopher Buckley and Ronald Legge in the Front Line with the Eighth Army

ON and around the desert ridge called by the Arabs Tel el Aqaqir, or "Hill of the Wicked," 15 miles west of Alamein and eight miles from the coast, the biggest armoured action of the Middle East campaign is being fought out to-day.

Both Gen. Montgomery and Rommel are believed to have thrown the bulk of their available tank forces into this savage head-on clash. All the indications are that it must prove of decisive importance.

The battle began at one a.m. yesterday. Under cover of another tremendous barrage from hundreds of our massed guns Eighth Army infantry, including units of the Highland Division, with tanks in close support, moved forward against the enemy.

This time our blow was aimed directly westwards on a 4,000 yards front.

Flares from British and enemy 'planes with the flashes of the guns and the light of a waning moon lit up the stony desolate landscape as the infantry went in with the bayonet.

They had to fight their way through minefields, strongpoints, booby traps and other obstacles, but they went steadily on, forcing a substantial gap in what are believed to be the enemy's last line of defences in this sector, and in every instance carrying their full objectives.

Then in the early dawn the tanks thundered forward, almost track to track. They were met with a hastily improvised line of anti-tank guns – and, as was expected, by the bulk of the Afrika Korps panzer force.

The main battle has since continued roughly along the line of the Rahman track, which runs SSW from the tiny coastal village of Sidi Abd el Rahman, whose solitary minaret is now clearly in view of our troops.

Quite clearly very hard fighting still lies ahead of our men, and it is important to emphasise the distinction between a breach and a break-through. The former implies that the enemy's line of minefields, earthworks and trenches – though one sees few continuous trenches here on the 1914-18 model – has been pierced.

That is what we have done.

By the term break-through the reader should understand that our armour and support groups have gone clean through into open country. That has not yet been achieved.

November 5 1942

AXIS FORCES IN FULL RETREAT: OFFICIAL

ROMMEL'S ARMY, OUTFOUGHT AND BROKEN IN THE 12-DAY BATTLE OF ALAMEIN, IS IN FULL RETREAT, WITH THE EIGHTH ARMY IN CLOSE PURSUIT.

THIS NEWS WAS GIVEN IN A SPECIAL MIDDLE EAST JOINT WAR COMMUNIQUE RECEIVED IN LONDON AT 10.10 LAST NIGHT. IT SAID:

"The Axis forces in the Western Desert after 12 days and nights of ceaseless attacks by our land and air forces are now in full retreat.

"Their disordered columns are being relentlessly attacked by our land forces and by the Allied air force by day and night.

"Gen. von Stumme, a senior general who is said to have been in command during Rommel's absence in Germany, is known to have been killed.

"So far we have captured over 9,000 prisoners, including Gen. Ritter von Thoma, commander of the German Afrika Korps, and a number of other senior German and Italian officers.

"It is known that the enemy losses in killed and wounded have been exceptionally high. Up to date we have destroyed more than 260 German and Italian tanks and captured or destroyed at least 270 guns.

"The full toll of the booty cannot be assessed at this stage of the operation.

"In the course of these operations our air forces, whose losses have been light, have destroyed and damaged in air combat over 300 aircraft and destroyed or put out of action a like number on the ground.

The remnant of Rommel's army is rounded up by the British

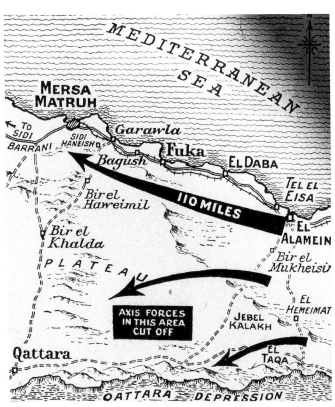

The British forces pursue the Afrika Korps
Right: The Prime Minister broadcasts to the nation

"At sea our naval and air forces have sunk 50,000 tons and damaged as much again of shipping carrying Axis supplies to North Africa.

"The Eighth Army continues to advance."

To-night, four months' deadlock is ended and the Axis position at El Alamein wiped out.

November 11 1942

"The End of the Beginning"

"THIS is not the end. It is not even the beginning of the end. But it is perhaps the end of the beginning."

This typical Churchillian summary of the Battle of Egypt delighted the great and distinguished audience gathered at the Mansion House yesterday, when the Prime Minister went to pay traditional compliment to the new Lord Mayor.

Mr Churchill spoke in the significantly named Egyptian Hall, the most magnificent banqueting chamber in the City, after having been played to his seat with the March of Scipio – Scipio Africanus, conqueror of Africa.

His summing-up of the present position was followed by the graver, more portentous statement:

"We mean to hold our own. I have not become the King's first minister in order to preside over the liquidation of the British Empire . . ."

The cheers which broke out came to an abrupt and anticipatory end, as Mr Churchill continued:

"For that task, if ever it were prescribed, someone else would have to be found. And in a democracy I suppose the nation would have to be consulted."

The interrupted breaker of cheers flowed on and came to a thunderous finale as he concluded: "Here we are and here we stand – a veritable rock of salvation in this drifting world."

Mr Churchill was inspired with the spirit of victory and the glory of British arms in Egypt. He paid tribute, each name italicised by cheers, to the troops of India, Fighting France, Czechoslovakia and the United States; but he went on with quiet emphasis:

"As it happened, the battle has been fought throughout almost entirely by men of British blood."

It was, he added, designed as a prelude to the tremendous enterprise devised by the United States at the western end of the Mediterranean.

"The President of the United States is the author of this mighty undertaking," he said. "In all of it I have been his active and ardent lieutenant."

He concluded with an effective quotation from Byron's "Childe Harold" on Waterloo and "the sword united nations drew."

November 14 1942

Joy and Resolve

WHEN the church bells, silent for many a grim month, ring out tomorrow, the country will not only be rejoicing in the historic victory of the Battle of Egypt but will be doing honour to the men and women of the Civil Defence services. It is a singularly fortunate coincidence that the Sunday assigned to commemoration of their work should also be given to general thanksgiving for a triumph which began the transformation of the war. We are, as the Prime Minister reminded us, only entitled to rejoice on condition that we do not relax. One of the paramount needs of the country is still that its civilian defenders should be well prepared and vigilant.

Between the autumn of 1940 and the summer of 1941 they were engaged in one of the decisive battles of the war, the attack of the Luftwaffe on British cities and industries. Without the unflinching courage and energy of the Civil Defence workers the battle could not have been won. There is still strength enough in Nazism for an air attack to frustrate which the country would need a thoroughly efficient Civil Defence. The spirit which made the defence services victorious in the past must stand on guard still.

The Union Jack replaces the Swastika over Tobruk

November 28 1942

FRENCH SCUTTLE FLEET WHEN NAZIS ENTER TOULON

SIX hours after German troops and tanks had swept into the great naval base of Toulon during darkness early yesterday, to seize the main force of the French Navy in the harbour, 230,000 tons of warships still there had been sunk by their crews. It was the greatest naval scuttle since the crews of the interned German fleet at Scapa Flow sank their ships – an estimated total of 400,000 tons – in June, 1919.

Munition dumps, oil tanks and all stores of value in the naval arsenal at Toulon were blown up by the French, as well as the coastal batteries. Some of the warships fired on the Germans to gain time for scuttling, and the captains of all the vessels stayed on the bridge till they sank. Many of these officers lost their lives.

The Germans, according to the Vichy news agency, entered the Toulon zone at four a.m. and by 10 a.m. no warship was afloat. A German version of events broadcast last night differed only to the extent of claiming that a few ships were saved.

The French fleet at Toulon, including the flagship, *Strasbourg*, is scuttled to keep it from falling into German hands

Red Army tanks advancing during the winter campaign in support of the infantry

November 25 1942

STALINGRAD RELIEVED AFTER 3-MONTH SIEGE

RUSSIAN troops advancing north of Stalingrad have joined forces with the defenders in the northern part of the city.

This was announced in a special communiqué issued last night by the Soviet Information Bureau and received in London at 9.45 p.m.

Together with other sweeping gains made since the opening of the Soviet offensive, this means the virtual relief of Stalingrad after a three months' siege.

In announcing the capture of 12 towns and villages on both flanks of the offensive, the communiqué indicated that the Russians have practically encircled the German forces between Stalingrad and the captured town of Sunovikhino, on the Stalingrad-Kharkov railway.

By clearing the ground north and south of this sector the Russians have made the escape of the enemy immediately before Stalingrad an extremely difficult operation.

The advance to the west into the Don Bend is deeper, and the German hold on the North Caucasus is threatened.

December 2 1942

The Beveridge Plan

IT is impossible to scan the Beveridge Report, or even an extended summary of it, without being moved to admiration at the commanding grasp of a very complicated subject and at the lofty idealism which inspires the constructive proposals. Whatever fate may attend specific recommendations in this brilliant State paper, we can already be certain in advance that the document, taken as a whole, will profoundly influence the whole future course of social evolution in this country. Yet, far-reaching though the plan is in scope and consequences, it codifies and extends rather than creates.

Sir WILLIAM BEVERIDGE himself describes the system of social provision which it is designed to supersede as "not surpassed and hardly rivalled in any other country in the world." The reforms amount not so much to a revolution as to the consummation of the revolution begun by Mr LLOYD GEORGE in 1911. What the author says of one of them might equally well apply to the whole: they rest "not on a denial of any good in the present system, but on the possibility of replacing it by a better system."

Perhaps the one really basic innovation among the multitude of changes is the establishment of a national minimum level of subsistence below which no one may be allowed to fall. Upon that primary objective converge all the other proposals, and this achieved in the main by two simple expedients, of which the first and more important is the doubling or trebling of all existing benefits and the adding of new ones, and the second is the inclusion of the relatively small sections of the community hitherto exempt from compulsory national insurance.

The rest of the Plan for Social Security consists chiefly in picking up all the ragged ends left over from the vast piecemeal social legislation of the past 30 years and bringing together the whole administration of social insurance under a single Minister of Social Security.

December 2 1942

German Failure Before Stalingrad

By A. T. Cholerton, Moscow Correspondent

"DON'T let us sing till we are out of the wood." Our foes have by now in the giant Russian offensive on the Stalingrad front lost over 150,000 men, dead, wounded and prisoners – at least half of the effectives of the 30 divisions at von Bock's disposal there.

Their loss in tanks, guns and vehicles, and, above all, in "organisation," is disproportionately greater.

Their strategic loss in terrain at one of the two most vital of Russian centres – Moscow being the other one – goes already beyond reckoning, and they are going to lose at least as much again in man-power before this battle is over.

Half a dozen divisions are trapped between Stalingrad and the Don, and all their attempts to break back westwards across the elbow have been foiled; great numbers of strong enemy units are encircled already between the upper and lower arms of the Don well back from the elbow, besides those already annihilated there.

In the west the right wing of the larger Russian army forcing its way southwards through the Chir River country towards the Don's southern arm is now almost within earshot of the heavy guns of the southern Russian army which is pounding its way more slowly westwards through more difficult country to meet it from the Kalmuk steppes.

The main reason why the German staff never fully guessed what was coming to them if they did not get Stalingrad or otherwise get out in time – assuming that they could – behind the Don elbow, was that despite everything they still were not quite cured of their contempt for the Russians, still failed to grasp that there is something more dangerous than their peerless quality in defence fighting – their aggressive morale, their bitterness of heart against all invaders.

The German Command, knowing how precarious their salient into Stalingrad might become as winter drew on – a child's atlas would show that – built a formidable system of trench-lines to protect its northern edge all the way from a point west of Kletskaya right to the Volga's bank, and on the south it was adequately fortified, too. But it altogether underrated the aggressiveness of the Russians and their swift, sudden initiatives in getting whole armies, even with their heavy equipment, across such a wide river as the Volga when ice-floes are swirling and packing.

Safety for the winter might have been secured if the Germans had held the entire city and all the high right bank of the Volga for 20 miles above and below it. Once again they underestimated their Russians.

A British escort opens fire on enemy aircraft to protect an Allied convoy bound for Russia

The Battle of the Atlantic

When after five and a half years it was all over, the Admiralty, which has never been given to gush, described the Battle of the Atlantic as "the most protracted and bitterly fought campaign in which the British Empire and her Allies have ever been engaged." Some of those who endured the rigours of storm-tossed life in tiny escort vessels, or the stress and weariness of thirteen-hour searches in aircraft of Coastal Command (its motto appropriately "Constant Endeavour"), considered that something of an understatement.

In 1940, victory in the Battle of Britain had prevented defeat. Concurrently and thereafter the Battle of the Atlantic – so named by Churchill in a directive of March 6, 1941 – was fought to keep Britain in the war. The Atlantic was the ocean conduit of raw materials for the weapons industry, fuel for the land, sea and air armed forces, off-the-peg arms and ammunition from North America and, not least, the transport of airmen for flying training in North America and Canadian troops for campaigns in Europe and North Africa.

If the RAF's victory of 1940 was by the narrowest of margins, the naval and air struggle to defend the convoy routes was frequently a matter of touch and go. At the Admiralty an operations room wall graph spelled out the peril – a thin red line delineating at the height of the U-boat offensive the proximity of defeat. There were moments from 1940 to 1943 when it seemed impossible that the red line would not be breached.

Sent to sea as a general reporter by the news editor of The Daily Telegraph, Hugh Chevins, L. Marsland Gander was at close quarters with the problem. He noted later: "I boarded the Vanquisher [a destroyer built in 1917] at a North-Western port [Liverpool] at a time when the Huns had sunk 500,000 tons of shipping in a month... Owing to the slow speed of convoys they [the U-boats] could quite comfortably shadow us, or by simply observing our smoke over the horizon when ships were hull-down." (See also Wartime Odyssey, p.203.)

When naming the battle in March 1941, Churchill had issued a directive setting up a Battle of the Atlantic committee under his chairmanship (it was disbanded that October), the battle was already at least nine months old. From the summer of 1940, U-boats and bombers operating from their newly won bases on the Atlantic coast of France gave rise to increasing difficulties. Convoys to and from North America and West Africa were now required to be routed at the greatest possible distance from such bases as Lorient, extending the length of passage. Threat of invasion that summer and early autumn deepened the peril as escort vessels were withdrawn for anti-invasion patrols.

U-boat commanders plunged gleefully into a period of sinkings which in more desperate days they fondly recalled as "the happy time." They attacked in "wolf packs." In June 1940, they sank fifty-eight ships, totalling some 300,000 tons. At night, surfaced U-boats in the role of torpedo-boats were an especial menace. Escort vessels were not as yet equipped with radar and surfaced submarines were invisible to Asdic underwater echo-sounding sets. New destroyers, fifty old American four-stackers, exchanged by the United States for bases, trawlers, sloops and corvettes (as portrayed in Compass Rose of Nicholas Monsarrat's The Cruel Sea), would be coming in. Meanwhile, the U-boat remained in the ascendant.

On August 17, 1940, Hitler announced a blockade of Britain and warned that neutral vessels would be sunk. U-boats from western France, operating more than 500 miles beyond the escort range and supported by long-range bombers, exacted an ever increasing toll. Sinkings in July, August and September nudged those of June, while in October, when 103 ships totalling 443,000 tons were lost, several convoys came close to massacre. But the invasion scare over measures were introduced which would pay later dividends.

Escort groups were formed; and co-operation in the Western Approaches between the Navy and Coastal Command improved – the latter were also vital to

Grand Admiral Karl Doenitz

U-boat survivors clamber on board the destroyer HMS *Escapade*

Admiral Sir Max Horton

countering the threat posed by German capital ships and armed merchantmen. In February 1941, the heavy cruiser Admiral Hipper, encountering nineteen unescorted merchantmen homeward bound from Sierra Leone, had sent seven of them to the bottom. At the same time the battle-cruisers Scharnhorst and Gneisenau were on the loose in the North Atlantic. In May, the battleship Bismarck and heavy cruiser Prinz Eugen moved onto the scene, Bismarck very soon heightening the threat to merchant shipping by sinking the battle-cruiser Hood. But, spotted by a Coastal Command Catalina flying-boat, and damaged by a torpedo from a Fleet Air Arm biplane Swordfish, she was finished off by the battleships King George V and Rodney. Yet capital ships remained a threat and while the pocket battleship Lutzow (formerly the Deutschland) was crippled by Coastal Command torpedo-bombers on June 13, others – notably the battleship Tirpitz – remained in the wings.

At U-boat level, availability of more escort vessels enabled the introduction of continuous sea escort. The growing effectiveness of Coastal Command was reflected in 1941 in the U-boat commanders' preference for working the 800-mile Atlantic gap, still out of range of Coastal Command. This would be further hampered until air to surface vessel radar was de rigueur and "Leigh Light" aircraft were illuminating surfaced U-boats at night. Establishment of naval and air bases in Iceland, with a consequent northward routing of convoys began to help, but alarming losses – fifty-eight vessels in May 1941, and not many less in June – continued. These sinkings preceded the battles between convoy support groups and U-boats which were to become such a feature of the mid-war Battle of the Atlantic.

As with the Battle of Britain, this ocean conflict had its stars. Ashore at Derby House, Liverpool, there was Admiral Sir Max Horton, commanding Western Approaches from late 1942. At sea, Captain Frederick ("Johnnie") Walker whose DSO and three Bars speak for his exploits as a support group leader. A brilliant submarine officer, Horton was the thief set to catch a thief in the shadowy person of Grand Admiral Karl Doenitz, master-mind of the wolf packs and inspiration of such aces as Lemp, Prien and Kretschmer. Walker, supremely professional at sea, could nevertheless unwind – he used to drink a pint of beer while standing on his head at wardroom parties. But before the war ended he succumbed to the stress of his task and died ashore of a cerebral thrombosis. A later Admiralty communiqué, somewhat uncharacteristically referring to him as an "ace killer of submarines," stated: "Captain Walker, more than any other, won the Battle of the Atlantic."

After a comparative lull in late 1941, brought about partly by diversion of U-boats to the Mediterranean, but also by greater American assistance and improving Coastal Command reconnaissance, U-boat commanders renewed the "happy time" in 1942. Between July and October that year 396 ships totalling more than two million tons were sunk, though much of the slaughter took place away from the areas of the convoy battles along the main Atlantic routes. In the early spring of 1943, however, events proved how vulnerable, despite the introduction of support groups and the first escort carrier, these routes remained.

That March, forty U-boats, attacking two convoys for five days, sank twenty-one cargo vessels totalling 141,000 tons. It was Doenitz's high noon. Thereafter, the support groups and Coastal Command, much assisted by Ultra intelligence – the reading of enemy Enigma code signals – gradually achieved the upper hand. This process was aided by Doenitz's insistence that summer on U-boats surfacing in daylight in the Bay of Biscay and engaging enemy aircraft. In early 1944, Doenitz conceded the Atlantic struggle, leaving but a handful of scattered submarines in its northern wastes. In the final reckoning, of 632 U-boats sunk at sea, at least 500 had been despatched by British warships or aircraft.

1943

Two members of a bomber crew on return from a night raid on Berlin

AFTER more than three full years of war the multiplicity of fronts and theatres began to strain even the manpower and material resources available since America's entry. Roosevelt, juggling with the claims of the Pacific against those of Europe, had also to select specific uses of American power within each theatre. In January his meeting with Churchill at Casablanca, in Morocco, went some way towards establishing priorities for the year ahead. Certainly, it set the pattern.

Operation Torch had ruled out – to some American dismay – invasion of France for at least a year, assigning the crescendoing aerial bombardment of Germany as the chief contribution towards its destruction and defeat, and to the relief of Russia. Once the Axis had been cleared from North Africa, as it was in May, Sicily was targeted for the next invasion.

That month in Washington president and prime minister looked beyond Sicily and, following its occupation in July – it brought about the fall of Mussolini – to landings on the Italian mainland. By the end of September these decisions had led to formal Italian surrender and, in October, its declaration of war on its former Axis partner.

Though the continuing campaign in Italy, stretching forward into 1944 and American entry into Rome two days before D-Day, further delayed the invasion of Normandy, German troop withdrawals from Russia to reinforce Italy helped Stalin to turn the tide. His armies, after driving the Germans out of the Caucasus earlier in the year – enforcing their surrender at Stalingrad, taking back Kharkov, Novorossisk, Smolensk and Dnepropretrovsk – recovered Kiev in November. Special Operations Executive subversive activities in Poland, the Balkans, occupied Europe and Scandinavia, and MI9 escape lines also helped to tie down German units.

But Bomber Command's night offensive, now complemented by the US 8th Air Force's developing day bomber raids, remained the chief Allied contribution to defeating Germany. It forced Hitler to keep and reinforce fighters in the west and double anti-aircraft defences in the Ruhr, eliciting from Albert Speer, Hitler's Minister for Armament and War Production, an admission of serious losses throughout the war economy. RAF and American fighter forces supplemented this effort as escorts and, in their own right, as intruders and in sweeps to pin down the Luftwaffe in Europe. Another vital bomber contribution was the build-up of attacks on U-boat bases.

As with land and sea victories, the air offensive – other than the tonic of retribution – provided the public with moments of badly needed consolation and much appreciated drama. One such, the Dambusters' raid (*separately described*), was to inspire the march and film which remains a popular television repeat. Another special target, attacked later that summer, was the secret rocket research station at Peenemunde on the Baltic. Leaving it holed like a solitaire board, Bomber Command set back the threat of the V-1 and V-2 terror weapons. The accuracy of the attack also confirmed the excellence of the Pathfinder Force.

In much the same moments as the raid, Churchill and Roosevelt agreed in conference at Quebec to locate a new South-East Asia Command at Colombo under Vice-Admiral Lord Louis Mountbatten, the 43-year-old former Chief of Combined Operations and second cousin of King George VI. The move was to have a profound effect on British fortunes in the far off war in Burma. There, since the long retreat before the advancing Japanese the one saving grace had been the exploits of Brigadier Orde Wingate's jungle long-range penetration groups operating behind the Japanese and popularised as the "Chindits." Mountbatten's restoration of morale in the 14th (the "Forgotten") Army and its honing by General Sir William Slim ("Uncle Bill") into a victorious jungle fighting force would eventually free Burma.

Further east, China, deprived of American commitment on the scale of Europe and the Pacific, was, nevertheless, aided to survive until such time as the Allies were ready to use its territory against Japan. But, following the fall of Burma and the loss of the link with Chunking along the Burma Road, supplying China created new difficulties. To overcome them the Americans organised a perilous airlift across the mountain ranges from India. Flying in officers to re-train the Chinese Army, they bolstered the economy with an Anglo-American loan of $550 million. The stroking of Generalissimo Chiang Kai-Shek reached its high point in November when he joined Roosevelt and Churchill at their Cairo conference and was promised the return of Manchuria, Formosa and the Pescadores after victory. But the Allied attitude was altered by events at the leaders' subsequent Teheran meeting with Stalin, whose neutrality towards Japan had kept him away from Cairo. Stalin's disclosure that after Germany's defeat Russia would go to war with Japan removed China's indispensability and forfeited Chiang his favoured relationship. The consequences were far-reaching.

George Formby entertains Londoners sheltering in the Underground

A convoy crossing the Atlantic

January 11 1943

ATLANTIC CONVOY BEATS 35 U-BOAT ATTACKS

THE curtain of secrecy which hides from the public gaze most of what goes on in the drama of the Battle of the Atlantic is drawn aside to-day for the telling of a grim story of the hazards which face our merchantmen.

Described in an official announcement as "an important convoy," an armada of ships recently reached this country after being attacked 35 times by U-boats in the Atlantic.

These attacks, spread over four days and four nights early last month, were repelled by escort ships of the British, Polish and Norwegian Navies.

By day British, Canadian and United States 'planes took a hand and gave the U-boats no rest.

The convoy did not escape without some loss. But the Allied forces almost certainly sank two U-boats, damaged a number of others, and finally drove off the enemy.

A full account of the epic voyage is given in a joint Admiralty and Air Ministry communiqué. This is accompanied by an announcement of awards to airmen who took part in the operations. One of those honoured is Sqdn-Ldr Terence M. Bulloch, Coastal Command's ace U-boat hunter. He receives a Bar to the DSO which he won last month.

The official joint report begins as follows:

First Day: Two or three U-boats attempted to close the convoy at about midnight. Visibility was good and the enemy was hotly engaged by the escort.

The Norwegian corvette Eglantine scored a direct hit by gunfire on one of the U-boats. The submarine at once submerged, either sinking or seriously damaged, and was then attacked with depth charges.

Other U-boats which attempted to take part in this attack were driven off without loss to the convoy.

Later that night, U-boats resumed the attack and a torpedo hit started a fire in one of the merchant ships in the convoy. By the glare of the flames the Eglantine sighted a U-boat ahead and engaged it with gunfire, scoring several hits in quick succession.

During this action the Eglantine's crew sighted a second submarine surfacing at close range to starboard. While still engaging the first U-boat, the Eglantine opened fire on the second submarine with every gun which could be brought to bear and forced the enemy to dive.

Meanwhile, HM destroyer Fame, commanded by Cmdr R. Heathcote, RN, whose award of the DSO was announced last week, and the Norwegian corvette Rose sighted and engaged two further U-boats. One of these crash-dived and was attacked with depth charges. The other was driven off.

Soon afterwards the U-boats resumed the attack. From then onwards, with hardly a pause throughout the night, they made repeated and unsuccessful attempts to close the convoy. Each time they were driven off.

January 6 1943

Ribbentrop has Corps of Art Thieves

An "Art Korps," known in Europe as "Ribbentrop's Own," systematically purloins and disposes of European art treasures, sometimes marketing them in neutral countries.

This is part of a mass of evidence available in London on the subject of German plundering of occupied countries.

This evidence has led the Allied Governments to issue a solemn declaration that all the property stolen by the Axis Powers will have to be restored. At the same time neutrals are warned against acting as "fences" for the thieves.

The treasures taken are carefully classified. The best are sent to Berlin, and the "seconds" are disposed of through agents in neutral countries. "Decadent" specimens are destroyed.

Classified as "decadents" by the Nazis are painters like Picasso and Braque.

January 16 1943

MALTA FIGHTS ON

By Richard Capell

HONOURABLE ruins!

When, approaching Malta the other week, I saw those famous yellow ochre cliffs and then the same coloured capital of the fortress island gleaming in the winter sunlight my feelings were those which must for generations to come fill English hearts at this sight.

Voltaire once said, "Everyone in the world has heard tell of Malta's siege." He meant, of course, the 16th-century siege of the Knights of St John by the Turks. Terrible it was, and crucial. But another siege will be uppermost in the minds of coming generations of travellers.

To-day many a noble palace of St John's knights is wrecked; often the stately Renaissance churches characteristic of the island are empty shells. Valetta's streets are gashed, nor Valetta's only, but also many of the courageous island's clustered villages.

But soon it is not ruins that one thinks most about. After all, half Europe shows similar sights – but not Malta's fighting energy.

To the island's millennial history a supremely glorious chapter has been added by British endurance and daring.

To-day, when Malta is alive, active, aggressive as never before, we can afford to contemplate the extremity of the island's peril in 1942. That thought will stir wonder in Mediterranean travellers and they will esteem lost monuments sacrificed in the best of causes.

Malta's trials are not over. No one entertains any illusions on that score; but future ordeals will not be those of 1942. Time was, at the beginning of the war with Italy, when the island's aerial defence consisted, so one hears, of but a few fighter aircraft – the three Gladiators were locally known as Faith, Hope and Charity. No one's imagination conceived Malta as the flaming sword it is to-day, flashing blows at the enemy north, west and south.

Malta has been transformed into one vast aircraft-carrier. It suggests a grain of radium, incessantly shooting off furious particles in all directions.

January 27 1943

President and Premier Meet in North Africa

PRESIDENT Roosevelt and Mr Churchill have met in North Africa to decide on future Allied operations in the war.

The conference took place at Casablanca, in French Morocco, where President and Premier spent 10 days together, each accompanied by Service Chiefs of Staff and expert advisers.

They completed their plans for the offensive campaigns of 1943 and have now separated to put them into execution.

These dramatic announcements disclosing the well-kept secret of the fourth war-time meeting of the two Allied leaders were made in a communiqué issued for publication this morning.

Premier Stalin, who was invited to the conferences, was unable to leave Russia on account of the great offensive he is directing. He has been fully informed of the decisions made, one of the objectives of which is to draw as much weight as possible off the Russian armies by engaging the enemy "as heavily as possible at the best selected points."

Generalissimo Chiang Kai-shek has been kept informed of the steps proposed for the assistance of China.

Gen. Giraud, High Commissioner for French North Africa, was invited to confer with the combined chiefs of staff and to meet Gen. de Gaulle, leader of the Fighting French. The French leaders recorded "entire agreement on the end to be achieved." Gen. de Gaulle is now back in London.

The Gordon Highlanders march into Tripoli

January 26 1943

11th HUSSARS WON RACE TO TRIPOLI

From Christopher Buckley with the Eighth Army

EXACTLY three months to the day after the opening of the El Alamein battle, Tripoli has fallen. It was a race between Highlanders advancing along the coast and armoured troops supported by New Zealanders coming across the desert by Beni Ulid and Tarhuna.

The first entry was actually made at five a.m. this morning by armoured cars of the 11th Hussars, who formed part of the southern column, but the coastal force followed them in within a very brief time.

When I entered shortly after sunrise British troops were already in firm possession and military police were directing traffic and patrolling the roads. On the Town Hall overlooking the Piazza Italia, the principal square of Tripoli, the Union Jack was floating in the morning breeze.

Precisely at noon Gen. Montgomery arrived at Porto Benito, the southern gateway of the city, to receive the formal surrender of the Libyan capital.

The Eighth Army Commander, who wore his familiar Tank Corps beret and battledress with full decorations, was accompanied by staff officers.

It was a profoundly impressive scene. The small, alert, grey-moustached figure of the British Army commander surrounded by officers of his staff.

Opposite them the three official representatives of Italy's last possession in Africa making the surrender. Around them a collection of armoured cars, staff cars and Jeeps, with a single Grant tank, and the outer fringe of interested civilian spectators.

Gen. Montgomery told them he had no intention of interfering in any way with the life of the civil population.

He wished the life of the community to continue, knowing that the town had a very big civilian population.

"My war," he said, "is with the German and Italian army. I have no quarrel with civilians. I shall do my best to see that the life of the civilian community continues."

February 8 1943

Nurses' Trek to Tripoli

WHEN Mr Churchill visited Tripoli last week a number of nursing sisters were among the first to welcome him. The full story can now be told of their experiences in the 1,500-mile trek from the Nile delta.

Throughout this long campaign these nurses travelled only a few miles behind the advance columns of the Eighth Army. They moved as self-contained units with their own army trucks, motor ambulances and stores – they were, in fact, a complete mobile hospital.

In their trim serviceable battledresses they have been responsible for saving the lives of countless soldiers during the past three months.

The colonel in charge of an advanced casualty station said to a military observer: "Usually the lads were prepared for a bad time until they reached the general hospital. But now these girls are right up at the casualty clearing stations you can see a difference.

"The best male orderly is not a patch on any woman. The atmosphere is different. Even the hospital tents do not look the same.

"In the most desolate spots they somehow manage to find a few flowers. And how the boys appreciate it."

The circumstances of their advance naturally involved these sisters in the general hazards and discomforts of the campaign, not the least of which are the interminable bumpings along the most shell-pitted, tortured stretches of road in the world.

Yet they have been ready immediately on arrival at their destination to jump out and set up hospital at a moment's notice, and with unfailing cheerfulness and expedition.

There was a great competition among the nurses in Cairo to be chosen to take part, since women in the Middle East are denied many opportunities of war service which are open to them at home.

Earlier in the war a successful experiment was made as a result of the initiative of Lady Spears, wife of Maj.-Gen. Sir Edward Spears, British Minister to Syria.

A small number of nurses were brought out to a military hospital, while the Fighting French also employed women nurses at their isolated desert post of Bir Hacheim last year.

It is a thoroughly representative body now in Tripoli. There are girls from every part of the United Kingdom and also from New Zealand.

"We have enjoyed every moment of it," said trim, dark-haired Miss Butland, Spencer-avenue, Coventry, who is sister-in-charge of the mobile hospital which entered Tripoli only 24 hours after the arrival of the first British troops.

"We had to rough it – bully and biscuits, sleeping on the ground, and very little water – but everyone of us here would do it again like a shot."

The Red Army re-captures Stalingrad

February 10 1943

GUADALCANAL EVACUATED

THE fight for Guadalcanal in the Solomons – Tokyo admitted its evacuation in a broadcast communiqué today – has cost the Japanese well over 50,000 troops, more than 800 'planes and crushing shipping losses.

It was the first time in this war that the Japanese people had been told officially of a major reverse.

February 13 1943

Britain's Greatest Trust Fund

ONE of the greatest gestures ever made by an industrialist as a vindication of his social faith is announced to-day.

Viscount Nuffield has allocated his shares in the Nuffield organisation to the value of £10,000,000 as a capital fund for a charitable trust.

The Nuffield Foundation, as it will be known, will be easily the best endowed charitable trust in Britain. Its net income, it is computed, will be in the neighbourhood of £400,000 a year.

February 1 1943

GERMANS' STALINGRAD C-in-C SURRENDERS

FIELD-Marshal Paulus – C-in-C of the German Sixth Army and Fourth Tank Army – and 15 other generals were captured yesterday when the remains of the enemy group in Central Stalingrad were liquidated.

A captured Nazi quartermaster-general confirmed that the force originally surrounded on Nov. 23 consisted of 330,000 men, not 220,000, as previously believed.

From Nov. 23 to Jan. 10, when the general offensive against the Germans at Stalingrad opened, the enemy lost 140,000 men.

In the three weeks since then more than 100,000 of the enemy have been killed and 46,000 taken prisoner. Of these 18,000 were captured in the last four days.

March 5 1943
178 Die in Tube Shelter Disaster

A total of 178 persons, many of them children, lost their lives and at least 60 were injured during Wednesday night's raid as the result of catastrophic overcrowding of the entrance of a Tube shelter.

There were no bombs. There was no panic. A woman and child fell on stairs leading to the shelter. Others tripped and fell on top of them. The disaster was simply and tragically a case of people pushing their way down and by their pressure crushing the life out of those who had preceded them.

The pitifulness of the tragedy is heightened by the fact that the shelter itself was in no sense crowded. Indeed, only a few feet beyond the stairs of death was a circular hall, 50 feet in diameter, that was practically unoccupied.

Two boys who have survived a bombing raid swap jokes and comics

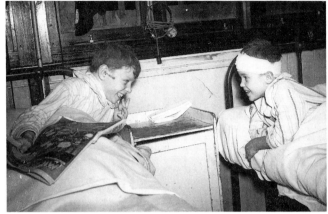

March 8 1943
"Wings for Victory"

GREAT crowds of Londoners flocked to the City and the West End yesterday to take part in the "Wings for Victory" campaign for £150,000,000 towards which £30,000,000 had already been collected by Saturday night.

The Stirling bomber standing near St Paul's and the Lancaster in Trafalgar Square were from morning till evening the centre of attraction for surging masses of people, young and old.

Trafalgar Square was packed with a singing, laughing crowd. People clung to every vantage point and the lions at the base of the Nelson Column were hidden by them.

Men, women and children moved forward in a solid stream towards the gaily decorated selling booths for Savings Stamps and Certificates. In one of the booths was Queenie, the bulldog mascot, whose target for the week is £25,000.

March 19 1943
NAZIS TORTURE RUSSIAN GIRLS TO DEATH

From A. T. Cholerton, Moscow

THE Moscow army driving south-westwards to Smolensk, toiling through waist-high wet snow, thawing swamp and tricky forest, retakes one ruined village after another.

Sometimes by fast flanking work they deliver their old people, women and children. More often, now that the going has become so bad, they find only a few old crones alive among the ashes.

All the rest have been driven like cattle before the retreating Germans.

The fate of these captives haunts me now. I talked in Rzhev with a few who had been rescued after several days' march in that caravan of slaves.

When the Russian troops retook Mishinka village, near Vyazma, they found three old grannies crouching among its cinders. But there was something else: a charred form wired to a charred fence.

That was little Nastenka –

15-year-old Anastasia Makarova, a bonny girl with long, dark hair and deep blue eyes. The tank men tenderly unbound the horror, placed it on a gun-limber, covered it with a flag, and drove slowly away.

Nastenka was not a guerrilla, but just a beautiful, strong girl, almost a woman. Oberleutnant Kluge wanted her. Throughout most of the winter she hid from him in a hole under a neighbour's barn.

Nastenka made a dash across the fields from the edge of the forest, where two soldiers caught her. Beating her shamefully, they dragged her back sobbing to Kluge in the market-place.

"So it's you, is it? Now will you come to Germany?" he sneered.

Nastenka shook her head, "No. I won't leave my village."

Finding her sulky, the Oberleutnant kicked her in the body. She fell, but soldiers got her up again and Kluge, smiling gently, pulled off her boots, stockings, coat and shawl, leaving her standing for a time knee deep in snow.

Then, "Now will you come to Germany?" he asked.

Quite calm now she sat down in the snow but a soldier kicked her to her feet again.

Her mother cried from the crowd, "Nastenka, come here to me." She tried to but her frost-numbed legs would not carry her. Time was now getting short. Kluge gave the order to tie her to the fence, drench it with paraffin and light it.

Nastenka stiffened her aching body and stood upright like a soldier. The flames crept nearer, but apparently too slowly. Kluge had two flaming boards put under her feet. She still remained silent.

It was really time to leave now. The Oberleutnant sent a soldier to get a can of petrol and pour it right over her. She only screamed for her mother – lying unconscious nearby – when the flames reached her hair. The whole village watched Nastenka's death.

I sometimes think that we Allied correspondents do not tell you enough of these atrocities.

Nastenka was not a guerrilla or even the daughter or sister of one. She was just a girl who would not have any truck with the Oberleutnant and did not want to go into slavery. In Rzhev we learned of cases of people murdered for failing to obey such round-up orders.

The Nazis make a practice of killing the families of those fighting them as guerrillas. The Mayor of Rzhev told us that they shot the wife and five children of one of his own guerrilla band.

A Kuban Cossack girl, Dusia Sorokina, aged 16, was tortured to death in the market place of Georgievskaya village for refusing to reveal her guerrilla father's hiding-place.

Her fellow villagers were forced to watch her die, but still they did not betray the other members of her family when the Nazis burnt down all their houses.

In the Kuban 12-year-old Davids have slain their Goliaths, and 13-year-old Judiths their Holofernes. But one of the jobs at which Cossack child guerrillas have proved best is "de-mining." They cut mine fuses and unscrew their detonators.

When caught they are shot, of course, and some tortured to death.

March 26 1943

MARETH LINE BATTLE OF HEAVY GUNS

THE full weight of the Eighth Army's heavy artillery has been thrown into the Battle of the Mareth Line, which, by last evening, had been raging without a stop for five days and five nights. A big gun duel has developed.

An Algiers report last night stated that the British continued to hold the bridgehead established in the coastal sector north-east of the village of Mareth, despite all the efforts of the Afrika Korps to re-establish its defence positions.

Rommel is stated to be suffering very heavy losses in men and material as his counter-attacks are caught by the British guns. Many embryo assaults have also been broken up by the Western Desert air forces before they could be launched.

Morocco radio said early to-day that while Rommel had been forced to use almost all his armour in the Mareth zone, Gen. Montgomery still had most of his still in reserve.

Meanwhile the British armoured force which is threatening the rear of the Axis Mareth positions in the north-east has made further progress in face of bitter resistance and is now only seven miles from El Hamma.

Rommel withdraws his troops to the Mareth line

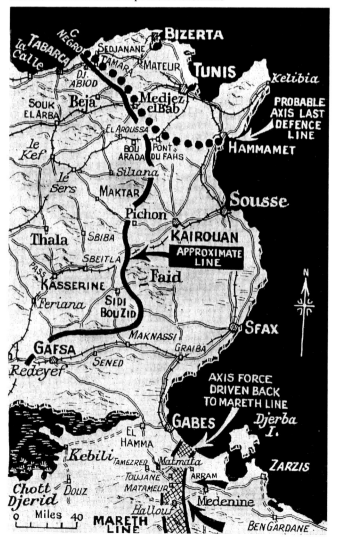

Land Army girls dig for victory on a drainage scheme in Epping Forest

March 20 1943

DAWN ATTACK BY BRITISH IN BURMA

BRITISH troops on the Burma front at dawn yesterday attacked a strong Japanese position before Donbaik, at the southern extremity of the Mayu peninsula. The advance began after our artillery had hammered the Japanese lines with concentrated fire.

The first three immediate objectives were attained and two small parties of Japanese isolated. An enemy counter-thrust from the direction of the village of Laungchaung has been contained, and from preliminary reports the position appears to be favourable.

If we succeed in pushing the Japanese from the Mayu peninsula the chief advantage would be to secure at least partial control of the mouth of the Mayu River. This is the most important artery of communication with the Arakan front.

March 29 1943

900 TONS OF BOMBS ON BERLIN IN 1½ HOURS

"A shattering assault on Berlin" was how Sir Archibald Sinclair, Air Minister, last night described Saturday night's raid, in which a force of Lancasters, Halifaxes and Stirlings dropped 4-ton bombs and a great number of 2-ton bombs.

It was the heaviest RAF attack yet on the Reich capital, 900 tons of bombs being rained on the city, or more than twice the weight dropped on London in its worst raid on April 18 1941. Two large explosions were caused in the last half hour of the raid, as if a gas-holder or fuel tank had been hit.

The weather was clear, the Air Ministry announced yesterday, and the bombing was concentrated. Berlin radio, describing the raid as "a terror attack," said that buildings were damaged and fires started.

Air Chief Marshal Harris studies aerial reconnaissance

April 12 1943

Queen Speaks to Women of Empire

THE Queen broadcast to the women of the Empire last night, telling them that "in these years of tragedy and glory" they had "earned the gratitude and admiration of all mankind."

Her Majesty said: 'I would like first of all to try and tell you just why I am speaking to you tonight – to you, my fellow countrywomen, all over the world.

It is not because any special occasion calls for it; it is not because I have any special message to give you; it is because there is something that, deep in my heart, I know ought to be told you, and probably I am the best person to do it.

Most of us, at one time or another in our lives, have read some fine book that has given us courage and strength, and fresh hope; and, when we lay it down, we have wished that, though we are strangers to him, we could meet the author and tell him how much we admire his work and how grateful we are for it.

Something of the same kind makes me feel that I would like to meet you this Sunday night.

For you, though you may not realise it, have done work as great as any book that ever was written.

You, too, in these years of tragedy and glory, of crushing sorrow and splendid achievement, have earned the gratitude and admiration of all mankind; and I am sure that every man, who is doing his man's share in the grim task of winning this war, would agree that it is high time that someone told you so.

Some of you may feel that I am exaggerating your own share in that task. "What have I done," you may ask, "compared to what my boy has to put up with, dodging submarines in the Atlantic or chasing Rommel across Africa?"

In your different spheres, believe me, you have done all that he has done in different degrees, endured all that he has endured. For you, like him, have given all that is good in you, regardless of yourself, to the same cause for which he is fighting – our cause, the cause of Right against Wrong; and nobody, man or woman, can give more.

There is no need, surely, for me to say in detail how you have done this. Perhaps, constantly travelling as the King and I do, through the length and breadth of these islands, I am fortunate in being able to see a clear picture of the astonishing work that women are doing everywhere, and of the quiet heroism with which, day in day out, they are doing it.

This picture I know is being reproduced in many similar aspects all over the Empire, from the largest self-governing Dominion to the smallest islands owing allegiance to the Crown. We are indeed very proud of you.

How often, when I have talked with women engaged on every kind of job, sometimes a physically hard or dangerous one – how often, when I admired their pluck, have I heard them say, "Oh, well, it's not much. I'm just doing my best to help us win the war."

In these last tragic years many have found in religion the source and mainspring of the courage and selflessness that they needed. On the other hand, we cannot close our eyes to the fact that our precious Christian heritage is threatened by adverse influences.

It does, indeed, seem to me that if the years to come are to see some real spiritual recovery, the women of our nation must be deeply concerned with religion, and our homes the very place where it should start.

It is the creative and dynamic power of Christianity that can help us to carry the moral responsibilities which history is placing upon our shoulders. If our homes can be truly Christian, then the influence of that spirit will assuredly spread like leaven through all the aspects of our common life – industrial, social and political.

The King and I are grateful to think that we and our family are remembered in your prayers. We need them and try to live up to them.

And we also pray that God will bless and guide our people in this country, and in our great family throughout the Empire, and will lead us forward, united and strong, into the paths of victory and peace.

Winston Churchill at 10 Downing Street

April 17 1943

CAPT. SCOTT'S SON IN SEA ACTION

NINE German E-boats and an armed trawler have been hit in the latest actions in the Channel and off the East Coast of England, stated Admiralty communiqués yesterday.

Strong forces of E-boats, whose positions were reported by naval aircraft operating under RAF Fighter Command, were routed early on Thursday morning by the destroyer Westminster and the sloop Widgeon. Both were set on fire.

One was seen to blow up. The other disengaged behind a smoke screen. Shortly afterwards the flash of an explosion was seen in this direction.

The Westminster and Widgeon scored hits on four other E-boats, which retired to the eastward. The rest of the enemy force also disengaged.

Albacore aircraft of the Fleet Air Arm took up the pursuit and later intercepted a number of E-boats and bombed them.

Whirlwind fighter-bombers also struck at E-boats in the Channel on Thursday night, destroying one and damaging two.

The trawler, one of three engaged 20 miles west of Le Havre on the same night by light coastal forces commanded by Lt-Cdr Peter Markham Scott, received many hits before she was left burning.

Our casualties in this action were one killed and four wounded.

Lt-Cdr Peter Scott, MBE, aged 33, is the son of the late Antarctic explorer, Capt. Robert Falcon Scott, and Lady Kennet. He was a godson of the late Sir J.M. Barrie and was named Peter, after Barrie's "Peter Pan."

A leading painter of wildfowl, he formerly lived in a lighthouse on the Wash, sharing his home with over 200 birds which he had collected on his travels.

He was mentioned in despatches for gallantry in the Dieppe raid, scenes from which he later painted.

April 21 1943

Church Bells Again

THE ban on the ringing of Britain's church bells is to be lifted. The bells will be heard not only on special occasions, but every Sunday, starting on Sunday next, Easter Day.

This decision was announced by the Prime Minister in the House of Commons yesterday.

No details were available last night as to what form of invasion warning will replace the ringing of church bells. Sounding of air-raid sirens for longer periods than for air-raids and in some different manner is expected to be the method chosen.

An announcement may be deferred until the authorities have reason to believe that invasion or enemy "commando raids" are imminent.

April 21 1943

HITLER SEES QUISLING

HITLER received Quisling, the Axis Premier of Norway, at his headquarters on Monday, the eve of Hitler's 54th birthday, it was announced in Berlin last night.

Quisling thus follows Mussolini, Antonescu, Horthy and King Boris, all of whom have been summoned to talks with their German master.

After Quisling's visit a communiqué was issued, which stated that questions of "the European battle for existence" were discussed.

May 8 1943

TUNIS AND BIZERTA CAPTURED BY ALLIES

THE great news of the capture of Tunis and Bizerta was announced in a communiqué from Allied Headquarters in North Africa which reached London at 11.25 last night. Their occupation was completed shortly after 4 p.m. local time. Ferryville, south-west of Bizerta, is also in Allied hands.

The Battle of Tunisia is thus virtually over within six months of the Allied landings in North Africa – Nov. 8. The entire Axis defence system in the north and centre has collapsed under the weight of Gen. Alexander's new offensive, launched at dawn on Thursday. Thousands of prisoners and vast quantities of munitions have been captured.

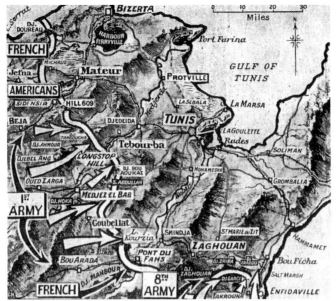

The German counter attacks in the Gulf of Tunis

Burgeoning allotments at Kensington Gardens

May 11 1943

First Wartime Racing at Ascot

THERE will be crowds here on Saturday for the first time since the war started. The thunder of hoofs will be heard again as the field flashes past the Royal Box to the finishing post.

Between races the crowds will stroll out from the enclosures across the course to the heath, where the gorse is in full bloom; saunter along the lawns and cast a critical eye at the parades in the paddock. But it will not be the Royal Ascot of former years.

The pageantry of the Royal Family's drive to the course in semi-state landaus, customary on the June days of the pre-war Ascot meetings, will not take place this year.

May 14 1943

Britain Now Better Fed

BRITAIN – particularly the working population – is better fed now than a year ago, declared Mr Mabane, Parliamentary Secretary to the Ministry of Food, in the House of Commons to-day.

He was hopeful that bread might continue unrationed through the war, but gave a warning that plans had been completed for severe control of catering establishments if they should make serious inroads on food reserves.

Mr Mabane said that the major work of the Ministry was concerned with long term global planning which enabled it in the fourth year of war to offer a balanced dietary and look forward with a reasonable degree of calm confidence to the fifth.

Earlier in the war stocks had been raised far above peacetime levels. "Provided, as I confidently believe," he said, "that home agriculture continues to produce as large a proportion of our own food as during this year the country can be confident that the national larder will continue to be well stocked."

May 17 1943

WELLINGTONS' HEAVY ATTACK ON PALERMO

ANXIETY among the Italian people, already harassed by fears of an imminent invasion and by a spate of alarming rumours, increased yesterday with news of further blows from the air.

Concern for the future was epitomised in a warning that the hour was at hand for "the supreme trial of strength."

A strong force of RAF Wellingtons of the Allies' Strategic Air Force in North-West Africa made a heavy raid on the important Sicilian port of Palermo on Friday night, dropping tons of incendiaries and high-explosive bombs. These started several fires, including a large one in the dock area. All our aircraft returned safely.

Elsewhere in Sicily and also over the foot of Italy 'planes from Malta attacked railways.

May 18 1943

RAF BLOW UP THREE KEY DAMS IN GERMANY

WITH one single blow, the RAF has precipitated what may prove to be the greatest industrial disaster yet inflicted on Germany in this war.

A force of Lancasters, loaded with mines and with crews specially trained for the task, early yesterday morning attacked and breached the great dams on the Mohne and Sorpe rivers, tributaries of the Ruhr, and also the dam on the Eder River.

To-day walls of water sweeping down the Ruhr and Eder valleys are causing widespread destruction to houses, factories and plants.

The Air Ministry announced last night that a partial reconnaissance of the Ruhr Valley and the district near the Eder dam shows that the floods are spreading fast.

"The waters are sweeping down the Ruhr Valley," it stated. "Railways and road bridges are broken down. Hydro-electrical power stations are destroyed or damaged, a railway marshalling yard is under water.

"The floods from the breached Eder dam are already as great as the floods in the Ruhr Valley, but the country here is flatter and the water likely to spread over a greater area."

The German communiqué yesterday, admitting that two dams had been "damaged" – it did not specify the area – said "heavy casualties were caused among the civilian population by the resulting floods." That was as much as the people of Germany were allowed to know. There was no reference to the disaster in later news broadcasts from Berlin.

The pilots reported seeing in the moonlight huge breaches in the dams with water bursting through. They saw a power-station below the Mohne dam swept away in the flood, and a 30ft high wall of water rumbling down the Eder Valley.

Reporting personally to Air Chief Marshal Sir Arthur Harris, Chief of Bomber Command, Wing Cmdr G. P. Gibson, who led the raid, said the immediate results of the destruction of the dams were far beyond their expectations.

Wing Cmdr Gibson was the first to attack the Mohne Dam. After dropping his load he flew up and down drawing the enemy's fire to give the following 'planes a better chance of success. It was not until the fourth load had been dropped that the dam was first breached.

Air reconnaissance yesterday showed that there was a 100-yard gap in it.

There was no indication last night of the number of Lancasters engaged, but, although the loss of eight machines and their crews on an attack on such an objective must be regarded as fairly heavy, the complete success of the operation tells its own story of the worth of the sacrifice.

May 19 1943

STATE OF EMERGENCY THROUGHOUT RUHR

A general state of emergency was proclaimed throughout the whole province of Westphalia at 4 a.m. to-day, following the breaching of the Mohne, Sorpe and Eder dams by the RAF early yesterday morning, states a semi-official report from Germany tonight.

At that hour the whole organisation of the army, the ARP services, the Labour Front and the Todt organisation in the Ruhr and Rhineland had failed even partially to stem the torrent sweeping down from the three mighty reservoirs.

The great sluices across the Ruhr at Duisburg, 58 miles below the Mohne dam, had been declared officially to be in imminent danger of yielding.

May 18 1943

Broken Dams

To break dams and flood the country against an invader is a manoeuvre well known in the wars of freedom. WILLIAM THE SILENT baffled the Spanish as his descendant, our WILLIAM III, baffled the French by opening the Dykes of Holland. So in this war the Russians blew up the great dam of the Dnieper to check the Germans. It is new tactics to flood the enemy's country far behind his front.

The onslaught of Bomber Command on the three biggest dams in Germany has shocked the Wehrmacht. The tone of aggrieved surprise in the German announcement that the dams were destroyed, "which caused floods resulting in heavy civilian casualties," confesses that an unforeseen and disastrous blow was dealt to the power of Germany's war machine.

The chief power house of the Reich, the Ruhr, requires enormous quantities of water to keep its coke ovens and its factories in production. Now that the 134,000,000 tons of water behind the Mohne dam have surged down the Ruhr Valley the Wehrmacht will go short of urgently needed armaments. The industrial organisation of the Ruhr depends to a large extent on water transport, and from the 200,000,000 tons of water in the Waldeck reservoir the Ems-Weser canal, a main artery, was fed. With railways strained far beyond capacity, the mutilation of the canal system is a grievous disaster. There are secondary effects – damage to hydro-electric plants, factories, roads and bridges – not much less grave.

Bomber Command have struck deep, and their achievement may well alarm the Reich. Successful air attack on a large dam was considered not long ago impossible. Germany will learn that other things outside the calculations of the Luftwaffe are now possible to the Allied Air Forces.

The Möhne Dam after it had been breached

A Lancaster bomber taking off

The Dambusters

The successful attack on the Möhne and Eder dams in the industrial Ruhr valley on the night of May 16-17 1943, resulted from a combination of the skills of Wing Commander Guy Gibson (awarded the VC afterwards) and his crews; the reliability of the Lancaster bomber and its four Rolls-Royce Merlin engines; the navigational aids developed by British scientists; and, of course, the bouncing bombs thought up on the Ducks and Drakes principle by the brilliant and intuitive inventor, Barnes Wallis.

To pinpoint and attack such a heavily defended target at low level required exceptional navigational and bomb aiming skills and to this end a new squadron, 617, was formed on March 20 at Scampton, Lincolnshire, under Gibson whose leadership, resolution and flying ability at the age of 25 were already a byword in "Bomber" Harris's 5 Group. Gibson handpicked his crews and led them through an intensive period of training. On the ground they pored over models of the dams, familiarising themselves with every feature. In low level practice in the Lake District, Gibson simulated the approach which must be made at 60 feet, a difficult and hazardous manoeuvre in such a heavily laden bomber. At Reculver, near Herne Bay, crews practised lining up on dummy towers resembling those of the Möhne.

Why were the dams rated so highly as targets? The Möhne controlled the level of the River Ruhr. Its lake contained more than 130 million tons of water for supplying pumping stations and electricity plants. A breach would flood the valley and disrupt industry. The Eder controlled the River Weser and a third target, the Sorpe, was also important.

In moonlight, Gibson led 19 Lancasters, briefed to attack in three waves, the first under him to take out the Möhne and the Eder, the second, the Sorpe, and the third in reserve. On the way one Lancaster in his wave was shot down.

Over the target the Möhne looked "squat and heavy and uncomfortable" and after circling for some time to choose a line of approach Gibson dived to 60 feet under fire from two flak towers. In the second attack Flight Lieutenant Hopgood's Lancaster was hit, crashed and his mine, or bouncing bomb, fell on the power house beyond the dam. Three other aircraft made successful attacks while Gibson flew up and down the dam so that his gunners could engage the defences. And then he heard the Australian, "Mickey" Martin (later Air Marshal Sir Harold Martin) shout: "Hell, it's gone. It's gone. Look at it for Christ's sake."

Gibson looked down and saw the water of the lake "like stirred porridge in the moonlight, rushing through a great breach." In the Operations Room at Grantham, Harris and Wallis waited anxiously for the signal that would announce success. There were smiles all round when it came – just one word: "Nigger," the name of Gibson's dog which had been run over and killed shortly before take-off.

Afterwards the Eder was also breached, but the Sorpe attack was less successful. By September next year Guy Gibson, VC, DSO and Bar, DFC and Bar, failing to return from a Mosquito sortie over Holland, was dead.

May 21 1943

BRITISH JUNGLE FORCE KEPT JAPANESE ON RUN

From L. Marsland Gander
New Delhi

To-night I am able to reveal details of a daring three-months' campaign carried out behind the enemy lines deep in the heart of Central Burma by a mixed force of British, Indian, Gurkha and Burmese troops.

The plan was that of Field-Marshal Wavell, C-in-C India, and he inspected the force before they set out on their adventurous expedition from Tamu, on the Assam-Burma border, in mid-February.

They were led by Brig. O. C. Wingate, DSO, who is a relative of Lawrence of Arabia. He was one of the small group of British officers who organised the Abyssinian guerrilla campaign in the Gojjam province.

"Wingate's Follies" his men called themselves. More officially they were known as "Chindits," after the fabulous gryphons that guard the Burmese temples.

Among them were Commando men who had raided Norway and France. Now, beating the Japanese at their own game of infiltration in the dark solitudes of the Burmese forests, as disclosed in a communiqué, they have:

Penetrated to within 50 miles of Mandalay; blown up the Mandalay-Myitkyina railway in 75 places; destroyed four railway bridges; and blocked the famous Bongyaung Gorge by starting a landslide.

In jungle clashes they killed at least 200 Japanese. Meanwhile they kept a whole Japanese division of 15,000 men occupied in hunting for them to prevent their reaching the Lashio railway.

The Japanese command was bewildered, and put out broadcasts saying these men were the remnants of Gen. Alexander's defeated Burma Army.

Some of the Chindits marched 1,300 miles in 58 days.

May 24 1943

BOMBERS DESTROYING ITALIAN AIRFIELDS

THE great Mediterranean Air Command under Air Chief Marshal Tedder is now being used for the all-out offensive to destroy Italy's airfields and communications. The Battle of Italy has, in fact, begun.

In the latest attacks, announced officially yesterday, a further 18 Axis aircraft have been destroyed, making a total of 303 since Wednesday. In this period Allied losses have been 17 aircraft only.

Details of the onslaught, received from North Africa last night, show grounded aircraft, hangars, barracks and buildings wrecked, and of big fires, chiefly on Sicily.

Orde Wingate (with the beard) briefs his "Chindits"

May 25 1943

"A Very Remarkable Woman"

By Peterborough

I heard a piece of news yesterday which brings home the fact that the siege of Malta is ended. This was that Miss Mabel Strickland is planning to take a holiday in England.

Lord Gort last February described her as "a very remarkable woman" – a judgment with which everyone who was in Malta during the siege would certainly agree.

Her work during the worst periods of the island's blitz in successfully bringing out her two dailies, "The Times of Malta" and "Il Berka," would in itself have justified the Field-Marshal's encomium. She has also been tireless in relief measures for the inhabitants.

Miss Strickland hopes to spend some time at Sizergh, the English home of her family in Westmorland.

May 28 1943

GIBSON, VC, DESCRIBES BOMBINGS TO KING

AN official announcement this morning of the award of the Victoria Cross to Acting Wing Cmdr Guy Penrose Gibson, who led the Lancaster bombers which breached the Eder and Mohne dams in Germany on the night of May 16, revealed that he himself attacked both dams.

He explained the way the attack was made to the King and Queen when they visited an air station in the North of England yesterday and met members of the Lancaster crews.

To illustrate the explanation Wing Cmdr Gibson showed their Majesties the miniature models of the dams with the aid of which the crews had studied their task for weeks.

The King and Queen examined through a lens pictures of the floods that swept a vast area of the industrial Ruhr after the raid.

Wing Cmdr Gibson also submitted two drafts of a proposed coat of arms for his squadron. One showed a hammer parting chains with the motto: "Alter the Man." The other, showing a breached dam, had the motto: "Après moi le déluge."

The crews of the 11 Lancaster bombers that returned of the 18 that set out for the raid were inspected in front of the plane in which Wing Cmdr Gibson led the attack.

Their Majesties spoke to every officer and NCO in the squadron.

A victory parade in Malta bearing an effigy of Mussolini

Pantelleria is bombed by the Allies

General de Gaulle

The King visiting the victorious troops in North Africa

June 11 1943

"I Resign" Threat by de Gaulle

A serious difference of opinion between Gen. de Gaulle and Gen. Giraud over the reorganisation of the French Army has led to reports in Algiers to-night that Gen. de Gaulle has threatened to resign or, alternatively, that he is "in a state of suspended resignation."

The first intimation of a crisis was the cancellation of to-day's meeting of the French Liberation Committee. After this Gen. de Gaulle was quoted as saying, "I resign."

Later it was announced that the Committee would meet to-morrow morning at 10 o'clock. Gen. de Gaulle's advisers and followers are urging him to reconsider his attitude, and there are some hopes of a settlement by the morning.

Gen. de Gaulle has put forward proposals for the future of the Army on which, his friends state, "a compromise is impossible for him."

June 3 1943

Leslie Howard Lost

Mr Leslie Howard, the film actor and director, is one of the people missing in a passenger plane shot down by a Nazi machine on the way from Lisbon to Foynes, Southern Ireland.

The plane left for England at 9.30 on Tuesday morning. At 11 o'clock it signalled "Enemy aircraft attacking us." That was the last heard of it.

June 1 1943

"Vinegar Joe"

Lt-Gen. Joseph Stilwell, the United States GOC in the Far East, who was in London yesterday, made a profound impression on the Chinese forces he commanded in Burma. Like his prototype "Chinese" Gordon, he was known for his impassive calmness under fire.

In battle, when the Japanese bombers were active overhead, he would be seen smoking a cigarette in a black holder and discussing operations in fluent Chinese with his staff. He received the American DSC last January for his "extraordinary heroism under fire."

"Vinegar Joe," as he is known in the American Army, is a man of few words – and these can be impatient. He is a specialist in understatement. "Heavy bombardment by large numbers of 'planes over long distances is a very interesting subject," was one example he gave yesterday of this characteristic.

Gen. Stilwell knows the Far East as do few soldiers. He began to learn Chinese in 1919, and from 1926, with one short break, was in China until the outbreak of war.

June 15 1943

COMIC OPERA OF PANTELLARIA LANDING

From K. Hooper, Pantellaria

Scenes reminiscent of Cap Bon were seen this morning as thousands of Italian prisoners forming the bulk of the 15,000 garrison wound their dusty tattered way from the surrounding hills into a foul ruin which once bore the name of Pantellaria.

Included in this clutch were several Luftwaffe Germans who had been showing a few of their flak tricks to their Italian Allies. These Germans were picked up whilst attempting to escape by a boat.

One of the most astounding facts about the reduction of this Mediterranean stronghold is that the attacking forces suffered no casualties whatever.

The only man to suffer any sort of injury was bitten by a donkey.

June 25 1943

Bombing will Save Lives

We must continue to use our superiority in the air as a means of ending the war as speedily as we can, says the Archbishop of York, Dr Garbett, replying in the York diocesan leaflet to letters protesting against the bombing of Axis towns.

"The real justification for continuing this bombing is that it will shorten the war and may save thousands of lives," he states.

"War is always horrible, and this is true of war from the air. Most of us would wish to see aerial warfare totally abolished, for the non-combatant is almost certain to suffer with the combatant.

"In its most hateful form it was used by the Germans when they bombed undefended Rotterdam, Belgrade and other cities, murdering thousands with the deliberate intention of striking terror into the hearts of the civilian population.

"The Allies have aimed at military objectives with the purpose of breaking down the military opposition of the enemy, though unavoidably many civilians have also had to suffer.

"Those who demand the suspension of all bombing are advocating a policy which would condemn many more of our own soldiers to death, and would postpone the hour of liberation which will alone save from massacre and torture those who are now in the power of the Nazis.

"Often in life there is no clear choice between absolute right and wrong. Frequently the choice has to be made of the lesser of two evils."

June 17 1943

THE KING FLIES TO SEE AFRICA VICTORS

THE King is in North Africa visiting the victorious Allied forces. His reception everywhere has been tumultuous.

He reached North Africa on Saturday morning after a 1,200-miles all-night flight from England in a four-engined bomber. But it is only to-day that we have been allowed to "break" the news.

It was his Majesty's first ocean flight and his second visit to forces serving abroad since the war began – he visited the BEF in France and toured the Maginot Line in December, 1939. On that occasion he crossed the Channel in a destroyer.

In these visits to his forces abroad he is following the example of his father, George V, who went to France six times between November, 1914, and August, 1918.

Since Saturday morning the King has had one of the busiest periods of his life. He has conferred with the Allied commanders; he has given a private luncheon, at which his guests were Gen. Giraud and Gen. de Gaulle; he has visited British troops, American troops – he has reviewed the United States Fifth Army – French troops, warships and airfields.

July 10 1943

Sir H. Oakes's Death

From Our Nassau
Correspondent

COUNT Alfred de Marigny has been arrested and charged with the murder of Sir Harry Oakes, his father-in-law.

Sir Harry Oakes, who was 68, was found dead on a bed which had been set on fire. There were four severe head wounds and burns on the body.

It was learned to-day that he had planned to leave for the United States last Tuesday.

He postponed his trip till Wednesday to show Press representatives over his 1,000-acre sheep farm. When a friend went to call him for the appointment he found him dead.

The inquest was opened to-day behind closed doors. After formal evidence it was adjourned till Tuesday.

The Duke of Windsor, Governor of the Bahamas, has cancelled appointments to keep in touch with the inquiry.

Sir Archibald Wavell

June 19 1943

Sir A. Wavell to be New Viceroy of India

IT was officially announced last night that Field-Marshal Sir Archibald Wavell is to succeed the Marquess of Linlithgow as Viceroy of India.

Gen. Auchinleck will be C-in-C, India, in succession to Field-Marshal Wavell, whom he will also succeed as Member of the Governor-General Executive Council.

Field-Marshal Wavell, who is now in this country, will vacate the appointment of C-in-C forthwith and will return to India to take up the Viceroyalty in October. Gen. Auchinleck will therefore assume the post of C-in-C immediately.

It is proposed to relieve the C-in-C, India, of the responsibility for the conduct of the operations against Japan and to set up a separate East Asia Command for that purpose.

July 6 1943

DEATH OF GEN. SIKORSKI

IT was announced in London last night that the King has sent a telegram of condolence to the Polish President, M. Raczkiewicz, on the death of Gen. Sikorski, Polish Prime Minister and C-in-C.

Gen. Sikorski was killed when a Liberator aircraft, in which he was travelling to Britain from the Middle East, crashed shortly after taking off from Gibraltar on Sunday night.

The cause of the accident is stated to have been engine trouble. The accident was seen from La Linea, the Spanish town just over the border from Gibraltar.

British troops of the 8th Army embarking for the invasion of Sicily, and (below) coming ashore

July 12 1943

ALL FIRST OBJECTIVES IN SICILY CAPTURED

CONTINUED progress in the Allied invasion of Sicily was reported in the following special communiqué from Gen. Eisenhower's headquarters received in London at 10.30 last night:

"Three Sicilian airfields are in our hands, and all first immediate objectives are believed to have been taken.

"American and British landing forces made contact with paratroops which had been dropped at selected points in Sicily on Friday night and Saturday.

"At the same time the main body of enemy forces has not yet been met.

"All reports of fighting say that contact has been made with Italian coastal defence units rather than with any mobile enemy forces."

One of the captured airfields is at Pachino, a small town on the south-eastern tip of the island, three miles inland from Cape Passero. Two are near Gela, a small port on the south coast, 20 miles west of Ragusa.

Throughout yesterday streams of reinforcements – men, guns, ammunition and stores – were being landed under cover of the guns of the Allied warships and of our air forces.

Thus the second phase of the attack – the first was the initial landings – has been opened within 48 hours of the first glider troops descending on the island about 10.30 on Friday night. They were followed after 11.30 p.m. by parachute battalions.

By destroying enemy strongpoints and disrupting communications these airborne forces paved the way for the great invasion armada of 2,000 vessels, which began to land the main advanced forces at 2.45 a.m. on Saturday along over 100 miles of the south and south-east coast.

The zone was not precisely indicated, but it may be assumed to extend from the region of Syracuse on the east coast to Gela. This region includes the best beaches in Sicily.

Guns of the warships pounded the enemy defence points; hundreds of aircraft swept the island, attacking airfields, road and rail communications, and enemy troop concentrations.

An inspiring message to all ships taking part in the invasion of Sicily was sent by Admiral of the Fleet Cunningham, Naval C-in-C Mediterranean, on Friday night. It stated:

1 We are about to embark on the most momentous enterprise of the war – striking for the first time at the enemy in his own land.
2 Success means the opening of the Second Front, with all that implies, and the first move towards the rapid and decisive defeat of our enemies.
3 Our object is clear, and our primary duty is to place this vast expedition ashore in the minimum time and subsequently to maintain our military and air forces as they drive relentlessly forward into enemy territory.
4 In the light of this duty great risks must be and are to be accepted. The safety of our own ships and all distracting considerations are to be relegated to the second place or disregarded as the accomplishment of our primary duty may require.
5 On every commanding officer, officer and rating rests the individual and personal duty of ensuring that no flinching in determination or failure of effort on his own part will hamper this great enterprise.
6 I rest confident in the resolution, skill and endurance of you all, to whom this momentous enterprise is entrusted.

The Allied landings in Sicily

July 19 1943

The Liberation of Sicily

IN the first week of the fight for Sicily the Allied forces have taken 30,000 prisoners. They have advanced more than 50 miles at the farthest point from their landing beaches, and they are firmly established across a great tract of the island from the Gulf of Catania to Agrigento. The central roads and railways are now not far beyond their reach. German concentrations of armour in defence of Catania have failed to prevent the advance of the Eighth Army into the suburbs of that city, the second in size and, for the organisation of the Axis resistance, the most important in Sicily. All this swift success has been won at a cost in casualties "amazingly light." By the week-end the moment was ripe for the establishment of an Anglo-American military government as the supreme authority in the occupied regions.

Seldom has the general of an invading army been able to set up organised government so quickly as Gen. ALEXANDER. The principles of his proclamation are well considered and certainly unlikely to fail to win the approval of the Sicilian people: they have made their feeling for Fascism and MUSSOLINI plain enough in the welcome they gave to the Allied troops. There are no half-measures about the proclamation. The powers of the Italian crown are suspended, the Fascist party is dissolved and its discriminating laws abolished. On the other hand property and the general body of law are guaranteed, and administrative and judicial functions will be left to existing officials who are trustworthy.

A Spitfire at a captured airfield in Sicily

Looting at Catania

July 24 1943

Palermo

WITH the capture of Palermo, organised defence of western Sicily has come to an end. The Axis troops in that part of the island have either surrendered or, as the Germans put it, are waging "elastic warfare with great mobility."

In a fortnight the Allies have conquered three-quarters of Sicily, though the spokesman of the German General Staff ranked the shore defences with those of the English Channel. Palermo is not only the capital and the largest city of the island but one of the best and most efficiently equipped of Italian ports. Holding the great harbour and its air bases, only some 125 miles from the Straits of Messina and 175 from Naples, Allied forces have enlarged opportunities of action against the Italian mainland.

At least five Axis divisions were still in the west of Sicily when the Americans made this swift advance to Palermo, but Italian weariness of the war and the Germans was again displayed. A whole division and a regiment of Bersaglieri, who are reputed first-class troops, surrendered to a man.

August 11 1943

Britain Makes Record Tea Purchase

LORD Woolton, Minister of Food, announced yesterday that his ministry had just completed the purchase of this year's tea crop, a total of over 700,000,000lb or 312,500 tons. This is a world's record single purchase of tea.

Allocations will be made not only to Britain, but to the whole non-Axis world – our Allies, the Dominions and neutral countries.

"Subject to the risks of war, I think the people of Britain can be satisfied that their tea ration for next year is secure," the Minister said. "Through the operation of the Combined Food Board we shall make allocations to all the countries concerned."

Other food news announced by Lord Woolton included:

Onions. Later this month there is to be a distribution of onions in selected urban and industrial areas, including London, of 1lb for each ration book holder. As supplies would be insufficient for every individual trader, Lord Woolton expressed the hope that those who received them would not limit their sales to registered customers and would display their onion stocks prominently.

Those who received this ration should have the fact recorded on the back page of their ration books, marked indelibly "On." That would prevent people with plenty of time from going from shop to shop for onions.

July 19 1943

"Resist, Resist, Resist," Cries Scorza

SCORZA, Fascist Party Secretary, exhorted Italians in a broadcast from Rome last night: "Resist, resist, resist. This is the order of the day for all Italians."

He told the Italian people the situation is grave and threatened them with severe penalties if they fail to resist and die in battle, if necessary, or at work.

"For two years," said Scorza, "Italy's fleet has dominated the Mediterranean against the most powerful fleet in the world. Italy's air fleets have dominated the skies against the riches of the most powerful industries of the world.

"To-day it is we who are obliged to defend ourselves, and to defend ourselves on our own soil. Should we despair for this any more than the enemy despaired when his life consisted chiefly of living in underground shelters, when the Japanese hit him out of the Pacific, when his fleet had to sail under Canadian escort?

"This is a war of religion, institutions and bread. Italy is defending her Catholic faith. Italy is defending her traditional and modern institutions.

"The Italians know that this is a war of distributive justice, and therefore a war for bread. Italy is battling desperately because she wants to save herself."

July 20 1943

1,000 Tons of Bombs Rained on Rome

A thousand tons of high explosive bombs were rained down on Rome in yesterday's daylight raid, the first ever made on the Italian capital. It is understood that up to 500 bombers took part.

The attack, the heaviest yet launched on any objective in the whole Mediterranean theatre of war, lasted two and a half hours and was carried out in 10 waves.

It was an all-American assault by Fortresses and medium bombers from the North-West African Command and by Liberators from the Middle East. The Liberators alone dropped 350 tons of bombs. It may be reliably assumed that at least double this load was carried by the North-West African aircraft.

Pilots returning from the attack reported vast damage in the railway marshalling yards – one of the main objectives.

Other targets, on which 4,000lb bombs were dropped, were Rome's three airfields, munitions factories and Government buildings, including the Ministry of War.

July 26 1943

Mussolini Resigns

MUSSOLINI, FASCIST DICTATOR OF ITALY FOR 21 YEARS, HAS RESIGNED. KING VICTOR EMMANUEL HAS ASSUMED COMMAND OF THE ITALIAN ARMED FORCES WITH ANTI-FASCIST MARSHAL BADOGLIO AS HIS PRIME MINISTER AND CHIEF OF GOVERNMENT.

This dramatic news, coming at a time when Italian forces in Sicily are surrendering in thousands, was contained in the following announcement broadcast by Rome radio at 10.45 last night:

"King Victor Emmanuel has accepted the resignation from the post of Chief of Government, Prime Minister and Secretary of State of his Excellency Cavaliere Benito Mussolini.

"The King has appointed as Chief of the Government, Prime Minister and Secretary of State his Excellency Marshal Pietro Badoglio."

Immediately afterwards the announcer read out a proclamation by the King of Italy. This stated:

"Italians, from to-day I assume the command of all the armed forces. In this solemn hour of grave anxiety which has occurred in the destinies of our country, each one must return to his post of duty, faith and battle. No deviation must be tolerated, no recriminations can be admitted.

"Every Italian must stand firm in face of the grave danger which has beset the sacred soil of the Fatherland.

"Italy through the valour of her troops and the determination of her civilian population will find in the respect of her old institutions, which have always ensured her progress, the way of recovery.

"Italians, more than ever before I am indissolubly united with you by the unshakable faith in the immortality of the Fatherland."

At an early hour to-day there was no indication of the whereabouts of Mussolini. Nor was there any indication of his present status.

The resignation of Mussolini, who will be 60 on Thursday, came six days after his secret meeting with Hitler at Verona in Northern Italy, a week ago to-day – the day Rome was bombed.

His resignation also followed within 10 days of the joint broadcast appeal by President Roosevelt and Mr Churchill to the Italian people. That call to the Italians declared that the sole hope for their survival lay in honourable capitulation to the overwhelming power of the military forces of the United Nations.

Throughout, the message laid the responsibility for war on the shoulders of Mussolini and the Fascist party, and confronted Italians with the choice between dying for Hitler and Mussolini or living for Italy and civilisation.

August 18 1943

ALL AXIS RESISTANCE IN SICILY ENDS

From Ronald Legge
Allied HQ, North Africa

THE whole of Sicily, bastion of Hitler's "European Fortress," is in Allied hands after a campaign of 39 days.

A special communiqué issued here to-night stated:

American troops captured Messina early this morning.

Some artillery fire is being directed on the city from the Italian mainland.

This was followed a few minutes later by the following official announcement:

"The Eighth British Army and the Seventh American Army have joined forces in Messina and all organised resistance has ceased on the island. The prisoners captured by the two armies have not yet been all counted, nor has all the enemy material which fell into our hands been ascertained."

The Eighth Army forces, whose advance up the coast the Germans had tried to delay with demolitions on a scale hitherto unparalleled, were only a few miles south of the city when American advance troops, who met no opposition, were entering it.

To-night British and American long-range guns were already engaging the enemy coastal batteries shelling Messina.

The whole weight of the Allied air attack has now been turned on targets on the mainland from the toe of Italy to the Bay of Genoa in the north. Railways, roads, airfields, troop convoys and beaches opposite Messina are being subjected to a round-the-clock onslaught.

There are already indications that the enemy does not intend to hold the toe of Italy. British warships, which are delivering widespread "softening up" bombardments along the coast on both sides of the Messina Straits, report that the Germans are already blowing up buildings and bridges at strategic points.

The waterfront at Messina after Allied bombing

August 31 1943

Verity's Last Order: "Keep Going"

From Our Leeds Correspondent

TWO soldiers who were close to Capt. Hedley Verity, the England and Yorkshire bowler, when he was wounded in Sicily have given an account of the action. Capt. Verity has been reported wounded and missing.

The soldiers are Pte. Frank Breckson, Stockton-on-Tees, Co. Durham and Pte. Leslie Rouse, Lower Ralston, Kent.

It was in the first attack on the German position on the Plain of Catania. Capt. Verity's company were moving forward through a cornfield behind a creeping barrage. Machine-guns fired at them from three sides. Mortar fire began and incendiaries set the corn blazing. Some of the men were badly burned in rolling on the fires to put them out.

Capt. Verity was leading one platoon forward to take a farmhouse when he was hit in the chest. Still at the head of his men, he ordered: "Keep going. Get them out of that farmhouse and get me into it."

The last seen of Capt. Verity was when he was being helped along by his batman. The company afterwards had to withdraw.

September 10 1943

LANDINGS AT NAPLES BIGGEST OF WAR

LATEST reports from Italy last night gave the following accounts of the situation:

At Naples, where progress was officially described as "satisfactory," thousands of Allied troops, with tanks, guns, transport and stores, are being landed to reinforce the assault force which went ashore at four a.m. yesterday and won a bridgehead from the German defenders.

Fighting has broken out between German and Italian troops in many parts of Central and Northern Italy. In the Balkans and elsewhere the Italian occupying forces are being disarmed.

Genoa, Verona and Brescia, in North Italy, are in German hands, but the Italians hold Venice, Milan and Turin, and are preparing to defend them against imminent Nazi attacks.

A British fleet is reported to be operating off Genoa, while a powerful Allied squadron is said to have been sighted in the Adriatic.

Germans have closed the French-Swiss and German-Italian frontiers.

The Naples operation, in which many Germans have already been taken prisoner, was described at Allied HQ as the biggest yet launched by the Anglo-American forces. After flying over the Fleet a Spitfire pilot said: "The whole area of approximately 1,000 square miles is swarming with Allied invasion shipping."

September 9 1943

BIG ALLIED LANDINGS IN ITALY

ALLIED TROOPS WERE AT 3 A.M. TO-DAY REPORTED TO BE LANDING ALONG THE WHOLE WEST COAST OF ITALY AND IN SARDINIA.

Tunis radio named landing points as north and south of Rome. Stockholm messages stated that further landings were taking place at Naples, Genoa and near Pisa, north of Leghorn.

Pisa lies 80 miles south of the Po line, which the Germans are reported to be holding in strength.

Another report from Stockholm stated that the Italian garrison in Corsica had overpowered the German forces in the island and seized control.

This news followed the official announcement last evening that Italy had surrendered unconditionally to the Allies and that the "Cease fire" order, so far as Italians were concerned, was given at 5.30 BST last evening.

Late last night the German News Agency had reported all telephone communication between Rome and Berlin had been cut. Swiss reports the Italian flag had been lowered at the frontier post at Ponte Chiasso.

According to Algiers radio the Italian Government has halted all ships, trains and road transport carrying German troops. No trains reached the Swiss frontier from Italy yesterday.

The cessation of hostilities was announced in a personal broadcast from Algiers by Gen. Eisenhower, who as recently as last Sunday flew to the Italian mainland to meet Marshal Badoglio, Prime Minister of Italy since Mussolini's fall on July 25.

An hour after Gen. Eisenhower's statement Badoglio told the Italian people by radio that an armistice had been asked for and granted.

In addition to ending resistance to the Allies, he said, the Italian armed forces would "oppose attacks from any other quarter," indicating that the armistice conditions, which are still secret, do not include a clause calling for immediate disarmament.

Troops push through Scafati

The first Allied convoy arriving at Naples

The Allied landings at Naples

September 13 1943

Nazis Claim to Have Freed Mussolini

THE Germans last night claimed to have freed Mussolini. A special announcement from Hitler's HQ, broadcast by Berlin radio at 9.35 p.m., stated:

"German parachutists and men of the security service and the armed SS to-day carried out an operation for the liberation of Mussolini, who had been imprisoned by the clique of traitors. The coup succeeded. The Duce is at liberty. The handing over of the Duce to the Anglo-Americans, agreed to by the Badoglio Government, has thus been frustrated."

Mussolini was reported to have been held by the Badoglio Government in various prisons, including islands off Italy's west coast. The most persistent report was that he was imprisoned in Fort Braschi, 27 miles north of Rome. Among the latest reports was an Ankara statement that he was suffering from a malignant growth.

The Berlin statement is the first definite news of Mussolini

since he resigned seven weeks ago, on July 25, after a stormy meeting of the Fascist Grand Council. It came 48 hours after Hitler, in a speech, told the German people, "I was, and am, happy to be able to call this great and true man my friend."

Hitler also described him as "the greatest son of the Italian land since the downfall of the ancient Roman Empire."

Should the report of Mussolini's liberation be true, Hitler might make propaganda capital out of it by placing him at the head of his puppet Fascist Government. It is not likely, however, that such a Government would muster any more Italian supporters with Mussolini than without him. Only those who are marked down as extreme Fascists would rally to it.

Three days ago, Berlin stated Mussolini was kidnapped on the steps of the Quirinal (the Italian royal palace) after his final interview with the King on July 24.

The Germans said he was approached by a colonel of the Carabinieri (police), who said: "I have orders to arrest you." Mussolini, it was added, resisted violently, but was dragged "by brute force" to an ambulance, where he was tied to a stretcher and driven away to the Carabinieri barracks.

Troops landing at Salerno

September 14 1943

ALLIED TANKS SMASH PANZERS AT SALERNO

THE first tank clashes of the Italian campaign have taken place in the Salerno area, south of Naples, where the Germans are putting up a bitter resistance to the Fifth Army, which is trying to break through their entrenched positions in the hills behind the city.

In counter-attacks to drive the Anglo-American forces back to the beaches – the Allies are reported to be holding a 50-mile front south from the Sorrento peninsula – Kessel-

ring, the German C-in-C, has thrown in formations of the 16th Panzer Division.

These attacks were met and smashed by Army gunners with the aid of salvoes from the Allied warships lying off the coast. The Germans have already lost more than 40 tanks in these engagements.

Allied armour, hurried ashore, has also been used to break up counter-attacks by enemy infantry.

The determined Nazi resistance is believed to be designed to keep open at all costs a corridor for the German troops retreating in face of the Eighth Army, which is now less than 100 miles to the south.

It is doubtful whether Gen. Montgomery's men will be able to maintain their present rate of advance of a mile an hour, an advance which has taken them beyond Crotone on the south coast and to south of Amantea on the west coast. They are again entering mountainous country where demolitions may delay them seriously.

Another threat to the Germans retreating from the Toe comes from the British forces in the Taranto-Brindisi area, who are pushing along the railway to Salerno, as well as north-west towards Altamura, which they were reported by Cairo radio last night to have captured.

September 22 1943

Premier's Promise of Mass Invasion

Mass invasion of the Continent from the west "at the right time" was promised by Mr Churchill today in a two-hour war review in the House of Commons. The second front, he said, existed potentially and was rapidly gathering weight. It had not yet been thrown into play. That time was coming – a main preoccupation with the enemy.

"The bloodiest fortunes of this war for Britain and the United States lie ahead," he prophesied. They would not shrink from the ordeal.

October 12 1943

MIDGET SUBMARINES HIT THE TIRPITZ

by Cdr Kenneth Edwards, RN, Naval Correspondent

THE Navy, using a new weapon, has broken the back of the German fleet. The great battleship Tirpitz, sister-ship of the ill-fated Bismarck, is seriously damaged.

The Tirpitz, by far the most important unit of the German fleet, is probably the most powerful battleship in the world. She will not be able to take part in operations for a considerable time.

The Navy has repeatedly tried to lure her to sea so that she could be brought to action, but the Tirpitz continued to skulk in a Norwegian fjord, so close to the mountains that she could not be attacked from the air.

So the Navy decided to attack her in harbour. For this operation midget submarines were used and picked crews selected for them.

These tiny craft were sent to seek out the main units of the German battle fleet, lying in the sheltered Alten Fjord, over 250 miles within the Arctic Circle, in the most northerly division of Norway.

October 13 1943

Oranges for All under 16

FOUR cargoes of oranges, totalling 28,000,000lb, have arrived from South Africa, Lord Woolton stated yesterday, adding: "And a pound is usually regarded as three oranges."

As this supply, he continued, was more than enough for the usual distribution to young children, and the oranges could not be stored, they would be offered to all children up to the age of 16.

An allocation would first be made at the rate of 2lb per head for young children with the RB2 ration book and 1lb per head for the RB1 ration book for older children. At the end of five days any oranges that might remain could be sold to customers free of restriction.

A deserted street in Salerno

A German submarine is bombed

October 22 1943

U-BOATS TRAPPED BY AIR SEARCHLIGHT WEAPON

TURNING night into day, the millions of candle power of the Leigh Light fitted to Coastal Command aircraft is revealed to-day as one of the outstanding inventions of the war.

It may well have done as much for shipping in its fight against the U-boat as the Burney paravane did against the mine in the last war and may prove to have provided the turning-point in the Battle of the Atlantic.

An Air Ministry statement discloses for the first time the story of its development and how it has enabled our coastal aircraft to "drown" the U-boats by night as well as by day.

Squadrons of planes equipped with these new searchlights have been in operation for more than a year and have achieved a high percentage of attacks to sightings in darkness.

These squadrons, which work in close co-operation with the Royal Navy, are named after Wing Cmdr H. de V. Leigh, OBE, DFC, who flew in the last war with the RNAS.

Many technical difficulties had to be overcome in fitting a powerful light in such a position as to be operationally effective without blinding the pilot or crew.

After practice attacks on a moored target had reached a certain standard of efficiency, an RAF experimental flight was brought up to squadron strength and taken over by Coastal Command.

On their first operational sortie the squadron, using their searchlight, sighted two U-boats, both of which were attacked.

Since that time more anti-submarine squadrons have been equipped with the "secret" weapon.

Before these aircraft appeared over the Atlantic, U-boats could submerge by day and surface with reasonable security by night to recharge their batteries. At that time attacks on them in darkness were necessarily haphazard and were practicable only on clear, moonlit nights.

In the intensive anti-submarine operations of the past year, the U-boats have been safe neither by day nor by night from the Leigh Light aircraft patrolling between dusk and dawn.

Many have been forced to cruise submerged by night and risk surface movement by day, when they hope to sight any patrolling aircraft and to crash-dive before it closes to attack.

October 25 1943

PENICILLIN IS SAVING THOUSANDS OF WOUNDED

From Douglas Williams
Algiers

RELATIVES of men serving in the Mediterranean theatre can rest assured that nothing has been left undone to care for the sick and wounded and that no expeditionary force has ever been so well protected medically. Compared with the last war the decrease of mortality is remarkable.

Of 400 operations performed recently in the battle zone after a beach assault fewer than one per cent proved fatal.

At base hospitals the mortality rate has fallen as low as one or two per 1,000, compared with from five to 10 per cent. in the last war.

The prevalence of malaria, especially in Sicily and Italy at this time of the year, has been the cause of considerable sickness, but the drug atebrine has reduced mortality in some areas by as much as 70 per cent.

Apart from this inevitable incidence of malaria, no field force has ever been healthier. Inoculation has produced immunity from such scourges as tetanus, typhoid and typhus.

Increasing use is being made of penicillin, which is producing astonishing results in curing bad wounds and severe cases of wound poisoning. A recent typical example was a badly wounded, delirious soldier who arrived by air in Algiers from Italy with symptoms of dangerous blood poisoning.

The penicillin team was immediately summoned by air from a place 300 miles away, and the man was about again within a fortnight.

November 8 1943

PATHFINDERS' CHIEF

It was officially announced by the Air Ministry last night that Air Cdre Donald Clifford Tyndall Bennett, CBE, DSO, is the commanding officer of the Pathfinder Force which guides RAF bombers to their targets in enemy territory. He was the first to wear the Pathfinders' special gilt eagle badge.

Flying in advance of the main force, the Pathfinders locate the target and identify it for the bombers by dropping large incendiaries and coloured flares. Some of them stay in the area to report on the raid.

Air Cdre Bennett, who is 33 and was born at Toowoomba, Queensland, Australia, won his DSO in 1941. He was captain of a bomber which was shot down attacking the German naval base at Trondheim, Norway.

With his observer he escaped into Sweden, evading German soldiers and quisling police, after an arduous journey across snow-clad mountains.

Before the war he was a well-known civil air pilot.

November 16 1943

Sir O. Mosley to be Freed

The Home Secretary, it was announced last night, has decided that on medical grounds it is necessary to suspend the Order of Detention, under Regulation 18B, made against Sir Oswald Mosley in May 1940, and to authorise his release in a few days, subject to certain security conditions.

Mr Morrison had before him reports on Sir Oswald Mosley's physical condition submitted by the prison medical authorities and by Lord Dawson of Penn and Dr Geoffrey Evans, who were brought into consultation.

The release of Lady Mosley, subject to restrictions, has also been authorised. She was detained in June 1940.

Sir Oswald married his second wife, a daughter of the second Lord Redesdale, and sister of Miss Unity Mitford, in Berlin in October 1936.

In December 1941, Sir Oswald was moved from Brixton Prison to a cell in Holloway Prison adjoining that of his wife. They had their own furniture.

November 25 1943

"Men of the Maquis" Defy Nazi Drive for Slaves

By Frida Stewart

"For your own safety – for the sake of France, of resistance – do not go, young men born in 1923!"

That was the impassioned warning uttered to the youth of France over the secret transmitter "Honneur et Patrie" when, a few weeks ago, it was known that Hitler was demanding the "1943" class to reinforce the 800,000 slaves he has already despatched from France to forced labour in Germany.

"Honneur et Patrie," speaking for France's resistance movement, told these young men not to present themselves at the medical examinations (for sick men, even consumptive and cardiac cases, are taken), but to escape from home as soon as possible and join the secret army of resistance.

This army now numbers some 200,000. Its members have chosen to live as "outlaws" in the woods and mountains.

Their formations are scattered all over France; some districts, such as Savoy, the Ardennes and Brittany, have become famous. It is Corrèze, with its deep valleys, its tangled copses, its small-holdings, its plateaux blessed with a mild climate, which beats all records so far.

A high official from Corrèze, responsible for executing Vichy's orders there, is said to have raised his hands to heaven in despair. "Not only do the youth of Corrèze refuse to respond to Laval's appeal," he lamented, "but they are reinforced by bands of young men from other districts and from the great towns, Paris, Toulouse, Bordeaux. They have formed camps of resistance against which we are helpless.

"All the population is in the conspiracy. It is difficult to find anyone, captures are practically impossible, and, in spite of German pressure, we cannot undertake to raise the number demanded . . . The whole 'class' has taken to the '*maquis*'!"

The term "*maquis*" has become proverbial. The word originally applied to the broom-covered cliffs of Corsica; it has now become a generic term for all the hiding-places – the grottoes, caverns, deserted huts, clearings – where France's youth in revolt is awaiting its liberation.

Berlin after heavy bombing by the Allies

France's "men of the *maquis*" are all defaulters from work in Germany. They consist of two main classes, apart from the simple truants who have not joined up but wander without papers from farm to farm hoping to escape capture "till things change."

Of the two main groups, the first, the Communists, or those recruited by the Communists, submit to an extremely severe discipline, intensive physical training, and military exercises as far as stocks of arms and munitions will allow. They are responsible for most of the "partisan" activity of bomb-throwing against German garrisons, captures of notorious Germanophiles, and executions of traitors prominent in the collaborationist Militia or Legion.

The second group are the military formations of young people of all political opinions training for the day of insurrection rather than present partisan warfare. They are led by former Army officers, usually Gaullist or Giraudist. They work hand-in-hand with the Communists, and though the Vichy Press does not accuse them of "terrorism," crop-burning or executions, they are none the less ready to use force when necessary to seize the food cards and supplies they need.

They capture police as hostages and rescue their comrades being taken off to captivity, holding up trains if need be.

New members are not taken lightly into the secret army. A

A typical story is that of Emile Delette, a young recruit who had left his camp at daybreak one morning for wood. The police had been watching the camp, reinforced by special brigades. Some 50 men fell on the boy, bound him, and one of them shot him in the stomach. They then opened fire on the camp huts but were forced to retire.

The incident made such a stir as soon as it was known in the district that next day 300 *gardes mobiles* were sent as reinforcements. They took Delette's body and buried it outside the village, hoping to avoid demonstrations; but the population from miles away assembled that afternoon, and a procession marched to lay a wreath at the village war memorial "in honour of Emile Delette, victim of Vichy's New Order."

It is still difficult and dangerous to be anti-German and anti-Vichy, for the Gestapo is pouring out money for its spies and stool-pigeons; it is easy for a well-paid spy to give away the employer who is helping his workers escape conscription, cheap for a Black Market profiteer to denounce the miller who gives his flour to the men of the *maquis* instead of the German Army. Yet, though a few traitors have been found to sell out, it is universally agreed that the people of France cannot be bought over.

November 24 1943

HITLER, RIBBENTROP AND GOEBBELS BOMBED OUT

MORE than 2,300 tons of high explosive and incendiaries were dropped on Berlin on Monday night in the greatest raid yet on the German capital; it was only just short of being the heaviest attack on any target in the history of air warfare.

Although cloud over Berlin made it impossible for RAF reconnaissance aircraft yesterday to photograph the damage, reports from neutral capitals last night made it clear that the havoc was on an unprecedented scale, particularly in the centre of the city.

Every hour there came fresh details of the damage:

Hitler's private house, adjoining the Reich Chancellery in the Wilhelmstrasse, burned to the ground. Goebbels's town house behind the American Embassy razed by fire. The Wilhelmstrasse Palace, formerly occupied by Hindenburg and latterly by Ribbentrop, in ruins.

The British Embassy was also destroyed. This also lies in the Wilhelmstrasse, which suffered more than any other street in the capital. It is virtually in ruins. Hundreds of four-engined bombers, Lancasters, Stirlings and Halifaxes, took part in the attack, which was concentrated into little more than 30 minutes. From the raid on Berlin (which was also attacked by Mosquitoes) and from minelaying operations 26 aircraft are missing.

The raid, one of the earliest yet carried out – the bombing began at eight o'clock – is regarded as one of the most successful ever organised by Bomber Command.

Unbroken heavy cloud lay along the whole route. This made it difficult for night fighters to intercept, and the enemy relied chiefly on anti-aircraft guns. Despite the weather conditions navigation and aiming was highly accurate, indicating the tremendous development that has taken place in area bombing by night.

The Pathfinder Force under Air Commodore Bennett was able to use its special technique to such purpose that we bombed Berlin "blind." The bombers followed the brightly lit "target indicators" these pathfinders dropped, although the target area itself was not seen.

young recruit has to swear an oath of fidelity and to renounce the sight of family and friends till after the liberation. He has to understand that the life is dangerous and un-rewarded by wage or even subsistence; he is threatened with death if he loses his weapon, for firearms are very precious; he must be ready to show a spirit of comradeship and sacrifice.

Hunger, cold, and the special police are the chief enemies. Humble folk and village gendarmes are very often sympathetic – witness the story of the policeman who went before day-break to warn the defaulters that they were to be arrested, and returned formally some hours later to find that the birds had taken his advice.

Or witness the conversation overheard near a Corrèze village between a gendarme and a wanted man who had been back by the main road to get some food from his father's house:

"*Mon vieux*, if you go by this road again I shall have to arrest you."

"OK, *gendarme*, count on me I don't want to upset you. I'll go back by the woods."

"At night?"

"At night."

The special police, Laval's men, are different; they are friends of Hitler and enemies of France and of all the men of the *maquis*. It is war to the knife between them, often with bloody encounters.

November 19 1943

THE LOSS OF LEROS

From L. Marsland Gander
Eastern Mediterranean Base

THE loss of Leros has taught another bitter lesson in air power. Though Leros had become practically an isolated strong-point behind the enemy lines, the decision to try to hold it was taken because of its strong natural defences.

It is a rocky switchback only 7½ miles long and at the narrowest point barely three-quarters of a mile wide. This wasp waist, roughly in the centre of the island, separates the two anchorages of Alinda and Gurna Bays.

Farther south, the fine harbour of Portolago Bay bites deep into the island, leaving another narrow neck of land only half a mile wide. The dangerous supply routes to Leros, hundreds of miles long, passed close to enemy airfields and were harried continually by the Luftwaffe.

Our ships had their best chance of slipping through at night, but had to endeavour to be under our own fighter umbrella by daylight.

Despite all the difficulties, we had, however, managed to land British troops of famous regiments in the island. These were additional to an Italian garrison, consisting of several thousand marines, soldiers and sailors.

Only about 2,000 of the Italians were first-line fighters, the remainder being technical and line of communication men. All the heights dominating the three main bays were commanded by Italian batteries, generally of 90 mm guns.

We had made determined efforts, chiefly by using HM warships as transports, to strengthen the anti-aircraft defences, but up to the time of invasion had only succeeded in landing some Bofors and a few heavier guns.

The garrison was, however, well equipped with automatic arms of all kinds, and the main defensive position, Mount Mereviglia, 600ft high, was studded with machine-gun nests.

Russian partisan women

November 26 1943

Even the Nazis won't talk to Haw Haw

From Our Special Correspondent
New York

THE woes of quislings who work for Goebbels as foreign language broadcasters are described in an article which has arrived here from Stockholm. It was written by Brita Bager, a young Swedish singer, who was known on the German radio as "the girl with the sex appeal voice."

Daughter of the former Swedish naval attaché in Berlin, she was a favourite of Hitler and other leading Nazis. Last month she threw up her job and returned to Stockholm.

"I have been a quisling broadcaster for Goebbels for two years," she writes. "Anyone who thinks this work is a bed of roses is sadly mistaken.

"Like crime, it does not pay. It means only hard work, long hours, for little money and ostracism even by Germans.

"Many of these radio quislings," states Bager, "are adventurers and people with whom the criminal law in their native land has some little score to settle. Others are purely and simply traitors. All serve Germany for ridiculously low pay.

"The most prominent, William Joyce [Lord Haw-Haw] received 3,000 marks monthly, which would be equivalent to £300 if it bought anything but bad and mediocre lodgings. But it does not, so the unspendable surplus is just paper.

"Eastern peoples, such as Syrians, Persians, Turks and others, are the best paid, averaging 2,000 marks.

"Americans were until recently in the same salary bracket, but Goebbels has evidently given up hope of sowing trouble in the United States. Therefore, the pay of American employees is being reduced.

"Many radio quislings are home-sick. They cannot go home, and that is their tragedy. Haw-Haw is a good example of this homesickness. 'I long for England – yes, with every fibre of my soul,' he said to me.

"Haw-Haw has not much of an existence in Germany. With his second wife he inhabits a poorly furnished two-room flat. His only luxury seems to be to drink occasionally in Goebbels's Press Club in the Leipzigerplatz, where the regular correspondents leave him strictly alone, detesting the sight of him.

"Germans don't like him any better. They appreciate his work, but cannot forget he is English, and desire no truck with him."

William Joyce

December 3 1943

Call-up for the Pits by Ballot

MR Bevin, Minister of Labour, announced in the House of Commons to-day that compulsory recruitment of men for the pits will begin shortly. They will be directed to such work by ballot. The selection will be made from men born on or after Jan. 1 1918.

November 30 1943

WOMEN TORTURED AND FLOGGED TO DEATH

IN 11 occupied countries Germans and Japanese have reduced women to the level of slaves. Reports of deliberate cruelties in this wave of terror have been collected by representatives of the Allied Governments in London, and are issued to-day by the Inter-Allied Information Committee in a pamphlet entitled "Women Under Axis Rule."

The material has been carefully selected from a mass of evidence based upon eye-witness accounts, official pronouncements from enemy-controlled newspapers and broadcasts, and similar sources.

It proves that the brutality is not just the temporary excess of an invading army, but a deliberate policy for more settled conditions of long-term occupation.

The Gestapo never hesitates to use its expert torturers in an effort to make women incriminate their men-folk.

Girls in Jugoslavia have been flogged to death and otherwise tortured to force them to reveal the secrets of the guerrillas. Many Norwegian women have died in the concentration camps.

Trifling offences are made the excuse for imprisonment and deportation to forced labour. Hundreds of women of occupied countries have been shot for "sabotage." Thousands more are dying daily in the concentration camps.

In Poland young girls are regularly abducted and sent to brothels for soldiers. These abductions are not isolated incidents, but are clearly the systematic policy of the German authorities.

When the Germans do not need women for slave labour, they watch them die. Women in Greece, trudging for miles with their starving children, plead with the Germans for food. They are told, "Even if half of you die, there will still be too many of you left."

Thousands and thousands of women are at present in concentration camps and prisons in France because of their resistance.

A woman who recently arrived in England gives the following particulars about a concentration camp near Paris where she was detained: "There were 300 of us in some old hutments, 48 in a room intended for 20. The daily fare consisted of two boiled potatoes. Stale bread was issued every four days. Two hundred detainees died from dysentery in one single night."

There have been many instances in which women have died in a concentration camp in Norway. The only official intimation ever given to their relatives is that they have died of "heart failure" or "natural causes."

Here is a case which may give an idea of the mental tortures which are inflicted on Polish women.

The famous Polish ski-champion Marusarz was executed by the Germans in Kracow. His wife was sentenced to death, too, but she was not executed until a month later.

She underwent the following torture: Every morning a Gestapo officer would come into her cell and she was made to believe that they were come to fetch her to execution. For 30 days this scene was repeated, and every time the German officer informed her that the execution had been postponed to the next day.

Finally, on the 30th day she was hanged.

To give some glimpse of the attitude of a typical German soldier towards the citizens of occupied Soviet territories there is the diary of Friedrich Schmidt, secretary of the 626th Group of the Secret Field Police, attached to the 1st German Tank Army. Schmidt's diary relates to his stay in the village of Budennovskaya, near Mariupol, in the Stalino region, and states:

Feb 25: Yekaterina-Skoroyedova, a Communist, expressed disapproval of Russians who collaborate with us. She was shot at noon. Four pretty 18-year-old girl students, young Communists, were brought to me. They had crossed over the ice from Yelsk. I beat them up heavily.

They were followed by six young men and a girl . . . Neither persuasion nor whipping was of any use.

March 9: At 10 a.m. two more girls and six young fellows were brought to me . . . I had to do some ruthless flogging. Then the mass executions began. Yesterday we shot five: to-day 33 . . . I cannot eat . . . I must admit that the Bolshevik youth behave heroically. Some of them, particularly the girls, did not shed a tear when we shot them. That is valour indeed. They were ordered to undress (we sell their clothing).

Heaven help me if I am caught here. I no longer feel safe in the village.

I ordered 17-years-old Lyudmila Chukanoca to be shot. I feel I must kill the young ones.

April 10: Flogged a few more girls and boys for not reporting for registration. Among them was the daughter of the Elder.

April 17: I flogged three men and an elderly woman. Yes, I beat an elderly woman because she confessed to having been a nurse.

April 17: I flogged two girls right to my apartment, whipping their bare backs.

April 18: A rainy, dreary day. I called in a lot of girls who had voiced their disapproval of the secret field police and flogged them.

These excerpts reveal both the amazing courage of the Soviet people in their hour of agony and the sheer brutality of the German invader.

President Roosevelt with Marshal Chiang Kai-shek and his wife

December 2 1943

Churchill, Roosevelt and Chiang Meet in North Africa

It is officially announced from Cairo that Mr Churchill, President Roosevelt and Marshal Chiang Kai-shek have held a five-day conference "somewhere in North Africa."

War moves in the Far East were discussed and a declaration was issued that Manchuria and Formosa would be restored to China and Korea made an independent State, and that Japan would be stripped of all the Pacific isles she has occupied or seized since 1914.

British, American and Chinese Chiefs of Staff and their advisers conferred, and it is understood that, in addition to the war in the Far East, operations in the Mediterranean and elsewhere in Europe were discussed.

The conference was an historic encounter. Although Mr Roosevelt and Mr Churchill have met seven times since the war – the first in 1941 when the Atlantic Charter was born – it was their first meeting with Marshal Chiang.

The talks ended on Friday. The Prime Minister and President left for unrevealed destinations.

The outcome of the North Africa conference, announced in a special communiqué issued at 12.30 a.m. to-day, was the drawing up of a Pacific Charter. The text of the communiqué

"The several military missions have agreed on future military operations against Japan.

"The three great Allies expressed their resolve to bring unrelenting pressure against their brutal enemies by sea, land and air. This pressure is already rising.

"The three great Allies are fighting this war to restrain and punish the aggression of Japan. They covet no gain for themselves and have no thought of territorial expansion.

"It is their purpose that Japan shall be stripped of all the islands in the Pacific which she has seized or occupied since the beginning of the First World War in 1914, and that all the territories Japan has stolen from the Chinese, such as Manchuria, Formosa and the Pescadores, shall be restored to the Republic of China.

"Japan will also be expelled from all other territories which she has taken by violence and greed.

"The aforesaid three Great Powers, mindful of the enslavement of the people of Korea, are determined that in due course Korea shall become free and independent.

"With these objectives in view the three Allies, in harmony with those of the United Nations at war with Japan, will continue to persevere in the serious and prolonged operations necessary to procure the unconditional surrender of Japan."

HMS *Duke of York* engaging the *Scharnhorst*

December 28 1943

SCHARNHORST SUNK

JUST before midnight last night the Admiralty issued a brief communiqué on the naval action which resulted in the sinking of the German battleship Scharnhorst (26,000 tons) while engaged on an attack on a Russia-bound convoy. This stated:

"It is not yet possible to give a detailed account of the action in which the German battleship Scharnhorst was sunk. It can, however, be stated that the convoy was unmolested and only minor damage was sustained by two of HM ships."

The Scharnhorst, almost the last effective big ship remaining to the Germans, was sent to the bottom after a battle fought in the Arctic Sea in the darkness of the Arctic day.

She was engaged by units of the Home Fleet under Adml Sir Bruce Fraser and was sunk on Sunday off Cape North, the most northerly point of Norway.

Details of the engagement will be made available when the exigencies of naval operations permit. The first news of her destruction was the following terse communiqué from the Admiralty late on Sunday night:

"This afternoon the German battleship Scharnhorst was brought to action by units of the Home Fleet, under the command of Adml Sir Bruce Fraser, which were covering a North Russian convoy. Scharnhorst was sunk this evening off the North Cape."

According to the version of events furnished by the Germans, the Allied convoy was escorted only by destroyers and cruisers when the Scharnhorst went in to attack.

Thereafter, by what the Germans describe as a surprise move not discerned in bad visibility, "heavy forces" of the Royal Navy came into action. This suggests that a battleship of the King George V class came within range with 14-inch guns against the Germans' 11-inch.

It appears that the Home Fleet units contrived to cut off the enemy's escape, for the German statement says that she was "encircled." She was sunk, the Germans say, at 7.30 p.m. after an engagement lasting in all for eight hours.

With the Scharnhorst at the sea bottom, it will be possible to release some of the heavier units of the Home Fleet for service in other seas, and this may have an important bearing on naval operations against Japan.

Survivors of the *Scharnhorst* under guard in HMS *Duke of York*

December 23 1943

Radio Ban on P. G. Wodehouse

A ban has been placed by the BBC on the revival of certain musical comedies the lyrics of which were written by P. G. Wodehouse, who since the war has broadcast from Germany.

Mr Leslie Henson, who has been broadcasting extracts from musical comedies, was forbidden to revive Mr Wodehouse's work in "Kissing Time," "The Cabaret Girl" and other pieces.

Mr Henson said to a reporter yesterday: "I think it is a little unfair. There is very great controversy about him, and my opinion is that under the English law no man is guilty until he is proved so.

"We shall not know the facts until 'Plum' Wodehouse is released from Germany. I shall stand up for my old friend until something is proved against him."

The BBC comment on the position was: "At present we are not broadcasting any of this author's works because of his broadcasts for the enemy."

December 30 1943

Mr Churchill's Nurse a Miner's Daughter

Mr Churchill is being nursed back to convalescence by the daughter of a colliery pitman whose home is in Chopwell Court, County Durham.

She is Sister Betty Clarke, of Queen Alexandra's Imperial Military Nursing Service. In an airmail letter to her mother, Mrs Mary Clarke, she wrote:

"Darling Mummy – Exciting news for you. I am nursing the Prime Minister. Isn't it an honour!

"Another sister and myself were chosen, and set forth at 4 a.m. last Sunday to an unknown destination. Quite the sort of thing that happens in a story book, and not to two rather ordinary sisters.

"We had a wonderful air trip. I sat in the cockpit, and at one period tried to navigate the plane.

"The Prime Minister is very much better, I am glad to say, and although we share the nursing duties there is not very much to do for him.

"It has been a wonderful experience living among so many distinguished people.

"We want for nothing. The countryside is lovely. Hedges of cacti and wild flowers."

December 28 1943

SIR A. TEDDER DEPUTY TO EISENHOWER

THE appointment of Air Chief Marshal Tedder to be Deputy Supreme Commander under Gen. Eisenhower for the British and American Expeditionary Force was announced last night.

It is notable for the fact that for the first time it places an airman in what is the second highest place in the Allied Command in the field, having control over forces not only from his own Service but from the Army and Navy.

The three men who have

co-operated so effectively in the operations in Mediterranean theatres of war are thus given the leading roles in the coming offensive, with Gen. Sir Bernard Montgomery as C-in-C of the British group of Armies under Gen. Eisenhower.

Air Chief Marshal Sir Arthur Tedder

December 31 1943

Past and Future

IN the last days of the dying year Germany has suffered a grim series of disasters fraught with evil consequences in the year to come. The ironical fate which derides the Nazi oracles made GOEBBELS boast of success in holding the "military positions which the German armed forces have gained during their great offensives" at the very moment when the Russians, attacking on a 190-mile front, have advanced farther west than ever and threaten to destroy the whole German defence system south of the Pripet Marshes. MANSTEIN and HOTH, the German generals entrusted by the High Command with the mass of its armoured forces to recover Kiev and restore the communications of the southern front, have been flung back with enormous loss. Their counter-offensive has finally failed.

Winter has not yet hardened the ground in the Ukraine. The Russian advance is still hampered by mud and unfrozen streams; yet it progresses in greater strength than ever. Small hope remains to Germany that any part of the Dnieper line will be held much longer. Retreat to the line of the Bug and on to the Dniester in the grip of frost looms as the next manoeuvre. The indispensable oilfields of Rumania and that softest spot in the German organism, the Danube Valley, are not far beyond. Germany must look forward to keeping the anniversary of the Stalingrad surrender in the gloomy fear of worse and, irreparable losses.

Stern lessons
This time last year, though MANSTEIN had failed to extricate the Stalingrad army by a counter-offensive, the Russians were still far to the east of Rostov and the Donetz, and they had not recovered the Caucasus. Those positions essential "for the security of the Reich," as GOEBBELS puts it – the cornfields and the mines of the Ukraine – were being vigorously exploited and strongly held. Germany will get neither food nor metals thence next year for the weary troops and dwindling munitions of the Reichswehr.

When 1943 began Axis armies were defending Tunisia. Now the Axis has been expelled from Africa, its Italian section

has collapsed and the Reichswehr has to provide many divisions for Italy and the Balkans lest the war should cross the frontier of the Fatherland. Along the Atlantic coast from the Arctic circle to Spain and from Spain along the Mediterranean to Turkey, the diminishing strength and reserves of the Wehrmacht are strained to meet imminent possibilities of invasion from many points. Germany has waged three wars for conquest without suffering war damage. All that has changed. The last "very heavy attack" on Berlin enforces the stern lesson of 1943 that the militarism which sought to dominate the world by air-power will perish by air-power.

Allied air bombardment of German industrial and military centres has been greatly increased this year with cumulative effect. Yet it is still far below the ultimate potential. The capacity of Germany to make war has already been reduced by an important fraction as the factories of city after city have been destroyed and communications broken. Russian recognition of the value of this air offensive to their battle is unstinted. It has played an important part in the Allied successes on the Mediterranean front and at sea. Its effects will have great influence on the vaster campaigns before us.

To take but one example already plain, it has weakened the Luftwaffe beyond German capacity of replacement, to say nothing of reinforcement. Thus the Allies open the new campaigns with the great advantages that air superiority brings.

Wasting defensive
The end of 1943 quenches the last German hope that U-boat and aircraft and commerce destroyer might avail to deprive the Allies of practical command of the sea. When the year began HITLER's revival of the old faith in the submarine promised an indefinite prolongation of the war by limiting the Allied capacity to deploy their forces. Now multiplication of escort vessels and extended use of aircraft over the ocean have put the U-boats on the defensive, and a wasting defensive at that. The Scharnhorst's fate and the failure of the German destroyers in the Bay of Biscay exhibit the incapacity of Germany to take effective action at sea.

From the successes of the past year we may conclude that nothing but unimaginable blunders in strategy or inconceivable failures of national determination could prevent the victory of the Allies. The unity of their operations and of the several arms engaged will speed the triumph.

Allied vehicles being landed on the Normandy beaches

AFTER a generally better year for the Allies in 1943, raising hopes of victory in Europe in 1944, the New Year disappointed. There was, after all, patently plenty of fight left in the Germans and recognition of this disconcerting truth came hard on Britain, dashing hopes of an easier life. Belief that the enemy was all but beaten had turned out, in the haunting wartime phrase, to be "wishful thinking," akin to counting the chickens, a lesson rubbed into Londoners, subjected to the "Little Blitz" from January to April, the heaviest series of raids since the Blitz of 1941. Even the Allied leaders' optimistic agreement at Teheran to launch "Overlord," the invasion of Normandy in May (in the event, in June) and conduct separate landings in the south of France looked somewhat premature; as did discussion on how to treat Germany after surrender.

News from Italy was especially disturbing. Anguished fighting on the Anzio beachhead and stubborn German defence of the battered Benedictine Abbey atop the brooding presence of Monte Cassino retarded the Allied advance. Retrospectively, its merciless bombardment, as with the later destruction of Dresden, seemed questionable. But progress was baulked by the stiffly defended Gustav Line and it was thought – erroneously as it turned out – that reducing the monastery stronghold (Indian and New Zealand troops had failed to take it) would ease the plight of troops pinned down at Anzio. Finally, in mid-May, Polish troops occupied the Abbey ruins.

On June 6, at long last, Stalin could smile. With the invasion of Normandy he had got, not the Torch invasion of North Africa, nor the landings in Sicily and Italy, but the true Second Front for which he had called so long and consistently. At home spirits soared, but Hitler, just when in the popular imagination he was supposed to be on the run, produced a strong card. Within a week of the landings, V-1 flying bombs, the "doodlebugs" or "buzzbombs", began nose-diving into London and village, town, hamlet and farmyard between the coast and the capital.

And there was worse to follow. Hitler, surviving attempted assassination in July, unleashed the full fury of his revenge weapons. In September, shortly after an official announcement that the doodlebug Battle of London was over, V-2 rockets, "flying gas mains," in public imagination until their identity was admitted, began their unheralded and indiscriminate barrage.

Nor was the news good from Burma, though, understandably, it was submerged by the doorstep interest of D-Day and home front hardships. Mountbatten's land forces under Slim were embattled with a Japanese offensive on the borders of India where sieges at Kohima, on the road linking Imphal with the 14th Army's base at Dimapur, and Imphal led to bitter hand to hand fighting. It was a testing start for the Supremo and his 14th Army commander, that, after they had proclaimed a march on Delhi in the early spring, the Japanese broke into India on the Imphal plain. But their preparation paid later dividends and, much assisted by the RAF (particularly its Hurricane squadrons), Slim's troops defeated Mutagachi's 15th Army. Mountbatten,

practising his own preaching of tireless pep-talk jungle visits ("We are not going to quit fighting when the monsoon comes, like drawing stumps at a cricket match when the rain comes"), astonished the Japanese. Supported by monsoon-defying air operations, Slim, advancing in the seasonal rains, pursued them eastward. As Burma dried, the road to Mandalay and on to Rangoon beckoned.

News was better from Russia and the Pacific, though, for all the headlines and reports of heavy fighting, both theatres yielded precedence in public interest to campaigns nearer home. The scale of war in Russia and the Pacific took some imagining and it was only after victory that how much had been achieved, and at how great a cost, could be absorbed and the better understood. The tally of Russian successes, paid for so massively in blood and resources, spells out the immensity of their campaigns – Leningrad relieved in January, Sebastopol and the Crimea recovered in May, Belorussia recovered and a Polish Committee of National Liberation established at Lublin in July, preceding the August to October Warsaw rising against the German occupiers. From the Pacific, too, reports, less meaningful than war closer at hand, reflected gradual American progress as, making costly beach assaults, they edged towards Japan. After opening an assault on the Marshall Islands, advancing through Dutch New Guinea, invading Saipan and recovering Guam in October, they landed in the Philippines, fought the Battle of Leyte Gulf and in November began the systematic bombing of Japan.

As much depended in the Pacific on air-assured supremacy at sea as in the Atlantic battle with U-boats where wearying long-range operations by RAF Coastal Command's Catalina and Sunderland flying-boats and land-based Liberators and Wellingtons obtained the edge and lessened the peril of losing men, arms, food and fuel that would equip and nourish Overlord. But, as late as November – following the September airborne setback at Arnhem and preceding that other sharp reminder not to underestimate enemy resilience, the shock December counter-offensive in the Ardennes – one lurking menace to the merchantmen had to be eliminated. Out of action for six months after Royal Navy midget submarines damaged her in Trondjhem Fjord, the battleship Tirpitz was yet again a threat. Bomber Command's Dambuster squadron, 617 (each Lancaster armed with a Barnes Wallis 12,000lb bomb), was briefed to eliminate her. And it did.

Soviet troops entering Lvov following their thrust (below) across the border towards the Lvov-Odessa railway

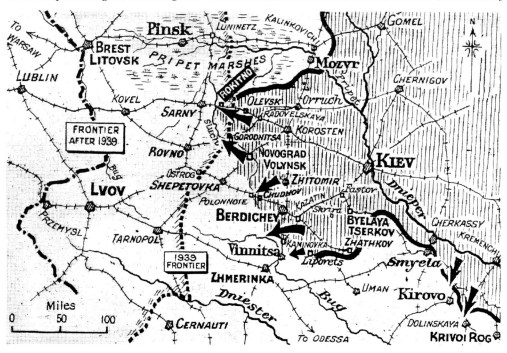

January 7 1944

RED ARMY 15 MILES INTO POLAND

THE first Moscow official indication that the Red Army had crossed the former frontier of Poland was given in last night's Soviet communiqué.

The communiqué reported the capture of the town and railway station of Rokitno, 15 miles on the Polish side of the border. It is 27 miles east of the important junction of Sarny, on the Kiev-Warsaw railway.

Rokitno is described as a district centre in the region of Rovno. The town of Rovno is a big German base 30 miles on the western side of the border.

Gen. Vatutin's First Ukrainian Army captured more than 80 places on this front. They included Gorodnitsa, south of Rokitno and about a mile to the eastern side of the border.

Another place captured was Lipovets railway station, 20 miles east of Vinnitsa and 30 miles from the Lvov-Odessa railway, the main supply line for the German armies in the Dnieper Bend. It is only 12 miles from an important line running from Kirovograd in the Bend through Vinnitsa and Zhmerinka.

At Novyi-Miropol and Chudov – an important highroad junction – the Russians are approaching the railway running from Berdichev to Brest-Litovsk, the big junction in 1939 Poland.

January 8 1944

NEW GLOSTER FIGHTER IS JET PROPELLED

By Air Cdre Howard-Williams, Air Correspondent

WITHIN 24 hours of the announcement that Britain had successfully developed a revolutionary jet-propelled propellerless 'plane, another secret of the RAF was disclosed last night.

This is that we have a new fighter, the Gloster, and it is propelled by the new jet device. Our latest aircraft promises great things.

This revelation was made by Mr E. Colston Shepherd, the recently appointed Secretary-General of the Air League. Describing the invention, he stated:

"The Italians talked about their jet 'plane as making a deep hum on the ground and a high-pitched whine or whistle in flight. Some of you probably know what our Gloster fighter sounds like.

"One of these days the enemy will know, too; until then we cannot say much more about its performance. But you can be sure that the jet is going to make a huge difference to flying."

The Gloster, latest product of the Gloster Company, remains on the secret list. Details of construction and performance cannot be given.

I can, however, say that it is a single-engined aircraft, the main features of which offer a very considerable advance on anything yet produced. It takes off in a comparatively short run and has an exceptionally good climb. Main features of jet propelled aircraft are:

No propellers – they are pushed forward by the jet flow;

Less overhaul head resistance, partly because of the absence of propeller and partly because of the simpler engine design;

Higher speed and power for the same weight;

Appreciably greater rate of climb;

Simpler engine control;

Less ground clearance necessary because of the absence of a propeller; this enables a shorter and stronger undercarriage to be used;

Greater overall efficiency.

Speeds of over 500 m.p.h. had been anticipated by Germany and Italy for experimental jet-propelled aircraft. This speed would give a very appreciable advance on any fighter in service in the air forces, of the world to-day.

As I wrote yesterday, some time must elapse before this new type of engine can be applied commercially.

Group Capt. Frank Whittle, inventor of Britain's jet-propelled 'plane, who is 36, said in a broadcast last night that he found "this sudden publicity very embarrassing." He had been devoting himself to the idea of jet propulsion for a long time.

It first occurred to him when he was an RAF cadet at Cranwell, and he paid further attention to it when he was taking an instructor's course about 18 months later. A great many people besides himself had contributed to the work. He believed there was a great future for this type of aircraft.

January 4 1944

MONTGOMERY'S FAREWELL TO HIS MEN

"THERE can be no possible doubt that the end of this war is in sight. In bringing about this wonderful fact the Eighth Army has played a very notable part."

These words were spoken by Gen. Montgomery today in taking leave of his troops before returning to England. Speaking from the stage of the battered Opera House in a town in South-East Italy, he said he found the occasion the most moving and difficult he had ever experienced.

In a speech lasting 30 minutes he addressed 2,000 officers and men, many of whom had been with him from El Alamein to the Sangro.

Gen. Montgomery said:

"It is not easy for me to say goodbye to this army, but we ought to regard to-day as a time for rejoicing and laughter and not as a time for sorrow. I have probably been long enough with this army. It is high time I moved on and somebody else came and gave you new ideas and new inspirations.

"I remember well August last year when I came to join the Eighth. In those days things were not good. Some people might say they were very bad.

"I was told the Eighth was in imminent danger of being attacked by Rommel, and that at all costs it was to be preserved and withdrawn down the Alexandria-Cairo road. Plans were actually being worked out to move Army Headquarters back to Cairo.

"It was clear the Army required a firm lead. The Eighth required somebody to say to it: 'If we are attacked we will fight where we stand – we will fight hard.' And once that had been said there was no further trouble.

"One of my corps commanders said to me: 'I'm awfully glad you've come, but you have a most difficult job. No Army commander has lasted here more than three or four months,' he added.

"I was determined I would last longer than that. You know what happened. Everything was swept before us, and the Eighth from that time to this day has never looked back."

January 12 1944

EXECUTION OF CIANO

From Our Special Correspondent Somewhere in Europe

COUNT Ciano, 40, former Italian Foreign Minister and Mussolini's son-in-law, and four other Fascist ex-leaders were executed this morning for treason, announced Rome Radio to-night.

The harbour at Anzio

January 24 1944

ALLIED SPEARHEADS NEAR ROME AIRPORT

THOUSANDS of British and American troops, their beachhead in the Nettuno area some 30 miles south of Rome secure, were last night thrusting swiftly eastwards to cut the key supply lines of the 100,000 German troops on the Garigliano front.

They were already several miles inland from the points where they landed early on Saturday, and had gained strategic heights. A number of coastal towns had been occupied and our forces were astride the southern end of a road leading to Rome.

Reinforcements in men and materials continued to pour in as an armada of landing craft with powerful naval and air cover kept up a shuttle service to the beachhead area.

Our forward troops were beginning to meet German patrols and increased artillery opposition, but there was still no news of the expected enemy counter-attack.

Everything goes well on the bridgehead south of Rome, *writes Reynolds Packard, with the landing forces.* All the objectives assigned to the landing forces on the first day are safely in our hands.

They include the coastal end of the highway to Rome. We can now truly say we are on the road to Rome.

The surprise achieved can best be judged by the fact that the first day's objectives were taken in four hours. They included several towns along the coast, the largest of which cost us only two casualties.

The Germans were obviously taken completely by surprise. They could have only found out what was going on as we started to move in on the beaches.

Certainly when I waded ashore from a small landing craft at four o'clock under the light of a jaundiced moon there was little opposition worthy of the name.

As I got on the beach I turned to right and then to left and saw a heartening sight – long lines of invasion craft moving in towards the beaches for miles, all of them loaded with guns, tanks, lorries and light vehicles.

My heart leapt, and I think the heart of every man on the beaches was stirred by that sight and the knowledge that the first, the vital move, was going to be a complete success.

There was no delay. Once the troops landed they fanned out to the north and south, striking like lightning towards their objectives.

One column swung inland. On them depended much. They had to seize some strategic hills and hold them against all possible attacks.

Remembering how Kesselring had made use of the high ground round the beachhead at Salerno we all knew how much the success of this column meant to us.

Then came a signal back, *"Objective attained."*

And there was still no sign of any enemy counter-attack.

January 28 1944

GEN. ALEXANDER: "WENT LIKE A FIELD DAY"

GEN. Alexander, Allied C-in-C, Italy, after his visit to the British and American forces on the Anzio-Nettuno beachhead, south of Rome, said: "Everything is very encouraging. We have had a terrific start.

"We have gained the advantage of complete surprise. We have not only seized a local beachhead, but we have built up our forces. Everything is going wonderfully.

"The port of Anzio had been highly prepared for demolition and the Germans were ready to touch it off. But they were so surprised they had no time to explode their demolitions. What damage exists in the port is largely due to its being knocked about by our own bombing.

"High praise is due to the Fifth Army and Gen. Mark Clark for the planning and the mounting of the operation. It went like a field day.

"The enemy had been drawn in to the main front just before the landings. The Third Panzer Grenadiers had been switched from the Eighth to the Fifth Army front. The 29th Division had just been brought down from the enemy's reserve and now it must go back. The Hermann Goering Division had been drawn in from Rome.

"The Germans had very little around Rome when the Allies landed. We were opposed by only a few troops on the front.

"They were so surprised by our landing that they did not even finish a drink and beefsteak waiting on a table in the German commander's house. We shot one German as he was getting on to a motorcycle in his pyjamas.

"I want to pay a special tribute to the Americans along the Rapido in the Cassino sector. They did a wonderful job in getting across the high, fast-flowing river and establishing two bridgeheads, although they later lost them.

"This action held down the German reserves, drawing them into the battle and thus facilitating the landings further up. We made the enemy lower his guard and then hit him on the chin. It was not quite a knockout but we rocked him badly.

"The Germans have bombed and hit one of our hospital ships off the beachhead. They are playing their old game of going for hospital ships, although the position of these is fully recognised under international law.

"The ship was well lit up. Fortunately, there were only a few casualties on board.

"He is the same old Hun. He will go for a hospital ship if he can. I suppose because he uses hospital ships for illegal purposes himself he thinks everyone else does."

Amphibious vehicles land troops and equipment at Anzio

A British soldier who has lost his foot on a mine is carried by captured German paratroopers

January 29 1944

Britain and US Indict Japanese Brutality

JAPANESE brutality to prisoners of war was exposed in British and United States official statements made public yesterday.

Sworn statements by American officers who escaped from their Japanese captors included an account of a six-day March of Death, during which prisoners taken in the Bataan peninsula of Luzon Island, in the Philippines, were murdered and tortured.

Mr Cordell Hull, United States Secretary of State, declared: "One would need to assemble all the demons and to consider all the fiendishness they embody to describe those who inflicted these unthinkable tortures."

The United States, he said, was gathering information to ensure that the Japanese war criminals would be punished.

In the House of Commons Mr Eden gave first-hand accounts of the torture of British and Indian prisoners, and disclosed that when a Japanese liner was torpedoed the crew battened down 1,800 prisoners and left them to drown. "Let the Japanese," he said, "reflect that the record of their military authorities in this war will not be forgotten."

The British attack at Carroceto, a key point in the Anzio beachhead

February 12 1944

BRITISH ATTACK IN ANZIO BEACHHEAD

BRITISH troops have returned to the attack in the Anzio beachhead south of Rome, and all messages from the front last night made it clear that a climax was near.

After a night of wild weather our troops advanced in a gale of wind in the battered area of Carroceto (Aprilia), 10 miles from the beaches, and were locked in a hand-to-hand battle.

Late last night the Fifth Army were reported to have pushed ahead slightly in fierce fighting in the area.

So close was this grapple with the enemy that the tremendous British artillery barrage that preceded the assault was stopped while the infantry fought with grenade and bayonet.

In this storm centre, which has changed hands several times, the Germans claimed earlier to have taken the railway station, outside the town. Gunter Weber, a Nazi front-line reporter, declared that the town itself had been captured and that Kesselring's forward troops had reached within some six miles of the ports of Anzio and Nettuno.

Salerno tactics were repeated by the Allied Command, who switched a big force of heavy bombers to smash five vital enemy road junctions within 10 miles of the outer defence lines of the beachhead.

A Nazi propaganda leaflet

Crossroads jammed with military traffic were cratered and blocked by tons of heavy bombs.

President Roosevelt, at his Press conference yesterday, described the situation as "very tense." The Allied forces, he said, still had air and sea superiority, and everybody was praying for good weather to ease the situation and enable the full weight of that superiority to be felt.

February 10 1944

The King And Queen Eat 1s Lunch At Pit

THE King and Queen yesterday sat down to lunch with 70 Yorkshire miners in the Elsecar Colliery canteen.

They were treated to the canteen's ordinary 1s menu of roast beef, sprouts, roast and boiled potatoes, golden pudding and coffee.

The Queen said to the men afterwards: "It is a long time since we have had a better meal." The King agreed.

The only difference made for the Royal visitors was that white linen tablecloths were used and there were jugs of free beer and mineral waters.

The lunch was in the middle of an all-day tour of West and South Yorkshire coalfields which the King made, it is understood, at his own suggestion, to study conditions at first hand.

With their Majesties at table was Mr A. E. Wilkinson, check-weighman. He said that the King, who discussed mining problems, "seemed a very sociable man and one of very open mind."

At Bullcliffe Wood Colliery the King and Queen were handed an illuminated scroll prepared by the men pledging themselves to do all in their power to keep up coal production.

At the Hickleton Main Colliery they were told that at one time the pits there held the national record output for the hour, the day and the week. The King remarked, "I hope you win it back," and the Queen added, "Yes, and send us a wire when you do."

The last call was at the Bentley Colliery, where the King donned a cloth cap and a linen overall over his uniform of Admiral of the Fleet, and the Queen also wore an overall.

Cassino: heavily shelled by the Americans

Allied 4.2 inch mortars in action

British soldiers rout out remaining Germans

February 16 1944

300 BOMBERS SMASH CASSINO MONASTERY

From Christopher Buckley outside Cassino

To-DAY, between 200 and 300 Allied 'planes bombed the Abbey of Saint Benedict. It had been used by the Germans as a fortified strongpoint, on the crest of the hill commanding Cassino, to hold up our advance in Southern Italy.

It was 25 minutes past nine on a cold, blue February morning when a formation of bombers – they were Flying Fortresses – passed overhead from the south in the direction of Monte Cairo, the massif north-west of the town.

They flew in perfect formation with something of that arrogant dignity which distinguishes bomber aircraft as they set out on a sortie.

For the moment they were the only moving objects that could be seen over the whole wide amphitheatre.

As they passed over the crest of the Monastery Hill flying at perhaps a height of some 6,000 feet, small jets of flame and heaps of black earth leapt into the air from the summit of the hill. Then a deep cloud of smoke enveloped the whole crest.

A series of thuds followed quickly, one on another, as the 'planes made for home. For the Abbey of Saint Benedict had been bombed. The German guns had been silenced.

Thousands of troops watched the 'planes' attack, in which Roman Catholic members of air crews were stated to have taken part.

One had known that it was coming. Cassino town commands the debouchment into the plains beyond, towards Pontecorvo and Frosinone and, ultimately, Rome. And Monastery Hill dominates the town.

One knew that every effort had been made to spare this ancient foundation, more than 1,400 years old, in which monastic Christianity came to birth.

Specific instructions had been given by Gen. Clark, Commander of the Fifth Army, that artillery, infantry and air forces were to take every precaution to avoid endangering the fabric of the monastery.

These undertakings were kept. But as the battle developed and American infantry pushed further and further up the slopes of the hill until in places they were only some 200 or 300 yards distant from the monastery, it was observed that the Germans were employing the building as a defensive point.

Not only was it being used for observation of the movements of the Allied Forces – that was already known.

But German machine-guns were identified as firing from cover of the monastery walls. German infantry were using it as a defensive position. German mortars were firing from the shadow of its walls. It had been converted into a fortress. Lives were being lost every day because no bombardment could be launched against it.

There was no alternative to the decision which was taken by the Allied Governments and executed by forces commanded by Gen. Alexander, C-in-C in Italy, and Gen. Clark.

The monastery had to be bombed, even though it meant the deliberate and carefully planned destruction of one of the oldest monuments of the Christian faith.

Leaflets dropped for the benefit of Italians yesterday stated that this step would be taken, "that the time had come" when we must train our guns on the monastery itself.

Aerial view of destroyed monastery and (below) British soldier bringing in two German prisoners

February 18 1944

Free Health Service For All After the War

A complete medical service, free of charge, for everybody in the country is to be established as soon as possible after the war.

Announcing in the House of Commons yesterday the publication of a White Paper explaining the Government proposals for a National Health Service, Mr Willink, Minister of Health, said:

"The proposals described are those which the Government believed to be best calculated to achieve an efficient and comprehensive national health service. But they are proposals – not decisions – and the Government have promised that they shall be discussed with all concerned, and will welcome constructive criticism in Parliament and the country."

The chief features of the Government's plan are:

· The services of a family doctor;

The provision of drugs and medicines and all but the more expensive appliances;

Improved hospital service;

Full specialist and consultant services;

A home nursing and midwifery service; and

Special care for the teeth and eyes.

Bomb damage at Krupps Works, Essen

March 4 1944

RAF DROPPING 12,000LB "FACTORY BUSTERS"

THE RAF are now using 12,000lb bombs, over 5⅓ tons, by far the biggest yet known in air warfare.

First disclosure of the existence of this devastating addition to Bomber Command's striking power was made last night when it was announced that two French works turning out 'planes, aero-engines and components for the Germans had been laid in ruins by the new "factory buster."

Almost simultaneously the news was released that Lightning long-range fighters of the American Eighth Air Force made an audacious feint sweep over Berlin in daylight yesterday as a big force of escorted Flying Fortresses and Liberators for the second successive day hammered targets in North-Western Germany.

These Lightnings were the first American formations to fly over the German capital. No fighter opposition whatever was met on their 1,200-mile flight there and back again to England. Some pilots reported heavy flak.

The RAF's newest bomb was invented by British scientists for precision attacks on special targets. It has already been proved to have enormous destructive effect.

A few of them sufficed to destroy the greater part of the big Gnôme-and-Rhône aero-engine works at Limoges on the night of Feb. 8. They were next employed against aircraft works at Albert, near Amiens, on Thursday night.

A 12,000lb "factory-buster" bomb

Allied tank moving up the Imphal Road

March 15 1944

Jungle Fighting

BETWEEN the Continental air and land battles of Europe and the oceanic operations of the Pacific, the war through the mountainous jungle of Burma must not suffer eclipse. The troops of the Fourteenth Army who have made their way across Manipur to the rear of the Japanese defences in Upper Burma have had to scramble up and down moun-tain climbers' gradients clothed in solid forest and scourged by floods of tropical rain. Besides these huge natural odds, they were faced by elaborately prepared and hidden positions in the mountainsides. There was never a war like this before.

Only air supremacy gained some few months since made the advance possible, and still the fighting is hard. The air bombardments which flatten out the mountain jungle fortresses also open a broad field of fire for the enemy upon our infantry. Though this front is small on the global scale and the operations are only at an early stage of development, they promise success which may have far-reaching future effects.

The Japanese hold on Upper Burma has been shaken and ground gained of value to the transport of munitions from Assam to China. Further advance would make the Japanese position southward and eastward towards the old Burma road to China precarious. Most important of all is the proof of Japanese failure in a jungle campaign.

March 15 1944

SECRET ALLIED MARCH IN BURMA JUNGLE

From Martin Moore, Calcutta

COLUMNS of British troops, crossing the Chindwin River, Upper Burma, in several places, have developed a new threat against Japanese positions based on Myitkyina, on the railway to Mandalay, in the valley of the Irrawaddy.

The crossing was a surprise manoeuvre, the climax to a march of 100 miles through fantastic country which the commanding officer described as "eclipsing Hannibal." The troops prepared for this expedition by months of secret training in Indian jungles.

The new thrust constitutes the second jaw of a pincer movement, of which the other is formed by Gen. Stilwell's Chinese troops to the north, pressing towards the Jambubum Pass, leading from the Hukawng Valley.

While the immediate threat appears to be to Mogaung, Myitkyina lies only about 50 miles beyond. It is probably the main Japanese air base in Upper Burma.

The aim of the river-crossing force has not been officially disclosed, but it is suggested by the mention in the official announcement that the crossings took place "in conjunction with other operations already in progress."

But the success and safety of these men depends on secrecy. Of their precise operations, objectives and special equipment nothing can yet be divulged.

They are going ahead and their commander is full of confidence. That is all that can be safely told now.

The crossings were made north of Tamanthi, which lies at the junction of the Tuzu and Chindwin rivers 90 miles to the north-east of Imphal. No Japanese resistance was mentioned in to-day's communiqué.

The river was crossed by several columns of the Fourteenth Army troops, organised on the lines of the famous expedition a year ago of Maj.-Gen. Orde Wingate, then a brigadier.

Penetration has been made possible this year largely by the great scale on which air supply-dropping has been organised.

Thirteen months ago I stood on the banks of the Chindwin and watched Maj.-Gen. Wingate's little band of men swimming across, battling with the strong current and pushing their kit on rafts or small native boats. This year the troops had petrol-driven craft and rubber dinghies. These were dropped to them on the river bank by a fleet of supply 'planes.

The men had made a march of 100 miles before reaching the river. On this first stage, though they passed through areas sometimes combed by enemy patrols, the chances of a clash were not great. They reached the river without meeting any opposition and without the Japanese having the smallest inkling of their presence.

They had to march often at night, always in silence, and to choose the difficult way rather than tracks where a chance encounter with local hillmen or enemy patrols might have betrayed their presence.

Bearded, dirty, some with tattered uniforms, but all triumphant, they came down the last steep hill to the river. On this arduous march they had suffered only 18 casualties.

The Japanese push into Manipur

March 23 1944

JAPANESE CROSS FRONTIER INTO INDIA

From Martin Moore, Calcutta

CONTRARY to rumours circulating here, I understand that the Japanese columns which crossed the Chindwin River and descended into the plain of Manipur, India, have not succeeded in cutting the Manipur road, which runs north to Imphal.

The invaders have been held at a point east of the road, but within 30 miles of Imphal, the capital of Manipur. This is the base from which, it is believed, the secret Allied expedition recently marched 100 miles east through the jungle to cross the Chindwin towards Mogaung. Fierce fighting is now going on inside the Indian border.

The general strategic position in the Pacific

April 1 1944

GEN. WINGATE KILLED IN BURMA PLANE CRASH

By Lt.-Gen. H. Martin
Military Correspondent

LATE last night the following official announcement was issued:

"The War Office regrets to announce that Maj.-Gen. O. C. Wingate, DSO, was killed in a 'plane crash in Burma on March 24."

Gen. Orde Charles Wingate was 41. Only last Sunday, two days after his death, it was revealed that he was in command of new operations launched in Upper Burma several weeks ago with the landing of British and Indian air-borne troops in the jungle east of the Irrawaddy 150 miles behind the Japanese lines and the crossing of the Chindwin River by several British columns.

Mr Churchill was so impressed by the achievements of Gen. Wingate's Chindits, or jungle commandos, who early last year penetrated 1,000 miles amid the Japanese positions, that he summoned him last summer to 10 Downing-street to discuss the repetition of that expedition on bigger and more ambitious lines.

Next day Gen. Wingate left with the Prime Minister to attend the Quebec Conference in August. There, after meetings with Mr Roosevelt, Gen. Marshall, United States Chief of Staff, and other Allied leaders, his plans for beating the Japanese in Burma were adopted.

At this juncture, when his methods are under trial for the first time on a large scale, his death is a particularly tragic loss, which the Allied cause can ill afford to bear.

Throughout the history of war the number of leaders who have invented a new technique of warfare is small indeed – and Wingate, with his Long Distance Penetration Group, will rank as one of them.

Major-General Orde Wingate

April 17 1944

RUSSIANS FIGHT IN SEBASTOPOL

THE remnants of nine German and Rumanian divisions in the Crimea were being killed and captured last night by the Red Army in Sebastopol, and near Inkerman and Balaklava on the south-western tip of the peninsula.

Last night, on the ninth day of the swift, overwhelming offensive, Marshal Stalin issued an Order of the Day announcing that Gen. Yeremenko's Independent Maritime Army had captured Yalta, the last big evacuation port apart from Sebastopol.

Yalta – described in the Order as one of the enemy's strongholds on the southern coast of the Crimea – is 30 miles south-east of Sebastopol. It had a good harbour, but few, if any, troops can have escaped by

sea. This is indicated by the annihilation of Germans and Rumanians trying to evacuate Sebastopol.

The troops of Gen. Tolbukhia's Fourth Ukrainian Army have taken Sebastopol's airport at Kacha, north of the city, and are fighting their way through the city suburbs. Here they are only two miles from the centre of Sebastopol.

About a dozen miles to the east the Russians are driving towards historic Inkerman, and to the south they are approaching the coast at Balaklava, which is eight miles from Sebastopol.

April 18 1944

Stage Door Canteen

AMERICAN Army officials in London are to-day waiting to hear from the Ministry of Works whether they can go ahead with plans to turn the Popular Café, Piccadilly, into a London counterpart of New York's Stage Door Canteen.

Forty American soldiers, sailors and British Wrens went there yesterday to start clearing stores from the blitzed building ready for the workmen, but they turned away, disappointed, when they were told that the Ministry of Works had refused a licence for building materials.

Changes have now been made in the application to the Ministry, I was told last night, and it is hoped that these will enable the permit to be given.

London's Stage Door Canteen is intended to be a contribution to Anglo-American friendship. It will be open, free, to all noncommissioned ranks of British, United States and Allied Forces, on the model of the New York show place for the Forces where stars give free entertainment.

April 25 1944

8 Weeks' Gaol Sentence on Ivor Novello

IVOR Novello, the actor and producer, was sentenced to eight weeks' imprisonment at Bowstreet police-court yesterday on a charge of conspiring to commit an offence against the war-time restrictions on the use of motor vehicles.

His co-defendant, Dora Constable, with whom he was accused of conspiring, he described as "stage struck," infatuated with himself and possessing a "great gift for self-dramatisation."

Miss Constable was fined £50, with £25 costs, on the conspiracy charge and £5 for causing a car to be driven in contravention of the Motor Vehicles (Restriction of Use) Order, 1942.

This provides that no person shall drive or cause to be driven a gas-producer car without a Ministry of War Transport licence.

Mr Novello was also ordered to pay £25 costs, or to serve in default a further month's imprisonment on the conspiracy charge.

THE DAILY TELEGRAPH

April 21 1944

Many Happier Returns

ONE of the privileges of Royalty – if privilege it be – is the right to be considered grown-up at an earlier age than ordinary folk. Thus it is that today the heiress-presumptive to the Throne passes at the age of 18 from the stage of tutelage to that of responsibility. It is, of course, a solemn moment in the life of the Princess ELIZABETH, though solemnity can carry with it no connotation of pomposity to a member of one of the least pretentious and happiest families of the Realm.

She may be strengthened at this moment by the knowledge that the people of the Empire already look upon her with special affection and hope. There is a ring of good omen about the name ELIZABETH in our annals, and it is as certain as anything can be in an uncertain world that just as this country repelled one great threat to its liberties when one ELIZABETH was on the throne, so it will repel another when another ELIZABETH is next in succession to the throne. If Queen ELIZABETH was her country's standard, let Princess ELIZABETH be her country's mascot in times of great peril.

The secret of the loyalty of their people towards the Royal family is the knowledge that they are not high and mighty, but essentially human. That was never more true than during this war, when so much of the ordinary savour of childhood has necessarily been lacking in all households from the highest to the humblest. Instead, therefore, of celebrating the Princess ELIZABETH's coming of age with any superfluous reminders of the new responsibilities now falling upon her, let her be offered the wish proper to all young ladies over whose normally care-free years a shadow has been thrown. May she have many happier returns.

May 5 1944

JAPANESE LOSE BATTLE FOR ARAKAN HILL

From South-East Asia Command HQ

HIGH ground overlooking the Maungdaw-Buthidaung road in Arakan is now firmly in Allied hands, announced to-day's communiqué, adding that the Japanese had fought for the possession of it "with great desperation."

The Japanese penetrated one of the Allied positions near Buthidaung, but were driven out in a counter-attack supported by tanks.

In the Imphal and Kohima sectors there has been only patrol activity north and south of Kohima.

The composition of the Chindits, who have been harassing Japanese supplies on the main route from South Burma to this area, has now been disclosed. About two-thirds of them are men from Britain; the others are made up equally of West Africans and Gurkhas.

May 6 1944

14th ARMY LAUNCHES KOHIMA OFFENSIVE

From Our Special Correspondent, Imphal

THE British have gone over to the offensive in the area north of Imphal, capital of Manipur State, where the Japanese hoped to cut the Allies' supply lines before the monsoon.

"Our troops are attacking at all points on the Kohima front," said the South-East Asia Command communiqué to-day, adding: "They are making satisfactory progress."

Kohima is about 60 miles north of Imphal on the road to the Dimapur railhead. North of Imphal plain itself there were minor clashes in which the troops of the Fourteenth Army inflicted casualties..

Elsewhere in the area there were no changes but, said the communiqué, patrols operating in the Imphal-Ukhrul area report finding "increased evidence of the enemy's heavy casualties.

Gurkhas and men of the West Yorkshire Regiment advance under cover of forward tanks

May 2 1944

First Pre-Fabricated House in London

THE pre-fabricated house, of which the Prime Minister in his broadcast speech promised 500,000 for demobilised members of the Forces and bombed-out families after the war, is in London.

It arrived in sections on Wednesday and was completely assembled and ready for occupation by four o'clock on Saturday afternoon.

To achieve this feat a number of workmen – the Ministry of Works would not divulge how many – were engaged through most hours of daylight on a plot of land specially screened from public view.

Although the public will not be able to inspect the house until Thursday, I had a preview yesterday. The house was standing in the middle of a lawn of newly laid turf flanked by beds of geraniums. It looked as if it had been there for at least a year.

In fact, it is not a house at all, but a bungalow. This in no way detracts from its merits. These are most apparent in the interior, which covers an area of 616 sq. ft.

With four windows front and back, no windows at all in the side walls, and a gently-sloping pent-roof with overhanging eaves, the outside appearance is not displeasing.

Inside are a hall, bath-room, kitchen, living-room, two equal-sized bedrooms, a lavatory and a fair-sized bicycle shed which is reached from outside.

A Ministry of Works "Pre-fab"

Extensive bomb damage at Stuttgart

May 24 1944

Nightmare Life of German People

From Noel Panter, Zurich

A picture of conditions now prevailing in Germany is given in an article from an authoritative source which is published to-day by the Swiss newspaper, *Neue Zuercher Zeitung.*

During the past few months the Gestapo terror has been intensified, it states. To counter the effects on the home front of military setbacks, the Nazi régime has been compelled to resort to ever more brutal coercive measures.

The crisis into which the German Army was plunged by the collapse of Italy could be surmounted only by intimidating the masses, who had grown critical. Force was openly used against them.

Nazism is like a nightmare to the country. All spontaneous impulses are smothered.

Burdens imposed by the air war, added to other afflictions, are especially oppressive because they are always present.

In danger areas a raid must at all times be reckoned with. One is never safe from the incalculable Allied bombers. As in the front line, the civilian no longer has even a quiet hour.

In fact, the air war dominates life. It is almost the sole subject of conversation. Events at the front and in politics recede far into the background.

The only important consideration in Germany today is: Does the weather indicate that another bombing attack is likely during the night? Absorbing interest is also shown in what happened in the latest raid.

Provision for the bombed-out is made by the State as best it can. But its resources are limited. People who have lost their possessions belong in a literal sense to those who fit into no class of society.

Priority purchase certificates for clothes and household necessaries are issued, but the time is passed when there was any certainty of getting goods with them.

Destruction of property has become so great that overburdened industries cannot easily satisfy the demand. Thus a sad fate awaits anyone who is bombed out.

Even those whose homes survive lead a life of privation. The glass industry has been unable to replace smashed windows. Hundreds of thousands of people lived and worked in cold rooms throughout the winter.

Travel in bombed towns has become laborious. As a result of all this the population's powers of resistance are beginning gradually to give way, says the writer.

Life consists of nothing but one terrible improvisation to which there seems no end.

With energy sinking, nerves overstrained, and many people suffering from insomnia, defeatism, non-political to an extent, is developing.

A growing number desire only to end their sufferings at any price. A condition of paralysing exhaustion, with a yearning for rest, is immeasurably increased. Apathy is manifesting itself everywhere.

May 25 1944

WVS – How It Works

By Sheila Birkenhead

DURING this war a new feminine army has come into being. It has no conscripts, no ranks, no pay; if the members want to wear the uniform they must buy it themselves. A year before war was declared the Home Secretary felt the need of some women's organisation to encourage training for Civil Defence. He asked Lady Reading, widow of the brilliant lawyer and Viceroy, to organise this work, and the WVS was born.

Its primary task is still that described in its full title, "Women's Voluntary Services for Civil Defence." Although its members now undertake work for 20 Government Departments, they still regard Civil Defence as their first and most important job. The Minister of Home Security has described them as "occupying, vis-à-vis my Department and Local Authorities, the same relationship as that of the Women's Auxiliary Services to the Armed Forces of the Crown."

WVS is responsible to local authorities in many places for staffing rest centres and casualty bureaux, and members also work at incident inquiry points, control centres and in Queen's Messenger food convoys and mobile kitchens. They will guide bombed-out people to the rest centres, feed and clothe the homeless, sit with invalids or expectant mothers during a raid, or help to save belongings from the shattered homes when it is over.

During the worst nights of fires and bombs WVS has been on duty, and many members have lost their lives. They are a pool of voluntary workers whose boast is that no job is too difficult, too dangerous, too small or too dirty – if it must be done they will do it.

But their work is not limited to ARP and post-raid work. At the outbreak of war local authorities were notified that WVS was "at their disposal to undertake any work for which the services of women volunteers were required in their own locality." At that time there were 335,924 members. To-day there are 1,000,000. They are everywhere – in every town, village and street of Great Britain.

"The Chairman"

This army of a million women has no general. Its head is known as "The Chairman." She travels all over the country, inspecting, advising, seeing for herself. During a week's tour recently, she made 18 speeches in six days. Always sympathetic and understanding, there is one thing she will not tolerate. That is the suggestion that anything is "impossible," or "inexpedient." Her only criterion is, "Will it help to win the war?" If she is convinced that it will, no regard for popularity and no apparent difficulties must be allowed to stand in the way. If the job should be done WVS will do it.

Lady Reading has drawn into the war effort thousands of women who cannot leave their homes. Almost all the younger, unmarried members left to go into industry or the Services when women registered for National Service; but it has proved possible by clever organisation to do urgent and important work with part-time labour.

Almost all the members have homes to run, children or relatives to care for. They could not leave their homes to work in factories or to join the Services. They are women who, though eager to serve, might never have been used if they had not been organised on a national scale to cook, to sew, to care for children, to help their neighbours in disaster, to deal with emergencies practically and promptly as they arise – in fact, to do for their country all the things that women have been doing in their own homes for generations.

A jubilant Rome welcomes the Allies: Allied soldiers (above) wave to the crowd from Mussolini's balcony

June 5 1944

ROME FALLS: MOPPING-UP ENDS AT DUSK

ROME fell to the Fifth Army at 9.15 last night, according to messages reaching London just after midnight.

Within a few minutes the German News Agency broadcast a special communiqué from Hitler's HQ stating that the Fuehrer had ordered a withdrawal to positions north-west of Rome to prevent the destruction of the city.

The communiqué added that Kesselring had submitted to the Vatican proposals for Rome to be treated as an "open city," and defining the limits within which no German troops would be maintained.

The Allies' mopping-up operations were carried out by tanks of the Anzio Beachhead Force. The German rearguards fought to the edge of the ancient Forum.

Operations ended with the knocking out of a German scout car outside the Bank of Italy a few yards from the Quirinal, in the centre of Rome and near Trajan's Column.

At 8.30 an official statement from Allied HQ had announced that Fifth Army troops had entered the city limits and that sporadic resistance was continuing. This came an hour after an announcement reporting heavy fighting all day in the outskirts of the city and between the Coll Laziali (the Alban Hills) and the sea.

A late report on the day's air operations stated that at least 300 German vehicles were destroyed and another 300 damaged in fighter-bomber attacks on transport jammed on the roads north of the city early yesterday morning.

The convoys stretched for 50 miles to the Bolsano area, and were the first indications that Kesselring was conducting an extensive withdrawal far to the north of the Italian capital.

Church bells were ringing throughout Rome when the first spearheads of the Fifth Army reached the suburbs of the Italian capital at 6.40 a.m. yesterday. They provided a background to the rattle of machine-guns and rifles and the heavy explosions of mortar bombs and anti-tank shells as the German rearguards continued their delaying actions.

As the first jeeps and tanks moved cautiously through the Maggiore Gate, where Highway Six enters Rome, people began to come up out of their cellars. They were nervous at first, but soon became bolder and began to shower the troops with roses and to press wine on them.

May 29 1944

Shot Prisoners Dug for 15 Months

Here is the first full and authentic account of reports current in Silesia, in South-Eastern Germany, of the mass escape attempted by 76 British and Allied Air Force officers from the remote war prison camp Stalag Luft 3. Mr Eden stated in the House of Commons on May 19 that 47 of the officers had been shot by the Nazis and 15 recaptured, while 14 were still at large. Searching inquiry, he said, was being made into the circumstances of the shooting.

One of the saddest heroes of this war is Wing Cdr Smith, *writes Ossian Goulding from Stockholm,* the man who worked and schemed for nearly a year and a half to organise the mass escape of 76 officers of the British, Dominions and Allied Air Forces from Stalag Luft 3, at Sagan, in Silesia, for nearly two-thirds of their number died in the attempt.

Smith is not his real name, nor is he a wing commander. Security regulations demand that that part of the story remain untold. But to-day he possesses the tragic knowledge that 47 of the comrades who took part in that gallant dash for freedom lie dead – murdered by the Nazis.

The epic of the Sagan Tunnel was first told to me just over three weeks ago by a friend from Breslau. But only now can its main details be made public.

Stalag Luft 3 lies on a specially cleared site in thickly wooded country south-east of the Silesian town of Sagan, between the River Bober and Highway 122, which runs from Cottbus to Breslau.

It is one of the largest prison camps in Germany, comprising several compounds with intercommunicating gates, which are closed and locked after dark. And it was from Sagan Camp that a mass break of British and Allied officers occurred one night in March.

Behind that escape lay 15 months of tireless planning and back-breaking labour. All this was carried out in the face of difficulties which must often have seemed insuperable and in constant fear of discovery by the Nazi guards, informers and security police.

The Germans have long boasted that Sagan Camp was "escape-proof." They have surrounded it with a complex system of electrified wire, guarded on the outside by sentries armed with tommy-guns and searchlight batteries which are switched on at intervals throughout the whole night.

Special Nazi officials, nicknamed "ferrets," visit the camp regularly. These men are armed with detecting apparatus and long steel skewers fitted with wooden handles with which they probe for tunnels. Their efficiency is shown by the fact that hitherto they have discovered over 100 of these painfully constructed roads to liberty.

Yet it was from this vaunted stronghold that the biggest prison-break in the history of modern warfare took place. The escape from Holzminden, in Brunswick, in the last war, which has held the record hitherto, was made by only 38 men.

It is considered certain that rage at this "loss of face" was the reason behind the Germans' suspectedly cold-blooded murder of the 47 unarmed Allied officers.

Otherwise it is difficult to explain why so many hundreds of men who escaped from other camps have been recaptured without an incident, while in this one case 65 per cent. of the fugitives were shot on what sounds the flimsiest of excuses.

At Stalag Luft 3 it is death to go within a certain distance of the outside wire. Sentries have orders to shoot on sight, and without challenge, anyone so doing.

Smith, therefore, began his tunnel far back from the wire inside one of the dormitory buildings in the officers' quarters.

Drawing on a peace-time knowledge of engineering, combined with the mathematical talent of members of the camp, he worked out designs for a shaft over 450 feet long. This, he calculated, would come up just outside the outer belt of encircling wire in the shadow of the surrounding trees.

The Germans estimate that it took Smith and his men one year three months to excavate that tunnel. During that time, some of the men were transferred to other camps, but still the job went on.

For 15 months they dug with improvised instruments. Working in relays, they hid the earth they took out of the excavation.

All these long months they scrabbled at hard under-soil in a narrow burrow which might at any time collapse and bury them. In air so foul that many must have been overcome and nearly suffocated, they tunnelled through what had recently been forest country and was still a maze of thick, gnarled roots around which they had to dig their tortuous way.

At last the work was finished. There followed a period spent in planning reconnaissance. Lots must have been drawn for the order in which the officers would leave.

Time-tables were arranged for each man. These they would have to follow to a split second to avoid the patrolling sentries and the sweeping, inquisitive fingers of the searchlights outside. The decision was taken as to what points each would make for on his journey to England.

Just after dark on a moonless night in March, the first man shook hands with Wing Cdr Smith and dropped out of sight into the dark mouth of the tunnel.

As the world now knows, 76 officers got away before the tunnel was discovered by the enemy sentries. Of these the Germans say 15 were recaptured while 14 were still at liberty a fortnight later, and 47 were shot "while resisting arrest or attempting to escape a second time following recapture."

Manhunt

That is the bald Nazi official announcement. Behind it lies a story which can only in part be told and which can still only be guessed at in all its horror.

The entire province of Silesia became a madhouse, the man from Breslau told me. A general alarm was issued.

In it was an extra note of hysteria, which was explained by the fact that the Germans regard the escape of more than eight prisoners at one time as a "major break." And this time it was a question of 76 – all officers.

Battalions of the military were turned out to comb the Silesian woods. Police dogs, bloodhounds, the whole civilian population over a wide area, were mobilised to join in man-hunts day and night after the fugitives.

Armed Gestapo and police patrols searched travellers at every little wayside halt from Breslau to Cottbus, from Dresden to Frankfurt-on-Oder. Trams and 'buses were stopped and their passengers ordered to descend to the road for investigation.

"It was a sensation which completely overshadowed for the time being all talk of invasion or the war in Russia," my informant told me.

"People walked or cycled or rode for miles to try to get a glimpse of the famous tunnel. But they found that the whole district of the Sagan Camp was cordoned off by armed detachments of the Sicherheitsdienst, Himmler's dreaded security police.

"Even these could not stop the tongue of gossip wagging. Within a few days practically everyone in Silesia knew the broad details of the escape and the story of the tunnel.

"Within a few more days we heard that the camp commandant and a whole contingent which had guarded Sagan on the night of the escape had been removed in disgrace and either shot or sent to Straffkommandos (penal battalions)."

Where are the 14 who got away? Some of them at least may be home in England by now.

In accordance with military regulations made to protect those who may come afterwards or who helped them to escape from Germany, their names, personal stories or details of the routes by which they travelled homewards may not be revealed until after the war.

June 6 1944

Less Choppy in the Straits

THE weather in the Straits of Dover improved slightly last night. Towards dusk the wind dropped a little and the sea became less choppy.

The cloud cover became higher and the barometer showed no further loss. The temperature at 10 p.m. was 55 degrees.

D-Day

No one in southern England was under any illusion in the New Year of 1944 that invasion of France was not coming. Villagers had become accustomed to Canadians, but now Americans and Sherman tanks, directed through narrow village streets by "snowdrop" American military police in white helmets, seemed everywhere.

At Portsmouth, in the Solent, and in harbours, creeks and inlets, assembly of an invasion fleet of warships, transports and landing craft left no one on the coast in any doubt. It was all too obvious that the amassing shipping and troops bivouacking with camouflaged tanks, artillery and motor transport in the hedgerows were destined for Normandy in direct line from the Isle of Wight.

Those who were kept guessing were on the receiving end across the Channel where Field-Marshal von Runstedt argued that the Allies might take the more obvious and so much shorter route to the Pas de Calais, poising them for a thrust to the frontiers of Germany. Although Rommel, despatched by Hitler to inspect defences between Dunkirk and Brittany, thought otherwise, a ruse under the codename "Fortitude" helped to convince Hitler that the Pas de Calais would play some part in the landings – be it merely a diversionary operation or an attempt to establish a follow-up front.

In the event, the deception, involving a fantasy US Army Group, duped the enemy who was taken in by pretend landing craft, motor transport, a phoney network of communications and the messages of turned spies, feeding back planted intelligence. Eisenhower could count his blessings that Fortitude kept the German 15th Army in the Pas de Calais into July. In reality there was a military presence in the area. It comprised two mobile brigades against the possibility of disruptive enemy landings.

In the Portsmouth-Southampton area, the anchorage was so busy that air reconnaissance could not have failed to miss it. Yet Allied total air superiority minimised the risk of comprehensive photographic intelligence. Though, once invasion was underway, U-boats and light naval forces sought to interfere, their efforts were frustrated by sea and air supremacy.

At the top, Allied commanders settled to their tasks under Eisenhower in supreme command. Air Chief Marshal Sir Arthur Tedder was his deputy and General Walter Bedell Smith, Chief of Staff. Montgomery was overall ground commander of the expeditionary Army with two other British officers, Admiral Sir Bertram Ramsay and Air Chief Marshal Sir Trafford Leigh-Mallory, responsible for sea and air. The preponderance of British brass did not please some Americans, but their 1st Army commander, General Omar Bradley, balanced General Sir Miles Dempsey leading the British 2nd Army.

No one who arrived off the five invasion beaches in the early hours of the choppy June 6 can ever forget the din of the bombardment which included the guns of seven battleships, their thunder laced with the whoosh of rockets racked in adapted barges. Nor will the memory fade of the roar of bombers overhead and the stately progress across the Channel of the majestic floating walls of the Mulberry prefabricated harbour.

How went the day? On the whole disappointingly, though British troops on the eastern end of the landings got within four miles of the first objective of Caen. Elsewhere British and Canadian troops advanced beyond the shore. Generally, the Americans were less successful. Yet, enabling more than two million men to step ashore by the end of July, D-Day had brought victory fractionally nearer. But it would be a hard and costly slog to free Paris at the end of August – let alone meet the Russians advancing from the east next May.

Troops and tanks on a landing beach in Normandy

June 7 1944

ALLIED INVASION TROOPS SEVERAL MILES INTO FRANCE

ALLIED ARMIES BEGAN THE LIBERATION OF EUROPE EARLY YESTERDAY MORNING WHEN THE GREATEST INVASION OF ALL TIME WAS LAUNCHED WITH LANDINGS FROM SEA AND AIR AT SEVERAL POINTS ON THE COAST OF NORMANDY. LATE LAST NIGHT FIGHTING WAS GOING ON IN THE STREETS OF CAEN, AN IMPORTANT ROAD JUNCTION 10 MILES INLAND AT THE BASE OF THE CHERBOURG PENINSULA.

Communiqué No. 2, issued from Gen. Eisenhower's HQ just after midnight, stated that "reports of operations so far show that our forces succeeded in their initial landings. Fighting continues."

Pilots returning from the front last night reported Allied troops moving inland, with the "beaches completely in our hands." They said soldiers could be seen standing up on the beaches, where convoys were already assembling, while Allied tanks were moving towards Caen. Concentrations of German armour were seen moving towards the battlefield from the back areas.

Mr Churchill made two statements to the House of Commons yesterday. In his first announcement of the invasion he said there were hopes that tactical surprise had been attained.

In the second statement later in the day he stated that operations were continuing in a "thoroughly satisfactory manner," with effective landings on a wide front and with penetrations in some cases several miles inland. Losses were very much lighter than had been expected.

According to German accounts, the landings were made at about 12 points along 135 miles of coast from west of Cherbourg to Le Havre.

Late reports from Berlin stated that the Allied beachhead was 13 miles long and several miles deep across the River Orne, about midway between Cherbourg and Le Havre. Heavy fighting was raging in the whole area, especially along the Cherbourg-Carentan-Caen road, where Allied paratroops had gained a firm grip on both sides of the road.

Paris radio reported heavy battles against new landings by airborne troops north of Rouen. Algiers radio quoted a German report which stated landings had taken place near

Troops at Sword Beach prepare to move inland
Below: Royal Marines from 48 Commando push out of the beachhead

Calais and Boulogne and that an airfield near Calais had been captured by paratroops.

First official news of the invasion came at 9.01 a.m. in Communiqué No. 1 from Supreme Headquarters, Allied Expeditionary Force, which said:

"Under the command of Gen. Eisenhower, Allied naval forces, supported by strong air forces, began landing Allied armies this morning on the northern coast of France."

It was revealed last night that the invasion was postponed for 24 hours on the advice of the weather experts. The original date was the fourth anniversary of the last evacuation from Dunkirk.

The landings, which involved the use of 4,000 ships, with several thousand smaller craft, were made under cover of the most gigantic air umbrella yet seen. Between midnight and dawn over 1,000 RAF heavy bombers dropped 5,000 tons of bombs on 10 coastal battery targets – the greatest single night bombing attack on record.

They were followed at dawn by 1,300 American heavy bombers supported by hundreds of medium and fighter-bombers, which hammered coast defences, roads, railway bridges and attacked troop concentrations. RAF Bostons laid smoke screens to conceal the movement of the transports and their escorts.

More than 10,000 tons of bombs were dropped in 7,500 sorties, with no opposition from enemy fighters, in weather which compelled the pilots to fly low to locate their targets. Between midnight and eight a.m. 31,000 Allied airmen were over France.

Opposition from the coast defences was not so serious as had been expected, it was learned at SHAEF (Supreme Headquarters, Allied Expeditionary Force) last night. The invasion armadas were led by 200 mine-sweepers which swept channels and marked them for miles against great difficulties.

The air preparation was described as "a magnificent job," which resulted in opposition from the coastal batteries being spasmodic. The bombing was supported by a bombardment from 640 naval guns, ranging from 16in. to 4in. Battleships, cruisers, monitors, destroyers and specially designed close-support vessels were engaged.

Naval losses were reported to be "surprisingly small." One battleship moved close to the shore to silence a group of fortifications.

Adml Sir Bertram Ramsay, the Allied Naval C-in-C, stated last night that the Allied Navies' task of landing the invasion troops had been "in effect" 100 per cent. successful. "We have broken the crust," he added.

Canadian troops coming ashore near Bernières

June 7 1944

Dedication

IN this hour, not only the armed forces battling across the waters but the whole nation is under test. Believing that God is using us to fulfil His high purpose, the King last night broadcast, in words which lift up the heart, a call to his people to dedicate themselves anew in the crusading spirit of the dark days of 1940. This is the message which His Majesty sends:

"Four years ago our Nation and Empire stood alone against an overwhelming enemy, with our backs to the wall. Tested as never before in our history, in God's providence we survived that test; the spirit of the people, resolute, dedicated, burned like a bright flame, lit surely from those Unseen Fires which nothing can quench.

"Now once more a supreme test has to be faced. This time the challenge is not to fight to survive, but to fight to win the final victory for the good cause. Once again what is demanded from us all is something more than courage and endurance; we need a revival of spirit, a new unconquerable resolve. After nearly five years of toil and suffering, we must renew that crusading impulse on which we entered the war and met its darkest hour. We and our Allies are sure that our fight is against evil and for a world in which goodness and honour may be the foundation of the life of men in every land.

"That we may be worthily matched with this new summons of destiny, I desire solemnly to call my people to prayer and dedication. We are not unmindful of our own shortcomings, past and present. We shall not ask that God may do our will, but that we may be enabled to do the will of God; and we dare to believe that God has used our Nation and Empire as an instrument for fulfilling His high purpose.

"I hope that throughout the present crisis of the liberation of Europe there may be offered up earnest, continuous and widespread prayer. We who remain in this land can most effectively enter into the sufferings of subjugated Europe by prayer, whereby we can fortify the determination of our sailors, soldiers and airmen, who go forth to set the captives free.

"The QUEEN joins with me in sending you this message. She well understands the anxieties and cares of our womenfolk at this time, and she knows that many of them will find, as she does herself, fresh strength and comfort in such waiting upon God. She feels that many women will be glad in this way to keep vigil with their menfolk as they man the ships, storm the beaches and fill the skies.

"At this historic moment surely not one of us is too busy, too young, or too old to play their part in a nation-wide, perchance a world-wide, vigil of prayer as the great crusade sets forth. If from every place of worship, from home and factory, from men and women of all ages and many races and occupations, our intercessions rise, then, please God, both now and in a future not remote, the predictions of an ancient Psalm may be fulfilled:

'The Lord will give strength unto His people: the Lord will give His people the blessing of peace.'"

No more difficult and hazardous operation has ever been undertaken than the invasion of Western Europe so brilliantly begun in the early hours of yesterday morning.

The Allied forces are attacking a coast line upon which the enemy has expended all his defensive ingenuity at high pressure for at least two years. They have to face an Army deliberately reinforced at the expense of all other fronts in obedience to the enemy's desperate strategy of defeating this invasion at all costs. They are putting to the test the inference that he has deliberately held in reserve for this hour every possible aircraft and every possible military unit. The coast from Narvik to Biarritz is long, but the sector open to a first assault has been limited to the range of effective fighter cover – much wider than it used to be, but still not very wide.

First reports of the battle are encouraging. The really surprising thing is that there does seem to have been, in Mr CHURCHILL's words, "a tactical surprise."

June 11 1944

PIN-POINT BOMBING AFTER BEACHHEAD REQUEST

From Cornelius Ryan

I LOOKED down last night over the Cherbourg peninsula from the nose of a Marauder, and saw bombs from my group blow a German six-gun battery out of existence.

The attack was made following an urgent request from the Allied beachhead for the destruction of a battery which was pinning down our advance.

It lay a mile and a half from the beachhead, past a point where the American troops first landed and so close to our lines that pilots were instructed to return with their bombs if they could not identify the target.

"If you miss," said the commanding officer, Col. J. W. Kelly, at the briefing, "you will kill our own men. You must hit the target at exactly nine o'clock."

The pilots were told that an attack would start as soon as the battery had been destroyed. They were allowed just eight minutes over the target in which to identify it.

We took off in exceptionally bad weather. At one time as we gathered formation over the field we were unable to see our low flight which was circling below us at less than a thousand feet.

In this inclement weather, and with the rain pelting madly against the glass nose, we set course for France a little before 8 p.m.

Beside me in the nose rode Lt-Col. H. Hankey, who was acting as bombardier and navigation officer. We crossed the Channel, just beneath the clouds, and above us flew the area fighter cover.

Bombers continually swept past us returning from France, and below on either side fighter planes swept in only a few feet from the water.

Col. Hankey was kneeling in the nose of the plane, his eyes following the leading ship. Ahead of me the bombs from the other formations spiralled downwards. They had found the target.

Suddenly I saw it – six rings, and in each a heavy artillery piece. At the end of the battery stood what looked like a small concrete fort. A quick movement of the colonel's left hand and our bombs had fallen.

I saw the whole area of the target covered in a second with a mass of explosions. The concrete fort disintegrated, and pieces of it flew up in the air. We had hit the target, and turning, we streaked for home.

As we left the target, which we had hit at exactly 21.01 hours, one minute after the set time, I saw our artillery open fire on the enemy battery site. Then we had crossed the coast and were out over the Channel.

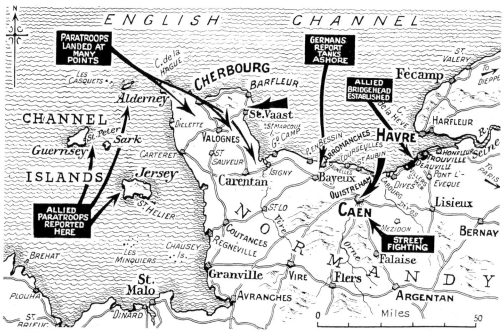

The Allied invasion of Normandy

June 13 1944

GEN. MONTGOMERY: "WE HAVE WON THE BATTLE OF THE BEACHES"

From Christopher Buckley with the Allied Forces in France

"WE have won the battle of the beaches."

Such was Gen. Montgomery's appreciation of the situation on the sixth day of the invasion of Europe when he spoke to war correspondents in France.

Wearing his familiar Tank Corps beret, corduroy trousers and grey pullover adorned only with the ribbon of the American Order of Merit, Gen. Montgomery received correspondents and discussed with them the development of the campaign.

He drew attention to certain significant aspects of the operation.

"The beaches," he said "are now behind us. The violence, power and speed of our initial assault carried us inland very quickly, leaving the beaches in our rear, with the exception of one very tough sector."

Summing up the results of the first phase of the campaign, Gen. Montgomery stated that we now held a continuous stretch of beaches some 60 miles in length from the eastern bank of the Orne on our left flank to a point some 20 miles short of Cherbourg on our right.

The various landing points had all been joined up and the invasion force now enjoyed a very considerable lodgement area ashore.

Its depth varied, but in places it was as much as 10 miles. It would form firm basis for developing operations in accordance with our plan.

"I am quite happy about the situation," said Gen. Montgomery, "but we must realise that there is a great deal to be done yet."

The Prime Minister visits the beachhead with General Montgomery

The V-1 flying-bomb

June 17 1944

Robot Plane Raids

MR Morrison, Minister of Home Security, who announced yesterday morning in the House of Commons the launching against Britain of the Germans' long-vaunted secret weapon, the pilotless plane, gave this assurance last night:

"There is no reason to think that raids by this weapon will be as heavy as the raids with which the people of this country are already familiar. The damage it has caused has been relatively small."

The RAF has been quick to accept the challenge of the aerial robot – a jet-engined monoplane generally described as a midget machine which is shaped like a Spitfire and painted a dark colour, and which flies fast on a straight course at a low level.

Apart from the intensive AA barrage which greeted these intruders in Southern England at their first onset on Tuesday morning and during their more extensive use on Thursday night and at intervals yesterday, RAF Typhoon fighters kept watch over the countryside.

After a daylight Alert had been sounded last evening a pilotless plane crashed on some houses, which were wrecked. At least three people were killed and several badly injured.

Before it crashed the robot plane was seen streaking across the sky with orange flame darting from its tail and with AA shells bursting all round it. Suddenly it dived and there was a terrific explosion.

After dark another Alert was sounded in Southern England.

An observer in one district reported that a plane showing a yellow light was shot at by tracer bullets.

Flares were dropped in one area by a plane, which was pursued by heavy gunfire.

The pilotless plane was described by the German Overseas News Agency yesterday as Germany's "first secret weapon."

The agency quoted a High Command spokesman as saying: "The new anti-invasion weapon which has been put into action against Britain has complete novelty and super-effect."

Suendermann, the Deputy Reich Press Chief, in a statement to the foreign Press, said that the new weapon marked the "beginning of retaliation" for the Anglo-American air attacks on Germany.

The German Overseas News Agency said that German military quarters were still extremely reticent about the new weapon. "It is a completely new kind of anti-invasion weapon which has a super-effect," it added. "Its operational importance can be compared to a powerful air fleet."

The German radio claimed yesterday that Daventry radio station was heavily hit by the new explosive.

It added that dense smoke clouds covered wide stretches of Southern England and that London suffered heavy destruction, warehouses and docks being in flames. Railway traffic for the most part has been paralysed.

"Kingston and Bromley seem to have been particularly hit," said the radio.

Sevenoaks, Sutton and Southampton were also claimed to have suffered.

The Ministry of Home Security yesterday issued the following advice to the public concerning the enemy's "secret weapon" raids:

"When the engine of the pilotless aircraft stops and the light at the end of the machine is seen to go out, it may mean that the explosion will soon follow – perhaps in five to 15 seconds: so take refuge from blast.

"Even those indoors should keep out of the way of blast, and use the most solid protection immediately available."

The pilotless plane can be launched by an artificial runway, a catapult, or under gyroscopically controlled engine power. Similarly there are probably various means of stopping its engines and sending it plunging to earth with its load of explosive.

When the planes are launched, possibly the propulsive force lifts them almost immediately to a height of about 300ft. They then probably climb gradually to 1,000ft, which is the altitude they probably maintain so long as their engines or batteries are running. They fly on a fixed course.

In good visibility they should be an easy target for fighters, and at night the tail-light, which appears to be an essential part of the robot's mechanism, must betray it to search-lights and to night fighters. It may thus be expected that pilotless planes will be operated under cloud conditions.

An observer said yesterday: "The planes have a distinctive rhythmic note, giving the effect of a pulsating low throb.

"Many of them have been observed in daylight and on several occasions RAF fighters, with total disregard of the danger, have dived into the AA fire around them in attempts to make a kill.

"They seemed to be painted a dark brown or black. Smoke issues from them in small thick puffs."

June 26 1944

CHERBOURG FALLS TO ALLIES

AMERICAN troops fought their way into Cherbourg yesterday and hold most of the town, it was learned at Supreme HQ at midnight. Full occupation was believed to be imminent.

This followed a German News Agency statement at 7.30 that numerous Allied tanks had penetrated into Cherbourg, and that "it is to be assumed that the Americans have taken possession of the town." At 9.20 a BUP despatch reported the entry of the Americans after reducing the outer forts.

A task force of battleships, cruisers and destroyers, commanded by Rear-Adml Morton L. Deyo, USN, flying his flag in the American cruiser Tuscaloosa, pounded the heavy coastal guns from 15,000 yards during the afternoon, their path being swept by a squadron of minesweepers.

Medium bombers hammered the forts during the morning. Bombing was later restricted because of the closeness of the fighting as the Americans smashed in from west, south and east.

From the other end of the bridgehead front between Tilly and Caen came reports of a new battle which began at 3.30 a.m. yesterday with a drumfire barrage, followed by an infantry attack on a front which New York reports estimated as being eight and a half miles wide.

June 27 1944

King's Nephew a Prisoner

THE following statement was issued from Harewood House last night:

"Lord Harewood has had official intimation that Lt Viscount Lascelles is reported wounded and missing and believed to be a prisoner of war."

A Canadian broadcast from Italy last night said: "Viscount Lascelles was wounded near a town which was later taken by the Eighth Army. His condition was such that he could not be moved except by a jeep, which a comrade volunteered to obtain, but on returning he found that Lord Lascelles and his men were missing."

A German war correspondent, Leonhard Osnitzki, stated in a broadcast from Italy last night, that "Lt Viscount Lascelles, the nephew of the King of England," was taken prisoner in the course of the fighting last week with the Sixth Tank Division. The report was quoted by the Berlin radio.

Viscount Lascelles, a lieutenant in the Grenadier Guards, is the elder son of the Earl of Harewood and the Princess Royal and is 21.

He joined the Grenadier Guards – his father's regiment – in 1942 and served in the ranks for eight months.

A French couple offer wine to an Allied soldier at Cherbourg

June 30 1944

King and Queen Visit Flying Bomb Victims

WHEN the King and Queen paid a surprise visit to a rest centre for homeless victims of flying bombs in the South yesterday they heard many stories of narrow escapes and individual bravery.

Several men, women and children were waiting at the centre to be given billets. Mrs Mullander, whose husband is a prisoner of war in Poland, summed up the feelings of everyone when she said to the Queen, "We're British and we can stand it."

With her were her two sons, seven-years-old Joseph and four-years-old Brian. The Queen wished them both luck and asked Mrs Mullander if her husband was getting his Red Cross parcels regularly.

The King talked to one of the oldest people in the centre, Mr John Ormrod, 85, who said to him: "I have been in five wars – the Burma Campaign in '85, the two South African Wars, the last war, and now this one."

"Well," said the King, "we may have more to go through yet."

"Yes, your Majesty, but we'll stick it," said Mr Ormrod.

Miss Elizabeth Steel, 81, lying in bed suffering from shock, clasped the King's hand in both her own and said: "God bless you for coming: it does buck our spirits up."

The Queen had a special word with 10-years-old Avril Gorman, whose arm was broken when her home was wrecked.

"I'm going on very well, thank you, your Majesty," said Avril, when the Queen asked her how she felt.

Both the King and Queen talked to Mrs Irene Searle, who is in bed with slight injuries. She told them how she had got her two daughters, Paulina, 7, and

Christine, 3, out of the Anderson shelter completely unhurt.

Another family party to whom the King and Queen talked were Mr and Mrs Sands and their three-year-old boy Ian. Mr Sands, in RAF uniform, said he was home on leave the night the bomb fell.

The Mayor of the area said afterwards: "What impressed the King and Queen most was the good spirits of everyone and the way they are taking it."

July 4 1944

Lady Louis and the Supremo

LADY Louis Mountbatten, who this month completes her second year as Superintendent-in-Chief, St John Ambulance Brigade, tells me that the Red Cross and St John War Organisation have not yet started to operate in South-East Asia, where her husband is Supreme Commander.

At present Lady Louis has no plans for going herself to Ceylon, where SEAC now has its headquarters. If necessary she may go there for a short visit later on.

She has also been invited by Mme Chiang Kai-shek to visit China to inspect the Red Cross and St John work there. So far she has been too busy at home, however, to spare the time.

Both Lady Louis and her husband have many close ties with the East. They became engaged at Delhi in 1922, when Lord Louis was ADC to the Prince of Wales, have visited Singapore many times, and know intimately much of the area now under his command.

Lord Louis is usually referred to as "The Supremo." A correspondent from Ceylon wrote to me recently: "Everyone thinks the Supremo grand. He is very friendly and easy to get on with."

July 7 1944

14th Army's Commander

AVERSION to the limelight explains why 52-year-old Lt-Gen. William Joseph Slim, commander of the 14th Army, which operates along the 800-mile Western Burma front, is one of our least publicised generals.

On the other hand, he gives every encouragement to officers to make known the work of his British and Indian troops, who have been so thoroughly tested in this hard campaign. He knows them well himself, for he served in a Gurkha regiment as far back as 1920.

His shyness, I hear, does not prevent him from being highly popular, for he tempers strict discipline with personal charm and a sense of humour. One of his characteristics is an intense consideration of "other ranks" when planning operations.

At the outbreak of war Gen. Slim was given the command of a brigade of the 5th Indian Division. This fought in Eritrea, where he was wounded by machine-gun fire from an Italian plane.

Some time later he commanded an Indian division in Irak during the rebellion. Later again he was a corps commander in Burma under Gen. Alexander in the campaign that ended in the retreat into India.

Commenting on his work during this difficult operation, Gen. Auchinleck recently stated that he "was an inspiration to everyone during that fighting withdrawal."

Like Gen. Alexander, Gen. Slim possesses in a high degree the indefinable quality of leadership. Both in consequence get every ounce out of the men who serve under them.

British tanks and guns in the centre of Caen

Despite its tragedy, the incident gave an example of the iron discipline of the Brigade of Guards. As the engine of the flying bomb "cut out," the King's Guard of 86 men had just been brought to attention.

The bomb rushed down and burst with a shattering roar in the chapel only tens of yards away. Not a man stirred in the ranks, and by strange good fortune not one was injured.

In the Chapel the congregation had finished a hymn and Lt-Col. Lord EDWARD HAY, of the Grenadier Guards, had just walked to the lectern to read the First Lesson when the bomb hurtled through the roof and exploded in the aisle in the centre of the congregation.

The roof with its heavy reinforced-concrete supports collapsed. The higher parts of the walls caved in. Masonry, timber and glass tumbled down on the congregation.

Two of the four massive Doric pillars over the west door toppled over and dragged the portico down with them. Only the apse at the east end remained.

Under the wreckage lay many of the worshippers and the chaplain.

Two other London buildings hit by recent bombs were the Regent Palace Hotel, Piccadilly Circus, and the Bankruptcy Court, in Carey-street, WC.

July 10 1944

CAEN FALLS: BRITISH REACH THE ORNE

CAEN, the most important road junction in Normandy, and the eastern bastion of Rommel's defence line, was captured by British and Canadian troops yesterday, when British tanks reached the River Orne to the east of the town.

British tanks and infantry, driving down from the north, were first into Caen. They met the Canadians thrusting from the west in Rue St Jean, the main street.

Early this afternoon I walked into the monument of debris that was once Caen. It was the most terrible spectacle of the war.

I had to walk from Labisy to Caen. It was better to walk. The road was under full enemy observation from the area of the tobacco factory on the far side of the River Orne. A walking figure drew less attention than a vehicle.

In fact, the only vehicles visible on the road were an occasional Bren-carrier and rather more frequent stretcher-carrying jeeps. These moved backwards and forwards along this bare, open road picking up battle casualties.

The road was a via dolorosa to the town. It was lined by a ghastly sequence of burnt-out and rusted trucks and Bren-carriers.

I breasted the very slight rise which goes by the name of Point 64. This was the scene of desperate fighting yesterday.

After that, the whole of Caen lay open to the view. It was such a view as took one's breath away. It left one barren of adjectives and epithets.

It was hard to tell where Caen began. Whole areas of the town have been obliterated by bombing and shellfire.

It was barely possible to recognise whether a particular heap of churned dust was once a house. It was impossible to pick out the lines of the streets.

Imagine a pleasant and prosperous country town lying in rolling, fertile country on either side of an almost Arcadian river. It raises spires and towers heavenwards. It is the very picture of contentment.

Now see this same town after the very masonry of its buildings has been ground, not only to fragments, but even to a fine white dust.

Heaps of such dust cover large sectors of Caen. Above them rise shattered, shambling ruins. Here is the corner of a house with some few splintered sticks of furniture poking irrelevantly outwards, or the pudding-like solidity of a mattress.

Elsewhere is the debris of what must have been a dining-room table and chairs, though one cannot be certain.

Everywhere rubble, rubble, rubble and bare matchstick trees in what were once gracious gardens.

That is what large-scale bombing and shell-fire does in modern war.

July 10 1944

Guards Chapel Wrecked by Flying Bomb

TO-DAY the famous century-old Royal Military Chapel, known as the Guards Chapel, in Wellington Barracks, near Buckingham Palace, lies in ruins. It can now be stated that the chapel received a direct hit from a flying bomb during a Sunday morning parade service.

There has been no official announcement of the death roll, but in the congregation, most of whom were officers and men of the Guards and their relatives, many were killed or injured. Most of the casualties were civilians.

July 11 1944

Leading U-Boat Killer Dead

CAPT. F. J. Walker, DSO and three bars, the leading anti-submarine ace, died in a Liverpool hospital over the week-end after a heart attack. He will be buried at sea after a service in Liverpool Cathedral to-morrow.

Ships and aircraft under his immediate control were officially credited with destroying 20 U-boats.

Capt. Walker led his sloops – the Wild Goose, Magpie, Wren, Woodpecker and Kite – into a fierce battle with U-boat packs in February by hoisting the famous signal "General Chase" from his senior ship, the Starling. He told one of his officers to "go in and blow the breeches off them."

The Guards Chapel, Wellington Barracks: hit by a flying-bomb

July 14 1944

SS MASSACRE A WHOLE FRENCH VILLAGE

THE French authorities in London last night issued a report on the massacre of Oradour-sur-Glane, one of the most barbaric atrocities in the list of crimes perpetrated by the Germans in France.

The account shows that of over 750 inhabitants of Oradour-sur-Glane, a village about 16 miles from Limoges, only seven escaped the German butchers.

The massacre was carried out without even the semblance of a pretext, the local German commander stating subsequently that "it was the wrong village."

On Saturday, June 10, at 1.30 p.m., several lorries carrying SS troops of the Der Fuehrer Division went into the village. An officer walked into the Mairie and gave the Mayor the order to assemble the whole population on the fair-ground.

The order was immediately given to the inhabitants by the town crier.

Men, women, children, taken by surprise while busy with their peaceful daily occupations, crowded to the assembly point, pushed brutally by the soldiers patrolling the streets with tommy-guns on their hips.

The soldiers went into the houses and compelled everyone, including old people and the infirm, to go out.

When the people had assembled, the Germans made the men leave the crowd of inhabitants and conducted them to a nearby barn. In groups of about 20, the men were pushed into the interior of the barn and shot on the spot.

On the fair-ground the wailing of the women and children mingled with the noise of shooting. After the men had been massacred, the women and children were taken inside the church. Some boys and girls were already there, preparing for their first communion, to take place the next day.

The SS then made the rounds of the houses, looking for anyone who might have stayed indoors.

Masters and pupils were also shut in the church. A few inhabitants who had hidden in their homes were dragged out with the utmost brutality, or shot on the spot if they attempted to escape.

A young woman and her eight-day-old baby were dragged out; she was taken to the church by a soldier who carried the baby in its cradle.

The SS treated the unhappy people in the church very brutally, profaned the high altar, forced the door of the tabernacle, and took the sacraments.

A little later a group of soldiers placed a large case in the centre of the church; then they left, closing the doors behind them. Other SS in the meantime went through the village, drenching the houses and barns with an incendiary product, probably phosphorus, and chasing the people who had tried to escape.

In the gardens and round the village were found several bodies of women and children shot down while trying to flee. Near a hut where she had sought refuge was the body of a woman with 18 bullet wounds.

At this moment the tram from Limoges to St Julien arrived at Oradour-sur-Glane. It was stopped and the Germans made the travellers get down.

According to one version they sent all of them to the church; according to another they sorted out the travellers, sending those who were inhabitants of Oradour-sur-Glane to the church and telling the rest to go back where they had come from.

Shortly afterwards the SS began to set fire to the village. The case in the church blew up an hour after it had been put in position, setting fire to the edifice, which began to burn all over.

It is not known precisely how this terrible hour and the minutes afterwards were passed by the unhappy people locked in the church. But the inhabitants of neighbouring hamlets declared that for a long time the air was rent by horrible shrieks.

Soon the entire village was a sheet of flame, filled with the crackling of the flames; the noise of houses collapsing in whirls of smoke, mingled with the terrifying cries of the people as the flames reached them.

The Germans had put a cordon of soldiers round the village. Isolated villagers who had been in the fields nearby and were seen were shot down by rifle and machine-gun fire, as were any who tried to escape from the fire.

When the church was alight one woman managed to climb up to a window and break the glass. As she tried to slide out a soldier fired two shots at her, one of which hit her shoulder.

She fell outside the church, fainting, which saved her life. During the night, she reached a neighbouring village. She is at present recovering.

Some soldiers entered the church as it began to burn and piled up chairs and benches on the mass of people, many of whom had already fainted or were wounded.

During the afternoon the roof of the church fell in with huge flames shooting up. The shrieks stopped.

July 14 1944

Bastille Day On Freed French Soil

From H.D.Ziman, Caen

TO-DAY the anniversary of the taking of the Bastille was celebrated openly for the first time in five years by people in the freed areas of France.

In Caen, which received a heavy shelling from the enemy last night and again to-day, it was decided to hold no large demonstrations.

The Tricolor was hoisted outside the Abbaye aux Hommes. Many families invited British and Canadian troops to spend the evening at home with them.

At a brief military ceremony in the early morning people of the town gathered to see five members of the resistance movement awarded the Croix de Guerre.

A wreath from the British Area Command was laid at the foot of the war memorial.

Otherwise the town's people were too busy clearing up the damage which the enemy are increasing. During the night 18 German shells hit the hospital of Le Bon Sauveur. One exploded in an operating theatre, wounding the surgeon.

In places not so near the front line July 14 was duly commemorated. I attended a moving ceremony near the damaged 12th-century church at Rots, a village five miles north-east of Caen. It is in the area where the Canadians recently did some of their hardest fighting.

Apart from the parish priest, the mayor and some 25 others who remained throughout the fighting, the village had been deserted. But for the past two days the inhabitants have been coming back.

At the suggestion of Capt. F.J. Connolly, a City of London police inspector now serving with Civil Affairs, British, Canadian and American representatives joined in the ceremony in front of a memorial of the last war. A guard of honour was mounted by Canadian troops.

British and American flags draped the churchyard wall. Occasional shellfire or mortar fire was heard in the distance.

The village priest said prayers for the King of England, for France and for the soldiers of all the nations fighting by the side of France.

He then spoke of the four years "without relaxation and without fear" in which they had faced the Germans during the present war. He welcomed the Allies as liberators.

The punishment for collaborating with the Germans

July 21 1944

REVOLT OF GENERALS IN GERMANY

Following the disclosure last evening that an attempt had been made to take Hitler's life, announcements were made on the German radio early this morning that a movement of revolt had developed in Germany in opposition to the Hitler régime.

Hitler himself made a broadcast speech, in which he declared that the attempt on his life had been made by a clique of officers.

He asserted that this clique was not connected with the Army. But this appears to be a very qualified denial, for Goering, who also spoke over the radio, disclosed that the leaders were former generals. Goering said:

"An unimaginably nefarious attempt on the life of the Fuehrer was made to-day by Col. Count von Stauffenberg on the orders of a miserable clique of former generals who had had to be relieved by the Fuehrer of their duties owing to their bad leadership.

"These criminal scoundrels are trying now as a new Reich Government to issue faked orders."

Hitler declared that the attempt on his life was made by a "small clique of criminal officers who had planned to kill him."

He asserted that these officers wanted to prepare Germany for the same fate as in 1918. These criminal elements would be ruthlessly exterminated.

One of the persons present at the conference in which Hitler was engaged at the time has died from his injuries. His name was not disclosed.

Doenitz, Chief of the German Navy, also came before the microphone. He referred to a "small clique of generals" as being responsible for the plot.

Soldiers examine a crashed V-1 flying-bomb

July 22 1944

Portent of Doom

There is no smoke without fire. Both the tone and the substance of Hitler's broadcast show that there really has been an attempt by a group of German officers to rid the Army of a chief whom many of them regard as a deluded and dangerous amateur. This feeling was known to be widespread. It has been expressed with evident sincerity by captured German Generals. It has been indicated by the recent dismissal of such Commanders as Von Rundstedt and Von Falkenhausen. There is therefore no reason to suppose that Goebbels has invented a sob story to restore the plumage of a moulting Fuehrer. Like Napoleon's Marshals, the lieutenants of a much lesser man are tired of being ordered to defeat.

The consequences can only be favourable to the Allied cause. The enemy has clearly been disconcerted by this drastic evidence that even the military worm will turn. Even Goebbels was caught off his balance. First he proclaimed that the authors of the attempt were enemy agents. Then Hitler blurted out that they were a "very small" clique of irresponsible and ambitious officers, and named, as the actual thrower of the bomb, a Colonel on the General Staff.

The latest story is that the guilty officers were in touch with an enemy Power. They were far more likely to be in touch with the spirit of Von Fritsch, murdered for holding independent views in 1939; or with the long succession of Marshals dismissed for offering sound but unpalatable advice. It is a matter of indifference to the Allies what may be the consequences to these or other military leaders in retirement. What matters is the effect upon the leaders and armies in the field.

We know what effect it will have upon our own, since it shows divided counsels in the German General Staff, and therefore finally dispels any idea that that body is a coherent and sagacious family. Nothing was more remarkable during the last war than the unremitting vigour of the Allied assaults during the last months, when every soldier knew they were the last months. That bit of history will certainly repeat itself now. What must not repeat itself is the mistake of allowing the German Army the shadow of an excuse for asserting later that it had never been beaten.

Let us therefore look for definite military consequences and not for theoretical political consequences of this event. It certainly justifies our beginning to count our eggs, but not yet our chickens, for they are not yet hatched.

July 22 1944

Suffering Flying Bombs Gladly

To the Editor of The Daily Telegraph

Sir – Not long after the flying bomb began to fall in a neighbourhood which had already been hard hit in the blitz, two boys, each 12 years of age, hit upon the idea of running a doodle-bug show for the purpose, in their own words, of taking the children off the streets and keeping them out of mischief.

The performance, which lasts about an hour and a half, is staged in a back yard measuring some 12ft by 20ft; at the rear is an Anderson shelter, the top of which provides the balcony. The programme includes a Punch and Judy show, Cinderella and Little Red Riding Hood, all with songs and dances.

Admission is ½d, half of which goes to the Red Cross. All the properties have been provided by the children themselves, even to the Punch and Judy box, which was home-made with timber from a bombed site.

The show has the backing of the mothers, who know where the youngsters are to be found should an alert be sounded while the performance is on. No one who has seen it can doubt that these little Londoners, who have preferred to remain at home rather than face the hazards of evacuation, are true to type.

Yours faithfully
(Rev.) J. W. FITKIN
East London

July 27 1944

Hitler Bomb was in a Suitcase

GOEBBELS, Propaganda Minister and newly appointed Reich Trustee for Total War Mobilisation, broke his silence last night when he broadcast what he termed a "full account of the events of July 20" – the attempted assassination of Hitler.

Points from his speech, which lasted three-quarters of an hour, were:

Count Stauffenberg brought the bomb to Hitler's headquarters in an attaché case and pushed it in front of the Fuehrer's feet.

He then went to Berlin by courier plane with the news that Hitler had succumbed.

The conspirators gave to the Berlin garrison the order to surround the Government quarters, forgetting that the garrison consists of fanatical Nazis.

The plot was practically finished in an hour. Officers and men of the garrison battalion took guns to settle accounts with the conspirators, whose headquarters were occupied without a shot being fired.

There is a vast potential of strength in this country not entirely used.

Himmler's task will be to send reserves to the front and to have many new divisions trained.

So many forces will be released for the front and for the arms industries that we shall be able to deal with all difficulties.

The flying bomb is only a prelude.

The results of our developments are partly still being tested, but mostly being manufactured already.

Recently I saw new weapons which not only made my heart beat faster but stopped it beating.

August 8 1944

CANADA'S FIRST ARMY IN THE FIELD

From H. D. Ziman in Normandy

It can be revealed to-day that the Canadian First Army, under Lt-Gen. H.D.G. Crerar, has been operating in France.

This is the first time that a complete Canadian army has been in the field. In the last war the Dominion had only an army corps in France.

Canadians have been in Normandy since invasion day. The main force, largely brought over in ships of the Royal Canadian Navy, landed that day on the beaches of Berni-eres-sur-Mer, while farther to the east Canadian parachute troops helped to seize the mouth of the Orne.

There has never been a day since the original assault when Canadian troops have been out of the line. One division has been continuously in battle for 53 of the 62 days since invasion day, while the paratroops have never been relieved.

August 14 1944

V-2 READY, SAY GERMANS

The Berlin correspondent of *Svenska Dagbladet* gives to-day what purport to be the details of Germany's secret weapon V-2. Germany, he says, is ready to launch the weapon, but is waiting for the supreme tactical moment.

The new weapon, he states, is not a variation of V-1 but something absolutely new. Unlike the jet-propelled robot bomb, which is a speciality of the Luftwaffe, it can be used by all branches of Germany's fighting services, in air, on land and on sea, "and with an effect more terrible than V-1's."

The German spokesman at the Wilhelmstrasse told the Swedish correspondent that V-2 is independent of distance from target. Even vessels at sea can use it.

Another version from a neutral correspondent is that V-2 is "in production following the conclusion of experiments."

Neutral correspondents are also being told that the bombing of London and Southern England by V-1 "will shortly be on a bigger scale."

"Soon the bombing will be so heavy that vital military targets in Central London will be wiped out," it is said, and the statement is repeated that "flying incendiaries" will be included in the attack.

August 8 1944

Channel Islanders Refused to Collaborate

From Christopher Buckley
On the Brittany Coast

THE Channel Islands, at the moment of writing, are still in German hands, but one cannot say how much longer the enemy will remain there.

The process of evacuation has already begun in the direction of St Malo, and possibly Brest, and it is reliably estimated that at least a third of the garrison has already been withdrawn.

With the American forces in control of the Cherbourg peninsula and also of almost the whole of the north coast of Brittany, the position of the remainder becomes extremely precarious.

Meanwhile, what of the conditions of life in these islands during the four years of German occupation, which began in June 1940? One might divide the occupation period into two phases:

1 The period of industrious wooing, which continued until about the time of Alamein and Stalingrad.
2 The period of intensive and increasing concentration upon defence, which really began something over a year ago.

During the earlier phase the Channel Islands were in the nature of a show place and holiday camp, which German soldiers on leave were encour-

aged to visit. Special passes and travel facilities were provided to give them the opportunity of seeing conquered British territory.

They were encouraged to spend, and did spend freely there, buying up such luxuries as could be obtained in the towns and also fruit and vegetables in the countryside.

Discipline generally was good, and my informants, themselves prominent citizens from Guernsey and Jersey, who have recently made their escape, knew of no atrocities committed during this first period.

In fact, the Germans were trying very hard to be liked, more especially, one gathered, by the English as distinct from the French population.

But they were not liked. Collaboration, in so far as it existed, was purely a commercial matter. It was conditioned by the necessity of keeping the economy of the islands running.

But there was virtually no social collaboration. All the efforts of the Germans to establish an Anglo-German cultural organisation fell absolutely flat in the face of the islanders' stoic refusal to co-operate.

German troops parade through St Peter Port, Guernsey

August 16 1944

LANDINGS IN SOUTH OF FRANCE

IT was officially announced at Allied HQ, Italy, last night that the beachheads secured in the South of France by Allied landings in the morning at points along 100 miles of coast from Nice to Marseilles had been extended and widened.

Substantial numbers of troops, together with guns, munitions and supplies, had been landed by nightfall. Enemy opposition remained sporadic and no German air attacks had yet been reported. Some of the high ground behind the beaches was in Allied hands.

During the operation two small enemy ships had been sunk and prisoners taken. On the beaches of the mainland where landings were successful against light opposition the operation was proceeding satisfactorily. Naval gunfire was reported to have been very effective.

The Navy was continuing without pause the landing of troops with their stores and equipment. Allied convoys were already leaving on their return voyage from the assault area and new convoys were arriving.

The first indication of the precise areas of landing was given in a statement at Allied HQ that the islands of Port Cros and Levant, in the Hyeres group 30 miles south-east of Toulon, had been captured.

The mainland peninsula of Cap Negre, about four miles east of Bormes, has also been occupied.

These captures were effected before dawn by American and French troops landed from ships of the United States and Royal Canadian Navies.

The only other invasion area identified from Allied sources up to this morning was at Frejus, near St Raphael, where, according to a war correspondent, seaborne forces were landed.

General de Gaulle returns in triumph to Paris

August 24 1944

PARISIANS FREE THEIR CITY AFTER 4 YEARS

" AUG. 23, 1944 – Paris is free." In these historic words Gen. de Gaulle's provisional Government announced the liberation of the French capital after it had been occupied by the Germans for more than four years – since June 14 1940.

The city was freed of the invaders' yoke by the citizens themselves after four days' fighting, in which 50,000 armed patriots of the French Forces of the Interior and several hundred thousand unarmed civilians took part.

Although there is no indication that the American troops who had closed in on Paris from the west and south had any share in these operations, a message early to-day from a correspondent with the United States forces said that strong patrols were operating last night outside Versailles, 20 miles west of the centre of Paris. It added that Versailles was invaded early yesterday by members of the French resistance movement.

The first news of the liberation of Paris was broadcast from a radio station in or very near the city just after 12.30 p.m. Within half an hour came a special communiqué from Gen. Koenig, the commander of the FFI and newly-appointed Military Governor of Paris.

The city is the first big Allied capital to be liberated and the news was hailed with tremendous enthusiasm by Frenchmen in many Allied countries.

When the order was given on Friday for a general insurrection in the French capital the revolt began in the Ile de la Cité, the original city of Paris. The Ile was seized and held by the Paris police, who were already on strike. By yesterday the patriots had occupied all the city's public buildings.

Within ten hours of the news of the liberation of Paris, it was officially announced last night that French troops had entered the great port of Marseilles, the second largest city of France.

American troops parade down the Champs Elysées
German prisoners are taunted by the jubilant Parisians

THE DAILY TELEGRAPH

August 24 1944

Great Days

IN all its long history, not even excluding the period of the Revolution, the city of Paris has known no more dramatic days than the week-end which has ended with its liberation. It was achieved by a mass uprising of the citizens themselves, the spearhead of which was a force of 50,000 armed men. Their strength and their achievement speak volumes for the efficiency of the quiet work which has been carried on despite Germans and quislings for four long years by men and women who have hourly risked their lives for this hour. "*Fluctuat nec Mergitur*," storm-tossed but unsinkable, is more than ever a fitting motto for the great city; and PEGUY'S "*peuple de Paris, peuple roi*" remains a true description of her people. The fall of Paris in 1940 struck a chill into every French heart and many more besides. It was the final proof that, for the time being, the game was up. The resurgence of Paris in 1944 sends a thrill through every heart then downcast. It is the final proof that the hunt is up.

Like the capture of Rome, the liberation of Paris possesses a military value largely symbolic. It is an omen of coming triumph so undeniable that the enemy has not yet dared to admit it. Moreover, in recapturing their city the Parisians have not only saved it from the risk of major damage, to the delight of the whole civilised world, but they have given the Allies, whose lightning advance inspired the signal for their rising, a first-class means to throw full strength into the task of destroying the German armies. Paris is a city of bridges, all probably intact and offering a channel for powerful forces to move swiftly north upon the rear of the German 15th Army.

Therefore not for the first time the *Maquis* has made a substantial contribution to Allied strategy, and has not merely recovered its country's capital city but has also greatly strengthened its country's claim to rank among the Great Powers. The importance to the Allies of not having to divert large forces towards so tempting an objective can hardly be exaggerated.

August 26 1944

Gen. de Gaulle Enters Liberated Paris

THE remaining German forces in Paris surrendered last evening after Gen. Leclerc, commander of the French Second Armoured Division, had sent their commander an ultimatum telling him to cease resistance, which had become useless.

Gen. de Gaulle entered the liberated city at 7 p.m. and was received at the Prefecture of Police and at the Hotel de Ville, the Town Hall, by the new Prefect. In a brief speech he said: "I wish simply and from the bottom of my heart to say to you, 'Vive Paris.'"

Captured German officers in the Hotel Majestic, former Wehrmacht HQ

THE DAILY TELEGRAPH

September 1 1944

Five Years

WE look back to-day upon five years of the sternest struggle which the British people have ever fought, a war for our national existence, for the rights of free peoples and for the life of Christian civilisation. Against us nearly all the resources of Europe outside Russia were soon combined, and over a long period the British Commonwealth stood alone and baffled forces far superior numerically in the air and on land. We may well be proud now of the achievement which brought into being the alliance of the United Nations and gave time for the deployment of their strength against the triple menace to mankind. It is a dismal anniversary for HITLER and German militarism. The wheel has turned almost full circle since that Sept. 1 which saw him with loud applause from German throats launch the Wehrmacht upon Poland. That tortured but gallant country has never given up the struggle then begun.

In 1941 the great alliance of freedom was built up. In 1942 the triple assaults in Russia, Africa, and the Far East were held and driven back. The campaigns of that year are the dividing line of the war, the line at which the Allies passed from the defensive to the offensive.

Through 1943 they obtained and kept the initiative all over the world. The Battle of the Atlantic against the U-boat went well. The German armies were driven back from the Volga to the Dnieper and the huge disaster of Stalingrad was equalled by catastrophic defeat in Africa. MUSSOLINI fell and in September Italy surrendered – another memory of the month for his imitator and master, HITLER. The Allied air onslaught on Germany grew to a scale which enfeebled the Luftwaffe and made its recuperation impossible.

To-day, at the beginning of September 1944, the Russians are on the frontier of East Prussia, the American Third Army in France well under a hundred miles from the German frontier this side of the Rhine. The battle of the air has been well and truly won before the battle of the land. Day after day Germans are told that their armies cannot withstand the striking power of the Allied air forces. The many brave words of HITLER and the High Command on the inevitable failure of an Allied landing are eaten wholesale by official spokesmen.

Even the propagandists are doubtful if they can now fool all the people all the time. The sagacious DITTMAR has posed the grim question whether the sacrifices and losses past, present and still to come are worth while, "taking a sane view of the situation." The announcement that sane Germans are anxious for peace now is, as Mr CORDELL HULL remarked, plain enough. Germany, as the sixth year of war begins, is still "vaunting aloud but racked with deep despair."

Canadian troops roll past Rouen

Canadian troops enter Bruges

September 6 1944

BRITISH CHASED NAZIS IN AND OUT OF BRUSSELS

From Christopher Buckley
Brussels

WE chased the Germans back into Brussels this evening and we chased them out at the other side. It was the climax of an advance in which the British armoured forces advanced 73 miles between sunrise and sunset – besides four short but brisk actions in the course of the day.

It is an achievement which has scarcely a parallel in the whole realm of military history.

There is no language adequate to express the enthusiasm with which a British uniform is greeted during these wonderful days. Whether it is Bayeux or Rennes, Paris or Brussels, the essential reception is the same – warm, spontaneous and generous.

Britain has never been more admired on the Continent – not even when she fought her lone and apparently hopeless battle in 1940. And we can retain this admiration if we choose.

Allied Dakota aircraft flying over Gheel, Belgium to Holland

September 18 1944

ALLIED ARMY LANDED BY AIR IN HOLLAND

A great force of parachutists and glider troops of the Allied First Airborne Army landed at noon yesterday in the Rhine delta area of Holland, striking at the right flank of Germany's whole defence line in the west.

A correspondent with these forces reported that by last night the enemy had been cleared from several Dutch towns and British and American troops had established their positions.

Strong British armoured columns from the Second Army's bridgehead over the Escaut Canal, 18 miles south of Eindhoven, drove across the frontier and were two miles inside Holland last night. Infantry rode on the tanks, which advanced behind a creeping barrage and with strong air support.

The whole of the Allied air forces based in Britain and Western Europe co-operated in the airborne invasion.

According to German sources the troops landed in the areas of:

Eindhoven, 10 miles across the Dutch frontier;

Tilburg, on the Wilhelmina Canal, 20 miles north-west of Eindhoven; and

Nijmegen, on the Rhine 35 miles north-east of Eindhoven and three miles from Germany.

September 12 1944

ALLIES FIGHTING FIVE MILES INTO GERMANY

ALLIED forces are now fighting on German soil, it was announced at midnight.

Troops of Gen. Hodges's American First Army crossed the German-Luxembourg border "in reasonable strength" some miles north of Trier, apparently across the River Sure, and advanced about five miles into enemy territory.

They made contact with the Siegfried Line, according to correspondents at Shaef, and are probing the strength of these defences, which are deep around Trier.

A fierce artillery bombardment of the frontier which preceded their entry indicates that their advance is being made with full artillery support and adequate air cover.

The Allies are now within range of the Siegfried Line all the way south from Aachen to Trier. Reports from the whole front confirm that the German Command is completely confused about where the Allies will strike next.

British paratroops landing on the outskirts of Arnhem

September 28 1944

Arnhem: Air Troops Withdrawn

THE survivors of the British First Airborne Division, after holding the Arnhem bridgehead against overwhelming odds for eight days and nights, were withdrawn to the south bank of the Lower Rhine during Monday night.

Supreme HQ, revealing last night that the operation had been completed, said that 1,200 wounded were left behind and were being well cared for by the Germans. The survivors were in rest billets and receiving every possible comfort.

Approximately 8,000 men were dropped in the Arnhem area and some 2,000 had been ferried across the Lower Rhine from the bridgehead, which became a trap when bad weather prevented adequate airborne reinforcements being dropped.

A despatch from Holland early to-day said that Field-Marshal Montgomery personally ordered the withdrawal from Arnhem.

Although the division failed to maintain its grip on the bridgehead – and at one period it actually held one of the river bridges – its dour stand 50 miles behind the German front was of inestimable value to the British Second Army's race across Holland to seize the Nijmegen bridge over the 600-yards-wide River Waal.

Large numbers of first-class German troops were immobilised at Arnhem and the enemy was barred from using the bridges there to stream south to Nijmegen.

One despatch said it was estimated that the air army killed or wounded 12,000 Germans during the battle. It added that there were reports of 1,000 men still hiding in the woods around Arnhem.

Other despatches said that among the reasons for the failure of the Second Army to reach the Lower Rhine in time were the exposed and elevated roads which made our tanks perfect targets for the German guns, the consequent delay while infantry cleaned up the hidden batteries and the cutting of the supply line by repeated enemy attacks.

A senior staff officer was quoted as saying the operation was a gallant but expensive success; "four-fifths of the risky plan succeeded."

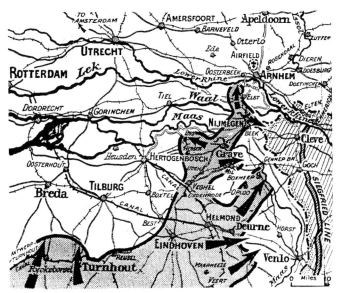

The attack at Arnhem

Maj-Gen. Urquhart plants the Airborne flag at his Arnhem HQ

September 29 1944

ARNHEM FORCE CHIEF ESCAPED AFTER CAPTURE

THE War Office announced last night that the Commander of the British 1st Airborne Division is Maj.-Gen. R. E. Urquhart, DSO and bar.

The Germans have said that he was a prisoner. He is believed to have been in enemy hands for a short time, said the War Office, but he subsequently escaped and is now safe.

Gen. Urquhart is 42. He went to St Paul's, the school which Field-Marshal Montgomery attended.

October 6 1944

GREEKS' JOYFUL WELCOME

From L. Marsland Gander
With the Land Forces, Adriatic

BRITISH parachutists and RAF aircraft began the liberation of Greece jointly some days ago. They came, they saw and they stayed.

Thus when the first ships carrying sea-borne troops arrived they found that the normal routine of invasion had been reversed. An airfield was already in operation, and supplies were being landed.

The first parachutists, dropped from Dakota transports, discovered that the airfield had been evacuated but that there had been extensive and thorough demolitions. There were no signs of the enemy, who had apparently cleared out hurriedly.

A Dakota then attempted a landing, touched down successfully and the parachutists began to consolidate.

A few hours later in daylight Spitfires landed, accompanied by formations of Dakotas of the Balkan Air Force bringing fuel, servicing equipment and more men.

The delirious enthusiasm of the peasantry at the sight of British troops was a repetition of that experience in Southern France and was tempered only by the grimmer living conditions and privations.

Spitfire pilots had flowers flung into their cockpits.

October 16 1944

ROMMEL DEAD: OFFICIAL

THE official German News Agency last night announced that Rommel is dead. He was 52.

It said: "Gen. Field-Marshal Rommel has died as a result of the severe injuries to his head which he received as C-in-C of an army group in the West in a motor-car accident.

"Hitler has ordered a State funeral. With the death of Gen. Field-Marshal Rommel, the soldierly life of one of our most successful army commanders has reached fulfilment.

"His name will be for ever linked with the two years' heroic fight of the German Afrika Korps."

Rommel was making a tour of the Germans' battle position in Normandy on July 17 when his car was attacked by two RAF planes.

He fell in trying to jump out of the car and was later found unconscious in a ditch. His aide-de-camp and chauffeur were killed.

H. D. Ziman, DAILY TELEGRAPH Special Correspondent, reported on July 30 that the Nazi field-marshal died at Bernay Hospital, near Lisieux.

October 16 1944

All Ranks' Civilian Kit

FROM to-day a private, on discharge from the Army, will receive a civilian wardrobe of exactly the same quality as that issued to a lieutenant-colonel. No distinction is being made between officers and men.

From to-day, also, he will no longer be able to take a cash grant of £2 15s 9d instead of a suit.

All discharged men leaving regimental depots will be dealt with in the same way as those who will eventually come under the Government's full demobilisation scheme.

Under that scheme there will be about 12 large demobilisation depots, but until they come into operation discharges will continue to take place through regimental headquarters in different parts of the country.

Soldiers will no longer return to civil life clad in inferior "reach-me-downs." Existing stocks of the old type of clothing have been collected for relief in Europe, and all future issues will be of the superior, non-austerity type.

At present-day values, each set of civilian kit is worth at least £20. It consists of a suit, chosen from a range of 100 patterns; shirt, collar, tie, pair of boots or shoes, raincoat or light coat, and a felt hat. In addition, each man will keep his Service socks and underclothing, of which he should have two complete sets.

October 18 1944

CAPT. DOUGLAS-HOME COURT-MARTIALLED

THE War Office last night confirmed a report that Capt. Hon. William Douglas-Home, of Royal Armoured Corps, had been court-martialled in Belgium on charge of "not obeying a lawful command" under Section 9 of Army Act. Findings of Court will be promulgated.

In a letter purporting to have come from Capt. Douglas-Home and published in a Maidenhead newspaper last month, it was stated he refused to attack when ordered at Havre, as he "could not bring myself to take part in operation against troops who admittedly did not want to fight but whose commander refused to accept unconditional surrender."

November 11 1944

Premier Reveals V-2 Damage Not Heavy

THE first official announcement that long-range rockets – Germany's secret V-2 weapon – have been falling on this country for several weeks was made in the House of Commons to-day by Mr Churchill.

He said that casualties and damage had not so far been heavy. Some rockets had been fired from Walcheren, now in our hands, and other sites would doubtless be overrun by our forces.

There was no certainty that the range of the rockets would not be increased, nor that new launching areas farther back would not in turn be overrun.

Mr CHURCHILL said: Last February I told Parliament that the Germans were preparing to attack this country by means of long-range rockets, and I referred again to the possibility of this form of attack in my statement in this House on July 6.

For the last few weeks the enemy has been using his new weapon, the long-range rocket, and a number have landed at widely scattered points in this country. In all the casualties and damage have so far not been heavy, though I am sure the House will wish me to express our sympathy with the victims of these attacks.

Americans in action on Leyte

October 21 1944

BIG US FORCES LAND IN THE PHILIPPINES

IN the greatest amphibious operation of the Pacific war powerful American forces under the personal command of Gen. MacArthur, Allied C-in-C, South-West Pacific, to-day landed on Leyte Island, in the Central Philippines.

By to-night two major beachheads had been firmly established on the east coast of the island, while tanks and infantry, advancing on the capital, Tacloban, a port of 32,000 inhabitants, had captured its airfield.

November 7 1944

Lord Moyne Killed in Cairo Outrage

From Our Cairo Correspondent

LORD Moyne, British Minister-Resident in the Middle East, died at 8.40 to-night in a military hospital here after being shot outside his home soon after 1 p.m. by two civilians. He was 64 and the third son of the first Earl of Iveagh.

Three bullets hit him in the neck, stomach and leg. The two assassins attempted to escape on bicycles but were arrested.

Gen. Paget, C-in-C, Middle East, in a tribute in Cairo last night to the dead Minister-Resident, referred to the "tragic death of Lord Moyne at the hands of Jewish assassins."

November 23 1944

Film of "Henry V"

By Campbell Dixon

RARELY, if ever, has a film excited so much curiosity as "Henry V."

The magic of Shakespeare's name, rich pageantry, a prodigious array of talent, and the fact that no British picture has ever before cost £500,000 – all this excited the highest expectations.

Much is magnificent. The battle scenes, made at Powerscourt, in Eire, owing to war-time difficulties in England, have the sweep and excitement one expects of Mr De Mille, with the gorgeous colour of a Flemish old master.

As the French cavalry came charging down the slopes while the English bowmen waited in deadly silence, the audience at yesterday's preview spontaneously applauded.

Some of the smaller scenes are as effective in their way: the French princess's English lesson, for instance; Henry's tempestuous wooing at first sight, saved from absurdity by its humour; and the talk of the soldiers around the camp fire on the eve of battle.

The acting, too, is for the most part admirable. Laurence Olivier, besides producing and directing, plays Henry with immense fire and dash.

November 21 1944

Lights Go Up in Piccadilly After 5 Years

THE lights were up again in Piccadilly last night. Three of the most famous streets in the world – Piccadilly, the Strand and Fleet-street – were among many lit up for the first time since the war began.

The Corporation of London and the City of Westminster sprang a pleasant surprise on thousands of people by switching on without warning the new "moonlighting." The result was not as in peace time, but it was enough to lighten the hearts of thousands of blackout-weary Londoners.

I walked from Fleet-street to Piccadilly-circus along streets in which the use of a torch was no longer necessary. Standing under one of the lights one could comfortably read a newspaper.

November 9 1944

Ensa Sending 300 Artists to Far East

Mr Basil Dean, Director of Ensa, said yesterday that by Christmas Ensa will have 300 artists in India and the Far East. Such well-known stars as George Formby, Josephine Baker, and Forsythe, Seamon and Farrell have already volunteered.

In addition, a dramatic company is going out to appear in the following repertory of plays: "They Came to a City," "How Are They at Home?" "Mr Bolfrey," "Ten Little Niggers," and "A Soldier for Christmas."

Six Allied Armies attacking on the Western Front

November 22 1944

RAF BLAST V-2 LAUNCHING SITE IN HOLLAND

A V-2 launching site in Holland was bombed "dead on the target" by Spitfire fighter-bombers of an Australian squadron of RAF Fighter Command yesterday, the Air Ministry stated.

Diving from 8,000 feet in difficult weather conditions, the formation placed bombs with pin-point accuracy.

"The site looked just like the illustrations in the Press. It had probably only recently been erected in readiness for firing," a pilot said.

"Our target was a V-2 storage erection and launching site, and there was a lot of cloud about when we finally located it in a clearing in the woods. We saw explosions on the site and in the woods nearby.

"After we had bombed we made a ground strafing attack on the target, spraying it with cannon-fire. We scored hits on a V-2 which was standing near the edge of the clearing, but it was not filled with its charge because it did not blow up when our shells struck it."

November 14 1944

TIRPITZ SUNK BY 29 LANCASTERS

BLASTED by the terrific explosions of three RAF 12,000lb "earthquake" bombs in a few minutes along her 790 feet of deck, the 45,000-ton battleship Tirpitz – last remaining pride of the Germany Navy since her sister-ship, the Bismarck, was sunk in May 1941 by the Royal Navy – lay capsized yesterday at the bottom of Tromsoe Fjord, in Northern Norway.

It was the third attack on the Tirpitz with 12,000lb bombs, but the first time that the plane crews had been able to see her properly.

Previously cloud, or the smoke-screen in which the battleship could be completely hidden in 10 minutes, had handicapped the RAF airmen.

The success they have now scored – a triumph of aerial precision attack from a great height, possibly about 16,000ft – was achieved largely by the development of the 12,000lb armour-piercing bomb.

The designer of this weapon, it was disclosed last night, is Mr B. N. Wallis, of Vickers-Armstrongs Ltd, the scientist who also designed the special mines which breached the Mohne and Eder dams in May 1943.

British tanks in formation between Gangelt and Geilenkirchen

December 31 1944

The Year's Work

IN these last days of the year RUNDSTEDT's offensive, which was, according to Berlin, "the most beautiful Christmas present for Germans one could wish," has been stopped and become a defensive and at some points a withdrawal. The German High Command has staked so much on this western blow that we must expect renewed and desperate efforts to make the gamble a success.

Thus at the end of the first round of the western battle for Germany hopes of swifter progress in the New Year are confirmed by the operations to which RUNDSTEDT has committed himself and his armies. He will have nothing to spare for the eastern battle, nor can he expect any help from the German forces engaged there. They are fighting to the death in Budapest and on the Hungarian plains, but they cannot stem the Russian advance upon the Austrian gate to Germany, the gap which was within 60 miles yesterday.

Such is the prospect as the year dies. A year ago HITLER's Order of the Day announced that the German front was south of Rome, that German forces were in command of the Balkans, and that "wherever a landing is attempted in the West it will fail." Yet the Allies saw great opportunities which have been brilliantly seized.

To-day the Germans, thanks to their professional and intuitional strategists, have the war on two fronts which has been their nightmare ever since they harvested their ill-gotten gains of 1870. The spoils which they hoped from this war are now beyond their reach. All the Ukraine harvests, the Rumanian wheat and the Hungarian wheat which fed Germany through the last war are now lost, with the oil and metals of the Danube valley and the Balkans. The satellites have deserted.

December 4 1944

The King's Farewell to the Home Guard

IN the presence of the King, contingents of Home Guards from all over Britain and Northern Ireland yesterday held their final parade following the recent "stand-down" order. From now they cease to exist as a force in being, but remain ready to answer in any emergency.

His Majesty took the salute in Hyde Park from 7,000 Home Guards. They marched through the West End of London on a three miles' long route lined with cheering crowds.

1945

"V" for Victory: searchlights illuminate St Paul's Cathedral

JUST when it really seemed to Britons that it was all over the drive on Berlin lost its impetus and the outlook was yet again bleak. Flying bombs, rockets, rationing, war work – however stimulating turbanned grannies found radio's *Music While You Work* – a hard, freezing winter and the Ardennes reverse on the western front, had taken their toll of morale. People were grey, pinched and war weary.

Away from it all, however, in the welcome February warmth of the Russian Black Sea resort of Yalta, Stalin, Roosevelt and Churchill agreed zones of occupation of Germany, considered the question of reparations and sketched the future map of Europe. As the leaders parted, they knew enough to justify their confidence. The Russians, reaching the Oder, and the Allies the Rhine, knew that defeat of Germany was but a matter of time. In mid-February, to help victory in Europe on its way and the Russian advance, the RAF – ostensibly to disrupt communications on the German front with Russia – added the destruction of historic Dresden to its unrelenting bomber offensive.

In the early spring, to the dismay of Churchill, the Americans lost interest in Berlin as the ultimate objective, Eisenhower maintaining that his first task was to seek and destroy the enemy. Not only did the Supreme Commander offer Stalin the German capital on a plate, but he briefed him on the Allied order of battle. Stalin failed to reciprocate and at first suspected a trick. He could not believe his good fortune. Generally, the Americans were reined back and on May 2 the garrison commander surrendered Berlin to the Russians. Hitler, his wife of a few hours, Eva Braun, and his dog were already dead. Among his last acts, Hitler had dismissed two of his closest and formerly most loyal colleagues – Goering, officially his successor, and Himmler – passing the chancellorship to Goebbels. But the creator of the Nazi propaganda machine, in his turn, committed suicide after killing his wife and children. In the same last testament Hitler had appointed Admiral Doenitz President and Commander-in-Chief of the Armed Forces, posts he held for a mere seven days.

On May 4, relishing the limelight and using "an ordinary Army pen that you could buy in a shop for twopence," Monty accepted the surrender of German forces in north-west Germany, Holland and Denmark at Luneburg Heath. Before the pen disappeared ("I suppose somebody pinched it") he signed also for the Supreme Allied Commander. At Rheims on May 7 the instrument of total, unconditional surrender was signed at Eisenhower's HQ by Lieutenant-General Bedell Smith and General Jodl and witnessed by French and Russian officers.

So much had changed so swiftly. London erupted in celebration and throughout careworn Britain people drew on the energy of success to celebrate. Hitler and Mussolini – executed by partisans on April 28 – were dead. In the mad, euphoric moments of VE Day the war in the Pacific and in South-East Asia seemed temporarily irrelevant.

More relevant than could be immediately recognised was the fact that the deaths of the Axis partners had been preceded in April by that of President Roosevelt, who had succoured Britain since well before America's entry into the war. Thus, when next the Allied leaders met at the Potsdam conference of mid-July in Berlin, the American seat was occupied by the new and un-tested figure of Harry Truman. In the event the abrupt conclusion of the wartime special relationship between president and prime minister was of no consequence. When the results of the July General Election were declared, Labour had romped home and Clement Attlee, Churchill's coalition deputy, was in Downing Street.

Now the full resources of the Allies could be turned against Japan, though Stalin delayed until the bitter end in August before declaring war. For those not in the know – and they numbered all but the scientists involved and people at the very top – an atomic bomb was at hand. Now that Slim's 14th Army was victorious in Burma, this weapon would bypass the bloody business of invading Malaya, liberating Singapore and the Dutch East Indies and invading Japan itself.

In Burma, Slim's troops moving forward "on the wings of the air force" (as Park, formerly leader of the Battle of Britain's key 11 Group and air commander in Malta, proudly claimed), had taken Mandalay and on May 3 obtained the Japanese surrender at Rangoon. The 14th Army was no longer forgotten, Mountbatten's publicity machine had seen to that.

At Quebec Churchill had promised to reinforce the Far East after Germany's defeat. Already, at the end of March a British Pacific Fleet (known as "Task Force 57"), was in its battle area east of Formosa. It greatly assisted the April landings on Okinawa, and shared with the Americans the horrors of the developing *kamikaze* suicide air attacks. The Americans offered Britain an air base on Okinawa and all seemed set for its participation in the assault on Japan.

Fortunately – as those who fought on Japanese shores understandably see it – nuclear destruction of Hiroshima and Nagasaki on August 6 and 9 removed the necessity. On August 14 Japan capitulated and on September 2, General Douglas MacArthur, Supreme Allied Commander – now more a god in the Pacific than Emperor Hirohito – accepted the Japanese surrender in Tokyo Bay. After six long years it really was all over.

Released British prisoners in a Rangoon prison camp

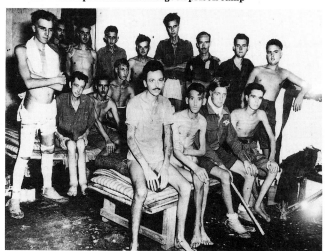

US tanks moving towards Bastogne, Belgium through the snow

January 1 1945

Hitler:"War Won't Be Over Before 1946"

HITLER this morning broke the long silence he has maintained since the attempt on his life last July.

In a 26-minute broadcast from his HQ to the German people, which he began at five minutes past midnight, he declared that the war would not end before 1946. Germany, he reiterated, would never capitulate.

The voice which came over the radio was recognised as Hitler's voice, but it was not clear whether it was a live broadcast or a recorded version.

The speech was delivered at almost breathless speed, far faster than usual, without the familiar rhetorical pauses and without any shouting.

Since his last public performance the voice has lost some of its bravado and acquired a clearly discernible lisp. At times the speaker had difficulty in pronouncing clearly some of his syllables. It was a very much older Hitler than the one who spoke at midnight following the attempted assassination.

160 people were killed by a V-2 attack on this store in New Cross, London

January 10 1945

GERMANS RETREATING IN ARDENNES BULGE

DESPITE bitter weather and heavy snow, with drifts 4ft deep in places, British and American troops are slowly but surely closing the gap between the northern and southern flanks of the Ardennes salient.

Little more than 10 miles to-night separated the armies of Gen. Bradley and Field-Marshal Montgomery at the narrowest part of the corridor between Longchamps to the south and Laroche to the north.

The enemy was still resisting savagely and bitterly disputing every yard we gained, but he appeared to be withdrawing from his advanced positions.

January 18 1945

WARSAW TAKEN

Warsaw captured by the Russians

Warsaw, the Polish capital enslaved by Hitler for five years and four months, has been captured by Russian and Polish troops – and last night Moscow and Lublin reported further sweeping Soviet victories in Poland along a front of more than 250 miles.

Moscow radio declared at midnight: "The victory march to Berlin is going on."

After Marshal Stalin had announced the capture, by Marshal Zhukov, of "the capital of our Ally, Poland," he gave the news of a break-through by the Polish-born Marshal Rokossovsky north of Warsaw on a 60-mile front to a depth of 25 miles.

Then Lublin radio stated that Krakov, the ancient Polish capital, the greatest German base in South Poland, and the centre of their "Government" in Poland, had been taken by Marshal Koniev.

January 20 1945

Polish Premier: "I Hold Out My Hand to Russia"

The Prime Minister of Poland, M. Arciszewski, broadcast to his country last night. He said:

"As a Pole, as one of the leaders of that underground movement which has not for one moment ceased from its life-and-death struggle against the German invader, as a Socialist, as Prime Minister of the Polish Government, I hold out my hand to the Soviet Union.

"I hold it out to achieve not a momentary understanding, but a lasting agreement, a lasting and honest co-operation.

"From the bottom of my heart, I believe that, in spite of all that has been said and all that has been done, such an agreement can be reached. Geography and history demand it.

"A tragic misunderstanding underlies the fact that the best of the Poles, those who have fought for the freedom of their own country and of the world, the architects of Polish freedom, democracy and social justice are to-day called traitors.

"A fact, which can never be obliterated or changed is the Polish people's five-and-a-half-year struggle for independent existence.

"Can it be imagined that in this great moment of her triumph, Russia will brush them aside to support a gang of little men who deny their reality?

"All we claim is the right of our nation to true independence. This means that no bayonet, however crowned with glory, shall dictate who is to govern a country.

"It means a Government not imposed by force, but based upon democratic elections without external pressure. If these principles are recognised, and all they imply fulfilled, then there is no Russo-Polish problem which cannot be easily and amicably solved."

January 24 1945

14th ARMY TIGHTENS ARC ROUND MANDALAY

As the Japanese mass considerable forces around Mandalay, 14th Army forces are threatening the city from the north, north-west and west.

Driving east towards the Irrawaddy from the Chindwin port of Monywa, Allied forces have reached Myinmu, 35 miles from the Upper Burma capital.

Troops closing in from the north-west have seized Tizaung, 31 miles from Mandalay, while farther north Yonbingan, about the same distance away, has been captured.

The capture of Monywa, on the east bank of the Chindwin, opens a new way of communication to the 14th Army, as the Chindwin can now be brought into use as a supply route.

Adml Lord Louis Mountbatten, Supreme Allied Commander, South-East Asia, has sent this telegram to the Combined Chiefs of Staff of Mr Roosevelt and Mr Churchill:

"The first part of the orders I received at Quebec has been carried out. The land route to China is open."

Steam pours from a Japanese train bombed by the RAF

February 13 1945

Three Powers Decide on Germany's Future

DECISIONS of far-reaching importance to the future of the world were announced in a communiqué issued last night at the conclusion of eight days' conversations between Mr Churchill, President Roosevelt and Marshal Stalin.

The meeting, which took place in the Crimean resort of Yalta, and is to be officially known as the Crimea Conference, was attended by the Foreign Secretaries, Chiefs of Staff and other advisers of the three Governments.

Agreement was reached for enforcing the unconditional surrender terms to be imposed on Germany, but these will not be revealed until after her final defeat.

The British, American and Russian forces will each occupy a separate zone of Germany. A Central Control Commission consisting of the Supreme Commanders of the three Powers will have HQ in Berlin.

France will be invited to take a zone of occupation and participate in the Control Commission.

Churchill, Roosevelt and Stalin at Yalta, February 1945

February 13 1945

Far-Reaching Decisions

WHEN the three leaders of the nations met in conference at Teheran they made plans which determined the course of the war. Their meeting at Yalta has completed great schemes by which the world's future will be shaped. What first strikes the mind is the number and extent of the problems dealt with; then the comprehensiveness of the conclusions. Nothing has been shirked. No difficulties have been ignored. In the long communiqué there are no loose ends.

Last, though by no means least, for it has been through centuries one of the most vexed questions of civilisation, comes Poland. It is evident that the Crimea Conference worked hard for a satisfactory settlement. The solution proposed is a compromise which would bring into the Provisional Government of Lublin "democratic leaders from Poland itself and from Poles abroad," give Poland an eastern frontier slightly more favourable than the Curzon Line and substantial extensions north and west, leaving the western frontier to be determined at the Peace Conference. Some controversial matters are at least modulated by this scheme.

There will no doubt be objections maintained with some vigour. On the whole it certainly provides a basis from which a settlement could be attained, with a will to peace on both sides. The building up throughout the world of the will to peace is the only means by which the future can realise the ideal "that all the men in all the lands may live out their lives in freedom from fear and want."

February 15 1945

MASSIVE RAIDS ON DRESDEN

By Air Cdre Howard-Williams
Air Correspondent

THE massive Allied raids on Dresden indicate that the plans made at the Yalta Conference are being implemented almost before the ink of the signatures is dry.

A heavy strain had already been thrown on routes to the Eastern front, other than that through Dresden, by recent raids on Chemnitz and Magdeburg, which were again attacked yesterday, and on Leipzig.

It is estimated that troops and civilians in Dresden may have numbered up to 2,000,000. The normal population is 640,000.

Many Berliners and evacuees from the east had fled to the city, which had excellent rail communications with the capital and had developed into a huge arms centre.

The confines of the city include over 30 miles of track and a huge marshalling yard on the left bank of the River Elbe, which is crossed by six bridges.

Most of the rail network there is located to the south-west and north-west in a system closely linked to the river docks and warehouses.

It is significant that the flak was not heavy. The Nazis may have sent their guns to protect Berlin, thinking Dresden safe from bombing owing to its distance from British bases.

Air Chief Marshal Sir Arthur Harris, Chief of Bomber Command, changed his tactics during the RAF raid. He sent his force on the 670-mile journey in two waves, with two separate master bombers.

"Give us a month of reasonable weather," said an Air Staff officer to me yesterday, "and we will paralyse the railroad system of the German armies in the East and in the West."

It is difficult to over-estimate the tremendous effect which the attack on the German rail junctions – all of them vital to the Wehrmacht at this time – will have on the German army attempting to hold Marshal Koniev's advance in Silesia.

The capital of Saxony, Dresden is the seat of a technical academy and of an academy of arts. The seventh largest city in all Germany, it can be compared in size with Manchester. I understand that the more valuable art treasures have long since been put underground elsewhere.

March 2 1945

Runner Beans at 30s a Pound

By a Woman Reporter

FOR the first time this year dwarf runner beans of the French type are in West End shops. Grown in Cornish and Devon hot-houses, they are 30s lb.

Grapefruit from the Middle East has arrived. They will be distributed in the same way as oranges and lemons at a controlled price of 8d lb.

March 5 1945

Princess Joins ATS

PRINCESS Elizabeth has joined the ATS and is taking a course at a training centre. This was disclosed in the following announcement issued at Buckingham Palace last night:

The King has granted to her Royal Highness the Princess Elizabeth a commission with the honorary rank of second subaltern in the Auxiliary Territorial Service.

Her Royal Highness is at present attending a course at a driving training centre in the South of England.

It is understood that this step has been taken at the Princess's own request. She is to be treated in exactly the same way as any other officer-learner at the driving training centre. By the King's orders she is to receive no special privileges.

Princess Elizabeth, who will be 19 on April 21, is the first woman member of the Royal family to join as a full-time active member of the women's services. The Queen is chief of all three women's services and the Princess Royal is Controller-Commandant of the ATS.

The ruins of Dresden after Allied bombing

March 14 1945

People of Ten Races in Freed Slaves' Camp

From Christopher Buckley, Krefeld

THE town prison I visited was not perhaps essentially different from those scores of hundreds of detention centres where people of all ages and races and callings have suffered, obscurely and hopelessly in Germany.

To-day it fulfils a new role. It is being used as an enormous transit camp in which many thousands of French or foreign workers of the Western Rhineland are being housed as a preliminary to repatriation.

Europe has never experienced anything resembling this forced migration of peoples which has been imposed by the German Reich in the past five years. None of the great depopulations in the Near East in mediaeval or biblical times is comparable in scale.

There are, at this moment, wandering about over Western Germany, tens of thousands of these hapless "displaced persons" whose lives were violently interrupted months or years ago by the Nazi demand for labour. Since then they have lived the life of slaves to the German war machine.

They tell me there are 17,000,000 of them, an appalling reflection.

To-day I saw over 3,000 of them, a cross-section of the foreign workers of the Rhineland. They included Russians, Poles, French, Dutch, Belgians, Italians, Spaniards, Czechs, Serbians and Armenians.

They sat patiently in the now open cells, wandered aimlessly about the tiled passages, or stood dutifully in queues waiting for their midday meal to be served.

Imagine the difficulties involved in providing these people with food and shelter.

Ack-Ack guns cover troops and supplies as they cross Remagen Bridge

March 7 1945

Milk Ration Increased

THE milk ration for non-priority adult consumers is to be increased from two pints to two and a half pints a week from Sunday, March 18, the Ministry of Food announced yesterday. A rise in milk production has enabled this seasonal increase to be made a month earlier than last year.

The January yield was 98,010,000 gal. compared with 95,940,000 gal. for the same month in 1944. In February 3,720,000 gal. a day were produced compared with 3,260,000 gal. in February last year.

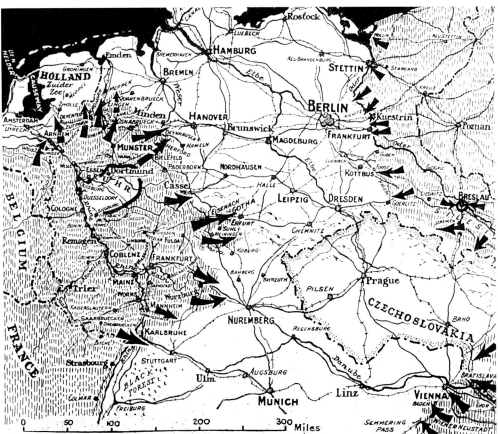

The Allies in the West and the Russians in the East drive on Berlin

March 9 1945

ALLIES ACROSS RHINE

TANKS and infantry of the American First Army have established a solid bridgehead across the Rhine at Remagen, nearly half-way between Bonn and Coblenz.

The first crossing, resulting from a junior officer's initiative, was made by armoured spear-heads at 4.30 p.m. on Wednesday. It was revealed last night, when First Army HQ partially lifted the security black-out on news from this sector.

Taken completely by surprise by this swift thrust, made under cover of drizzle which prevented air observation, the Germans put up only the lightest opposition and their defences were rapidly overrun.

Gen. Hodges at once pushed infantry forces across to consolidate the ground gained. Throughout the night and all day yesterday further reinforcements – tanks, troops, guns – and supplies poured over the river.

March 23 1945

LAST STAND WEST OF THE RHINE

From Cornelius Ryan
Mainz-Worms Front

THE Germans are making a last stand west of the Rhine. In desperation they are feverishly trying to hold open the sides of the last sizeable pocket between Gen. Patton's American Third Army and Gen. Patch's Seventh while they extricate the scattered remnants of their First and Seventh Armies.

This last bridgehead extends along a 30-mile stretch of the Rhine between Ludwigshafen and a point above Lauterbourg. It is roughly triangular, with its apex west of Pirmasens.

On both sides of this triangle the enemy are fighting savagely to hold back the crushing pressure of the two American armies. While they fight, a convoy of 1,000 vehicles has been observed racing madly for the Rhine.

It is a race against time, and the probability is that the greater part of the convoy will not reach the eastern bank. Already a column of Gen. Patton's tanks have cleared a path from the northern side of the triangle to a point within six miles of Landau.

This has narrowed the pocket in this area to nine miles, while at two other points American armour has cut into it for distances of up to two miles.

In these thrusts the Americans have reached the small towns of Annweiler and Munchweiler, both on the main road to Speyer, a town at the base of the triangle on the west bank of the Rhine.

It is a hopeless venture for the Germans. They cannot hope to hold out very long because of the terrific weight of men and material that threatens them from either side.

March 15 1945

FIRST 10-TON BOMBS FALL ON GERMANY

A stupendous explosion, dwarfing even the effects of the RAF's 12,000-pounder, revealed to the Germans yesterday afternoon that Britain had a new biggest-ever bomb. It was the 22,000-pounder – nearly 10 tons – and specially adapted Lancasters of RAF Bomber Command were dropping it for the first time.

The target was the railway viaduct at Bielefeld, 40 miles east of Muenster, which carried the last remaining double-track line out of the Ruhr.

Some details of the bomb and of the havoc it causes were released by the Air Ministry last night. Placed on end, the bomb is as high as the average suburban house. It is 25ft 5in long and 3ft 10in in diameter. It takes a crew of six half an hour to load it into a Lancaster.

The designer is Mr B. N. Wallis, CBE, of Vickers Armstrong's, and the bomb was worked out and perfected by the experts of the Ministry of Aircraft Production.

A man who saw one of the bombs land, Flyg. Off. H. R. Short, of Abbotsford, British Columbia, said: "There was a tremendous pall of black smoke and a fountain of debris."

Sqdn Ldr C. C. Calder, DSO, DFC, of Forres, near Inverness, said: "I thought the new bomb would have a surprising effect, and I was not wrong."

April 13 1945

SUDDEN DEATH OF PRESIDENT ROOSEVELT

THE Daily Telegraph profoundly regrets to announce the death last night with tragic suddenness of President Roosevelt.

Cerebral hæmorrhage was the cause of death, which took place at 3.35 p.m. [9.35 p.m. British time] at his summer cottage at Warm Springs, Georgia. A White House statement at 11.50 British time, giving the news, said:

"Vice-President Truman has been notified. He was called to the White House and informed by Mrs Roosevelt. The Secretary of State [Mr Stettinius] has been advised. A Cabinet meeting has been called.

"Our Roosevelt boys in the Services have been sent a message by their mother, who said that the President slept away this afternoon. He did his job to the end as he would want to do."

April 2 1945

BIG PACIFIC INVASION

From Our New York Correspondent

AMERICAN soldiers and Marines combined into a new American Army, the Tenth, stormed ashore on two beachheads in Western Okinawa, a strategically situated island in the Ryukyus group, only 370 miles from Japan, early this morning.

They have advanced to a depth of three miles at several places and have made the landing beaches secure. Opposition has been light.

Adml Nimitz, Pacific C-in-C, emphasised the importance of the landings, the largest amphibious operation which has yet taken place in the Pacific, by personally reading the text of his communiqué.

A British Pacific Fleet task force under Vice-Adml Rawlings aided in the preparations for invasion by bombing and shelling the Sakishma group, the southernmost of the Ryukyus.

April 5 1945

BRITISH COMMANDOS WALK INTO OSNABRUECK

From Christopher Buckley

WHEN British troops entered Osnabrueck in the early hours of this morning they were welcomed as liberators by the citizens. Women turned out to wave to them and applaud them.

Osnabrueck was taken by a Commando force acting with the Sixth Airborne Division. While the paratroops by-passed the town on either side and proceeded to push on in pursuit of the scattered enemy, the Commandos, moving down the road from Langflich on foot in single file, burst into the town at about 2.30 in the morning.

Within four hours they had virtually cleared the town with the exception of a few snipers.

April 13 1945

Mr Roosevelt

IN the hour of the triumph of the cause for which he did so much President ROOSEVELT has passed away. The news will be greeted with profound sorrow and sympathy for the people thus robbed of the leader who has served them faithfully for longer than any President of the United States in history. Through all the great strain of his great position, a strain never greater than during the past four years, Mr ROOSEVELT has borne a physical frailty with a courage which has been the admiration of the civilised world. He will be remembered with ABRAHAM LINCOLN as a leader who set and kept his country on the path of true greatness with a humanity, a steadiness of purpose, and a grandeur of vision unsurpassed in the records of mankind.

His passing leaves a gap in all our hearts and in the counsels of the Allies which it will be hard to fill. This country, in particular, owes him a debt which can never be repaid for his understanding, help and confidence in its darkest hours. When we had few confident friends he was an unremitting and undespairing one. That is why we venture to share with peculiar poignancy in the sorrow of the American people.

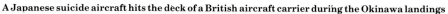

A Japanese suicide aircraft hits the deck of a British aircraft carrier during the Okinawa landings

April 12 1945

Slave Women Lived Like Nomads in Nazi Camp

From Our Paris Correspondent

A grim account of how the Germans treated their women "slave labour" at a camp at Ravensbrueck is now disclosed with the arrival home of the first batch of French women deportees liberated and repatriated by the Russians.

Because some of the women, belonging to all nationalities, even German, refused to do munitions work they were set to work as navvies for 12 hours a day. They were given only half a pound of bread and two plates of soup to sustain them.

Details were given by Marie, a student of medicine, who was deported with her mother and 680 other French women last July. Only 23 of them survived.

Ravensbrueck contained 30,000 women permanently, but many more came through in transit bringing the number up to 120,000.

They lived in large huts filled with three-tier beds; they had two blankets but no sheets or towels. Sometimes seven women had to share two beds.

"We lived like animals," Marie said.

Sanitary and hygienic conditions were appalling. Paper bands were used as wound dressings and changed only once weekly. Admission to hospital was granted only when the patients' temperature exceeded 104.

I asked Marie whether the women who had been freed with her had made any plans for the future. "Oh, yes," she said. "We did. We want to eat and eat and eat, and we have been dreaming of having a room each with a real bed and a pair of sheets."

A delegation of British MPs at Belsen

April 12 1945

ADMIRAL SCHEER SUNK BY RAF AT KIEL

LAST but one of Germany's pocket battleships, the 12,000-ton Admiral Scheer, sister ship of the Graf Spee, is out of the war. She was capsized and sunk in Kiel Harbour in an attack by RAF Bomber Command last Monday night.

She now lies almost upside down in the inner dockyard basin in Kiel. She is in much the same position as the great 41,000-ton battleship Tirpitz after she was bombed in Tromsoe Fjord.

Reconnaissance on Tuesday revealed the full success of Monday night's raid, stated the Air Ministry last night. It was only two days before the attack that the vessel had been detected moored at Kiel, where she had been driven to seek safety when the Polish port of Gdynia was threatened by the Russian advance.

The attack on Monday night was by a strong force of Lancasters and was made in clear weather. Marking and bombing was extremely well concentrated around the aiming points.

Many crews reported a violent explosion which they thought at the time was caused by a hit on either a ship or an ammunition dump.

"The explosion came just as I began my bombing run," said Flt Lt Albert N. Marshall, a pilot from Runcorn, Cheshire. "A sheet of flame rose high in the air, and in its light we could see the docks and the port very clearly. The whole target area seemed to be a mass of flames, with the fires starting from two aiming points and merging."

April 19 1945

VICTIMS STACKED IN HEAPS AT BELSEN

THE Senior Medical Officer of the Second Army has been for 48 hours at the German concentration camp at Belsen, liberated three days ago by Gen. Dempsey's Army. He said it was "the most horrible, frightful place" he had ever seen.

This brigadier found 40,000 half-dead prisoners, corpses in great heaps, and thousands of cases of typhus, typhoid and tuberculosis.

He described on his return what he had seen, and said, "Anything you have ever read, heard or seen does not begin the story."

His revelations follow those made on the recent liberation of the two other camps at Nordhausen and Buchenwald.

"I am told," he said, "that 30,000 prisoners died in the last few months. I can well believe the figure."

Here is his description of what he saw, and of the steps taken to alleviate the sufferings of the victims:

The unclothed bodies of women formed a pile 60 to 80yds long, 30yds wide and four feet high, within sight of children.

Gutters were filled with dead. Men had gone to the gutters to die.

There was bunk accommodation for only 474 of the 1,704 women suffering from acute typhus, typhoid and tuberculosis. An additional 18,600 women who should have been in hospital were lying on bare bug-ridden boards.

In the men's quarters there were 1,900 bunks for 2,242 acute cases. Another 7,000 men should have been in hospital.

"The prison doctors tell me that cannibalism is going on," the brigadier said. "There was no flesh on the bodies, but the liver, kidneys and heart were cut out."

April 19 1945

Murder Camps

NAZI concentration camps have always been a synonym for horrors, but the worst ever reported or imagined about them is far outmatched by the realities being disclosed daily to the eyes of the Allied troops as one by one these ghastly charnel heaps are overrun. It is difficult to know which is the more horrible, the piles of naked bodies of men, women and children awaiting cremation or the emaciated forms of the half-dead racked with disease, filth, hunger and hopeless misery.

It is not a matter of scores but of hundreds and thousands. Nor are all these people the victims of mere neglect or of any breakdown in supplies of food and medical stores. They are the subjects of organised mass murder by starvation, by unbelievable tortures, and by deliberate overcrowding in hovels unfit for the habitation of beasts far less of human beings. Their "guards," all of them HIMMLER'S SS men, betray something more than an utterly callous indifference to their suffering; they actually shoot any found trying to rifle the swill bins. The most merciless of the mediaeval torturers would shrink in horror at what is being enacted in the twentieth century in the heart of a country that has been professing to hold something like a monopoly of "culture."

Next to the imputation of war-guilt there was nothing that aroused so much resentment among Germans between the wars as atrocities charged against them in the conflict of 1914-18. This time the Allied High Command is taking praiseworthy pains to ensure that the eye-witnesses of concentration camp outrages shall include enough ordinary German civilians to rule out any attempted self-exculpation. A thousand Weimar citizens of both sexes, for example, have made an enforced tour of inspection at Buchenwald, and this is a method which should be repeated in every case. Responsibility for these barbarities rests with the whole German people, who were ready enough to applaud HITLER and his gangsters in the heyday of success.

That responsibility cannot be expiated merely by defeat. But apart from the general punishment that will fall upon the German people as a whole, the facts now brought to light will redouble the determination of the United Nations that every identifiable executant of these crimes shall be condemned and punished with the utmost rigour of the law. It would be an affront to all civilised decency if such unspeakable miscreants were to be left at large and inviolate.

April 30 1945

Mussolini Executed by Patriots

Two British war correspondents who entered Milan ahead of the Fifth Army yesterday saw the bodies of Mussolini and 17 of his henchmen being publicly exhibited in a square in the city, it was officially announced in an Allied HQ statement last night.

Mussolini and the other Fascist leaders were reported earlier by partisan-controlled radios to have been executed by Italian patriots after a brief trial by a people's tribunal.

Those who died with Mussolini – the executions took place on Saturday afternoon – include Clara Petacci, his mistress, Carlo Scorza and Allessandro Pavolini, former secretaries-general of the Fascist party, and Francesco Baraccu, Vice-President of the Council of Ministers.

The two war correspondents said that Mussolini and his associates were seized in Como while trying to escape into Switzerland.

The account brought back by the correspondents was released in the form of an announcement by AFHQ.

They said that Mussolini and other Fascists were executed at 4.20 p.m. on Saturday in the town of Guliano di Mezzegere, near Como. The bodies were then taken by lorry to Milan for public display in the same square where 15 patriots were executed by the Fascists.

The AFHQ announcement said that both reporters stated that they personally saw the bodies of Mussolini and his henchmen lying in the Piazza Loretto, where the populace passed by to view the corpses and revile them.

The corpses of Mussolini, Clara Petacci and other Fascists

Large crowds from the surrounding countryside also flocked to Milan yesterday to see the bodies, according to the Italian resistance radio.

The radio said Allied tanks which entered Milan were stopped by this unexpected sight.

One report said that the remains of Mussolini, Petacci and Scorza were hung from a petrol pump station in the square.

Partisan-controlled Milan radio stated that one woman fired five shots into the already bullet-riddled body, crying "Five shots for my five assassinated sons."

May 2 1945

Hitler's Death Announced: New Fuehrer Once Certified Insane

THE DEATH OF HITLER WAS ANNOUNCED OVER THE GERMAN RADIO SHORTLY BEFORE 10.30 LAST NIGHT. THE STATEMENT SAID IT TOOK PLACE AT HIS COMMAND POST IN BERLIN, NOW ALMOST COMPLETELY OCCUPIED BY RUSSIAN TROOPS. THE TEXT OF THE ANNOUNCEMENT WAS:

"It is reported from the Fuehrer's HQ that our Fuehrer, Adolf Hitler, has fallen this afternoon at his command post in the Reich Chancellery fighting to the last breath against Bolshevism and for Germany. On Monday the Fuehrer appointed Grand Adml Doenitz as his successor."

This thin-lipped man who has made the study of submarines his life-work has always hated Britain. He fought against us in the last war. As a junior lieutenant he was in the Breslau when she escaped to Constantinople with the Goeben. He afterwards volunteered for U-boat work.

In October 1918, he attacked a convoy off Malta. But his U-boat was attacked by a British ship, depth-charged, and when she surfaced damaged by gunfire. Doenitz then scuttled his craft and he and his crew were taken prisoner.

Doenitz was afterwards certified insane and transferred to Manchester Lunatic Asylum from his prisoner-of-war camp. In 1919 he was repatriated as insane.

May 2 1945

"Haw-Haw" Drunk

WILLIAM Joyce ("Lord Haw-Haw" of the German radio) appeared at 9.30 p.m. at the microphone of Hamburg radio obviously drunk. Stuttering, coughing, choking and at times nearly crying, he spoke with a hoarse and heavy voice, trying without avail to show bravado.

May 4 1945

Eire Visitors to Reich Legation

From Our Dublin Correspondent
THE Secretary to the President of Eire, Dr Douglas Hyde, called on Hempel, the German Minister in Dublin, to-day and conveyed his condolences on the death of Hitler.

Among previous callers were Mr De Valera and Mr J. P. Walshe, Secretary to the Department of External Affairs.

The bunker where Hitler died, showing the entrance (left) and the cone-topped ventilation shaft

May 3 1945

BERLIN FALLS: HITLER AND GOEBBELS COMMIT SUICIDE

BERLIN, "THE HEART OF GERMAN AGGRESSION," AND THE CAPITAL WHICH THE NAZIS SAID WOULD NEVER CAPITULATE, HAS FALLEN TO THE RED ARMY. AN ORDER OF THE DAY FROM MOSCOW SAID THAT THE REMNANTS OF THE DEFEATED GARRISON SURRENDERED AT TWO P.M. B.D.S.T. YESTERDAY.

Shortly afterwards came a statement by Dr Fritsche, Goebbels's Deputy, who was captured in the capital. It was quoted in the Russian communiqué that Hitler, Goebbels and Gen. Krebs, newly-appointed Chief of the General Staff, had committed suicide.

British occupation forces enter Berlin

May 25 1945

HIMMLER TAKES HIS OWN LIFE

From Douglas Williams
SHAEF

HEINRICH Himmler was captured on Monday near Bremervoorde, 35 miles north-east of Bremen, and at 11 o'clock last night committed suicide by taking poison while being examined at British Second Army Headquarters.

Himmler was crossing a bridge near Bremervoorde at 7 p.m. on Monday, accompanied by two men, one his adjutant and the other his bodyguard, when he was stopped by the British guard. He gave the name of Hitzinger and produced papers purporting to identify him as a discharged member of the German Field Security Police.

All three were taken to a prisoner-of-war camp where they told such conflicting sto-ries that the camp commandant sent them on to Second Army HQ. During interrogation there Himmler admitted his true identity. After being stripped and searched he was segregated.

Later he was examined by a doctor. As the doctor put his finger into Himmler's mouth to make sure he was not hiding poison, Himmler jerked back his head and bit a tiny phial held between his teeth. He swallowed the contents, later found to be potassium cyanide, and died 25 minutes later after desperate attempts at artificial respiration had failed.

The British doctor acted with the greatest promptitude in trying to prevent the suicide. He seized Himmler by the throat to keep him from swallowing the poison, but all his efforts were in vain.

When arrested Himmler was disguised in plain clothes and was wearing a black patch over an eye.

Field-Marshal Montgomery signs the Instrument of Surrender at Luneberg Heath, May 4 1945

May 5 1945

SURRENDER: THIS IS THE END

From Christopher Buckley on Luneburg Heath

AT 6.25 THIS EVENING, IN A TENT ON A WINDSWEPT HEATH UNDER GREY, LOWERING CLOUDS, FIVE GERMAN PLENIPOTENTIARIES, IN THE PRESENCE OF FIELD-MARSHAL MONTGOMERY, PUT THEIR SIGNATURES TO THE SURRENDER OF THE GERMAN ARMIES OF THE NORTH. THIS IS THE END.

The capitulation of Luneburg, as it will in all probability be known to history, practically puts an end to the second Thirty Years' War – the war which began in August 1914, and continued through the period of uneasy peace into the second and more deadly phase of the war which has lasted through five years and eight months.

It has been preceded by other capitulations of great significance, notably the surrender in the Ruhr and the surrender in Italy. It will be followed by others. But the scene in the little dun-coloured tent this evening is the most important act of capitulation of the entire war. Of that there can be no possible doubt.

Himmler photographed shortly after his suicide

May 24 1945

Streicher Found in Farmhouse

JULIUS Streicher, the Jew-baiter, was captured yesterday in an isolated farmhouse at Walding, 40 miles east of Berchtesgaden. He was picked up by a patrol of the 502nd Parachute Infantry Regiment of the 101st United States Airborne Division.

A young woman who was with him made a terrific scene. At first he denied his identity. He remained arrogant throughout and ordered his companion to put his shoes on for him.

May 30 1945

"Haw-Haw" Captured

From L. Marsland Gander
Luneburg

WILLIAM Joyce, alias Wilhelm Froelich, alias "Lord Haw-Haw," who had been broadcasting from Germany since Sept. 19 1939, was arrested yesterday afternoon in the Flensburg area, near the Danish frontier. He is wounded and in a serious condition.

An English-speaking woman who described herself as his wife was arrested some days before in the same district. The two were brought to Second Army HQ here this afternoon.

Joyce's vanity, it seems, led to his discovery. Two British officers were gathering wood for a fire in a forest when a well-dressed civilian came up and spoke to them in German.

It was Joyce, who had been a fugitive since the British took Hamburg and occupied the broadcasting station.

Joyce, who was apparently leading a gipsy existence and also gathering wood, was so confident of his ability to fool the British officers that he lapsed into English.

One of them recognised his affected voice and challenged him, saying: "Surely you are William Joyce!"

Joyce said "Yes," and made a movement with his right hand towards his pocket as if to draw a revolver. Whipping out his pistol, one of the two officers shot Joyce through the thigh.

May 23 1945

Bacon, Cooking Fats and Soap Cut

REDUCED rations, including cuts in bacon, cooking fats and soap, were announced by Col. Llewellin, Minister of Food, yesterday.

He gave an assurance that the new food allowances, coming into force on May 27, will be "sufficient to maintain full health and vigour."

It was also made clear yesterday that there is no immediate prospect of an increase in the clothing ration. It was announced that not more than 24 coupons would become available on Sept. 1.

Mr Dalton, President of the Board of Trade, said it was not possible to decide for how long these must last, but he hoped for an increase before the end of the next rationing year.

Countries better supplied with food than Britain will also make sacrifices to help people in the liberated Allied countries, he said. A new principle of share and share alike had been accepted by the United States and Canada.

In future, these countries will eat only as well, approximately, as Britain. To give effect to the principle Britain must reduce her stocks in the United Kingdom by 300,000 tons and consume slightly less than in 1944.

May 30 1945

YOKOHAMA BLITZED

THE greatest daylight Super-Fortress raid – by 450 machines – on Yokohama, Japan's chief ocean port, followed neutralising attacks by Mustangs, which smashed Japanese fighters on the ground.

The raid on Yokohama began at 9.30 a.m. yesterday and lasted for an hour and a half, said Japanese reports. The city was still burning block by block last night.

The attack – again on a "Super-Berlin" scale – gave more evidence of the American plan to reduce the big centres of Japan one by one. The paralysing of neighbouring air bases beforehand is the reply to the enemy's recently increased AA and fighter opposition. Only two Super-Fortresses were lost.

A bonfire party in Stepney, East London, celebrating VE Day

May 8 1945

GERMANY CAPITULATES! TO-DAY IS VE-DAY

THIS is VE-Day. The war in Europe is over. After five years and eight months "complete and crushing victory" has, in the words of the King, crowned Britain's unrelenting struggle against Nazi Germany.

Germany has surrendered unconditionally to Great Britain, the United States and Russia. Resistance has ceased in all areas where the German Government is still in touch with its remaining forces.

May 8 1945

Victory!

AT last, after five years and eight months, the end crowns the work, and the enemy has been beaten into total surrender. After so long a period of struggle and suspense, the news may seem too big to evoke at once outward signs of exhilaration. Nevertheless, even in these first hours, certain feelings emerge clearly and demand expression.

The first is surely thanksgiving for a great deliverance. In retrospect it is more apparent even than it was at the moment that five years ago our country was in greater peril than at any time since the Armada. Indeed, the reason why "Dunkirk" will have a special echo in British hearts as long as the English tongue is spoken is that, though it was a military disaster of the first order, there was a deliverance within the disaster and, as Mr CHURCHILL pointed out at the time, a victory – that of the RAF over the Luftwaffe – within the deliverance. Thus even in logic there was a grain, and in spirit a mountain, of hope that the mortal peril might be averted; and so it was. Yet the deliverance was so miraculous that we must, in all humility, feel that it owed something to more than human effort and human resolution. "Except the Lord keep the city..."

Within the compass of human reasons for survival then and victory now, the fact is outstanding that our cause was recognised by many who despaired it as involving something greater than the fate of the British people. Wherever falsehood or fear had not banished reason, it was recognised that upon our fate depended the survival or the death of what makes life worth living – those things which President ROOSEVELT so nobly epitomised later as the Four Freedoms. Let history say what else it likes of events anteced-ent or subsequent to that period when, physically speaking, we were alone in arms against a triumphant foe, it will at least say, "This was their finest hour." Our second feeling at this great moment can therefore be one not of vulgar pride but of consciousness that we did give the forces of freedom a chance to rally and thus to triumph.

In the actual counter-attack upon the powers of darkness the whole Empire has played a valorous and ungrudging part. Our enemies both in Europe and Asia may have hoped for dissension or at least luke-warmness. They have seen and felt a spontaneous outpouring in the common cause of men, money and material by the Dominions and Colonies which a few captious and carping critics could do nothing to lessen or to sully. It has been the Empire's "finest hour," too. Nevertheless, it cannot be said or thought that the peoples of the United Kingdom have allowed or arranged that the rest of the Empire should do their fighting for them. The casualty figures alone show that they, in spite of their modest numbers, have put into the forefront of the battle forces which both in size and in quality challenge comparison with the effort of any other people in this or any other age.

Where modesty comes in is not that our effort has been short of our utmost, but that admittedly our utmost alone could not have achieved this victory. Our feelings, therefore, must include unstinted gratitude and admiration towards our Allies, great and small, both those who withstood or never had to endure on their own soil the enemy's fiercest blows, and those who temporarily succumbed. Looking back, which could say that it would have won without the others? All are entitled to our thanks, whether they gave the widow's mite or the giant's strength, whether they suffered more than ourselves or less. It is a natural transition from gratitude towards others to gratitude towards those who have nerved and served our own nation. This is a total victory and has been won by the whole people.

Indeed, "the civilians have held." Nevertheless, they would be the first to require that the palm should be given to the men and women of the Services, including the Merchant Navy, who, whether in defeat or in victory, have never failed to respond to the calls upon them. As for their leaders, selection is inevitably invidious. Much of the material of victory is often supplied by those not in the public eye at the time or at all. About one name there can be no invidiousness – HM the KING, who has shared the perils and sustained the hearts of all his subjects.

Fame will crown ALEXANDER, modest architect of victory in the Western Desert and in Italy, and an instrument, under EISENHOWER, of victory in Tunisia; MONTGOMERY of the Eighth Army, of D-Day, and of the final triumph in Germany, with his unequalled capacity for acquiring the trust of his men and his fierce skill in using it; BROOKE, CIGS, with his overriding responsibility for the whole British Army and therefore the predominating credit for making it the finest in our history; PORTAL, HARRIS and TEDDER, who tore the wings and so much of the armour off the enemy and made RAF the sign of hope to the afflicted and of terror to the oppressor; CUNNINGHAM, SOMERVILLE, VIAN, RAMSAY, HORTON, who saw to it that the Navy was once again our "sure shield." Let us also remember those who held the field when the spears were against us – POUND, GORT, WAVELL, AUCHINLECK and DOWDING.

Not least our thoughts will go out in this hour to Mr CHURCHILL, Prime Minister and Minister of Defence from the darkest hour to the brightest. No words can express what his country owes to him. At every turn of the war, he has been able to express the feelings in magnificent language and to direct the actions with un-flinching resolution of a people whom he loves in a cause worthy of them and of him. His task is not over; but he may pause in it one moment to hear those whom he has led say, "Well done." Lastly, after thanksgiving, modest pride and gratitude comes the prayer that the future may be worthy of victory. The great enemy of freedom and of peace lies prostrate and we have played our part in one great purpose not unworthily. We shall now be called upon to play it in another. As the tumult and the shouting dies, let us turn to it with the resolution displayed during the long ordeal by fire.

May 9 1945

Nation's VE Outburst of Joy

A GREAT NATIONAL OUTBURST OF RELIEF AND THANKSGIVING AT THE END OF NEARLY SIX YEARS OF WAR IN EUROPE WAS EPITOMISED YESTERDAY, VE-DAY, BY TREMENDOUS SCENES OF REJOICING IN LONDON, WHICH BEGAN IN THE AFTERNOON WITH THE PRIME MINISTER'S ANNOUNCEMENT OF THE END OF HOSTILITIES AND CONTINUED ALL NIGHT.

The floodlighting of prominent London buildings and public places last night, including Buckingham Palace, St Paul's, the Houses of Parliament, Trafalgar Square and Piccadilly Circus, aroused great enthusiasm among the crowds still celebrating VE-Day.

British family instinct inspired tens of thousands of men and women to go to the London home of their King and Queen on VE-Day to share with them the joy of peace in Europe.

A vast crowd was assembled outside Buckingham Palace throughout the day and until a late hour a joyous and colourful crowd whose enthusiasm rose to a crescendo of patriotic fervour at the occasional appearances on the balcony of the smiling King and Queen and the Princesses.

Eight times their Majesties came to the balcony in response to the insistent roar of the crowd. On most of these occasions, they were accompanied by Princess Elizabeth and Princess Margaret.

On their third appearance the Prime Minister joined the Royal party. He stood between the King and Queen, waved his cigar to the great assembly and gave the Victory sign. The cheers continued for at least five minutes.

In the evening a crowd of 100,000 listened silently to the King's broadcast. They then clamoured for his appearance, and when he again came out on the balcony he was given the greatest ovation of the day.

Then just after 10 o'clock came the moment that many people in the crowd had waited for all day. As the left-hand wing of the Palace was suddenly lit up by the glare of the first floodlights cheer upon cheer burst from the delighted crowd.

The two Princesses, escorted by Guards' officers, left the Palace after nightfall to mingle with the great crowds outside. Then they appeared again on the balcony with the King and Queen.

With flags treasured through five long years for this occasion, with pealing church bells and in some places floodlighting and fireworks, towns and villages throughout the country celebrated VE-Day.

Here are descriptions of the scenes in some of the big centres:

Manchester

A crowd of more than 15,000 gathered in Albert Square to hear Mr Churchill's broadcast.

A speech by the Lord Mayor, Ald. W. P. Jackson, which followed, was punctuated by the bangs of fireworks hurled into the air by youths and Servicemen.

An illuminated tramcar and 'bus toured the city from early

The crowds outside Buckingham Palace on VE Day

evening and the Town Hall was floodlit. There were dances in all the parks and bonfires in many districts.

Liverpool

Sirens of beflagged liners were the background to 20,000 voices singing "Land of Hope and Glory" outside the Town Hall and on St George's Plateau in acknowledgement of the victory proclamation.

Birmingham

Led by the Lord Mayor, crowds in Victoria Square sang patriotic songs for hours on end. Principal buildings were floodlit and huge bonfires were burning in every suburb while crowds danced and sang.

Cardiff

At the City Centre 30,000 gathered to hear the Prime Minister and an address by the Lord Mayor, Ald. Walter Parker. Sailors of all nations left their ships to join in the celebrations.

Glasgow

Ships in the Clyde sounded their sirens. For miles around the noise was heard. People defied the coast black-out and allowed their lights to blaze out.

Belfast

The streets were smothered with flags and emblems. Even lamps and flagstones were painted red, white and blue in some districts.

Nottingham

Effigies of Hitler and Mussolini were burned in the streets. Bells of the main churches had been re-hung just in time to ring victory peals.

Churchill and the King on the balcony of Buckingham Palace

July 27 1945

Mr Churchill: "I Have Laid Down My Charge"

THE Socialist party has been returned to power with a working majority for the first time in the history of the country. Election results declared yesterday were:

SOCIALISTS	390
CONSERVATIVES	195
OTHERS	42
SOC. MAJORITY OVERALL	153

Mr Churchill has issued the following statement:

"The decision of the British people has been recorded in the votes counted to-day.

"I have, therefore, laid down the charge which was placed upon me in darker times. I regret that I have not been permitted to finish the work against Japan.

"For this, however, all plans and preparations have been made, and the results may come much quicker than we have hitherto been entitled to expect.

"Immense responsibilities abroad and at home fall upon the new Government, and we must all hope that they will be successful in bearing them.

"It only remains for me to express to the British people, for whom I have acted in these perilous years, my profound gratitude for the unflinching, unswerving support which they have given me during my task, and for the many expressions of kindness which they have shown towards their servant."

July 27 1945

Japan Given Chance to Surrender

From Ossian Goulding, Potsdam

The final ultimatum to Japan to end her futile resistance and get out of the war was released to the world to-night from Berlin.

The text of the ultimatum, which was signed by President Truman and by Mr Churchill, was communicated to Chungking by the British and American Army cable and wireless.

A reply was received by the same route from Marshal Chiang Kai-shek, in the form of a personal message to President Truman, concurring in the terms of the document. It is now being communicated to Japan by the Office of War Information in its radio services in Japanese.

August 7 1945

ALLIES INVENT ATOMIC BOMB: FIRST DROPPED IN JAPAN

THE Allies have made the greatest scientific discovery in history: the way to use atomic energy. The first atomic bomb has been dropped on Japan. It had:

Over 2,000 times the blast power of the largest bomb ever before used, which was the British "Grand Slam," weighing about 11 tons; and

More power than 20,000 tons of TNT.

Yet the explosive charge is officially described as "exceedingly small." A spokesman for the Ministry of Aircraft Production said last night that the bomb was one-tenth the size of a "blockbuster" yet its effect would be "like that of a severe earthquake."

The first atomic bomb, a single one, was dropped on Hiroshima, a town of 12 square miles, on the Japanese main island of Honshu. Tokyo radio said that the raid was at 8.20 a.m. yesterday Japanese time, and that the extent of the damage was being investigated.

August 9 1945

Russia at War with Japan To-day

PRESIDENT Truman announced at a hurriedly summoned Press conference this afternoon that Russia was now at war with Japan.

After correspondents had entered his study the President, with Adml Leahy, his personal Chief of Staff, at his right, and the Secretary of State, Mr Byrnes, at his left, made his nine-word statement. He said: "Russia has declared war on Japan. That is all."

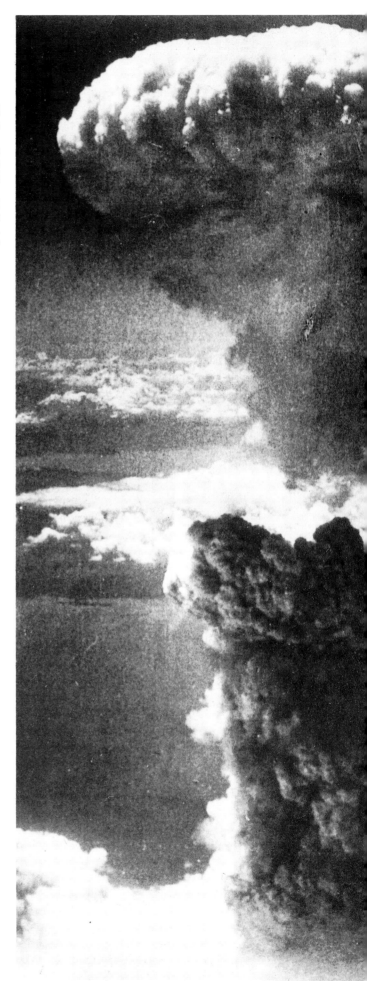

The mushroom cloud over Nagasaki of the second atomic bomb

The ruins of Hiroshima: 80,600 people were killed instantly

August 15 1945

JAPAN: UNCONDITIONAL SURRENDER

JAPAN has surrendered unconditionally. This was announced simultaneously at midnight in London, Washington and Moscow – by Mr Attlee, President Truman and in a state broadcast by Moscow radio.

Gen. MacArthur has been appointed Supreme Allied Commander to receive the Japanese surrender, stated President Truman. Britain, Russia and China will be represented by high officers.

In the meantime, Allied armed forces have been ordered to suspend offensive action.

In Britain victory holidays will be to-day and to-morrow. The King will broadcast at nine p.m.

Mr Attlee and President Truman both read the Japanese reply to the Allies' surrender terms. The reply was received through the Swiss Minister in Washington last night. President Truman said it was "a full acceptance of the Potsdam declaration, which specifies the unconditional surrender of Japan."

The Emperor of Japan was due to broadcast to his people at midnight.

August 15 1945

The End

FINAL and total surrender by the last of our enemies. That is the message which Mr ATTLEE was able to give to the country at midnight. Peace descends upon the world again after six years, within three weeks, of war which had devastated civilisation on a scale never seen before.

Recovery will take many a year, but the carnage has ceased and the nations are free to turn to the tasks of reconstruction with such speed as concentrated resolution may wring from the material impoverishment that is the aftermath of war. In the hour of triumph solemn resolves will mingle with the joy of a public holiday – resolves to apply every resource to overtake the heavy tasks which lie before us and determination that no aggressor shall be allowed to provoke such a conflict again.

The Telegraph at War

Bʏ way of an Appendix, this section of the book reflects on the way *The Daily Telegraph* itself coped with the exigencies of producing a daily newspaper in wartime. W. F. Deedes, then as now an adornment of its pages, contributes a personal reminiscence of 1939; and Simon Heffer, a leader writer on *The Daily Telegraph*, scrutinises his predecessors' attitude to appeasement. Clare Hollingworth, *doyenne* of war correspondents, describes her experiences in Poland at the outbreak of war, and Edward Bishop, himself a former war correspondent, surveys the *Telegraph* staff in the field.

Items from the contemporary newspaper touch on its production, paper shortages, distribution, personalities and own "bit" for the war effort.

The Daily Telegraph

AIR RAID PRECAUTIONS SCHEME

It is YOUR DUTY to read this book. In air raids there are two enemies, the raider and panic. Panic comes from ignorance of what to do and where to go.

---

2. PROTECTION OF STAFF.

Immediately an Air Raid Warning is sounded, every member of the Staff will proceed by the PRESCRIBED ROUTE to his or her Shelter. All movements are to be carried out at WALKING PACE.

If hostilities seem likely Shelter Cards will be issued to all members of the Staff. These Cards must be completed immediately—ready for handing to the Shelter Superintendent on taking refuge.

The " Civilian " respirator (which, during emergency conditions, should be kept ALWAYS AT HAND) must be taken to the Shelter.

SHELTERS.

" A " SHELTER—MAIN OFFICE BUILDING BASEMENT.

" B " „ STORES BASEMENT.

" C " „ MACHINE ROOM BASEMENT.

" D " „ „ „ (GROUND FLOOR).

SHELTER EQUIPMENT.

The following Equipment is to be maintained in every Shelter:—

Tools.—Cold chisel and hammer, hack-saw, crow-bar, axe, pick and shovel.

Furniture.—Tables and Chairs or benches.

Lighting.—Electric torches and lamps.

Sanitation.—Chemical closets for " B," " C " and " D " Shelters.

Fire.—Chemical extinguishers—2 in each Shelter. Also supply of sand.

Gas-proofing material.—Reserve to be kept against emergency.

Games.—Card games, darts, etc.

First Aid.—First Aid Section will be responsible for all arrangements and equipment.

Refreshments and stimulants will be under the control of Mrs. Robertshaw.

Radio.—One wireless set.

3. PROTECTION OF BUILDINGS, etc.

Fleet Street frontage to be sandbagged on timber over pavement lights; front door and windows to be protected.

Wine Office Court walls to be sandbagged on timber over pavement lights.

Area in yard (outside women's lavatories) to be timbered and sandbagged.

Area in yard (outside boys' room) to be timbered and sandbagged.

Back-door and wall between above areas to be sandbagged.

Area beside yard lavatory to be timbered and sandbagged—allowing below improvised communication between electricians' mess-room and yard lavatory (the latter will be the Decontamination Post and Men's Cleansing Centre).

Wall from Old Returns Department to around end of Mr. Pethers' office to be sandbagged.

Entrance to yard lavatory to be sandbagged.

Commissionaires' box and adjoining oil-store to be sandbagged.

Lights on ALL flat roofs and the tops of lift shafts to be protected by ¼-in. steel plate or heavy timber, with sandbags.

Glass roof of Linotype Room and other Rooms to be fitted underneath with two layers of ½-in. mesh wire netting, to prevent injury from falling glass.

Smaller light in Composing Room to be reinforced on underside with sandbags.

All windows in the Front Hall to be fitted on the inside with ½-in. mesh wire netting.

4. COMMUNICATION OF AIR RAID WARNING.

PUBLIC WARNING. A public general Warning of an impending Air Raid will be given by means of a fluctuating or warbling signal of two minutes' duration, sounded by sirens on police stations and " key " buildings.

A continuous signal of two minutes' duration will denote " Raiders Passed."

Extracts from The Daily Telegraph's wartime booklet, issued to staff of its Fleet Street offices

Bill Deedes joins the TA

Subs and Subalterns

W.F.DEEDES

FOR most people the Second World War began on Sunday, September 3, 1939, but for *The Daily Telegraph* it began a few days earlier than that. One evening at the end of August, I was filling sandbags at the headquarters in Buckingham Gate of our Territorial Army battalion, 2nd Queen's Westminsters, when I was called to the telephone. It was the editor of *The Daily Telegraph*, Arthur E.Watson. He was in distress "We appear to have lost half our sub-editors," he said. "It will be difficult to get the paper out…" He sought my help.

But no, I have begun this account at the wrong end. It opens properly in April 1939. About that time there were two relevant events. The Government doubled the size of the Territorial Army and Mussolini invaded Albania – on Good Friday of all days. Among his principal victims were King Zog and his lovely young wife, Queen Geraldine. This rape of beauty stirred young hearts. Enough was enough. The enlarged TA offered to put a sword in one's hand.

Neither event was calculated to disturb Arthur E. Watson; but there was a third. Michael Killanin, 3rd Baron, man about town and a reporter on the *Daily Mail*, thought it would be a fine idea to recruit for the new TA a company composed of actors and journalists. The TA drilled in the evenings, when all actors and most journalists work. This company, exceptionally, would drill in the mornings. The idea was warmly received by

2nd Battalion Queen's Westminsters. The press gang went to work.

After we had recruited about a dozen journalists in the *Daily Telegraph* office, I was called in by the then general manager, Lord Burnham. A little bird had told him, he said tactfully, that *Daily Telegraph* journalists were enrolling in the Territorial Army. I should be aware that in the event of war, the newspaper would continue to be published and it would need journalists.

I thought this rather saucy, coming from a man who had won a DSO and MC with the Hussars in the First World War, who was then a TA brigadier in the Royal Artillery – and who, incidentally, not many months hence, was to win high distinction on the beaches of Dunkirk. So I replied, with equal tact, that we were not pressing people on the staff to join but that they were seeking to join. We parted uneasily.

It was true that certain members of *The Daily Telegraph* staff wanted to join this company in the 2nd Queen's Westminsters. Not all of them were moved by heavy patriotism. They sensed it was a fun thing; and so it was. We drilled twice a week – at Wellington Barracks, which is a good address for a soldier. Furthermore, our ranks, in conformity with Killanin's idea, embraced stars of stage and screen. Hugh Williams, then appearing in *The Barretts of Wimpole Street*, became a rifleman. Nigel Patrick, Guy Middleton and Frank Lawton, who remained a lifelong friend, and many others joined the ranks. Their observations on parade, as the drill sergeants tortured their muscles, made our parades one of the best shows in town. No wonder humble journalists at *The Daily Telegraph* wanted to join in.

The fact was also that, after Munich in the autumn of the previous year, those of us who were professionally engaged in reporting the news had a sense of the direction events were taking. *The Daily Telegraph* had encouraged me to specialise in air raid precautions, or civil defence. That bridge afforded a glimpse of our woeful unpreparedness.

There is a moving passage in Hilaire Belloc's book, *The Cruise of the Nona*, describing the vision he had early one morning in 1914 while sailing his boat round the coast: "Like ghosts, like things themselves made out of mist, there passed between me and the newly risen sun, a procession of great forms, all in line, hastening northward. It was the Fleet recalled. The slight haze along the distant waters had thickened, perhaps, imperceptibly; or perhaps the great speed of the men-of-war buried them too quickly in the distance. But, for whatever cause, this marvel was of short duration. It was seen for a moment, and in a moment it was gone. Then I knew that war would come, and my mind was changed."

It would be wrong to say we knew war would come; yet our minds were changed. So Lord Burnham's cautionary words fell on deaf ears. That August we all bundled off to camp, Burley in Hampshire. It rained unceasingly. I find a letter on my files from Mr Goodliffe of *The Daily Telegraph*, dated August 1 of that year. "I am sorry to hear that you are having such a damp experience. I am enclosing your corrected proofs in booklet form for you to go through finally before I submit the copy to his Lordship."

In order to preserve as many *Daily Telegraph* readers as possible, Lord Camrose had asked me to write a guide on air raid precautions, which appeared just before war broke out. My last pre-war letter from *The Daily Telegraph* is dated August 31, and is from the company secretary, H.J.C.Stevens: "His Lordship is very anxious that I should send you the enclosed cheque for £52 10s for the excellent work you did in connection with the ARP booklet." The Inland Revenue chased me for tax on that cheque – worth about £1,000 today – until there was some sort of amnesty in 1945.

Not many days after our return from camp, the bugles struck a more urgent note. I forget exactly which day we had to clear our desks in Fleet Street and report to Buckingham Gate for attestation; but it must have been during the last ten days of August. "You will be ARP officer," said the Colonel, which is why I was filling sandbags when the editor of *The Daily Telegraph* rang me up.

Arthur Watson had been an artilleryman in the First World War and had, I believe, won a DSO. But he was a sub-editor by training and the suddenly depleted subs' room went to his heart. He begged me to reason with the Colonel. Could not one or two subs be released just for a night or two while *The Daily Telegraph* adjusted itself?

I had a lot to learn, and so I approached the Colonel with this request. His response was unprintable in a family newspaper. That is how war came to *The Daily Telegraph* a few days early.

The Daily Telegraph and Herr Hitler

SIMON HEFFER

THE *Daily Telegraph* had the measure of Adolf Hitler from the start. On February 1, 1933, two days after he became Chancellor of Germany, a leading article described him as one "who, in floods of mob oratory, poured out incessantly for years past, has threatened…destruction."

Readers, however, were reminded that "all public men in Germany who acquiesced in the signature of the Treaty of Versailles have been told by Herr Hitler that their 'heads would roll on the sand' as soon as he came to power, and that the Treaty itself would, from that auspicious moment, be as dead as they. But they and the Treaty are admittedly not in the slightest danger to-day."

This contradiction – recognising Hitler as a thug but regarding him as a lightweight figure towards whom disdain was the appropriate attitude – was maintained to varying degrees in leader columns until the crises of 1938. This was despite reports in the *Telegraph* describing Nazi excesses in unadulterated terms. It is unlikely that the leader-writers of the day did not read their own newspaper; rather that a generation used to the horror of the trenches could not, until there was no choice, find the intellectual honesty to acknowledge the likely results of the policy of brutality, concentration camps and persecutions reported on the newspages.

In this respect *The Daily Telegraph* has more of which to be proud than some other newspapers. It is well documented that Geoffrey Dawson, Editor of *The Times*, re-wrote dispatches from his European correspondents to keep the stark truth from his Establishment readership. It seems that no such censorship was imposed on *The Daily Telegraph*. In May 1933, a series of articles entitled "Germany under the Swastika" outlined Nazi terror, the beatings of Jews by storm troopers, suspicious "suicides", and tales of brutality coming out of Dachau. Also in the same year, the *Telegraph*'s German correspondent confidently predicted the *Anschluss*.

Yet the leading articles were not always prescient. "Herr Hitler in office is very far from being the national and international peril that he has so often vowed himself to become," said one in February 1933. Even after Hitler's "night of the long knives" in July 1934, when he murdered von Schleicher, the former Chancellor, and massacred the Brownshirts, the paper took a detached view, even saying that "the infamous character of Rohm [the Brownshirt leader and notorious homosexual] and his associates actually invests the stroke with a quasi-moral sanction." In 1937 the paper saw no reason why the Hitler-Mussolini axis could not be girded to ensure the peace of Europe. It was not long before the fatuity of such hope became clear.

By 1938 contacts between the proprietor, Lord Camrose, and Winston Churchill ensured that the *Telegraph* was more aware of the approaching peril. Before Hitler moved into Austria in March 1938 the paper was concerned about Britain's preparedness for conflict, saying there was "no room for complacency." The editorial line throughout the crises of 1938 was one of loyalty to Chamberlain and the Government, not borne out of party sympathy, but patriotism. Unlike other papers, particularly *The Times*, *The Daily Telegraph*'s definition of patriotism did not include abrogating responsibility towards other nations.

On March 12, the day after Hitler delivered his ultimatums to Vienna, the *Telegraph* said: "It would be difficult to find any parallel in modern times for the manner of this onslaught by one State against another. What is tantamount to annexation by ultimatum at a moment's notice is a step which cannot be excused or condoned by any canon of international intercourse. The claim that Austria, by reason of race, is an 'internal affair' of Germany is inadmissible and indefensible." Five days later, it looked to the future: "The violence of the manner [of the *Anschluss*] has aroused a universal sense of foreboding as to the next point where arms might, once more, and perhaps more fatally, supplant diplomacy in the realisation of Germany's ambitions…There can henceforward remain no possible room for doubt, if, indeed, any has existed hitherto, that an attack on Czechoslovakia would unloose a European war."

The attack came at the end of the summer: by August the paper's loyalty to the efforts of the Government, and the desperation to avoid war, muffled some of its springtime roaring. Talking of efforts to solve the Czechoslovak problem, a leading article on August 2 spoke of the "earnest protestations of the Führer that he seeks a peaceful settlement". It continued: "There is no reason to doubt his good faith, since the situation in Czechoslovakia is such that it is essential to reach agreement if a European conflagration is to be avoided." The infection of appeasement, and the scale of the retreat from the principles propounded at the time of the *Anschluss*, come with the next sentence: "Necessarily there must be concessions from both sides."

Later in the month, as Viscount Runciman of Doxford was engaged on his mission to Prague to find a settlement, the *Telegraph* sought to make the best of a bad lot and expended yards of column inches wondering whether it could placate Hitler with honour. Soon the tone changed again, though, because meat offered by Dawson's *Times*, in a scandalous editorial, was too strong for an honourable newspaper to endorse: "A suggested alternative, put forward by *The Times*, that the Czech Government might consider the surrender of minority areas of its territory has been promptly repudiated by our Foreign Office. No more sinister blow could have struck at the chances of settlement. The suggestion has been seized upon by the German press with avidity and denounced by the Czechs as the dismemberment of their country. Such encouragement to the intransigence of the Sudeten Germans must embarrass the Czech Government, make infinitely more difficult the delicate task of Lord Runciman, and encourage German resistance to every effort at settlement. There could be no more dangerous or deplorable misrepresentation of British views at this crisis."

Yet dismemberment happened, and *The Times*'s leader damaged the prospects of a more favourable settlement as much as the *Telegraph* feared. On 10 September the *Telegraph* warned that "peace is not to be preserved by indifference to the coercion of a small nation by a powerful neighbour", a line that turned out to be somewhat stiffer than Chamberlain's. Two days later, maintaining its resolve, the paper argued that Hitler's designs on Czechoslovakia were "a growing challenge to all systems of Government that have not bowed the knee to the Nazi ideal. To that, if it were seriously intended, the world would offer an unexampled resistance."

Churchill's influence became more apparent as September 1938 wore on. The *Telegraph* stood up again and again for the rights of the Czechoslovak republic, and warned again that the provocation by the Sudeten Germans meant our own preparations for war should be stepped up. It must have been a bitter disappointment when the Anglo-French plan for Czechoslovakia, constructed after Chamberlain's visit to Hitler in mid-September, was shown to advocate dismemberment. On 22 September the *Telegraph* continued its support for Chamberlain – despite his actions contradicting the line the paper had taken since the *Anschluss* – saying the plan was a "concession difficult to make but justifiable as an effort to avert an immediate outbreak of war." The message of this leader becomes quite confused thereafter.

Speaking of the concessions, it says: "Obviously the effort will not have been worth the candle if it is to bring no more than a few weeks, or a few months, respite from German demonstrations of bellicosity – if, in other words, this is but the first instalment of a Danegeld that Europe is to go on paying for ever afterwards, in ever larger sums, as the price of immunity from military aggression." These fears were borne out by events, but were immediately contradicted: "Any such idea is too ridiculous to merit a moment's consideration."

The next day, this undue effusiveness seemed to have been recognised: the plan of Britain and France "offered no small challenge to their national pride," the paper said. Three days later, as Chamberlain was shuttling back and forth to Germany, the *Telegraph* was even more caustic about "Herr Hitler's dictatorial demands", saying they would mean "the Czechs are to be subjected to superfluous humiliation" and that "The German system of saying 'thank you for nothing' to every concession and perpetually raising the price of peace has reached the point of exhausting the patience no less of the two Western powers than of the Czechs themselves."

The following day, September 27, the leading article noted: "Herr Hitler said that the satisfaction of his claim against the Czechs would mark the last territorial demand he had to make in Europe. That would be the promise of a substantial step forward, if past experience could permit us to take statements of this kind at their face value." It hoped that Chamberlain, at Munich, would "impress on him [Hitler] that in the event of his resorting to force Great Britain and France would stand united in resistance." When Chamberlain first reported, on September 28, on the hopeful signs in his discussions with Hitler, the *Telegraph* spoke of this as "a transformation in which the shadow of death seemed turned into morning."

Yet it quickly qualified this: "The present respite must be hailed with a certain reserve…peace cannot be founded on mere effusiveness…this nation cannot prudently afford to purchase present ease at the expense of future trouble… throughout this crisis all the concessions have come from one side, and all the exactions and provocations from the other… every new concession has provided the occasion for a new demand."

This was two days before Chamberlain returned with his piece of paper, again having ignored the *Telegraph*'s attempts to stiffen his resolve. The paper nonetheless congratulated him on October 1 – "Peace, even at a price, is a blessing so inestimable" – while reminding the Government of its greater obligations than hitherto to the Czechs, whose exclusion from the negotiations it deplored.

That was a Saturday. By the Monday Duff Cooper had resigned from the Government, and the paper's patriotic support for Chamberlain was stretched to the limit. It upbraided Chamberlain for saying "I am not going to be browbeaten", noting that when the crunch came "he feels that his position is not strong enough to present a sufficiently firm front". It continued: "Not the least ground for uneasiness is the consciousness of the impunity with which Herr Hitler has been allowed to gain his ends by the methods of threat … great as is the debt we owe to Mr Chamberlain. It would have been greater still if he had stood out more forcefully on this issue."

The *Telegraph*'s patience had been severely tried by the Prime Minister it had so dutifully supported, and that it should snap after the Sudetenland had been given to Hitler was entirely forgivable. Its waverings throughout the five years before Munich, and especially during 1938, merely reflected the uncertainties of a desperate nation, and may be considered forgivable too.

Never, when it mattered, did *The Daily Telegraph* give our enemies any cause to believe that popular opinion in Britain would lie down and be trampled upon by Hitler. If the editorial line sometimes showed frailty, it also showed honour.

1939: A good "gas"

The Day War Broke Out ...

CLARE HOLLINGWORTH

WHEN the editor of *The Daily Telegraph*, Arthur Watson, offered me a job late in August 1939, his orders were: "Get to Warsaw as quickly as you can and report to Hugh Carleton Greene" [*The Daily Telegraph*'s former Berlin correspondent then encamped in Warsaw].

By luck, there was an aeroplane the following morning via Berlin. I was thrilled to be returning to Poland, a country I knew well from working there for seven or eight months trying to help refugees from Czechoslovakia and Germany flocking illegally into Silesia.

As I packed my clothes around midnight I realised that I needed a smaller suitcase so I telephoned a famous store and they delivered one, within an hour, to my flat in Westminster—a service not restored after the war.

Among the passengers travelling to Warsaw was a fellow correspondent, William Forrest, of the *News Chronicle*. When we landed in Berlin we were amazed to find the normally over-crowded Templehof airport completely devoid of passenger traffic.

Cafés and bars were closed and fighter 'planes lined up near the runway. Within minutes of landing Willie and I were taken into what looked like a wire cage by the German police and told that Hitler was going to make a speech that evening at Tannenbaun when war against Britain would be declared.

Thus it was "necessary" to detain the British press who, in any case, had all, already, been expelled from Germany. I do not know why we were not more frightened. Maybe it was just youthful naivety.

After twenty minutes, however, we were informed that the Führer had decided to postpone his speech and we could proceed to Warsaw. The pilot was ordered to fly low on a set course but we landed in Warsaw late in the afternoon and I set out to find Hugh Greene at the Europeski Hotel.

Few senior correspondents at that period would have welcomed a young and inexperienced female as their number two. But Hugh did and immediately got down to planning, saying "one of us must go to the border where there will be action."

"Let it be me", I suggested, "because you already have good contacts here, while I have spent much of the last six months in Silesia near the German border."

Then Hugh urged me to leave at once and I caught the night train to Katowice. As it stopped at stations moving south I noted men posting on the walls orders for the mobilisation of the Polish Army.

The Consul-General offered to put me up and told me the border with Germany was already closed except for flagged, official cars which enabled the Germans to come and go as they wished. Old Polish friends were alarmed and many were moving from Katowice to Warsaw to get away from the dangerous border.

Early the next day I borrowed the Consul's car with his permission and drove over the closed frontier into Germany. The Nazi officers I encountered saluted the flag and looked amazed when they saw it was the Union Jack.

But I enjoyed a good lunch and then bought some German wine, films and aspirin—goods already unavailable in Poland. On my return journey I was driving down a steep valley and noted the view had been blotted out by a screen of hessian sacking.

Fortunately, a sudden strong gust of wind blew the dark brown cloth away from its wooden frame and I saw below me scores, if not hundreds, of tanks obviously lined up and ready for the invasion of Poland. I drove back quickly to Katowice and told the Consul what I had seen. He was torn between gratitude for having produced such sensational information and anger that I had actually dared to drive his car into Germany.

I wrote a report for *The Daily Telegraph* on German tanks poised for the invasion while the Consul locked himself in an inner office and sent a top secret message to the Foreign Office. I then drove around the border and noticed that the Polish Army was busy constructing concrete gun emplacements all of which were unhardened and unusable when the invasion took place.

Early in the morning of September 1, I was awakened by the sound of artillery and the distant roar of tanks. I had been told by the Embassy that should the German army move, I should inform them in Warsaw before I did anything else.

I therefore put through a telephone call. The duty officer at the other end of the line was an old friend, Robin Hankey.

"Robin", I said, "the war has begun."

"Are you sure, old girl?" he replied. I recall taking the telephone to the window, saying "Can't you hear it?"

Robin then ordered the consular staff to leave Katowice as quickly as possible because he feared the town would soon be occupied by German troops. I then telephoned the sensational news to Hugh Carleton Greene; but when he, in turn, telephoned to the Polish foreign ministry they initially denied that the German invasion had begun—even though an air raid warning could be heard on the line while Hugh was talking with them.

Eventually, however, some minutes later, they confirmed they were now at war with Germany. I walked to the consular offices where we quickly burned the cyphers and the secret files as well as telephoning to warn the few remaining British subjects of the situation.

Before piling into the Consul's car I telephoned Hugh to tell him that we were leaving for Krakow. But the journey took far longer than we had expected—not only due to the roads being overcrowded with cars carrying household equipment but to constant "straffing" by low-flying German aircraft that naturally caused havoc.

When we arrived late in Krakow we were given good accommodation but there was no chance to sleep as the security forces insisted we spend the night in an uncomfortable air raid shelter. Nor was it possible to telephone to Hugh in Warsaw.

Next morning I drove south towards the German border and met some of the dying and wounded cavalry returning after they had attacked German tanks. Otherwise Krakow seemed peaceful. I bought a car for a song as the Consul's vehicle was becoming too crowded.

After a second night in the air raid shelter, I was trying hard to tune in to the BBC, when suddenly I heard Neville Chamberlain's voice, loud and clear, saying "that a state of war now exists between Great Britain and Germany." A few minutes after this the local authorities informed the Consul he must move on as Krakow would soon be occupied by the Germans.

We travelled north, experiencing great difficulties after dark in persuading the Polish security forces to allow us to cross bridges or enter towns. Naturally, I drove just behind the Consul's car. Influenced by his passengers, he decided to head towards Warsaw but officials persuaded him to move towards Lublin. While spending the night in a bug-ridden dormitory on the way, we heard, over the German radio, that the route to Warsaw was already in German hands.

When we reached Lublin a temporary consulate was opened as the Polish government had moved in secret to a town nearby. The road from Lublin to Warsaw was still open, though it was impossible to make telephone calls. But as the authorities claimed trains were still running from Warsaw to the north, I agreed to drive two British subjects to the capital to put them on a train.

The journey was uneventful but when we arrived at the British Embassy the military attaché, Gen. Carton de Wiart, told me that the Ambassador and his staff had left for a secret destination where the government had already moved. Hugh Carleton Greene's room was empty and I heard that foreign correspondents had been ordered to follow the government to the Lublin area.

I remember my passengers becoming almost hysterical and refusing to take the train. I went round the city begging for petrol, which was ultimately vouchsafed by the Americans. We drove back through the now familiar blackout to Lublin which, in the course of 48 hours, had become an overcrowded, foodless city.

We met Robin Hankey on the road with his dog Smallsize. His morale was high and he calmed my passengers but could not help me locate Hugh. I sent three or four press telegrams, assisted by the Consul, not only to London but also to New York. None, however, arrived.

After two nights in Lublin, where there was a strong anti-British atmosphere because we were not sending aircraft to bomb the invading Germans, the shortage of petrol became critical and Poles were paying in gold for a few litres. I saw one man sell a car loaded with possessions to obtain sufficient petrol to get to the border.

Fortunately, we were moved on to Lwow and then to a remote country house near an airfield where operations had ended through lack of fuel and spare parts. The Polish pilots gave me some petrol which enabled us to move on to a town near the Russian border, Krecheminitz, to which the Polish government had already moved from Lublin. The British Embassy had been allocated a small house — only the Ambassador had a room to himself. Mrs Clifford Norton (better known as "Peter") welcomed me with a glass of gin and I shared an egg with Robin Hankey at the canteen set up for diplomats.

Strange to report, the road to Warsaw was still open and I was offered petrol to go if I was willing to take passengers beyond Lublin. This I did but failed to make Warsaw. On my return journey I crossed an area occupied by the Germans. The tanks had passed and with the help of the local peasants I was fortunate to cross the area before the infantry took over.

An American diplomat I met shortly after this adventure told me that the Polish government was leaving Krecheminitz. He also told me a story — which was to have enormous significance — that the Russian Ambassador had crossed the border into Russia and on his return announced to the Polish foreign ministry that he had been recalled to Moscow.

I went to the border with Roumania where I made contact with Hugh Carleton Greene and the Consul from Katowice. Naturally, Hugh expressed disappointment that none of my information had reached him or London. I then stayed in Kuty, a small village on the Roumanian border — which was to be the last home of the Polish government. The foreign ministry was located in a farm and the British Embassy in a small peasant's house.

I drove Hugh along the border towards the east. A few days later, to our astonishment, we saw tanks ahead. The awful truth dawned upon us that they were Russian tanks moving into Poland.

"This is where we get out", Hugh said firmly. I turned the car and drove to the bridge which marked the border between Poland and Roumania where we were able to file our report. We returned to watch the British Embassy followed by the Polish government leave Poland for Roumania across the same bridge.

The three weeks' war in Poland was over.

The Telegraph 'WarCos'
EDWARD BISHOP

ON receipt of 'Hadrian' [a codeword] you will report within two hours of the timing of the message to the Guard Room, Duke of York's HQ, King's Road, Chelsea. You will carry your war correspondent's licence. Luggage will be restricted to one attaché case, a portable typewriter, a haversack if of service size, a steel helmet, and gas respirator."

On reading this as I opened a cardboard box labelled "Leonard Marsland Gander" lodged in the Imperial War Museum's Department of Documents, I was on the trail of the wartime career of the sometime *doyen* of Fleet Street radio and television correspondents and of some of his *Telegraph* colleagues whose bylines occur in this chronicle.

'Hadrian' was perhaps more appropriate than its military authors intended. At the outset the services erected a wall between themselves and the Press. The War Office hoped that it would be as impenetrable as the Maginot Line and war correspondents were disparaged as "WCs". But eventually the wall crumpled before the resolution of Gander and others.

Nor, early on, was the Ministry of Information – which, among its multifarious "Ministry of Morale" duties, housed the blue-pencil brigade of press censorship – much less obstructive. As a callow seventeen-year-old volunteer awaiting the call, I frequented it. The supreme frustration was to be summoned to the rostrum in the great rotunda of Senate House in Bloomsbury and receive the remains of emasculated stories for transmission to my newspaper.

Conditions improved as the war progressed – an increasing liberality being reflected in this chronicle's selections. Towards the end of 1944, by which time I had joined *SEAC Newspaper*, the inter-service daily of South-East Asia Command, the turned tide had relaxed the authorities.

Gander and Co. – who, epauletted with the war correspondents' green and gold insignia, spearheaded *The Daily Telegraph*'s coverage in the heat of the struggle – inherited a tradition of courageous newsgathering. This had been established by Hugh Carleton Greene and Clare Hollingworth in Poland and Douglas Williams with the British Expeditionary Force in France. Courage, coolness, resourcefulness and patience were essentials in the composition of a competent correspondent – and not only in combat conditions.

Clare Hollingworth, stranded with Carleton Greene in a Polish inn in September 1939, was obliged to share a single bed with the towering torso of the future director-general of the BBC. Douglas Williams, on leave from the front, as France and the Low Countries were invaded, bluffed a speedy return by walking on to an RAF transport and braving the displeasure of a party of brasshats.

Gander, frequently in the frontline at Dover after the fall of France, commented in a 1940 diary: "The nearer danger comes the less terrifying it seems" – an opinion he modified after campaigning on fronts from North Africa to Burma. But his diary and notes scribbled on the back of an envelope under shellfire at Dover are reminders that the south coast of England *was* the frontline in 1940. At Angmering in July 1940, he noted the incongruity – as a dogfight took place overhead – of his beloved wife, Hilda, asking whether he would prefer "the machine-gun or the anti-tank beach this afternoon?"

Not yet a uniformed and accredited war correspondent, Gander found the Battle of Britain from the viewpoint of the ground to be a comparatively gentle blooding. Later he was to report from the Battle of the Atlantic, North Africa and Burma and – as the only journalist covering the Dodecanese campaign – escape in the destroyer *Echo* when the defenders of the island of Leros were overwhelmed by the Germans.

Papers preserved at the Imperial War Museum throw an interesting light on the relationship between *Daily Telegraph* correspondents and the office; and to some extent relationships between themselves. At one point Gander notes: "My relations with *The Daily Telegraph* office were peculiar. Skelton, the assistant editor in charge of news, usually had no idea where I was and equipped apparently with a penny atlas sent impossible demands when he did not know. I was now ordered to Rangoon. His cable ran, 'Agree Calcutta and Lashio [China] *en route* for Rangoon, but want you Colombo earliest'."

Gander remarked: "Skelton's magic carpet proposals were plainly impossible." So he went to Colombo. At another point he noted the frustrations: "After nearly five months of travel by sea, air, gharry, taxi and my two feet I had achieved virtually nothing." But one occupational frustration of absence abroad, the non-arrival of expenses, seems fortunately to have eluded him: "They... cabled £200. This was one of the joys; the paper never refused funds."

He adds: "Undeniably the correspondents were privileged, free from the rigorous discipline of the forces, paid by their offices and supplied with lavish expenses. If they did not relish a particular job then it was fairly easy to dodge it. Nevertheless many were killed and at the end of the war the only honours were a meagre sprinkling of MBEs and campaign medals, a big difference from the First World War when knighthoods were conferred."

Other than the obvious competition between correspondents of rival newspapers, there seems to have been an element of watchfulness between *Telegraph* men in the field. Gander noted: "In the late summer of 1943 I was ordered back to the Middle East [from India] to await accreditation to the Eighth Army. Curiously, the *Telegraph* also had another man there, Richard Capell, and the two of us, eyeing one another jealously, sat about twiddling our thumbs and waiting." Gander solved the problem by persuading the Army to despatch him to the "doomed island" of Leros, an experience which led to his book, *Long Road to Leros*.

Capell, after starting the war with the French Army in Africa, had taken in South Africa *en route* for Egypt. From Libya – he was in Tobruk during the siege – he had gone down to East Africa in 1942 before returning to the North African desert where the groundwork had been laid by Arthur Merton and was to be consolidated at Alamein by Christopher Buckley.

Merton was an old-timer in wing collar and bow tie until uniformed. At the outbreak of war he had already spent thirty years in the Middle East. Covering Libya, Iraq, Iran, Syria and Greece, his movements were closely observed by other correspondents. When they tumbled to it that he had left Cairo for somewhere, they feared that his experience, instincts and brilliant anticipation had inspired him to arrive in an area where something was about to break. He enjoyed numerous "firsts", beginning before the war with what he called his "old Tut scoop", as the first journalist to enter King Tutankhamen's tomb. Later he was first into Benghazi when Wavell's push captured the Libyan port from the Italians. But for all his Middle Eastern omniscience, Merton was generous in his assistance to younger colleagues and those new to a region he knew so well. It was an irreparable loss when in 1942 he was killed while driving between Alexandria and Cairo beside the prime minister's son, Randolph Churchill, who survived the accident.

Buckley, popularly known as "The Bishop" and whom Gander relieved with the Eighth Army (so that he could move eventually to the Second Front before the Normandy invasion became a reality), had a busy and ubiquitous war as his bylines show. Given to quoting the Lord's Prayer or Shakespeare under fire, he was found lunching at the Lion d'Or, a Bayeux café, shortly after D-Day and reporting the Japanese surrender in Burma in 1945. He survived the war, but died together with Ian Morrison of *The Times* when, in 1950, their jeep was blown up by a landmine in Korea.

Gander and Buckley shared the hardships of Burma with Martin Moore, also of *The Daily Telegraph*. At the outbreak Moore was in Lisbon, making use of that important neutral listening post. Assigned to Singapore in 1941, but redirected to New York when the Japanese invaded, he became one of the first British correspondents accredited to the United States Army. In 1942 he accompanied American and Australian troops in New Guinea before transferring to Ceylon and covering the China, Burma and India fronts from 1942 to 1944. He was with Wingate's Chindits during their first operations behind Japanese lines in Burma, but was switched in 1944 to Italy where he remained as Rome correspondent until 1949.

When it was time to invade Normandy and fight the campaign in North-West Europe, the skills of the *Telegraph*'s key correspondents were finely honed and, in some respects, produced their finest hour. Cornelius Ryan, the Dublin-born naturalised American citizen with the United States forces in Normandy, needs no introduction. His reputation and talents survive him in his books, *The Longest Day* and *A Bridge Too Far*, both turned into feature films.

Gander, after training with the airborne forces to accompany the Rhine crossing, was somewhat fazed when his glider crashed in a field well behind the German lines, but survived to write the tale. "We were busting with pride in our red berets," he wrote of himself and other correspondents. "For once writing men had been in front of fighting men."

Late in the day, Edmund ("Teddy") Townshend entered the scene. For four days and three nights after baling out of a blazing Stirling bomber miles behind German forward positions in Holland – the mission was to drop supplies at Arnhem – he evaded capture. Then he filed from Brussels: "I am probably the first war correspondent ever to be shot down on his first flight with the RAF." He led the paper. The wreath ordered by colleagues was cancelled.

Let L. Marsland Gander – to recall that familiar byline – have the last word. Selected to appear in the London Victory Parade of June, 1946, he sat in the back of a jeep, wearing uniform for the last time. Dismayed momentarily to find the jeep sandwiched between a mobile laundry and mobile canteens, he wrote off this tactless separation from frontline troops with whom he had so often served, as a compliment to his "strictly Chocolate Soldier attitude".

November 19 1943

War-time Odyssey

MR Marsland Gander, whose despatches from almost the four quarters of the earth have appeared in THE DAILY TELE-GRAPH since the war, has now capped his many adventures by escaping from Leros.

Dover during the Battle of Britain, Iceland, hunting U-boats in the Atlantic, then India, have been some of his experiences.

From my knowledge of Mr Gander, I am sure he has been unperturbed through them all. His philosophy is proof even against Assam in the wet season, where he saw the end of the retreat from Burma.

If he has a weak spot it is for the Royal Navy, and he has written a book about his Atlantic cruise in a destroyer.

It pleased him particularly that the ratings classified him with the ship's mascots: "The dogs and the cats," one sailor wrote home, "are delightful."

The Daily Telegraph
and
Morning Post

TELEPHONE:
CENTRAL 4242.

FLEET STREET, LONDON, E.C.4.

TELEGRAMS:
TELENEWS, LONDON

RLS/M

9th April 1945

Dear Gander,

Your airborne story was most excellent, and gave us a clear beat over every other paper in the Street. It must have been a frightening experience, and I congratulate you on coming out of it unscathed. I will take up the matter of salary at the first opportunity.

Yours sincerely,

Marsland Gander, Esq.

L Marsland Gander's identity card, a letter from his news editor and part of his dispatch from the Atlantic (below)

Name GANDER Leonard Marsland

Description War Correspond

Unit G.H.Q. M.E.

Height 5': 11"

Colour of Eyes Blue

Colour of Hair Fair

Signature of Holder

For Censorship by admiralty

From L. Marsland Gander

On Board H.M. Destroyer -----,
At Sea.

Tuesday night

This ship, one of many gallant craft fighting to keep open the North Western Approaches to Britain, is at sea again, after a rapid turn round, to resume her part in the Battle of the Atlantic. On with the U-boat hunt and the never ending work of convoy.

She lately returned from a 1600 miles voyage and landed a number of 152 survivors from a convoy, which, as stated in an Admiralty communique, lost twelve ships. I am writing this, as the dizzy plunging of the ship permits, in a small cabin that accommodated eleven Dutch officers rescued from their boats.

Two stories of the survivors illustrate the stubborn courage and fortitude of Allied and British seamen that has won the admiration of the Navy. This destroyer stood by a bombed Dutch steamer in mid-Atlantic for 56 hours. Her Dutch master Captain J.S.T. Rietbergen, aged 52, had been asked to leave with his officers and crew but clung obstinately to the hope of saving her, although she had been holed by one bomb and had another, unexploded, in one of the bathrooms.

Persuaded at last to abandon ship, as she was obviously sinking, he attempted to lower a boat, but it capsized throwing him into the water. He drowned before a boat's crew from the destroyer could drag him out.

Dear Chevins,

I have unexpectedly had a chance of sending this dispatch ashore written hurriedly and with some difficulty, as you may imagine. I cannot tell you the name of the ship but perhaps the Admiralty will oblige. Her Captain is Lieut. Hortney, D.S.C. R.N. We have temporarily left the convoy but have not completed our job.

This destroyer had a very rough time last voyage. God knows when this letter will reach you but I am not able to phone or telegraph. I suggest you ask the Admiralty for news of our movements.

The survivors I speak about were put ashore before I arrived.

Yours, aye,

L.M.G.

The News Editor
Daily Telegraph.

December 31 1940

BOMBS FALL ON THE DAILY TELEGRAPH

THE DAILY TELEGRAPH building was one of the first to suffer in Sunday night's raid on London.

A shower of incendiary bombs fell on it 15 minutes after the Alert and others dropped all around.

Despite this and the fires which raged in the building and adjoining property, the preparation and publication of the paper proceeded steadily.

Difficulties that had to be overcome in its production included the failure for some time of the electricity and gas.

The women's editorial department on the third floor was destroyed by flames, but bombs in the composing-room and machine-room were promptly put out.

One of the tragedies of the night occurred when a burning building adjoining THE DAILY TELEGRAPH in Shoe-lane collapsed.

Several volunteer fire-fighters were buried beneath a mound of red-hot rubble.

Volunteers from all parts of THE DAILY TELEGRAPH hurried to the spot and tore with bare hands or such implements as were available at the smoking ruins.

The search continued until last night without any bodies having been recovered. It will be resumed to-day.

A boy of 17 on the staff of the paper was injured when trying to put out an incendiary bomb by jumping on it. He returned to help in rescue work after his hurts had received attention in hospital.

August 6 1940

Daily Telegraph in US 34 Hours after Issue

New York

THE resumption of the direct British passengers and mail service over the Atlantic, marked by the arrival last night at La Guardia Airport, New York, of the flying-boat Clare, impressed Americans as a remarkable undertaking at the moment when Britain is threatened with invasion.

The flight was made more dramatic by the fact that Capt. J. C. Kelly Rogers brought over copies of THE DAILY TELEGRAPH printed in London on Saturday morning, and this afternoon the New York World Telegram printed a five-column wide photograph of the top half of the front page of THE DAILY TELEGRAPH.

Capt. Rogers told me this morning that while war conditions compelled him to refrain from giving any details of the journey from England which he and the crew of four made in approximately 34 hours, he could say it was uneventful and that no ships were sighted during the crossing.

"We did see plenty of icebergs off Newfoundland," he said. "We circled one, a particularly big one, to have a good look at it on top. It is the first time I have seen them while flying over the Atlantic."

Expressing the hope that the service would be maintained with regularity, Capt. Rogers added: "It proves one thing – that the Germans have not shot us off the air any more than they have shot us off the seas."

October 19 1940

Making a War-Time Paper

WIRELESS listeners on Thursday night heard a graphic description of the production of a newspaper under wartime emergency conditions from the offices of THE DAILY TELEGRAPH.

The broadcast was arranged by Mr Michael Standing, assisted by Mr Vaughan Thomas of the BBC staff, and it was designed to show the general public how the staffs of a national newspaper carry on during the long, nightly air raids, so that it can receive its paper at the usual time in the morning.

Announcing the broadcast, Mr Standing explained that they were taking listeners "to the offices of one of the country's leading newspapers, to hear something of the general activity as the first edition is going to press."

Message received

The tour of the building began in the sub-editors' emergency room in the basement, where there is a tape machine on which news is received from all parts of the world. As an illustration Mr Vaughan Thomas selected a message cabled from THE DAILY TELEGRAPH's New York Correspondent, and then proceeded to follow it through the various departments until it appeared as a front-page story in the printed paper.

Mr Vaughan Thomas first read the message in the abbreviated cabelese in which it comes over the tape machine. He then explained that it was sent on to the copy-taster, whose job it was to read the continuous flow of messages.

There being some doubt as to the value of this particular message, the copy-taster consulted the chief sub-editor, and then followed a brief dialogue between the chief sub-editor and the night editor with regard to the length and the position that should be given to it. "Not a top," decided the night editor, "but it should go on the front page."

Working in a blitzkrieg

Mr Vaughan Thomas then proceeded to give a short description of the emergency rooms to which the various editorial departments moved when the "spotters" high on the roof above signalled "danger near." He referred to the underground telephone exchange and interviewed a reporter on his night's work.

Afterwards a visit was paid to the "Manchester" room, where, as he said, "item by item the contents of the London issue is transmitted by teleprinter to feed the Northern offices and plant that produce the North-country edition of the paper."

Before the typesetting and printing departments were visited Mr G. P. Simon, the general manager, made a short statement in which he said that working in a *blitzkrieg* had become very much a routine matter.

"I suppose," he added, "that most newspapers, like ourselves, have moved hundreds of thousands of pounds worth of plant from one part of the building to another to ensure the maximum safety for their workers." He paid tribute to the courage of the men who volunteered for the dangerous work of "spotting" for enemy 'planes on the roof.

Finally, the microphone was taken along to the mechanical departments, and the announcer briefly indicated the various processes through which every item of news destined for the paper passed before it became part of the completed newspaper, during which he interviewed the senior printer, the "copy-cutter-up" and one of the linotype operators.

The microphone was taken 50ft below the road level. There, beside the linotype and moulding machines, were the mighty presses, which, whirling over at great speed, turn out the printed pages.

November 21 1940

CORPS OF CORRESPONDENTS

IN the new Libyan campaign which has opened with so much promise THE DAILY TELEGRAPH will be served by a corps of correspondents of notable ability and experience.

Mr Arthur Merton's brilliant accounts of the earlier campaign under Gen. Wavell will be well remembered. Later he reported the repression of the revolt in Irak, the fighting in Syria and Iran, and the course of events in Turkey. Mr Merton has an intimate knowledge of the Near and Middle East.

Mr Richard Capell, who was formerly well known as a music critic and is a remarkable linguist, served through the last war as a stretcher-bearer. Refusing to take a commission, he received as sergeant the Military Medal.

He won his spurs as a war correspondent last year, when he was our representative with the French Army. He saw the evacuation from Crete to Egypt, and sent vivid pictures of life with our Forces in the Western Desert last summer.

Mr Christopher Buckley, an authority on Balkan affairs, saw the fighting in Albania and Greece. After the arrival there of the British Forces he was with them until the evacuation.

Since then his despatches from Cairo have shed light on all the Middle Eastern operations and on the resistance to the invader in the Balkans.

THE DAILY TELEGRAPH has also the exclusive services in the British Press of Mr W. J. Munday. He is Australian born and has practised journalism in Sydney and in London. During Gen. Wavell's campaign in the desert he accompanied the Australian Forces.

May 2 1944

War prison life reproduced in the Mall: The Daily Telegraph Exhibition

By Alan Dick

JACKBOOTS in the Mall, barbed wire and bayonets in St James's – these two hard facts brought home the realism of a war prisoner's life of guarded monotony to the crowds which gathered in the grounds of Clarence House yesterday to hear the Duke of Gloucester open THE DAILY TELEGRAPH Prisoners of War Exhibition.

The exhibition was organised with the help of the Red Cross and St John War Organisation.

For half an hour, under May skies and surrounded by the throb of a free city, men and women of the Services and men and women of the war organisation at home met in the replica forecourt of a German prison camp to express their concrete sympathy with the men who suffer behind wire.

A Nazi look-out post glowered down upon them. Nazi guards in steel-grey uniform paced every exit. Drab huts formed a rectangle of unrelieved monotony around them.

But behind the barbed wire, behind the look-out post and behind the bayonets was evidence of how the British spirit has conquered the turgid Nazi régime.

The evidence was inside the huts, in the things which those imprisoned hands have made and in the diplomas which those imprisoned minds have gained. It was there, too, in the upsurging desire of every British prisoner to prepare himself to take part in the new world after the war.

This exhibition is inspiring. Its inspiration comes from the triumph of the spirit above circumstance.

Following his introduction by Viscount Camrose, the Duke of Gloucester was given a great ovation when he rose to declare the exhibition open.

He said: "It gives me great pleasure in opening this exhibition to thank THE DAILY TELEGRAPH for sponsoring it and defraying its cost.

"The thought of staging such an exhibition was a most helpful inspiration. It has provided an opportunity to demonstrate the high morale of our fellow countrymen in captivity, and the ingenuity with which they occupy themselves.

"At the same time, the part played by the Red Cross and St John in supplying them with food parcels, educational courses, books, games and sports equipment and many other things has, I understand, been illustrated.

"The effect cannot fail to bring comfort to relatives and friends of prisoners of war whose patience, however stoical, must sometimes need to be fortified.

"And it will help to confirm to the public, whose sympathy for prisoners of war has been so generously demonstrated by contributions to my Red Cross and St John Fund, that the money they provide for the numerous services rendered by the Red Cross and St John is used to good purpose."

The Duke made a tour of the exhibition. By the sign in German letters *"Eingang,"* he passed behind the barbed wire to open the first hut with the bronze key presented to him by Judith Sussman.

He showed great interest in every detail of the exhibition, from the pilchard tins converted by prisoners into little pens to the "roll of honour" of prisoners who have passed examinations in their camps.

He spent some time examining the "Prospectus of the Barbed Wire University," an illuminated noticeboard reproduced from one in Stalagluft 6. It reads like the noticeboard of a college of any university at home at the start of term, with its lists of lecturers and subjects, lecture rooms, and examinations past and future.

At the bottom of the board he read, "The only qualification for entry is to have faced death."

Among the handwork and models he was particularly taken by a model train. He tapped it with his fingernail to test the tin, shaped from melted-down tinfoil from Red Cross parcels and tins.

He also admired a wooden jewel casket with an inlaid design in the lid made from the pink, yellow and green bone handles of old tooth brushes, and a Thames sailing barge constructed from the wood of a camp hut, with dyed khaki handkerchiefs cut into sails.

From the very special interest shown by His Royal Highness in every form of regimental badge, from badges moulded out of molten tinfoil to those laboriously stitched in petit point, it appeared that he would have chosen that for his self-imposed soldier's task in a prison camp.

March 14 1941

Notice to Readers

By Lord Camrose

AS from Monday next the consumption of newsprint used in the production of the newspaper Press of the country is to be reduced, at the request of the Government, by approximately 17½ per cent.

For the past eight months all penny morning papers, by arrangement between themselves, have made six pages their standard size. The smaller amount of newsprint now available can only be met in one of two ways – a lesser number of pages or a reduction in the number of copies printed.

THE DAILY TELEGRAPH has decided to adopt the latter course. In peace times the normal issue of this paper varied from 20 to 34 pages daily. It is felt that a further reduction in size from six pages would mean the sacrifice of too much that the reader of THE DAILY TELEGRAPH expects to see and read and the loss of features which, over many years, have become an integral part of the paper.

Far better that five people should read a DAILY TELEGRAPH true to its character and traditions than that six should read what could in four pages be, at the best, only an approximation to it.

In contradistinction to other penny papers, THE DAILY TELEGRAPH will, therefore, be maintained as a six-page paper. To do this means, unfortunately, a substantial reduction in the number of copies which can be printed with the newsprint available.

The inevitable result must be that a large number of present readers will be unable to secure THE DAILY TELEGRAPH in future. The war has, however, led to a spirit of co-operation in many ways unknown in normal days, and we hope that in this spirit those readers who are able to get their copies regularly will share them, wherever practicable, with less fortunate friends.

April 18 1944

"A" Flash

THE DAILY TELEGRAPH correspondent with the United States Third Army, Cornelius Ryan, who is on leave, is the first man I have seen in London wearing the flash of Gen. Patton's Army.

This is a large "A" on a blue ground circled in red. He tells me it is the same insignia as the United States Third Army wore when it was the American occupational force in Germany in 1918. The "A" circled by the red "O" stands for "Occupational Army."

Ryan flew home in one of American Air Transport Command's Dakotas. His companions were American prisoners of war returning from German camps.

April 14 1945

Universal Loss

THE Stars and Stripes over THE DAILY TELEGRAPH building was symbolical of the feeling in Fleet-street yesterday.

Never has the death of a great public figure from a country not within the Empire caused such a sense among us of universal loss.

This feeling was also reflected in the appearance of this paper with its front-page columns in black borders.

The passing of a foreign head of State has never before, I believe, been announced with this mark of mourning and respect.

May 8 1945

VE Day

FLEET-street in the afternoon of VE Day appeared gay with flags.

The façade of THE DAILY TELEGRAPH building was adorned with the French tricolour and the Red Soviet flag. From the two flagposts on the roof fluttered in the breeze the Union Jack and the Stars and Stripes.

The cries of hawkers with their barrows of flags and bunting, added to the holiday air. So did the planes that frequently zoomed overhead, dipping low over the City.

Afterword by John Keegan

HOW well had British newspapers in general, and *The Daily Telegraph* in particular, passed the test of the Second World War? As Max Hastings emphasised in his Introduction, the war imposed an unprecedented burden on newspapers, editors and journalists in this country. The heart of the newspaper world in Fleet Street itself came under direct attack by German bombing, threatening production and interrupting distribution at the height of the Blitz, while at the front journalists found themselves faced by risks unknown to their predecessors of the First World War.

Then the trench lines had clearly delineated the zone of danger, which journalists in any case were rarely permitted to enter. The fluid nature of the fighting in the Second World War meant that the front often overran the journalist, pitching him into the heart of action whether he liked it or not. Many, in fact, soon came to feel that unless they were as close to combat as persuasion or deception could get them they were not doing their jobs. Thus was born the modern ethos of war reportage. No group obeyed it more completely than the war photographers, of whom as high a proportion suffered death on the battlefield as front-line infantrymen.

The war was also a test, as Max Hastings has pointed out, of editorial responsibility and journalistic objectivity. In Britain at war the two were potentially in conflict. There is no tradition of the "government newspaper" in Britain. Indeed, here, as in the United States, newspapers have always prided themselves on their independence of official control and suspicion of official favour. Yet the newspaper, though its coverage and status were encroached upon by broadcasting, was still the principal means by which the public heard of events and learnt to interpret them. If British newspapers did not want to curry favour with government, they even more strongly shrank from giving favour to the enemy. The foreign press was eagerly studied in Germany, both as a source of intelligence and as an index of public and private morale.

Editors and journalists alike had, therefore, to tread a narrow path between reporting and commenting on the truth as they saw it and betraying vital fact or disloyal sentiment to the enemy. At the immediate level the censorship saw that they did not. But external censorship is the enemy of good journalism, as Fleet Street was the loudest to argue in the early months of the war when it was evolving its working relationship with wartime government. Self-censorship, on the other hand, can be a creative state of mind, and it was towards self-censorship that newspapers progressed as the war drew out. *The Daily Telegraph* with its strong tradition of eclectic and objective news coverage, was particularly successful at working within the bounds of self-censorship to produce daily copy that was truthful both to the events

and mood of the war. Even during the "Phoney War" of September 1939 to May 1940 the news columns contained stories which stand up well in hindsight. Our Special Correspondent in Montevideo, for example, describing the scuttling of the Graf Spee on December 18, 1940, after its action with the British cruisers Ajax, Achilles and Exeter, embroidered his account by suggesting that Captain Langsdorf was ordered by Hitler to destroy his ship and then committed suicide after the Führer had branded him a coward. As we now know, he was merely authorised to scuttle if he could not bring the ship home, and then shot himself in a fit of depression. As an account of the event, however, the story is almost completely accurate and little of substance could be added to it even today.

In the same vein, Douglas Williams, reporting the return of some "little ships" from Dunkirk at "A South East Port", gives a picture of the evacuation which can have left readers in little doubt of how chaotic the situation was on the beaches or how grave the disaster. The newspaper's editorial two days later rubbed home the message. It emphasised that Dunkirk had been, in Mr Churchill's words, "a colossal military disaster".

In reporting the effects of the Blitz, the newspaper also achieved high standards of objectivity, though it thereby reflected the government's decision not to disguise the extent of the damage done to London, and the provincial cities which were also attacked, by German bombing. With hindsight we can see that the policy of openness was encouraged by the comparatively ineffective nature of the German campaign. No British city suffered as Hamburg did, where 50,000 inhabitants were killed and a million driven out of the city by the RAF raids of July-August 1942. This firestorm horror forced Goebbels to disguise the truth from the German population, for fear of causing panic in cities which had not yet felt the growing weight of the Combined Bomber Offensive. Rumour spread, nonetheless, devaluing official pronouncements. Similar rumours might have circulated with similar effect in Britain, had not the government issued lists of damage done – as, for example, to 2,659 churches published on March 21, 1941 – and newspapers printed them as a staple item.

"Colour" reports of the Blitz were also notably objective. If a note was struck which sounds at all false to modern ears, it is that of the chorus of "We can take it" from blitzed Londoners to visiting leaders. Wartime reportage of morale – British, Allied, German or in the occupied territories – strikes a consistently unconvincing chord. "Paris Taunts the Invader", of July 15, 1941, for example, is embarrassingly off key. It describes young Frenchmen mocking German officers with impunity and ordinary citizens walking the streets wearing RAF badges. Nothing, of course, could be further from the truth.

The Germans, though "correct" in their behaviour as occupiers, exacted correctness in return. Moreover, pro-British sentiment in France, whether in the occupied or unoccupied zones, was weak in 1941. The French had not forgiven the British for their destruction of the French fleet, with heavy loss of life, at Mers el-Kebir in July 1940. Not until 1944, after two years of imposed labour conscription and with Germany clearly heading for defeat, would pro-Allied sympathy become strong and widespread in France. Even in March 1944 Marshal Pétain was to be received in Paris by cheering thousands as the hero who had saved the nation from the worst consequences of military catastrophe in 1940.

There were blind spots in the coverage of the war. Reports from the Western Desert, the only land campaign which Britain waged with a share of the initiative, were of high quality, no doubt because the best of the *Telegraph* reporters, notably Christopher Buckley, served there. His report of what we now call the Battle of Alam Halfa in July 1942 is an excellent narrative, which does not disguise the shortcomings of British tactics. Accounts of the fighting in the Far East, however, and of the bombing of Germany in 1942 fall below his standards. The year of 1942 was a low point for the British, and for Britain's Prime Minister, as he freely admitted in his post-war memoirs. The loss of the Prince of Wales and the Repulse in December 1941, the fall of Singapore, the surrender of Tobruk were all deeply depressing events.

The *Telegraph* summary of the Singapore fighting whistles against the wind. It describes "heroic" and "sustained" resistance. As we now know, much of the garrison gave up without a serious fight and nearly all the Indian troops subsequently went over to the Japanese to form the anti-British Indian National Army.

Bombing, too, was exaggeratedly reported. Though the "1,000 bomber" raids opened in March, and the campaign did for the first time seriously begin to hurt German civilian morale, it was still a clumsy instrument of strategic power, which continued to cost Bomber Command heavily in aircrew casualties. The newspaper conveyed little of that. All raids were reported as successes, and the crews as bubbling with enthusiasm at the effect achieved. As we now know, crew morale was severely affected by losses which, when they passed five per cent per raid, as they frequently did in 1942, threatened the sustainability of the campaign.

By 1944 the shift in advantage to the Allies was clear for all to see and the need to sustain morale at home by overpainting the state of morale in the forces and in the occupied lands had passed. The *Telegraph* editorial summing up the achievements of the year that had passed set the tone. "We may conclude", it stated, "that nothing but unimaginable blunders in strategy or inconceivable failures of national determination could prevent the victory of the Allies".

Nevertheless, there was understandable anxiety over the prospects of the Anglo-American invasion of France which every British citizen could see, from the evidence of his or her own eyes, was gathering in the spring of the year. There could naturally be no detailed reporting of the preparations but, from the moment of the landings, coverage of the course of operations was very full. News, moreover, arrived from both sides of the lines, thanks to the intelligence service of the French resistance, which began to come into its own as the invasion forces pressed inland. One of the most remarkable items included in this collection is a detailed and highly accurate report of the massacre of the population of the village of Oradour-sur-Glane by troops of the SS Das Reich Division after it had been attacked by the *maquis* on its way to the Normandy battle four days after D-Day.

The initiation of the German secret weapons campaign against Britain came as an extremely unpleasant surprise to the British, particularly to Londoners who were its main victims. Reports of the effect of the flying bombs, from June 12 onward, appeared in the paper daily; on August 14 it printed a warning that London was also about to be attacked by the V-2 rocket, and V-2 stories continued to feature until the spring of 1945, when the last German launching sites in Holland fell into Allied hands.

By then the worst revelations of what Hitler's rule had meant for Europe were being disclosed. Reporters were entering the concentration camps and attempting to describe the horrors they experienced to their readers at home. Nevertheless, one of the great values of this collection is that it disposes of the belief, which has gained currency in the years after the war, that the West's leaders and peoples were ignorant of Hitler's racial extermination policies until the moment of liberation. In fact it is clear that newspapers, *The Daily Telegraph* foremost among them, were aware that some terrible act was being perpetrated inside occupied Europe from early in the war and published extensively and accurately on the facts as they emerged.

On VE – Victory in Europe – Day, May 8, 1945, the newspaper's editorial prudently warned that the ordeal of the war was not yet over. But the sense of the worst having come to an end was uncontainable. "At last, after five years and eight months", it began, and went on to chronicle the sufferings and triumphs of Britain's epic. The forces, land, sea and air, which had won the victory were then already undertaking their transfer to the Far East, to seal the defeat of Japan.

Fortunately, before large reinforcements could be sent, the Americans had tested their first atomic bomb, to the making of which British scientists had significantly contributed, and dropped the second on Hiroshima on August 6. Nine days later the Japanese Emperor announced his country's capitulation.

For *The Daily Telegraph*, quintessentially the organ of conservative opinion in Britain, the news of final victory was overshadowed by the defeat of Winston Churchill and his government in the July general election. The political rewards of the victory to which it had looked forward throughout the war were therefore dashed from it. It was not a point of view, however, that it laboured in its editorial columns. The survival and welfare of the nation throughout the six years had always been its overriding concern and it had served that cause with diligence and dignity from beginning to end.

Acknowledgements

We would like to thank the Imperial War Museum for their invaluable assistance in this project and also the following for their practical help and advice: Robert Bodman, Valerie Boyd, Jane Carmichael, Roy Castle, Brian Coulon, David Twiston Davies, Philip Ide, Lewis Jones, Paul Kemp, Joyce Meachem, Teresa Moore, Glen Swann, Harry Smith, Philip Warner, Graham Windram, and the staff of *The Daily Telegraph* Dark Room.

Picture credits Imperial War Museum: Page 1, 12, 13 (bottom), 16 (bottom), 21, 31, 34, 35, 36, 38, 39, 40 (bottom), 41 (top), 44/45, 46, 51, 52, 53, 54, 55, 56/57, 60 (bottom), 61, 63, 64, 65, 67, 68 (bottom), 70, 71, 72, 73, 77, 78, 84/85, 87, 88 (top), 89, 92/93, 95 (top), 96, 98, 100 (top) 101 (top), 102, 103 (bottom), 104, 106, 110 (top), 111, 115, 121, 122, 123, 124, 136 (top), 137, 142, 143, 148 (bottom), 149 (top), 150, 151 (top), 152 (top), 154, 155 (top), 156, 157 (top right & bottom), 162, 164, 166, 174, 175, 176, 179, 188, 190, 191, 194/195, 199; Novosti Press Agency: 118/119, 140, 146; United Press: 83 (top), 86; Bundesarchiv: 110 (bottom); Ullstein: 94; Rijksinstituut voor Oorlogsdocumentatie: 83 (bottom), 88; Paul Popper: 17. Other photographs come from *The Daily Telegraph*'s own sources. (Some of the photographs of the events recorded in this book which were not available to *The Daily Telegraph* at the time of publication, have been included for their historical interest.)